JUDAISM IN BIOLOGICAL PERSPECTIVE

Studies in Comparative Social Science
A series edited by Stephen K. Sanderson

Revolutions: A Worldwide Introduction to Political and Social Change, Stephen K. Sanderson (2005)

Plunging to Leviathan? Exploring the World's Political Future, Robert Bates Graber (2005)

The Depth of Shallow Culture: The High Art of Shoes, Movies, Novels, Monsters, and Toys, Albert Bergesen (2006)

Studying Societies and Cultures: Marvin Harris's Cultural Materialism and Its Legacy, edited by Lawrence A. Kuznar and Stephen K. Sanderson (2007)

The Supernatural and Natural Selection: The Evolution of Religion, Lyle B. Steadman and Craig T. Palmer (2008)

Judaism in Biological Perspective: Biblical Lore and Judaic Practices, edited by Rick Goldberg (2008)

Conflict Sociology: A Sociological Classic Updated, by Randall Collins, updated and abridged by Stephen K. Sanderson (2008)

Judaism in Biological Perspective

Biblical Lore and Judaic Practices

Edited by Rick Goldberg

Paradigm Publishers
Boulder • London

All rights reserved. No part of this publication may be transmitted or reproduced in any media or form, including electronic, mechanical, photocopy, recording, or informational storage and retrieval systems, without the express written consent of the publisher.

Copyright © 2009 by Paradigm Publishers

Published in the United States by Paradigm Publishers, 3360 Mitchell Lane Suite E, Boulder, Colorado 80301 USA.

Paradigm Publishers is the trade name of Birkenkamp & Company, LLC, Dean Birkenkamp, president and publisher.

Library of Congress Cataloging-in-Publication Data

Judaism in biological perspective : biblical lore and Judaic practices / Rick Goldberg, editor.
   p. cm.
  ISBN 978-1-59451-563-7 (hardcover : alk. paper)
  ISBN 978-1-59451-564-4 (paperback : alk. paper)
  1. Judaism and science. 2. Religion and science. I. Goldberg, Rick. II. Title: Biblical lore and Judaic practices.
  BM538.S3J77 2008
  296.3'75—dc22
                                                                                                                2008005909

Printed and bound in the United States of America on acid-free paper that meets the standards of the American National Standard for Permanence of Paper for Printed Library Materials.

Designed and Typeset in Adobe Garamond by Straight Creek Bookmakers.

13 12 11 10 09   2 3 4 5

I have been blessed by the transforming influence of two outstanding teachers, Rabbi "Yitz" Greenberg and Dr. Lyle Steadman. Without their willingness to reach out, my ability to envision this book would never have developed.

I would also like to acknowledge the helpful comments of Rabbi Eliezer Langer, Prof. Esther Raizen, and Marsha Walker during the preparation of this book.

Contents

Editor's Preface: How This Book Came About   ix

Foreword: Why Explore Aspects of Judaism from a Biological Perspective?   xi

First Principles

Chapter 1   Judaism's *Yetzer* as a Biotheological Construct   2
Rick Goldberg

Chapter 2   Jewish Knowing: Monism and Its Biological Implications   18
Michael Satlow

Biblical Lore and Biological Theory

Chapter 3   The Fertility of Prominent Men in the Bible and Ancient Middle East   42
Laura Betzig

Chapter 4   Intrafamily Conflict in the Bible and Biological Theory   62
David Barash

Chapter 5   Toward a Sociobiology of the Jews: Sexual Selection, Circumcision, and the Centrality of Texts in a Coevolutionary Framework   84
Melvin Konner

Inheritance for Intergenerational Success

Chapter 6   Biosocial Regulation of Husband and Wife: The Requirement for Periodic Conjugal Separation and Reunion   118
Rick Goldberg

| Chapter 7 | Traditionalism and Human Evolutionary Success: The Example of Judaism
Craig Palmer, Lyle Steadman, and Rick Goldberg | 139 |

Costly Signaling (Handicap) Theory and Jewish Life

Chapter 8	The Handicap Principle in Human Social Interaction *Amotz Zahavi*	166
Chapter 9	Making Biological Sense of Judaic Sacrificing *Rick Goldberg*	173
Chapter 10	Why Are Synagogue Services So Long? An Evolutionary Examination of Jewish Ritual Signals *Richard Sosis*	199

Contributors — *234*

Index — *237*

Editor's Preface

How This Book Came About

IN GRADUATE SCHOOL MANY YEARS AGO, I took a required course in sociological theory taught by a professor who thought social science should require the same exacting theory and hard data as natural science. He insisted that biological theory be the primary source for all explanations of human social action. That seminar kindled my desire to follow closely discoveries as they emanate from the fields of evolutionary psychology and anthropology.

My interest in sociology of religion, especially Judaism, began much earlier. Over the years, my increasing Judaic literacy, combined with my enthusiasm for the power of natural and sexual selection to explain the living world, stirred me to consider how bridges might be built between the two. Assuming evolutionary theory should be applied to human behavior generally, then its application to the values and behaviors of Judaism could prove interesting. As I searched to see if this approach had been used elsewhere, I noticed that, while there were books connecting Judaism to physics and cosmology, there were none interpreting Judaism knowledgeably and respectfully through the lens of biological theory. After deciding it might be timely to develop such a book, I began putting together my own thoughts while soliciting those of well-respected scholars of Judaism and biological psychology/anthropology.

Assembling and editing this book has been a labor of love. My intention is to bridge, where possible, the deep chasm between Darwinism and the religious principles/behaviors of Judaism. Like all structurally sound bridges, this one must be built from the ground up, one supporting component at a time. Relating religion to science and vice versa is a tricky business given the quarrelsome rhetoric swirling around the differing perceptions of mankind in the natural world. My hope is that this book makes a positive contribution to what I see as a worthwhile effort.

Foreword

Why Explore Aspects of Judaism from a Biological Perspective?

DOES BIOLOGICAL SCIENCE REALLY *DISPROVE* RELIGION? Can there be cases of coexistence and even compatibility between natural science and religious behaviors? This book's premise is that the mutuality between the two not only exists but deserves to be fully revealed.

Using the Passover phraseology, why is this book so different from all other books about science and religion? In all other books, the conflict between evolution and faith takes center stage. In this book, we refrain from dipping even once into this omnipresent, 150-year-old disputation.

This book is also different because our method of analysis is novel—the dispassionate focusing of biological theory on selected aspects of the history, ideas, and practices of the Jewish religion. Our respectful scrutiny of these objects of study should come as a relief to those weary of the endless debate between Darwinians and defenders of the Bible. In these pages, biology asks permission to speak about Judaism, and that permission is respectfully granted.

Biology-related stories appear daily in the popular press to satisfy the public hunger for information about genes found to be associated with common diseases and behaviors. As a reader with interest in natural science, you probably have a strong measure of confidence in scientific method and its many achievements. If, at the same time, you are intrigued by Judaism, although perhaps not that familiar with it, these biological interpretations can serve as a point of entry for understanding this ancient and modern way of religious life. For those with some Judaic knowledge, there are biological constructions in these chapters that you will not see elsewhere, because these authors delve with creativity into regions of intersection between Judaism and biological thinking. A major purpose of this book is to introduce recent scholarship on human evolution to readers who have an ongoing interest in Judaism and/or the Jewish people. This perspective may also suggest new approaches for readers well versed in evolutionary theory. If you like reading about natural science and appreciate Judaism, this book was written for you.

Classical social science never neglected the central project of constructing human nature, a task modern social science has, unfortunately, avoided and even disdained. The proper role for biological theory in social science is the exercise of coercive surveillance. No respected evolutionary thinker would say that genetic predisposition or cultural norms *determine* the behavior of Jews or anyone else. Although human *nature* is surely the product of our evolutionary history, human *behavior* cannot rightfully be called a "hard-wired" outcome of the process. On the other hand, research attempting to explain behavior without referencing our biologically derived nature runs the risk of scientific irrelevance. Curiously, many who would think appropriate the application of evolutionary theory to the mating strategies of grasshoppers or elephants might dismiss out of hand the notion that certain *mitzvot* (obligations) constitute a *Judaic* mating strategy. Regrettably, many social scientists think we humans are so unique that employing biological theory to help explain our behavior is unnecessary and insulting.

The social scientific quandary was expressed well by anthropologist Robin Fox:

> Those who are uncomfortable with an evolutionary approach to human behavior insist that through our mental activity we reorder nature, thereby imposing our will on both the world around us and our place in the world. While this assumption is true, it is really only half-true, since it requires the Cartesian distinction between mind and nature which, like its counterpart distinction between mind and culture, is so fatal to scientific inquiry or even imaginative good sense. When biological science describes the emergence of a human being from the fusion of sperm and egg and, subsequently, produces a thoroughly predictable human anatomy and physiology, no one cries "biological determinism" in protest. Nor is there protest when natural science predicts that our life cycle events will be triggered by hormonal changes, and physiological dysfunction will cause every person eventually to die. Yet some think it should be forbidden for scientific theory to explain and predict those behaviors that human beings have shared in common throughout the historical development of our species.[1]

When exploring human behavior and institutions, our biological inheritance surely deserves a seat at the table. Human exceptionalism need not be challenged by the presumption that we are evolved and embodied creatures. Although our behavior has much in common with other living creatures, illuminating that commonality can construct only partially what it means to be human. But let me state unequivocally that the naturalistic approach neither delegitimizes nor excludes other interpretive approaches to human (or, more specifically, Jewish) behavior. Additionally, these chapters should not be taken as evidence of Judaic uniqueness. To my knowledge, there are no categories of religious claims or behaviors that belong exclusively to the Jewish way of life. In fact, the resemblance of some Judaic traditions to those of other religions should spur even further a biology-based exploration of similar religious behaviors.

Nature *and* nurture ("these *and* those"[2]) constitute unified man living in the natural world. Differentiation between "nature" and "nurture" as categories is only artificial; in reality, they are intertwined subdivisions that constitute our unitary evolutionary experience. The preeminent thinker of Modern Orthodox Judaism, Rabbi Joseph Soloveitchik, asks a question about the perspective of two of his ideally constructed "men": is Judaism-centered "*halakhic* man" precluded from understanding the natural world of which he is a part? The Rav answers that "*halakhic* man" should exhibit the same curiosity about natural phenomena as science-oriented "cognitive man," because Torah can be more fully understood by incorporating lessons from the natural world (מדע).[3] In the spirit of *Torah umadda*,[4] argument and evidence are presented here to suggest how a biological hermeneutic sheds light on Torah-based principles and practices. Our premise is that an evolutionary analysis of Judaism can reveal facets of interpretation not otherwise discernable. Our overarching message is that elements of Judaism can be interpreted as evolutionarily successful.

As behavioral mandates constituting a way of life, Judaism does not require individuals to transcend their natural selves; rather, the Judaic method of transcendence neither promotes nor permits the illusion that our nature can be overcome. Acquiring knowledge of the natural world and the place of Jews in it has been one of the foundational tasks of Jewish religious texts. For example, the laws requiring conjugal separation cannot be implemented without knowledge of the menstrual cycle; rules for keeping kosher cannot be enforced without expertise in the physiology of permitted animals; arrival of the new month in the Jewish calendar cannot be announced and blessed without the ability to measure lunar phases; and when fruits can first be harvested *(orlah)*, associated with grafting, layering, or dwarfing of fruit trees.

We should be clear that the modern science of "biology" is impossible without its basis in Darwinian natural and sexual selection. The ongoing effort of evolutionary psychologists and anthropologists to flesh out the modalities of human nature should be trumpeted as an outstanding scientific achievement. Analyzing human behavior from an evolutionary perspective has the advantage of elegantly joining the intellect with common sense. The accomplishments of modern life science, however, stand in sharp contrast with those of our contemporary social science. Today's social scientist constructively agrees with anti-Darwin fundamentalists by rejecting biological causation. His fear, perhaps, is that if he gazes too long in the mirror he might see a monkey in it. As a result of biology denial, and bent on the moralistic mission of "social change," most social scientific research engages in social advocacy masquerading as science. Consequently, many of today's university-based, public policy missionaries characterize the application of biological theory to humans as "reductionist" and "determinist." They use these pejorative terms to marginalize the biological analysis of human behavior by characterizing it as reducing to a single (biological) cause that results in a predetermined outcome.

One frequently heard criticism of attempts to study religion from a naturalistic perspective is the claim that science and religion are separate and incompatible. Here is a claim made by a prominent psychologist reflecting this commonly held notion:

Religion and science are independent approaches to knowledge, and neither can be reduced to the other. Religion and science are fundamentally different, with the former relying on faith as a source of wisdom and the latter demanding evidence.[5]

Contrast that opinion with this opinion, from an interview with a young Orthodox rabbi knowledgeable of the Darwinian selection process:

Many [religious] people believe there are certain phenomena that science can't explain, and that God may be found in those inexplicable phenomena. This formulation is problematic, because it restricts God's role to those things that science can't at present explain—an area constantly shrinking in size. I believe God can and should be found in all natural phenomena, including those that science *can* explain.[6]

In pursuit of a noble calling, much current social science aims to "solve" societal problems like war, injustice, and inequality. But, unlike this program of social advocacy, our method contains a perspective without promoting an agenda. Our natural scientific orientation aims to be purely descriptive—if the reader wishes to conjure up religious or social agendas, he or she is free to discover them between the lines. Although our authors do designate certain Judaic values and behaviors as "biologically correct" (having been adaptive), their purpose is neither to praise nor to disparage Judaism. As the reader, you are left to draw your own conclusions based on the evidence presented.

In many books debating science versus religion, we have become accustomed to the polemical arguments of both scientific rationalists and religion defenders, combatants in the war to win the hearts and minds of the public. Polls, however, show the vast majority of Americans trust both science *and* religion. Despite this fact, the creationist-evolutionist debate most often consists of the two sides talking past one another. Quixotic scientists like Richard Dawkins and Daniel Dennett do battle to break the spell of religion over the "deluded" multitude with religious sensibilities who lead religious lives. Following the path of enlightenment thinkers who claimed religion was a human invention and a blockade to reason, their antireligion crusade of philosophical scientism asserts that natural science is all we have to tell us what is valuable in the world. When well-known scientists proclaim their exclusive insights about the meaning of life, including the deficiencies of centuries of inherited religious wisdom, keep in mind that their standing as scientists does not qualify them as moralists. Leon Wieseltier cautions that cultic Scientism is never content for science to be *one* of the things you need to know. It demands that science be the *only* thing you need to know.

On the other side of the chasm, science-denying Creationists live in a world of great hope seasoned with deep denial. For them, failure to recognize the primacy of self-evidently true biblical narrative is the fatal flaw of those who utilize evolutionary theory. A goal of this book is to demonstrate that biological thinking and aspects of Judaism can be compatible. Even more optimistically, we suggest that biological theory can reveal novel interpretations within the Tradition. Using close readings of Judaic texts, our goal is to discover aspects of Judaism from the perspective of biology, not biology from the perspective of Judaism. The pseudo-biological argument from Intelligent Design, therefore, lies well beyond our scope due to its lack of overall scientific verifiability. The scientific task is to explain the natural world based only on *knowledge* of the natural world. That knowledge is called data, and, to qualify as *scientific* data, it must be self-evidently verifiable by the senses.

Our view is that both materialist scientists and serious-minded Creationists (including most Orthodox Jews) are often too heavily invested in denying or demolishing the propositions of their supposed antagonists. In this book, neither science-based secularism nor God-fearing religiosity will be attacked or even trivialized. As you will see, these pages exhibit familiarity with and respect for both science and religion. We aim to build our own case, not diminish the credibility of someone else.

The reader may wonder why no part of this book deals with the Jews or Judaism *as a comprehensive whole*. Unlike some scholarly work, this book does not represent the Jewish people or Judaism as a discrete, biological category. Our surgical approach is modeled on that of Solomon Schechter's *Aspects of Rabbinic Theology,* in which topics are discussed individually but not panoramically. Simply put, Judaism in its entirety is much too diverse and complex to be treated as a unified whole from *any* perspective. These authors have chosen a limited number of subjects amenable to evaluation by the light of biological theory. No argument is made here that *all* Judaic values and standards of behavior are successful adaptations, although *some* aspects clearly appear to have had evolutionary success. Our goal is not to reduce Judaism to *extrinsic* materialisms; therefore, the reader should not view our work as Judaism "tricked out" as biology.

The revelations in each chapter are not offered intentionally to promote Judaism as a way of life. The presumption is that behaviors practiced by many Jews for hundreds or even thousands of years would not have proved so durable had those behaviors denied human nature. To that end, we focus on those perspectives (*hashkafat olam*) and behaviors (*mitzvot*) with biological compatibility. The common thread running through these chapters, each of limited scope, is that Judaism's affinity with human nature is one reason it continues to be venerated and practiced by so many Jews after so many centuries.

—Rick Goldberg, Editor

Notes

1. Fox, R., *The Red Lamp of Incest* (Notre Dame, IN: University of Notre Dame Press, 1980, pp. 197–198).
2. According to the Talmud, conflicting opinions are *both* the word of God (Er. 13b; Chag. 3b1; Yev. 14a2; Gittin 6b3).
3. Soloveitchik, J., *Halakhic Man* (Philadelphia: Jewish Publication Society, 1983, pp. 1–98).
4. Torah combined with and revealed by secular knowledge.
5. R. P. Sloan, *The Chronicle Review,* November 3, 2006.

6. Natan Slifkin, *The Zoo Rabbi*. For a Torah-centered (*nishtaneh hateva*) approach to both evolution and the animal world, Rabbi Slifkin's recent book, *The Challenge of Creation* (2006), is recommended.

References

Fox, R. 1980. *The Red Lamp of Incest*. Notre Dame, IN: University of Notre Dame Press.
Soloveitchik, J. 1983. *Halakhic Man*. Philadelphia: Jewish Publication Society.

In these chapters, references to citations in the Jewish religious texts begin with the (abbreviated) name of the tractate, followed by a page number plus an "a" or a "b" side. When there is another number after the "a" or "b," the reference is specifically to The Artscroll Talmud Bavli Series, The Shottenstein Edition, Mesorah Publications, Brooklyn, 2006.

First Principles

Chapter 1

Judaism's Yetzer *as a Biotheological Construct*

Rick Goldberg

> The only reason why the love of [physical science] has been implanted in man is to support the [rational study] of religion, both together making an excellent combination.
> —*Saadia Gaon, tenth-century Judaic sage and rationalist*

The Jewish Religious Texts and Liturgy Construct Human Nature

In the first verse of the Bible, God is described as initiating creation of the universe *ex nihilo*. As the beginning had begun, chaos was transformed into natural order.[1] Once the inorganic features on earth had been finished, the origin of life ensued, depicted as a systematic progression of biological categories. The passage in which man's origin is first described[2] uses a different Hebrew root, י-צ-ר (y-tz-r), than the verb ב-ר-א (b-r-a) used in Genesis 1:1 to describe the overall process. The root ב-ר-א, used in Genesis for creation of the inorganic (earth, water, heavens), means bringing into existence from elements *not* preexisting.[3] The root y-tz-r, on the other hand, means "to form," a developmental process of reconfiguring existing elements into new forms. To illustrate using modern Hebrew, a *yotzer* is a potter or craftsman, one who refines existing materials into more useful forms. Along those lines, man is described as being of natural origin, having been crafted from the dirt of the earth.[4] In his biblical commentary, Rashi describes God's fashioning of man as similar to the way a baker prepares and kneads his dough.[5]

Further along in the Genesis account additional clues for fleshing out the biblical concept of *yetzer* can be found. After man has eaten the fruit of the tree of knowledge, God comments on man's changed status: "Behold, the man becomes one of us by knowing good and evil."[6] As God observes mankind operating in the world, He displays disappointment in man's innate propensity for "only evil thoughts all day [continually]."[7] In the Hebrew, "evil thoughts" is a word construct containing "*yetzer*."[8] To extend further, the text tells us that "man's imagination is evil from his youth,"[9] utilizing the word *yetzer* again to mean "imagination."

In interpreting this verse, the Rabbis discussed at which stage of life this elemental urge (*yetzer*) enters man. The consensus was that, like a genetic trait, the *yetzer* is inborn, having been established at the time of conception.[10] Evidence of the *yetzer*'s dominance during childhood is said to be found in children's self-centeredness. Reinforcing the biological nature of the *yetzer*, it was declared that the *yetzer* exists in men but not in angels, and in this world but not the world to come. The angels are viewed as "free from it (the *yetzer*) because they do not carry earthly corporeality."[11] In summary: the *yetzer* inclination is seen as the basic, embedded ingredient of man's biological nature in this world, but absent in the world to come when man ceases biological functioning.

What we know about *yetzer* from Genesis is that it is an inherent propensity, compelling man's narcissistic thoughts. As I have mentioned, the *yetzer* was characterized by the Rabbis as an inborn mechanism (*élan vital*), included by God from the beginning in man's biological packaging.[12] Genesis makes it clear that animals were formed (*yitzar*) in the same way, providing evidence that this *yetzer* essence is not unique to humans.[13] In his nineteenth-century reconciliation of evolution and Genesis, Naftali Levy argued that because Genesis uses the term "He formed" instead of "He created" for animals, the intention is to tell us that animal species transform from one to another in the ongoing process of creation.[14] In modern Hebrew, the adjective form *yitzri* means "instinctual," a biological term applicable to all living organisms.

Within the daily and Sabbath liturgy, the natural order is often referred to as the product of creation. During the morning blessings God is thanked for many things, including the "rooster's ability to differentiate between night and day" (and therefore knowing when to crow), for "numbering the stars and giving each one a name,"[15] for "giving to the beasts their food and the ravens that for which they call,"[16] and for creating a world "by whose laws nature abides." Man's physiological necessities have their own blessing, in which God is thanked for forming (*y-tz-r*) us, and causing the various valves and openings that regulate our bodily activities to function properly. Mirroring biology's evolutionary process is the blessing in which God is acknowledged for "day after day, continually, renewing the work of creation." Judaism teaches that "creation is not an act that happened once upon a time, once and for ever"; rather, "the act of bringing the world into existence is a continuous process"[17] in which God "renews the face of the earth."[18] When God is praised for creation, the verb referring to the process of creating (*b-r-a*) is stated in the present rather than the past tense, signifying the process as ongoing.[19] We can say, therefore, that Judaism views the creation of life not as a onetime event but, rather, a process of continual re-creation.[20]

Proper functioning of the natural order is viewed as essential in biblical theology. In describing the conditions predating the Flood, the Bible generalizes that "all flesh had corrupted its ways on earth."[21] Natural processes became so perverted that all life, except the remnant saved on Noah's Ark, was seen as needing to be destroyed. Rabbinic commentary explained the nature of pre-Flood corruption by describing a pandemonium of sexual anomalies—"cattle had perverse relations with wild beasts, and man with both cattle and wild beasts."[22] "Even the earth acted like a harlot ... farmers harvested weeds though wheat had been planted."[23] Ibn Ezra, twelfth-century commentator, added more pre-Flood aberrations: "dogs copulated with wolves and chickens with peacocks." He summarized the vivid discussion of the subject: "No living creature adhered any longer to the laws of its procreation, flagrantly perverting the known path implanted in it." Jewish tradition has adopted the explanation that the Flood was visited on the world as a result of the perversion of what should have been a fixed biological order first established during the six days of creation.

Normative Judaism has always insisted on a monistic understanding of the natural world as the product of both the mind of God and His ongoing creative impulse.[24] As I have noted, in the Genesis account living creatures come to exist after having been *formed* from preexisting matter. Additionally, as I previously suggested, even nonhuman *forms* of life can be said to contain the genetic foundation of *yetzer*. Once all other creatures had been formed, God proclaims, "Let *us* now make man in *our* image."[25] Since Judaism claims God as the sole Creator, why is plural language used instead of singular? This dilemma might be resolved by suggesting that existing plants and animals were cocreators of human descent—our formation depended on an antecedent process in which less complex creatures provided the prior conditions for man's appearance. That process of natural descent would be characterized biologically as evolution by natural selection.

Rabbinic Discovery of Two *Yetzers*

> Healthy-mindedness is inadequate as a philosophical doctrine, because the evil facts which it refuses to positively account for are a genuine portion of reality; they may be the best key to life's significance, the only openers of our eyes to the deepest levels of truth.
> —*William James,* The Varieties of Religious Experience

In rabbinic exegesis, the biblical *yetzer* as a unified, innate propensity was bifurcated into a good *yetzer* and an evil *yetzer*. The rabbinic division of the *yetzer* into two distinct aspects is never self-evident within the biblical wording; nevertheless, the Rabbis read between the lines to discover the existence of two *yetzers*—within the text of Genesis 2:7 the letter *yod* (י) in the verb *vayyitzer* (וייצר) had been doubled.

Since not even one letter of the Bible can be dismissed as extraneous, the Rabbis declared that the two *yods* represented the existence of two *yetzers* within man, one a force for good and the other for evil.[26] As further rabbinic proof, the most repeated biblical verse in Jewish liturgy, the *sh'ma*,[27] contains the requirement to "love God with all your heart." There are two words used in biblical Hebrew for "heart" and, in this instance, the verse uses the word *levav* (לבב) instead of *lev* (לב). Noticing that the conjugated form of *levav*[28] has the letter *vet* (ב) doubled, the Rabbis deduced that the obligation to love God with *all* one's heart means with both one's good and one's evil *yetzer*.[29] As Schofer states, this rabbinic deduction created a "small anthology of binary contrasts."[30] Although the bifurcated *yetzer* became well accepted in rabbinic commentary, the two-*yetzer* construct has no explicit biblical origin.

The evil *yetzer* is given great biological amplitude by the Rabbis and characterized by embodied action; the good *yetzer* is seen as not inborn but the product of acculturation (Torah training). There is rabbinic disagreement regarding at which age each *yetzer* becomes operative. One source claims that (in an individual) the evil *yetzer* is thirteen years older than the good *yetzer*,[31] implying that the evil *yetzer* is innate at birth. In other passages from Avot, the evil *yetzer*'s origin is to be found preconception in the father's semen.[32] As I have mentioned, the inability of children to control their desires and impulses is seen as evidence of the primordial existence of the evil *yetzer*. The good *yetzer*, on the other hand, gains strength only after a good measure of Torah instruction, vesting at the time of one's social maturity (bar mitzvah). As the child becomes fully developed, control over budding sexual desire is made possible only by dedication to Torah study.

Although Judaism depicts the human as having a monistic nature, rabbinic texts model that singular nature as dialectic in structure.[33] As a result, an argument can be made that the evil and good *yetzers* are not parallel, built-in propensities as the Rabbis assume. Rather, evil behavior can be seen as innate as our genetic blueprint, and good behavior seen as derived from years of Judaic learning. As Biale confirms, "The good inclination is learned; the evil one instinctual."[34] Seen in this light, Judaism's standards of behavior derive from the systematic instruction of Torah-based rules that are binding on all Jews.[35] Although all men are seen as instinctively evil, for "Judaic man" good behavior emerges only to the extent that religious law (*halachot*) constrains natural behaviors. Properly characterized, the good *yetzer* is a *potential* discipline that requires social development; in contrast, the evil *yetzer* functions as an *instinctual* appetite. An example might be the sociopath, who is amply equipped with an evil *yetzer*, but lacks potential for the learned acquisition of a good *yetzer*.

Evolutionary Psychology's Short-Term Male Reproductive Strategy

In reproductive terms, males typically produce millions of tiny sex cells (sperm gametes) daily, even as females typically produce a few hundred much larger sex cells (egg gametes) in a lifetime. This overwhelming asymmetry, called anisogamy, is thought to be a primary reason why men and women pursue widely differing mating strategies. The other major reason, stemming from anisogamy, is that the level of parental investment required of females is much greater than that of males. There is a great disparity in the minimum cost of offspring production and care: males are much less constrained by the necessities of infant and child care than females, who gestate, give birth, and lactate. Accordingly, in our polygynous species, females generally employ a reproductive strategy characterized by far greater choosiness in the matter of sexual partners.

Continuous male superproduction of gametes brings by itself no great penalty for the squandering of semen in marginally rewarding sexual encounters. As a result, men are much more likely than women to desire sexual variety per se.[36] Although men do discriminate in choosing sex partners, the value of impersonal novelty is more influential in male than in female sexual choice.[37] That men are more partial to variety and prejudicial against familiarity can be termed the short-term male reproductive strategy, described anecdotally as the Coolidge Effect:[38]

> One day President and Mrs. Coolidge were taking separate tours of a farm. As Mrs. Coolidge passed the chicken pens, she paused to ask the man in charge if the rooster copulates more than once a day. "Dozens of times a day," replied the farmer. "Would you please tell that to the President when he comes by?" she requested. When the President passed the pens, he was told the answer given to his wife. Coolidge then asked the farmer, "Same hen every time?" "Oh, no Mr. President," said the farmer, "a different hen each time." The President then nodded, saying, "Tell that, please, to Mrs. Coolidge."

In the evolutionary history of polygynous species like chickens and humans, male reproductive success was often attained through opportunistic copulations with willing females. To characterize the short-term male strategy, "men who impregnated as many women as possible produced more children, even if they didn't stay to help raise them."[39] The long-term male reproductive strategy, featuring greater spousal and offspring investment over long periods of time, is at odds with the short-term strategy of sexual variety featuring opportunistic copulations (and offspring) with less per capita investment per woman and per child (polygyny).

Female sexual allure for men includes a combination of youthfulness, healthfulness, status, facial features of average size and shape, nubile waist-hip ratio, and comparatively bilateral symmetry. In their normally visual erotic imaginings, men are likely to view females as reproductively valuable *objects* of interest.[40] Although physical attraction is not the only factor in (short-term) male sexual choice, it remains the most important one.[41] Selection in human evolutionary history places a premium on a woman's physical appearance because of the "abundance of reliable cues it provides to her reproductive potential." For men, female attractiveness is a "deeply ingrained psychological mechanism" driving mating desires and decisions.[42]

The common expression for short-term male reproductive desire is lust, the pursuit of which can result in philandering. As Ridley states, "Humanity shares the profile of ardent, polygamist males ... with about 99% of all animal species, including our closest relatives, the apes."[43] To paraphrase Fisher, regardless of local marriage traditions, divorce customs, and cultural mores about sex, all forty-two ethnographies (to which she refers) describe peoples past and present who acknowledge the influential presence of adultery. "There exists no culture in which adultery is unknown, no cultural device or code that extinguishes philandering... even where adultery is punished by death."[44]

It is certainly not suggested here that the short-term male reproductive strategy governs all male sexual desires and mating behaviors. Both sexes also have a long-term reproductive strategy, selected to influence the provisioning of resources to their children. More so than most other species, the long human gestation period and nonviability of children at birth require substantial investment by kinfolk to ensure that offspring survive to reproductive age. Thus it becomes clear that the short-term male strategy is not coincidentally parallel to Judaism's biological construction of the evil *yetzer*.[45]

Rabbinic Construction of *Yetzer*: ?למה הדבר דומה (To What Does This Compare?)

Man's biblical *yetzer* refers to purpose or function as well as formative matter. As a result, *yetzer* can also be construed as *imagination* or *disposition,* a rendering as unconsciously purposeful as a biological reproductive strategy. In Rabbinic discourse, the evil *yetzer* is attributed as the source of anger, revenge, greed, deceit, pride, religious unbelief, and idolatry, a broad range of transgressive emotions and behaviors.[46] For purposes of this chapter, however, the evil *yetzer* is being referenced in its most common rabbinic depiction, male lustfulness. My purpose is to explore the mating strategy correlate of the *yetzer* construct through the lens of Darwinian theory.

The colorful talmudic personifications of the evil *yetzer* as beguiler and seducer can be seen as the origin of lust and is consonant with, as I am suggesting, the short-term male reproductive strategy. Like one's genetic inheritance, the wellspring of the *yetzer* is antecedent in origin and operation, portrayed as a sexual force with deterministic power:

If the evil *yetzer* says to you, "Sin, and God will forgive you," don't believe it.[47]

The Rabbis taught: We should not give an opportunity to sin even to an honest man, much less a thief, for the sages say this is like putting fire next to a burlap sack.[48]

The evil inclination (*yetzer*) is sweet at the beginning and bitter at the end.[49]

The *yetzer* appears as a "modest traveler," even a "welcome guest," only, in the end, to exact obedience from the master of the house.[50]

The *yetzer* represents himself as harmless but, later on, overwhelms with masculine strength. He deals with man by feigning weakness (like a helpless dog), but when a man is off his guard, he jumps on him and makes him sin.[51] At first the *yetzer* is as fragile as the thread of a spider, but eventually the thread becomes as strong as cart ropes.[52]

Commenting on the verse, "Let there be no strange god within you,"[53] R. Jannai says that one who obeys his *yetzer* (the "strange god") is practicing a form of idolatry.[54]

When the evil *yetzer* sees a man swaggering [so women will notice], showing off his clothes and arranging his hair, he says, "That man belongs to me!" He who spoils his *yetzer* by tender and considerate treatment (allowing it to slowly gain dominion) will end by becoming his slave.[55]

When an attractive man gazes into his reflection in the water, his *yetzer* will attempt to gain control and stimulate his lustful behavior.[56]

The *yetzer* is the "tempter," inciting to sexual impropriety. All sexual intercourse performed more with the purpose of satisfying one's sexual appetite than with perpetuating the human species is tainted by one's *yetzer*.[57]

Yetzer is the "foolish old king" who accompanies man from earliest youth to old age, and to whom all the body's organs show obedience.[58]

He is the "spoiler" who spares none, bringing man to lust even in old age.[59]

As is apparent in the above personifications, the *yetzer* inclination is a potentially self-destructive animus, almost beyond control, exerting power over an individual's behavior. As such, this natural force can be seen as an evolved, inherited complex of traits referred to above as a mating strategy. As was discussed, a mating strategy is a set of behaviors for choosing mates that predisposes individuals to act according to "preexisting" inclinations that have proven to be reproductively successful over the lineage's evolutionary history.

Commenting on Genesis 6:5 ("man's thoughts are only evil, and all day"), R. Isaac comments that the *yetzer* masters man by renewing itself all day.[60] What is the biological corollary to this rabbinic characterization? The answer is found in the paradigmatic development of human males: the production of sperm, and the desire to ejaculate "renews itself" forcefully every day.

Below are three passages, two from recent books written by evolutionary thinkers, and the third of talmudic origin. The first excerpt is the last paragraph of a self-help book:

> We should enjoy our animal passions and even indulge them but prevent them from controlling us. The key to a satisfying life is finding a middle ground that combines free-flowing pleasure, iron willpower, and the crafty manipulation of ourselves and our situations. Our temptations are powerful and persistent, but we are not destined

to succumb. Ancient and selfish, our mean genes influence us every day in almost every way. But because we can predict their influence, self-knowledge plus discipline can provide a winning strategy in the battle to lead satisfying and moral lives.[61]

In the second excerpt, a *yetzer*-type inclination is described in the folkways of many peoples:

> Time and again we see [in religious myth] an evil being that tries, in the guise of innocence, to entice people into seemingly minor but ultimately momentous wrongdoing.... For example, natural selection "wants" men to have sex with an endless series of women.... The concept of evil doesn't fit easily into a modern scientific worldview.... There is indeed a force devoted to enticing us into various pleasures that are (or once were) in our genetic interests but do not bring long-term happiness to us and may bring great suffering to others.[62]

Compare the core concept of these two excerpts with the following talmudic dictum:

> When the Evil Inclination takes control, there is no one to remind you of the Good Inclination.[63]

Like the talmudic pronouncement, the ideas expressed in the first two passages could have been written by modern rabbis suggesting ways to acknowledge and overcome the influence of the evil *yetzer*. Just as the Rabbis assert that failure to control the evil *yetzer* undermines long-term, multigenerational well-being, so may biological psychologists (and others) see pursuit of the short-term male reproductive strategy as hindering the preferred long-term strategy of investing in a wife and children. When men pursue the short-term strategy ("cads"), they diminish their potential success as long-term investors in their children ("dads"). Men are free (but are required) to obey the Law despite the acknowledged power of the evil *yetzer*.[64] "At the time when man becomes excited and goes to do an immoral act, his entire body becomes involved, because the evil *yetzer* rules over him."[65] As the Talmud suggests, when individuals habituate themselves to immorality, there can also be profound social consequences, comparing their *yetzer*-driven behavior to a "spark that ignites a coal" (i.e., incites others).[66] It is the obligation of the righteous person to overcome his baser self by "slaying" the evil inclination "all day long" and every day.[67] The following, from a latter rabbinic source, illustrates the social consequences of an individual's *yetzer*-driven immorality:

> To what can the evil *yetzer* be compared? To two people who entered an inn (to commit a robbery). One was seized for robbing, and they said to him, "Who is with you?" He could have said, "My friend was not with me," but he thinks, "Because I will be killed, let my friend be killed with me." So thinks the evil *yetzer*, "Because I am lost to the world to come (afterlife), I will make the entire body perish with me."[68]

The Evil *Yetzer* Viewed as Good

By fleshing out the biological *yetzer*, Judaism's approach to human nature becomes more complex and nuanced. Good and evil are not viewed in Judaism as inclinations acting separately or necessarily in opposition to one another; rather, they are seen as two aspects of a larger, unified whole. Consequently, the rabbinic characterization of the evil *yetzer* was enlarged to include all of what today would be called man's competitive initiative and productivity.

In reading the Genesis account of creation, one may notice that the process ends on each of the first five days with the words, "And God saw that it was good." But at the end of the sixth day (when man was created), the text reads, "And God saw everything that He had made and, behold, it was *very* good." In the additional word "very," the Rabbis saw a reference to the creation of the evil *yetzer*, implying its *positive* quality.[69] By this favorable light, the evil *yetzer* emphasizes self-aggrandizement by the exercise of competitive and productive power. In the same way, Freudian psychology uses the term *libido* to mean the "driving force behind human action."[70] And Rabbi Lamm captures the subtle distinction, "The good [*yetzer*] is good, but the evil [*yetzer*] used for the good is even better."[71] Thus interpreted, the "evil" *yetzer* becomes the capacity for self-interest, which, if properly channeled, leads to human achievement; if left undisciplined, to immorality and ruin.

The Talmud raises the issue of self-control with a direct question: "Who is the mighty individual? He who conquers his *yetzer*."[72] To promote self-discipline, the biblical command to "blot out the name of Amalek" was psychologized by the Rabbis to mean domination of one's own internal Amalek, the evil *yetzer*. The more learned the individual, the more powerful is his *yetzer* urge.[73] By this is meant that "greater" men invariably engage in more difficult moral struggles with more at stake. With sharper illustrative focus, the Rabbis wrote that "were it not for the sexual impulse (evil *yetzer*), no man would build a house, marry a woman or engage in an occupation. All labor and skillful work comes from a man's competition with others."[74] Ecclesiastes adds that "all labor and skillful enterprise come from men's envy of each other."[75] Giving credit to those who made productive contributions to the completion of his Temple, King Solomon thanks his followers for "remembering the *yetzer*-thoughts of their hearts."[76]

So the evil *yetzer* is not viewed *simply* as shameful or sinful. Judaism sees human initiative (including sexual desire) as a healthy, even necessary, life force when kept within prescribed limits. The struggle against the evil *yetzer* does not mean withdrawal from or denial of the world and its activities; rather, it includes conquering one's *yetzer* while living fully in the world.[77] As Rashi wrote, "If a man alienated his desire completely, he would reduce the propagation of the species."[78] Proper balance is the rabbinic objective: "Man has a small organ—starve it and it is sated, overuse it and it remains hungry."[79] In sum, the Rabbis see sexuality in general as a powerful drive with very destructive possibilities, but nonetheless necessary as both a creative and procreative force.[80]

What would ensue if the evil *yetzer* were totally destroyed? According to rabbinic legend, on a certain occasion (the People) Israel prayed that the Evil Impulse be handed over to them for destruction. The prophet Elijah warned them that if the *yetzer* were destroyed, the whole world would collapse. Nevertheless, when Israel's prayers were answered, they imprisoned the *yetzer* for three days. But during that time, when they looked for a fresh egg, none could be found in all the Land of Israel. Then the people prayed that if they agreed to free the *yetzer*, would God agree that henceforth all urges and desires would be licit ones? To their disappointment, the response of Heaven was that no conditional prayers would be answered. Since it was acknowledged that without the *yetzer* the world could not survive, the people blinded the *yetzer* (to keep him under control) and released him (disabled) back into the world.[81] The dialectical instruction of this tale is that in order for there to be desire in men at all, there must also be illicit desire.[82] And licit desire, productive and vital, is necessary for the continuation of life. Although influenced by Platonic and Christian mind-body dualism,[83] the Rabbis nonetheless reject ethical dualism in favor of a monistic construction of *yetzer*. Comprised of both constructive and destructive forces, the *yetzer* retains its own singular existence and essence.[84]

The Rabbis' view of *yetzer*-driven sexuality situated ideal behavior within the scale of human fragility. Controlling one's *yetzer*-related urges was viewed as a great challenge. It was told that R. Akiva (first-century sage) mocked those who could not withstand the power of their *yetzer*, yet he himself was saved from falling before the "tempter" only by heavenly intercession.[85] If a man sees that his *yetzer* is getting the best of him, he should go to a place where he is not known, put on black garments, and do what he desires in private.[86] It is better that a (Jewish) man commit a sin in secret than profane the Name in public.[87] The Rabbis also understood the power of self-deception: a person forever thinks that no matter how he acts he is right, since the *yetzer* causes him to (rationalize) his course of action.[88]

The Jewish religious texts at times use food-related, biological metaphors to characterize the *yetzer*. In one such instance, God is described as having given the Law as a *tavlin* (seasoning or spice) to temper the harshness of the *yetzer*.[89] The *yetzer* as "leaven in the dough" is the rabbinic characterization most impregnated with biological possibility. The metaphor comes from the final daily prayer of R. Alexander: "Master of the World, it is revealed and known to You that it is our duty to do Your will, but what prevents us? The leaven in the dough."[90] Leaven (yeast) is a biological agent, a catalyst used in baking to "enliven" the taste and texture of breads and other foods. The process by which yeast does its work is fermentation, which, if kept within control, can add value to food and drink. When fermentation is excessive, however, the preparation will be spoiled, the food unpalatable.[91] Like the *yetzer*, leaven is a ferment that can either induce decay or be a source of productivity and growth.[92] Like the *yetzer*, yeast is an external agent inserted by the (B)baker to function internally, transforming the flour and water into risen dough ready for the oven. As we see, "leaven in the dough" is an especially appropriate metaphor that portrays the *yetzer* as dialectic in nature—useful, even necessary, for human functioning and progress, yet fraught with license and immorality if not controlled. As additional evidence, the Rabbis equate the evil *yetzer* with *chametz*, the leavening agent (yeast) prohibited during the eight days of Passover when Jews are restricted to unleavened bread. In Judaism's critical view, "any man who permits his appetites to dominate his faculty of cognition is undisciplined [literally, 'uninstructed']."[93] The *Zohar* warns that "the evil *yetzer* seduces with food and wine."[94]

In summary, rabbinic synthesis of the *yetzer* posits Judaism, a learned framework, as an overlay imposed on man's instinctual, biological inclinations. The Rabbis regarded the forbidden as precisely that which man desires the most, but is able to forgo when Torah-infused limitations rule those urges elemental to his nature.[95] Avot d'Rabbi Natan relates the following: "Rabbi Simeon ben Elazar says, the evil *yetzer* can be compared to iron that is placed in a flame. All the time it is in the midst of the flame, people can make from it any utensil they might want. So too, the evil *yetzer*: its only means of reform are the words of Torah, for they are like fire."[96] The Talmud advises, "Drag the *yetzer* into the study house. If it's made of rock, it will be crushed; of iron, it'll be smashed to pieces."[97] Study of the God-created Law is an "antiseptic" to the *yetzer*'s urgings.[98] Biologically speaking, controlling one's *yetzer* results in the triumph of the long-term male reproductive strategy of high-investment, strict monogamy over the short-term strategy of low-investment polygyny. As the biological counterpart to the polygynous male strategy, the *yetzer* embodies a powerful, innate drive with both destructive and beneficial possibilities. Man's *yetzer* has the potential to lead human beings to both enormous feats of creativity and love and, conversely, to enormous deeds of self-destruction or even violence.[99]

Is There a *Yetzer* Instinct in Females?

Women also have a short-term reproductive strategy that can reward opportunistic mating with high-quality men willing or unwilling to invest in their children.[100] Pursuing this strategy, women may seek male investors either by design ("sugar daddy") or deception (cuckoldry). Since the Sages of tradition were men, it is not surprising that the rabbinic discourse on *yetzer* sexuality is heavily androcentric.[101] As was the case in traditional rabbinic deliberation, the *yetzer* was constructed by men for the purpose of instructing other men. Nowhere in the religious texts is the *yetzer* relegated *only* to men, but, as we have seen, descriptions and personifications of the *yetzer* better conform to the male than the female short-term reproductive strategy.[102] In most rabbinic sources, "[uncontrollable] sexual desire is envisioned as that of a man for women."[103] Female sexuality is usually left as an unexamined given, although there are indications that wives are assumed to be more in control of themselves than husbands[104] but sometimes flirt with young men.[105] In addition, the *yetzer* can also be applied generally to female sexual desire[106] and can function as a force that drives a widowed or divorced woman to remarry.[107] I would conclude that even though the sexuality of women is clearly recognized (and the *yetzer* is nowhere said to be limited to men only), the Rabbis viewed males as the more *yetzer*-activated sex in need of legal restraint.[108] For men, "the visual temptations of forbidden women are everywhere, and only sexual satisfaction within marriage [displacing the *yetzer* urge] can overcome them."[109]

Conclusion

> Our descent, then, is the origin of our evil passions!!
> —*Darwin*, M Notebook *(1838), quoted in Wright, p. 327*

In a lecture at Oxford University in 1893, T. H. Huxley, historically known as "Darwin's Bulldog," insisted that proper behavior not be learned from nature: "Let us understand, once for all, that the ethical progress of society depends not on imitating the cosmic process [or] ... running away from it, but in combating it."[110] Like Huxley, Judaism contends that the capacity to do evil is inherent in all people. Although detecting potential danger from others has certainly been selected for, strategies for deceiving one another have also evolved in the ongoing "arms race" known as sexual selection. Regarding deception, the Talmud comments on the biblical tension between Laban and Jacob. After Rachel warns Jacob about her father Laban's habits of deception, Jacob responds by saying, "I am his equal in the ability to deceive." The Talmud asks, "Where did Jacob learn to be so crafty?" The answer given is, "when dealing with the evil *yetzer* [of Laban], one [Jacob] must be wily, too."[111]

During the past century and a half, the gap between what science and religion claim as truth has expanded into a wide chasm. In this chapter, I have attempted to at least partially bridge the chasm by demonstrating how Judaic law and the construction of *yetzer* regulate the nature of male sexual instinct. To this end, the religious texts depict the protoscientific *yetzer* as a dialectically operating, biotheological construct.

In his book *Darwin's Dangerous Idea*, Dennett suggests that evolutionary scientists be on a sharp lookout for areas of conflict between science and religion.[112] This book suggests the opposite approach: it would better serve the interests of both science and religion to seek areas of intersection. Evolutionary science lessens its validity as overarching theory in direct proportion to its tendency to dismiss or trivialize the embodied human universals guarded by religion. Our goal as evolutionary thinkers should be the mutual accommodation, when possible, of religious culture and biological theory.

Notes

1. See n. 3; Gen. 1:1.
2. Gen. 2:7.
3. *Yesh mi ain,* or "something from nothing."
4. Ps. 103:14.
5. Rashi commenting in the Artscroll Siddur on Gen. 2:6–7, p. 11.
6. Gen. 3:22.
7. Gen. 6:5.
8. Note God's pessimistic prognosis using the *y-tz-r* construct in Deut. 31:21.

9. Despite the existential nature of man's *yetzer,* God decides to never again destroy all life (Gen. 8:21). Hirsch confesses an inability to understand the reasoning of this verse, since implantation of the *yetzer* had been, after all, God's work (p. 165).

10. Gen. Rabbah 32, 34; Eccl. Rabbah 9:14.

11. Lev. Rabbah 24.

12. In contrast, the Christian doctrine of original sin posits the origin of evil in the *choice* made by Adam and Eve to disobey God.

13. Gen. 2:19.

14. From *Toldos Ha-Adam*; referenced in Slifkin, *The Challenge of Creation,* p. 273.

15. Ps. 147:4.

16. Ps. 147:9.

17. Heschel, 1951, p. 100.

18. Ps. 104:30.

19. Neh. 9:6; Mishnah Berachot 7:5 and 9:2.

20. In Ps. 92 (read on the Sabbath), God's "designs" (of the natural order) are described as "deeply profound," a wording that can be seen as paralleling the complex, semihidden Darwinian dynamic.

21. Gen. 6:12.

22. Mishna Tanchuma Noah 5; Talmud Sanhedrin 108a.

23. Gen. Rabbah 28.8.

24. Freedman, 1993, p. 63; for a full elaboration of Judaic monism, see the chapter "Jewish Knowing."

25. Gen. 1:26.

26. Berachot 60b. Rashi inferred another dualism from the double *yod*: that two human formations are represented, one for this world and one for the resurrection (see Slifkin, 2006a, pp. 77–78).

27. Deut. 6:5.

28. לבבך (*levavekha*, "your heart").

29. Mishnah Berachot 9:5.

30. Schofer, 2003, p. 27.

31. Avot, Nos. 1–6.

32. Ibid. Nos. 7–10.

33. Boyarin, 1993, p. 64.

34. Biale, 1992, pp. 44–45.

35. See the chapter "Traditionalism and Human Evolutionary Success" for full exposition of this idea.

36. The Talmud confirms that promiscuous men are commonly seen (Ket. 36b2).

37. Ridley, 1993, p. 266. Interpreting the phrase "stolen waters are sweet" (Prov. 9:17), Rashi explains that men naturally desire and pursue that which is forbidden to them (Sotah 7a3, n. 26).

38. See Symons, 1981, p. 211, and Buss, 1994, pp. 79–81.

39. Ackerman, 1995, p. 156; see the chapter "The Fertility of Prominent Men in the Bible and Ancient Middle East."

40. Ellis and Symons, 1990, p. 529.

41. See Symons, 1994, p. 87.

42. Buss, 1994, p. 70.

43. Ridley, 1993, p. 178.

44. Fisher, 1992, p. 87.
45. Identified without reference to Judaism by Tiger, 1999, p. 75.
46. Porter, 1901, p. 132.
47. Hag. 16a, quoted in Montefiore and Loewe, 1938, p. 296.
48. Tan. B. Metsora 26b.
49. Shabbat Rabbah 14:3.
50. Suk. 52a.
51. Gen. Rabbah 22:6.
52. Suk. 52a.
53. Ps. 81:10.
54. Tan. I:284.
55. Gen. Rabbah 22:6.
56. Naz. 4b3, including n. 26.
57. Lev. Rabbah 14:5.
58. Eccl. Rabbah 4:13.
59. Gen. Rabbah 54:1.
60. Ked. 30b.
61. Burnham and Phelan, 2001, p. 252.
62. Wright, 1995, pp. 367–368.
63. When we are seized by the desire to sin, we ignore the advice of our good *yetzer* (Ned. 32b1).
64. Ezek. 36:26.
65. Avot, 2002, p. 63.
66. Yev. 63b5, n48.
67. Fishbane, p. 138.
68. From Schofer, 2003, p. 45.
69. Gen. Rabbah 34.
70. Patai, 1977, p. 500.
71. Lamm, cited in Patai, p. 500.
72. Pirkei Avot 4:1.
73. Suk. 52a.
74. Ber. Rabbah 9:7.
75. Eccles. 4.4.
76. 1 Chron. 29:18; in rabbinic parlance it is the heart, not the head, that is the seat of thoughtful judgment.
77. Urbach, 1987, p. 475.
78. Quoted in Urbach, 1987, p. 477.
79. Sanhedrin 107a. The Talmud's advice for personal *yetzer* management is to "push it away with the left hand but draw it close with the right." By this is meant one should embrace the evil *yetzer* for licit procreation but reject it for the illicit. (Sotah 47a4, n.36).
80. Boyarin, 1993, p. 74.
81. Yoma 69b.
82. Porter, 1901, p. 120. This act of blinding (thus limiting) the *yetzer* is considered the origin of the incest prohibition in Jewish law (one of the forbidden sexual deviancies, *giluy arayot*).
83. See the chapter "Jewish Knowing" and Porter, 1901, pp. 93–97.
84. Boyarin, 1993, p. 62.

85. Ked. 81a.
86. Chag. 16a; Meg. 17a2.
87. Ked. 40a.
88. Ber. Rabbah 10.
89. Ked. 30b.
90. Ber. 17a. In describing the need to control the "dark side" of human nature, naturalist Lyle Watson uses the same metaphor: "We need to *leaven* [italics mine] the single-mindedness of our unconscious attitudes with conscious flexibility" (1995, p. 283).
91. Jacobs, 1995, p. 608.
92. Gordis, 1988, p. 106.
93. Saadia, 1948, p. 361.
94. Ber. 100.
95. Biale, 1992, pp. 47–48.
96. Referring to Prov. 25:21–22.
97. Suk. 52b.
98. Sifre, chap. 45, quoted in Moore, 1962, p. 481.
99. Boyarin, 1993, p. 75. As one of many recent examples, does Elliot Spitzer, former governor of New York, come to mind?
100. Rav Idi comments that a woman's evil *yetzer* will influence her desire to get married. Thus it is asserted that, unlike the male *yetzer,* the female *yetzer* affects the long-term sexual strategy (Ket. 53a3).
101. An exception in Soloveitchik, 2002, pp. 134–135, refers to the female inclination for primping by using mirrors.
102. In a full discussion of the "value" of various women to men, the Talmud says the most determining factors are her family status, her occupation, and her relative health (Ket. 40a2–b1).
103. Schofer, 2003, p. 49. Women are generally seen as more in control of their sexual urge (Ket. 4b1).
104. Note the discussion in Ket. 4b1. Interestingly, follow the graphic depiction of a wife who carried out her adulterous scheme in Sotah 8b4–9a1.
105. Ket. 72b1.
106. Ket. 54a3.
107. Ket. 53a3.
108. For example, a man's sexual desire may be visible (by erection), but a woman's is internal (Ket. 64b1, including note 3).
109. Biale, 1992, p. 78.
110. Quoted in Watson, 1995, p. 250.
111. Meg. 13b.
112. Dennett, 1995, p. 515.

References

Ackerman, D. 1995. *A Natural History of Love.* New York: Vintage Books.
Artscroll Siddur—The Stone Edition. 2005. Brooklyn, NY: Mesorah Publications.
Avot d'Rabbi Natan. 2002. Version A, Ch. 16, translated by Jonathan Schofer in a paper given at the meeting of the Association of Jewish Studies.

Biale, D. 1992. *Eros and the Jews.* New York: Basic Books.
Boyarin, D. 1993. *Carnal Israel.* Berkeley: University of California Press.
Burnham, T., and Phelan, J. 2001. *Mean Genes.* New York: Penguin Books.
Buss, D. M. 1994. *The Evolution of Desire.* New York: Basic Books.
Dennett, D. C. 1995. *Darwin's Dangerous Idea.* New York: Simon & Schuster.
Ellis, B. J., and Symons, D. 1990. Sex differences in sexual fantasy. *Journal of Sex Research* 27(4): 527–555.
Fishbane, Michael, 1998. *The Exegetical Imagination.* Cambridge, MA: Harvard University Press.
Fisher, H. 1992. *Anatomy of Love.* New York: Ballantine Books.
Freedman, S. 1993. *Life as Creation.* Lanham, MD: Jason Aronson.
Gordis, R. 1988. *Love and Sex—A Modern Jewish Perspective.* New York: Hippocrene Books.
Heschel, A. J. 1951. *The Sabbath.* New York: Noonday Press.
Hirsch, S. R. 1966. *Commentary on the Torah—Genesis.* Brooklyn, NY: Judaica Press.
Jacobs, L. 1995. *The Jewish Religion.* New York: Oxford University Press.
Montefiore, C. G., and Loewe, H. 1938. *A Rabbinic Anthology.* New Haven, CT: Meridian Books.
Moore, G. F. 1962. *Judaism in the First Centuries.* Cambridge, MA: Harvard University Press.
Patai, R. 1977. *The Jewish Mind.* Lanham, MD: Jason Aronson.
Porter, F. C. 1901. The Yecer Hara—A study in the Jewish doctrine of sin. In *Biblical and Semitic Studies.* New York: Charles Scribner's Sons.
Ridley, M. 1993. *The Red Queen.* New York: Penguin Books.
Saadia Gaon, 1948. *The Book of Beliefs and Opinions.* New Haven, CT: Yale University Press.
Schofer, J. 2003. The redaction of desire: Structure and editing of rabbinic teachings concerning *yeser* ("inclination"). *Journal of Jewish Thought and Philosophy* 12(1):19–53.
Slifkin, N. 2006a. *Man and Beast.* Brooklyn, NY: Yashar Books/Lambda Publishers.
———. 2006b. *The Challenge of Creation.* Brooklyn, NY: Zoo Torah/Yashar Books.
Soloveitchik, J. B. 2002. *The Rav Speaks.* Brooklyn: Judaica Press.
Symons, D. 1994. Beauty is in the adaptations of the beholder. In *Sexual Nature Sexual Culture.* Chicago: University of Chicago Press.
———. 1981. *The Evolution of Human Sexuality.* New York: Oxford University Press.
Tanakh—The Holy Scriptures. 1985. Philadelphia: Jewish Publication Society.
Tiger, L. 1999. *The Decline of Males.* New York: St. Martin's Press.
Urbach, E. 1987. *The Sages.* Cambridge, MA: Harvard University Press.
Watson, L. 1995. *Dark Nature—A Natural History of Evil.* New York: HarperCollins.
Wright, R. 1995. *The Moral Animal.* New York: Vintage Books.

Chapter 2

Jewish Knowing

Monism and Its Biological Implications

Michael Satlow

Editor's Introduction

Thousands of years ago, the ancient Greeks used the word know *with two separate meanings: to know by the senses and to know by the mind. As heirs to the Greek intellectual tradition, Western thinkers have generally assumed that knowledge has two origins and areas of influence, mind and body. Dualistic epistemology reflects the view that human beings are constituted of these two irreducible elements.*

As was discussed in the previous chapter on the bifurcated yetzer, *Judaism has also been influenced by classical dualism. But, as Michael Satlow explains in this chapter, Judaic thought as a whole requires a monistic source of knowledge. In contrast to essential dualism, monism acknowledges the human being as a unitary, organic whole with no independently functioning parts. In Judaic thinking, the monistic nature of human beings stems from the basic unity of God Himself. Rabbi S. R. Hirsch explains Moses's desire to understand both God's essence[1] and his attitude of encounter with human beings.[2] In his biblical commentary, Hirsch insists on the harmonious relationship between the diversity and uniformity of both God and His ways.*

In contemporary social scientific research, "bodies" and "minds" are seldom studied monistically (i.e., as inseparable). Satlow suggests in this chapter that Judaism's insistence on the monistic unity of God might also be appropriate as a model for the social scientific study of human behavior.

> Like the Jewish monotheistic intuition,... modern [natural] scientists instinctively believe that a fundamental unity underlies all natural phenomena.
>
> —*Rabbi Norman Lamm*

The perceived conflict between reason and revelation troubled Saadia, the early tenth-century Gaon (head) of the rabbinic academy of Sura (in modern day Iraq). Conversant with the rapid advance of scientific knowledge throughout the Islamic world, along with the sophisticated methods that Islamic philosophers were developing to reconcile this new knowledge with traditional theological positions, Saadia offered a bold Jewish alternative. At the beginning of his tractate, *Book of Doctrines and Beliefs,* written in Arabic for a Jewish audience, Saadia complains that Jews are increasingly falling into error. These errors, he explains, derive from an inability to properly reconcile the knowledge derived from reason with the knowledge derived from tradition. The result was that Jews did not know whether to trust their reasoning or their tradition:

> When I considered these evils both in their own nature and in their particular manifestations, my heart grieved for my race, the race of mankind, and my soul was moved on account of our own people Israel, as I saw in my time many of the believers clinging to unsound doctrines and mistaken beliefs while many of those who deny the Faith boast of their unbelief and despise the men of truth, although they are themselves in error. I saw men sunk, as it were, in a sea of doubt and covered by the waters of confusion, and there was no diver to bring them up from the depths and no swimmer to come to their rescue.[3]

Saadia argued that, in fact, the choice between reason and revelation was a false one. His position followed naturally from his assumption that there is a single, God-given, truth. God has endowed humans with sensory perceptions and intellectual resources that, when used properly, lead to the discovery of this truth. Scripture, especially the Torah, does not as a result contradict the truth attainable through reason. By his logic, contradictions are only apparent, not *real*. A "contradiction" between the results of one's reasoning and one's scripturally informed faith is actually an error either in reasoning or scriptural interpretation. One purpose for writing his book, he says, is "to find out for ourselves what we know in the way of imparted knowledge from the Prophets of God."[4]

Although the answers have changed, the problem confronted by Saadia remains remarkably persistent. In today's language, it is the conflict that some see between science and faith. Religion, many think, exists in a distinctive epistemological domain in which critical inquiry does not apply. Science is found here and religion there; at best, they exist in tension with one another. This perceived tension has been so great that Darwin's theory of evolution has been a frequent visitor to the American legal system and political process for more than a century.

The binary thinking that underlies the common conception of science and religion as occupying opposite poles on the same line expresses itself in other, subtly related domains of knowledge. The phrase "nature versus nurture" expresses a similar epistemological dichotomy. Are human beings born as blank slates (tabula rasa) upon which culture imprints itself, or are we genetically determined? As applied to the theory of evolution, this is largely a false dichotomy: all biological social scientists recognize that culture (nurture) plays a critical role in mediating the fitness of genetic mutations. For most social scientists, however, the choice is starker, with biological influence most always omitted in the chain of causation. This division between nature and culture, and the privileging of the latter over the former, rarely result from a disinterested weighing of the data. Rather, the "conflict" results from an *a priori* commitment by many to see humans fully embedded in culture *rather than* the process of natural selection.

The compartmentalization of religion as a unique and disconnected area of human knowledge, and the binary thinking that grows out of it, are a legacy of Reformation and Enlightenment science. By emphasizing human interiority and subjectivity, the Protestant Reformation reinforced the notion that religion (and matters spiritual) constituted an independent domain of human experience. As such, religion was made into a discursive category instead of an integral part of culture. One's beliefs now stood apart from, and frequently in opposition to, other domains of knowledge, such as science. This binary thinking spilled over into anthropological models. The sharp distinction between body and soul during the Reformation was shifted to the material body, on one hand, and one's faculty for thought on the other. The soul was seen as the seat of rational thought, which, in turn, was identified as that which was distinctively human. The philosophy of René Descartes exemplifies this dualism—he pithily located the essence of human existence not in overall biological vitality but in the thought process itself.[5] For most religious thinkers of the Reformation, there was tension between belief (associated with soul and spirit) and rational thought (science, associated with the material world). In the context of this oppositional thinking, belief won out: religion trumped science hands down. Enlightenment thinkers were only too happy to adopt dualistic thinking even as they reevaluated aspects of it. In turning the tables, they accepted the dichotomy accompanied by the possibility of tension, but reversed the conclusion: science and rational thought now claimed the upper hand.

As we saw from the words of Saadia, the assumption that science and religion are in tension is in no way "natural." Yet just as dualistic thinking would have appalled Saadia, it remains dysfunctional well into our own time. On a cultural and legal level, it strains the fabric of our society, as in the "nature vs. nurture" debates and the policy conclusions derived therefrom, often hopelessly enmeshed in religious claims. On the level of academic research, there is an increasing awareness that epistemological dualism impairs rather than promotes the generation of predictive data and the acquisition of general knowledge. The learning process itself is instinctual. The human mind learns within the parameters of what it is predisposed to learn: our evolutionary history has endowed us with special mental devices, each content-sensitive and expert at extracting needed information from our environments.[6] A well-known modern critic of epistemological dualism is Steven Pinker. In his book, *The Blank Slate: The Denial of Human Nature and Modern Intellectual Life,* Pinker argues strongly that nature versus nurture is not an either/or issue. To lean so heavily toward cultural explanations (nurture) of human behavior, he argues, is to willfully and irrationally neglect the powerful influence of biology and genetics. Human beings share certain behavioral propensities, modes of behavior inherited from our evolutionary past, and these must be consulted to achieve a richer account of modern human behavior.

Such criticism, however, has not been limited to the work of cognitive scientists like Pinker. Paul Bloom, a psychologist, has recently argued for a biological basis for human belief in supernatural forces and an afterlife. He posits that the evolutionary development of human cognitive faculties led, quite incidentally, to the natural development of these beliefs; they are, to a certain extent, hardwired. Lawrence Sullivan, a professor of religion, has argued for the relevance of neuroscience in understanding religious experience. Each of these authors (among many others) chips away at the epistemological dichotomies of what has been referred to as the (dualism-based) Standard Social Science Model.[7] This chapter reflects my own continuing attempt to grapple at the intersection of religion and science. Over the last forty years, scholars who study religion from academic perspectives have been moving fitfully toward an understanding of "religion" from a scientific perspective. Bloom perhaps exaggerates the biological basis for, and the universality of, religious phenomena. Can scientific theory and data contribute to a more accurate understanding of religion? Can religious reflection and behaviors be interpreted as making sense scientifically?

Our starting point here is the observation that classical Jewish texts understand the human being from a monistic perspective. Judaic epistemological dualism, however, is more prevalent now than it was in antiquity due to the influence of Platonic and Christian anthropological dualism. According to some passages in Plato, human beings have a body and a soul. The ethereal, eternal soul is the seat of rational thought, and, though it lives imprisoned in the body, it yearns for a more spiritual existence. This dualistic anthropology is entirely foreign to the Hebrew Bible and, quite secondary, to the classical rabbinic literature of late antiquity.[8] Both the biblical and rabbinic writers believed that humans are largely indivisible. Human bodies were seen as battlefields in which different desires and urges fight for dominance, but "our bodies are us." That which is essential to and distinctive about the human being is within each body and inseparable from it.

Whether empirically correct or not, the premise that humans are monistic rather than dualistic carries in its wake several implications. Perhaps most important are the epistemological issues: if the human being is seen as a single, organic unit that does not decouple the rational element ("soul") from the flesh, what does it mean to "know" something? The point of this exploration is to show that a shift of presuppositions can lead to far-reaching shifts of understanding, which can cause us today to see traditional Jewish concepts with new eyes. I am not arguing that these monistic understandings are more "authentic" but, instead, that ancient presuppositions can be useful to modern understandings. What impact does a monistic model have on the way we understand knowledge? How does the explicit uncoupling of "thought" and "knowledge" from the "mind," "brain," or "soul"—and its concomitant assimilation into the body as a whole—change the way we understand certain traditional Jewish concepts?

In this chapter I will focus on a monistic epistemology for understanding biblical and rabbinic positions regarding God and the *mitzvot* (commandments). These two topics are useful to juxtapose because they highlight the two epistemological poles referred to earlier. If knowledge and being are synonymous, what does it mean to "know" God? And if *mitzvot* are performed by the body, how is "knowledge" influenced? More broadly, the assumption of a monistic human invites into the conversation insights from evolutionary biology. In what ways do these theological implications relate to—or even collapse—the biological categories of cognition and conation, thinking and acting instinctively, respectively? Similarly, how might Darwinian adaptation—understandable as a kind of embodied knowledge—play a role in analyzing Jewish norms and practices?

I should be clear that this chapter is my tentative and experimental attempt to explore the usefulness of applying scientific concepts to the study of Judaism. This is *not* a claim that "Judaism" functions in some evolutionary fashion, like a living organism. Judaism is a second-order scholarly construct, a loose category by which we more easily refer to a particular religious community's range of belief and practices.[9] People, not abstract second-order categories, can adapt, and one of the interesting questions that lies behind this chapter and throughout this volume is the nature of those adaptations and the utility of using scientific models to describe them.

Monism

The Hebrew Bible understands humans to be monistic beings. "And God created man in His image," the Bible relates. "[I]n the image of God He created him, male and female He created them."[10] The human in this account is not divided into parts, but is a single organism made as an indivisible being in the image of God.[11] Whatever the precise relationship of this account to the second human creation story in Genesis 2:7–22, both are consistent in regarding humans as monisms. In the second story, unlike the first, "the Lord God formed man from the dirt of the earth. He blew into his nostrils the breath of life, and man became a living being."[12] Here, the human is singular, but the force that vivifies him—God's contribution—is separable. Indeed, without God's force of breath the human remains a lifeless corpse. The Torah tells us nothing further about this force, but it appears to be that which causes humans to come alive rather than that which makes them distinctively human.

As has long been noted, there is a connection between the biblical assumption of a monistic anthropology and biblical eschatology. The Bible has only a very shadowy, if any, exposition of an afterlife. Generally, the Hebrew Bible assumes that nothing remains "alive" after a person dies; i.e., that there is no future corporeal "life." This lack of attention to the afterlife also helps account for biblical notions of theodicy, the problem of God's justice. Biblical writers, unlike later Judaic thinkers, could not shift reward and punishment from the body to some kind of separable eternal soul. Nor did they have the option of deferring deserved reward and punishment to the period of some "world-to-come," an eschatological moment when all who ever lived will be judged. For the most part, the Bible assumes that good people are rewarded in their lifetimes with long lives, prosperity and plentiful descendants. On the other hand, those who do wrong will face the divine reckoning before they die.[13] At the same time, the Bible is perfectly aware that this bad behavior–causes–bad consequences relationship does not always obtain. One biblical response is found in the passage known as the "thirteen attributes":

> The Lord passed before him [Moses] and proclaimed, "The Lord, the Lord, a God compassionate and gracious, slow to anger, abounding in kindness and faithfulness, extending kindness to the thousandth generation, forgiving iniquity, transgression, and sin; yet He does not remit all punishment, but visits the iniquity of parents upon children and children's children, upon the third and fourth generation.[14]

The claim that God punishes descendants for the sins of ancestors solves the problem of why it appears that bad things happen to good people. At the same time, it raises a sensitive moral problem: can a just God punish a person for the sins of ancestors? This problem so troubled the prophet Jeremiah that he flatly rejected it as unjust: "But every one shall die for his own sins: whosoever eats sour grapes, his teeth shall be blunted."[15] Job recognizes the problem, but refuses to offer a solution. God *must* be just, however much the evidence of the world suggests otherwise. God's justice, Job asserts, is simply beyond the ken of human understanding.

Rabbinic anthropology is somewhat different and not entirely coherent, but it too leans strongly toward monism. The Sages of antiquity,[16] authors of classical Jewish texts such as the Palestinian and Babylonian Talmud, primarily use the terms "body" (*guf*), "spirit" (*ruach*), and "soul" (*nefesh* or *neshama*) to refer to the human.[17] The biblical "spirit" is seen as God's vivifying force. At least one understanding of the complicated relationship between the body and the soul, though, is captured well by a rabbinic parable:

> "Speak unto the children of Israel: When a *nefesh* (soul) [unwittingly incurs guilt ...]"[18]: Why [does it say] *nefesh* [and not "person" or "man"]? [The guilt] overpowers the soul. R. Yishmael taught a parable: [It is similar] to a king who had an orchard containing nice figs. He placed two guards in it, one lame and the other blind, to guard it. He said to them, "Be careful about the figs." He left them and went. The lame man said to the blind man, "I see nice figs." He said to him, "Come and let's eat [them]." He said to him, "Am I able to walk?" He said to him, "Am I able to see?" What did they do? The lame man climbed on the blind man and they took the figs and ate them. They went and returned, each to his place. After some time, the king came and said to them, "Where are the figs?" Said the blind man to him, "Can I see?" Said the lame man to him, "Can I walk?" The king, who was sharp, what did he do? He placed the lame man on the blind man and judged them

together.... Thus, in the world-to-come, the Holy One says to the *nefesh*, "Why did you sin before Me?" She says before Him, "Master of the world! Am I the one who sinned before You? The body sinned. From the day that I left it could I sin?" He then says to the body, "Why did you sin?" He says before Him, "Master of the World! The *nefesh* sinned. From the day that she departed from me, can I not be compared before You like dirt on a trash-heap?" What did the Holy One, blessed be He, do? He returned the soul to the body and judged both of them as one.[19]

Body and soul here are portrayed as both separable and inseparable; they are conceptually distinct while being inextricably bound. The body is incomplete without the soul, and the soul is powerless without the body. Body and soul are thus seen as different parts of the same morally responsible human being. The Rabbis of antiquity frequently return to the construct that human beings have parts and yet are single, integral organisms. A Talmudic passage attempts to work out one aspect of this complex relationship:

Our Rabbis taught: There are three partners in a human being, the Holy One, blessed be He, his father and his mother. His father sows the white stuff [semen] from which [are formed] the bones, sinews, fingernails, the brain in his head and the white of the eye. His mother sows [!] the red stuff from which [are formed] skin, flesh, hair, and the black of the eye. The Holy One, blessed be He, gives breath and soul, beauty, eyesight, hearing, speech, ability to walk, discernment, and mental alertness. When his time arrives to depart the world, the Holy One, blessed be He, takes His share and leaves the share of his father and his mother before them. Rav Pappa said, "That is like the folk-saying, 'Shake off the salt and leave the flesh to the dog.'"[20]

This is a brilliant, if incorrect, display of rabbinic embryology. The Rabbis are working from an implicit "two seed" embryological theory that posits contributions to the embryo by both the father and the mother. Hence, just as the father "sows" (literally, "emits seed"), so too is the woman imagined to be emitting seed. This "seed," though, contributes not genes but colors, and the two dominant colors of the (white) human body are thought to arise (more or less) from the colors of their respective seed. Mother and father together make only a body—God contributes not only the vivifying force but its animating characteristics. Without God's contribution—likened by Rav Pappa to salt—the body is but a hunk of flesh.

God's critical contribution is explored in another rabbinic interpretation:

And when a [man's] time to depart (from this world) arrives, the Holy One, blessed be He, takes His share and leaves that of his father and mother before them, and his father and mother weep. The Holy One, blessed be He, says to them: "Why do you weep? Have I taken something of yours? I have taken only that which is Mine." They answer Him: "Sovereign of the universe, so long as Your portion was integrated with ours, our share was preserved from worms and maggots; but now that You have taken away Your share from ours, our portion is lying exposed to worms and maggots."

R. Judah the Patriarch illustrated this with the help of an analogy:

> To what can the matter be compared? To a king who had a vineyard, which he leased to a tenant farmer [for a share of the crop as compensation]. The king (one day) instructed his servants: "Go, pick the grapes in my vineyard, taking my share and leaving that of the tenant in its place." Forthwith they went and carried out the king's command, whereupon the tenant began to cry aloud and weep. Said the king to him: "Have I taken anything of yours? Is it not my own that I have taken?" He replied: "O my lord, the king! So long as your portion was with mine, my share was preserved from spoliation and theft. But now that you have taken your share, mine lies exposed to spoliation and theft."[21]

God's contribution to the human being is but a single portion, but it is also the critical one. Without the contribution by God, the remainder is without value or irreparably damaged.

The ambivalence between a purely monistic and a more nuanced understanding of the human pervades the classical rabbinic literature, and no doubt derives at least in part from rabbinic struggles to understand what it means for a human to have been created, according to Genesis 1:27, "in the image of God." Humans, they note, are at once different than animals and yet not quite divine.[22] Balanced precariously between heaven and earth, complete with the ability to tilt one way or the other, the human being, in the rabbinic imagination, is a complicated yet integral compound. The point is that God cannot simply remove His portion and leave an animal; it's all or nothing.

While the Rabbis struggled with understanding their biblical heritage, they were also heirs to a classical tradition. Many years earlier, Plato suggested that there was a radical dichotomy between the body and soul. These statements portray the soul, which contains the uniquely human rational or thinking ability, as if trapped in the prison of the flesh. This is the strain of platonic thought that many (but not all) later Christians would highlight when they developed both elaborate theologies of the soul's afterlife and monastic orders whose disciplinary practices served to degrade the flesh to "release" the soul. During later periods, many Jews lived in Christian societies that took the firm distinction between body and soul for granted. Similarly, rabbinic discourse, influenced by the Christianity of these environments, developed its own theologies of the soul, with some also adopting harsh ascetic practices meant to degrade the body.

Plato and the tradition he engendered, though, is hardly unequivocal on this issue. In addition to his harsh evaluation of the body, he articulates a much more nuanced anthropology. In Plato's "other" writings we find something that much more resembles the rabbinic passage above.[23] For this "other" Plato and many of the late antique philosophers who built upon his legacy, body and soul were mutually necessary: true perfection of the self could only be achieved in an embodied state. Although also not unequivocal, the Jewish philosopher Philo[24] thought the human self was located in body and soul as an integral unit, not in the rational soul alone.[25] In their monistic anthropology, the Rabbis of Palestine stood well within the classical tradition of the broader culture in which they lived.

As this chapter asserts, however, this is a nuanced monism, one that has room in some regards for divisions within the self. Just as today we distinguish between different parts of the body (e.g., brain, heart, liver, arm) but call them all "body," so too in antiquity the Rabbis made their own distinctions about what constitutes the self while maintaining their essentially monistic orientation. In addition to notions of body, spirit, and soul, the Rabbis engaged in intricate analysis of human "desires" or "inclinations." Much like St. Augustine in his *Confessions,* the Sages were confronted with the basic theological problem that humans, though created by a good, beneficent, and just God, desired to do, and actually did, bad things. Why did God endow our nature with evil propensities? The Rabbis explained this with the notion of *yetzer*: God created in us an "evil inclination" (*yetzer ha-ra*) so we would procreate, build houses, and earn a living. Though capable of bestowing creativity and productivity, the *yetzer ha-ra* needed to be carefully reined in because trouble ensues when humans do not exercise proper control over it. Again, the *yetzer* is not detachable from the self as a whole; we are obliged to control it, but it is not something that can or should be eradicated.[26] The Rabbis recognized human beings as living organisms and discrete individuals dominated by conflicting yet necessary tensions. Many of these tensions are distinctive to human beings, so the Rabbis never suggest that we can fully resolve them. Our inner struggles, along with our monism, are part of the rabbinic understanding of the human condition.

The Rabbis' monistic orientation is reinforced by their eschatology. The Hebrew Bible, as discussed above, maintained a less complex anthropology and, correspondingly, a less complex (but perhaps more problematic) eschatology. As previously noted, all reward and punishment, according to the dominant voice of the Torah, was to occur in the here and now. Not all biblical authors or later Jews subscribed to this theology. Josephus, for example, relates that the Pharisees believed in transmigration of the souls.[27] This concept imputes that souls are separable and reborn into other bodies where, presumably, they receive their just reward or punishment (an idea that would return in kabbalistic thought). The Rabbis, however, rejected eschatological scenarios that involved separating body from soul. They were thus compelled to develop an eschatology that would take into account both their monistic anthropology and a "World-to-Come," an afterlife in which God metes out true and final justice.

The rabbinic answer was the doctrine of resurrection of the dead. There is no single rabbinic eschatology—ideas of what occurs at the "end of days" are scattered and largely incoherent, part of the *aggadah* (oral law) rather than normative *halakhah*. Uniting these disparate eschatologies is the notion that God will ultimately resurrect the dead *in their flesh,* and judge each of them. As the previous rabbinic passage illustrates, judgment can come in no form other than embodied. This doctrine became so fundamental to the Rabbis that they declared: "All Israel has a share in the World-to-Come ... And those who do not have a share in the World-to-Come [are those] who say the [doctrine of] resurrection of the dead is not found in the Torah ..."[28] The Rabbis here go beyond an insistence that Jews *believe* in resurrection of the dead; they now acknowledge its authority as rooted in the Torah.

This importance the Rabbis placed upon the *body-as-self* makes better sense of other rabbinic norms relating to bodily treatment. Bodies are not to be mortified because mortification serves no function. With a monistic anthropology there is every reason not to degrade the body. Humans might fast and mortify themselves on occasion as a penitential rite or in order to petition God, but neither the intent nor result of these practices is allowed to be self-abusive. Dead bodies are treated with respect and left whole because they are still considered the "self," albeit without God's enlivening spirit. When I die, "I" remain located in my body rather than becoming a disembodied spirit. To disrespect a corpse is viewed as abusing the whole individual, not just his or her body.

Knowing

The epistemological implications of divesting the "soul," "mind," or "brain" of its monopoly on thought are both clear and radical: now the *whole* person "knows." Knowledge is acquired not only through what one reads, memorizes, or watches others do, but also by what one himself does. To juxtapose, just as the body then "knows" what one reads, memorizes, and watches, so too does the mind "know" what one does. A physical activity can give knowledge as valuable and well integrated as knowledge acquired in a classroom. The *acquisition* of knowledge becomes also a bodily activity, one that involves a person's entire being. To say that one's "mind" knows something, or that one knows something only in a certain way (e.g., cognitively), becomes a case of non sequitur. While the acquisition of certain forms of information might involve one method of "intake" more than another, the transformation of that information (or, as Saadia might say, that acquired through sense perception) into knowledge is diffused throughout one's entire being.

The radical corollary to this approach is that *knowledge* and *being* are synonymous. If one can know only by using one's whole being, then knowledge *transforms* being. Viewing knowledge through the prism of the monistic body means that the truest knowledge of a thing lies in *doing* and finally *being* that thing.

There is nothing philosophically unproblematic in this formulation. Although existentialists such as Martin Buber never phrase the issue as I have, they end up at the same conclusion. Buber acknowledges the possibility of knowledge-without-being, but this formulation is possible only in the "I-It" relationship between subject and object, necessary but far inferior to the "I-Thou" relationship between two subjects. Many of the same objections leveled at Buber are equally applicable to the monistic epistemology elaborated in this chapter.

However philosophically questionable this epistemology may be, it does raise important general issues applicable to evolutionary thinking. As mentioned previously, the monistic anthropology of the Rabbis collapses the modern-day, social scientific distinction between cognition and conation. Behaviors produce knowledge with high quality equal to that of cognition. Herein lies a developmental model that centralizes personal behavior within the process of adaptation. As a result, human actions become personally transformative. If adaptation is seen as embodied knowledge, then we can also see this rabbinic anthropology in the same light. Just as generations of organisms can adapt to their environment, aided and constrained by their biological flexibility, so can humans over time be transformed through their behaviors.

This is not, however, a knowledge that can be genetically transmitted. In the rabbinic model there is a hint of Lamarck—behaviors create transformations. Unlike Lamarck, the Rabbis never suggest that these personal transformations pass to the next generation. Instead, as we will see, they prefer to transmit *traditionally* those behavioral patterns. Adherence to the normative standards may produce or maintain *culture*, a range of adaptations that share a family resemblance.

This way of thinking can be pushed more speculatively to consider tradition a form of adaptation.[29] Human societies develop and sustain traditions because they "work"; they adapt over the generations to the environmental needs of that society. We are accustomed to thinking about traditional knowledge as disembodied knowledge easily manipulated and separable from behaviors. A monistic cultural anthropology, however, suggests a different perspective. In most societies, tradition is always considered an organic part of culture. Let me suggest, then, that tradition can be seen as a mode of transmitting embodied knowledge that a society considers true not because it stands the test of reason but because it becomes an embodied part of each individual.

Let's now consider how tradition as *embodied knowledge* plays out against environmental factors, using the language of evolutionary biology. According to a phenomenon known as the Baldwin Effect, certain behaviors can convey an evolutionary advantage to organisms.[30] The organisms that learn these behaviors gain an advantage in natural selection, creating a cycle that reinforces the behavior. Over time, the behavior becomes ingrained in the species. Evolutionary biologists debate whether the Baldwin Effect really occurs and, even if it does in some species, if it applies to humans. Nevertheless, traditions work within a reinforcing cycle that confers advantages within certain environments. The same traditions conferring advantage in one setting, however, can easily confer disadvantage in another. This fact can account for tradition's far greater intergenerational fragility and malleability than genetic inheritance.

The *idea* of an anthropological monism can provide a fresh way of reframing some old problems. Anthropological monism helps us better understand the biblical and rabbinic discussions of God and idolatry. How, after all, is one to *know* God short of *becoming* God? It also opens a new perspective on the *mitzvot*, which, through a monistic perspective, can be seen as creating embodied knowledge by means of obligated physical activities. The notion of embodied knowledge explains why and how different Jewish communities come to radically different conclusions when making *halakhic* decisions.

God and the Problem with Idolatry

Paradoxically, the Torah acknowledges the human desire to know God while noting its impossibility. The best-known expression of this desire is attributed to Moses: "Now, if I have truly gained Your favor, pray let me know Your ways, that I may know

You and continue in Your favor,"[31] *to* which God replies, "I will make all My goodness pass before you, and I will proclaim before you the name Lord ... but ... you cannot see My face, for man may not see Me and live."[32] "Seeing" God's face and living in this world are, as rabbinic *midrash* emphasizes, mutually exclusive. The impossibility of true knowledge of God is why Moses requests to know God's *ways*: "One who is created does not have the ability to know the Creator, only His *ways*."

Why can humans not know God and live? Because, if knowledge and being are the same, then knowledge of God is equivalent to *being* God, the One who transcends all categories, including life and death. Death occurs only on this side of the heavenly firmament; it is impossible for one who lives to know the One who does not die. The importance of Exodus 33:20 is not "one who sees God will die" but, rather, one who lives cannot know God. Human beings, as biological organisms, are constructed and constrained through the selection of traits. In the biblical understanding, God exists beyond selection. Humans are subject to environmental pressures that can cause evolutionary changes; God, in many later Jewish philosophical understandings (although not in the Bible itself), is eternally static. For Maimonides, God is the great "unmoved Mover," that indefinable being that cannot experience passion or change. Whether humans evolve directionally, perhaps toward a greater perfection, or, conversely, fitfully and randomly, is a question well beyond the scope of this chapter. My point here is that we, unlike God, do evolve according to constraints that God is seen as not having.

This difference might help us understand better the problem with idolatry. Yehezkel Kaufmann has noted the biblical obsession with idolatry:[33] though God inveighs against idolatry numerous times in the Torah, the Torah never makes explicit exactly what the problem with idolatry is. The problem with idolatry is commonly understood as a denial of monotheism, yet when Israel turned to idolatry the idol is portrayed as God Himself, not as a substitute for God or an addition to the pantheon of Gods. Israel, for example, only turns to the molten calf when she loses contact with God.[34] Idolatry springs from the otherwise commendable desire, expressed by Moses himself, to know God.

Thus the Judaic problem with idolatry is twofold. On the one hand, humans have by their nature a capacity to understand something, however small, of the divine. That part of us made in the divine image really *can* understand God. To focus that knowledge on an idol, an iconic representation, is to critically mistake the nature of that image. While God bestows on us fully functioning bodies, idols, as the psalmist says,

> have mouths but cannot speak, eyes, but cannot see; they have ears, but cannot hear, noses but cannot smell; they have hands, but cannot touch, feet, but cannot walk; they can make no sound in their throats. Those who fashion them, all who trust in them, shall become like them.[35]

Just as it is impossible for a human to fully know God, so too it is impossible for us to know that which is inanimate. To attribute divine qualities to rocks and wooden statues is to misapprehend not only God but ourselves as well.

The second and more serious problem with idolatry is that, although it might arise from the best of intentions, it assumes that knowledge of God is possible in the first place. This, as we can see from our analysis of the epistemological ramifications of monistic anthropology, is an arrogant error of misconception: to know God is to become God, a process requiring an impossible ontological leap.

The issue of human arrogance is at the center of the rabbinic understanding of the Tower of Babel story. According to the biblical account:

> Everyone on earth had the same language and the same words. And as they migrated from the east, they came upon a valley in the land of Shinar and settled there. They said to one another, "Come, let us make bricks and burn them hard" (brick served as stone and bitumen as mortar). Then they said, "Come, let us build a city and a tower with its top in the sky to make a name for ourselves; else we shall be scattered all over the world." The Lord came down to look at the city and tower that man had built, and the Lord said, "If, as one people with one language for all, this is how they have begun to act, then nothing that they may propose to do will be out of their reach. Let us, then, go down and confound their speech there, so that they shall not understand one another's speech."[36]

The problem at the center of this story, which is only alluded to, is the human desire to climb to heaven—to "make a name for ourselves," and thus gain the power that will prevent them from being scattered. God fully understands the arrogance inherent in the human attempt to know or become God. Curiously, the Bible's account does not regard the human attempt as fanciful—God acknowledges that, left unchecked, the plan has a chance of success! As interpreted by later commentators, the Tower of Babel story becomes a cautionary tale of human arrogance that attempts to storm the heavens.

Though the Rabbis do not formulate the issue in this manner, they do excoriate those who have thought themselves divine. Pharaoh and Nebuchadnezzar are singled out for their arrogance in thinking themselves gods. Making an idol, like building a tower, expresses an intolerable arrogance by presuming we can cross a line forbidden to us.

When body and self are seen as inseparable parts of an integral whole, the problem with idolatry is the presumption that in a certain object we can know God. When knowing is seen as being, this knowledge of God was seen as transformative, implying a crossing over the firmament that separates heaven from earth. Knowledge of God is therefore construed as dangerous not because of its content—no matter how much we try, we humans can never truly know God—but because it implies that humans think they can know God and thereby become God-like. Idolatry reflects the same mistake, denying not only God's existence, but, more importantly, God's otherness. To reduce God to an idol, a lifeless object, is to place God in the material world. Idolatry engages in category confusion when thinking that humans can aspire to divine status.

Mitzvot

While the assumption of "knowledge as being" can help us see idolatry in a new light, a more interesting application of the concept regards the relationship of human behavior to human adaptation. In one of the Torah's versions of the giving of the Ten Commandments on Mt. Sinai, Israel is said to have responded to Moses, "we will *do* and we will *hear*."[37] A well-known rabbinic interpretation of that pledge is that the Jewish people committed itself to covenantal standards even before knowing what they are. The traditional understanding is that the people had such faith and love of God that they were ready to do whatever it was that God required of them. Just as plausible, however, is that this *midrash* reflects a recognition of the consequences of a monistic anthropology that attributes transformation to knowledge. Traditional religious behaviors can be, as I said before, embodied knowledge in which ingrained cognition and conation blend together.

The modern Jewish theologians Franz Rosenzweig[38] and Abraham Joshua Heschel[39] have insisted that the value of the *mitzvot* can be realized only through their performance. This position has been criticized on philosophical grounds, for it removes their theological justifications from the possibility of critique.[40] But the presumed need for cognitive critique is evidence of Athens and Jerusalem passing by each other in the night. The critics of Rosenzweig and Heschel are correct that neither gives the *mitzvot* the rational explanation and justification that Western philosophy demands. In fact, both thinkers remove the *mitzvot* from the possibility of purely intellectual comprehension. Though they do not explicitly say this, both Rosenzweig and Heschel are doing no more than denying the dualism of bodily and cerebral understandings. In their explanation of *mitzvot*, they reclaim the holistic biblical and rabbinic presupposition of bodily integrity. We can use this language to rephrase their argument as follows: performance of *mitzvot* imparts a particular knowledge, which then effects personal transformation.

This conception of theology as "embodied" helps explain the ambivalence of Jews for purely theological speculation and attempts to justify Judaic law theologically (*ta'ame ha-mitzvot*). The Rabbis themselves eschewed theology, preferring to work out theological issues in the form of ad hoc stories and biblical interpretations. It is not accidental that one can open a tractate of the Talmud entitled "Blessings," "Shabbat," or "Levirate Widows" but none entitled "God," "Torah," or "Israel." Until Saadia Gaon, there were very few attempts to articulate a Jewish theology, a systematic and rigorous exploratory process we today call "theological." Until recently, theological explanations for performance of the *mitzvot* have typically been *post facto*, assuming the importance of first observing the commandments, and only then ascribing the reasons for observance. Traditionally, Jewish theological justifications assumed a very secondary role compared to the religious behaviors themselves.

Here the evolutionary parallel is intriguing. Lamarckian thinking assumed a purposeful evolution—organisms cumulatively embodied the traits they needed. The theory is attractive because it is so straightforwardly teleological. We would like to think the justification precedes the action but, in the Darwinian model, the reverse is true. Many things change with unpredictable variety, and the test of outcome suitability will depend on natural selection. We first *become,* only to see whether or not what we *became* proves beneficial or detrimental for descendant-leaving in future environments.

Evolutionary thinking can also extend to the transmission of *mitzvot.* Within all forms of Judaism, revelation alone is never enough; rather, it must lead to actions for which a body is required. If Torah, defined as the continually unfolding process of revelation, is seen as the word of God, then its translation or embodiment into the will of God occurs in the *mitzvot.* The bodily execution of *mitzvot* is crucial to the rabbinic enterprise, for only with a body can a Jew fulfill God's will. And as Jews act in an embodied way by performing *mitzvot,* so too do the *mitzvot* act upon their performers.

There is a way in which Jewish law, *halakhah,* resembles the random variations that impact the process of natural selection. Prior to the modern period, *halakhah* was determined locally, by individual rabbis making specific decisions potentially in conflict with rabbis of other localities. During the Middle Ages, these individual decisions would occasionally be compiled into a code that would then adjudicate between competing rabbinic decisions, resulting in an array of decisions labeled as authoritative. But just as quickly as codes were written and disseminated, local rabbis began to challenge their authority, and the process began anew. *Halakhah* does not follow a straight line but, instead, develops out of a tree of options, some that survive the test of time while others do not. *Halakhah* is clearly a product of culture rather than genes, nor is it a single, culture-based "meme." At the same time, evolutionary theory raises for *halakhah* the issue of selection and survival: does adherence to a particular set of embodied commandments confer benefit on those who observe them?

"Benefit" can be taken in different ways. We might first ask if adherence to *halakhah* confers a *direct* benefit in the evolutionary sense of "advantage." Might the observance of certain *halakhic* practices lead to longer lives and more offspring? This question has a long genealogy; for example, it has been argued that superior Jewish hygiene resulting from ritual practices led to fewer Jewish deaths during the plagues of the Middle Ages. This issue even today remains unresolved, with more rigorous investigation yet to be done.

It is also possible to understand "benefit" in an *indirect* sense. Adherence to a constellation of *mitzvot* can be judged as conferring the "benefit" of increased group cohesion. From the social scientific perspective, the group effect of ritual has been well noted. Rituals function to mark group boundaries and internalize group identity. The Jewish food laws, *kashrut,* can be explained as having this kind of function. Observance of *kashrut* requires individuals to "sacrifice" by restricting social action with outsiders. At the same time, it creates metaphorical kinship feelings among those who submit to the discipline. Such camaraderie can create a larger network of mutual support that extends the assistance members can be called upon to render to each other.[41] Group differentiation through differential *mitzvot* observance hardly stops at the level of "Judaism." Adherence to common *mitzvot* creates strong identities among different *sectors* of Jews; if Judaism can be seen as a *genus*, these individual groups of Jews represent its different *species*. Jewish history is replete with discrepancies in traditions differentiating rather than unifying Jews. The introduction of *glatt* kosher meat in eighteenth–century Eastern Europe, for example, helped create a distinctively Hasidic identity. Those Orthodox Jews today who insist on a more restrictive standard for dairy products (*chalav yisrael*) are also consciously differentiating themselves from other Orthodox Jews for whom *chalav yisrael* is unnecessary for proper *kashrut* observance.

Given the great variety of *halakhic* variation, on what basis would an individual find one *halakhic* position more compelling than another, since both contain perfectly valid legal reasoning? For a possible answer, we can return to the notion of knowledge as embodied. Because knowledge is not confined to a special compartment of our being (e.g., soul, brain), it is part of our whole being, informing who we are. Failure to understand the totality of how *mitzvot* affect a person explains why nearly all Jewish thinkers have been stymied when trying to articulate the value of the *mitzvot*. The universe of those who only *ponder* the problem convince only each other, while those who *practice* the *mitzvot* remain unfazed by theological explanations. Rosenzweig and Heschel consciously try to articulate what cannot be articulated; those wishing to understand the *mitzvot* solely by contemplating them inevitably become frustrated.

To assert that *mitzvot* are beyond intellectual investigation would, of course, be an exaggeration. Students of rituals in a cross-cultural framework describe the interaction as reinforcing relationships between concepts and rituals. Judaism contains, for example, many prohibitions against "mixing," like *shatnez, kashrut,* and hybridization of species. In Jewish religious texts, these negative *mitzvot* are related to myths of both *creation,* as when God created the world's creatures in distinct categories, and *chosenness,* in which God separates Israel from the other nations to be a holy people.[42] While we cannot know whether the ritual practices or the associated theology came first, we can see how Jewish myths and *mitzvot* are mutually reinforcing, strengthening the core truth that together they manifest. What is less visible is "unified truth," the transformation effected in *mitzvot*-performers themselves by a combination of ideas and rituals. Since all cultures contain complex interactions between myths and rituals, those cultures that presuppose supremacy of the intellect to define rituals would expect a ritual participant to be willing and able to articulate this "single truth." When Judaism assigns to rituals the power of creating their own knowledge, the ability of the performer to translate ritual knowledge into words fully intelligible to a nonpractitioner is denied.

Throughout this chapter I have contrasted those who localize human knowledge in a rational element with those who disperse knowledge throughout the whole being. I have placed *mitzvot*-performers in the latter group, treating them as a single community. Yet this is a forced commonality. While all historical manifestations of Judaism have considered *mitzvot* to be actions that reflect the will of God, various historical expressions of Judaism have understood the theological basis of the *mitzvot* in different ways. The logic of this chapter—that from a rabbinic perspective religious behavior provides transformative knowledge—leaves the door open for differences of understanding by different communities of observance. A monistic anthropology predicts that someone who strictly observes *kashrut* is likely to be a different person, everything else being equal, than a person who does not keep kosher. One whose *mitzvot* observance includes wearing garb of a style fashionable a century ago is unlikely to *be* like someone who wears more contemporary clothing. What are the implications of these differences?

Recognition of the transformative, nonintellectualized knowledge generated by *mitzvot* can help explain the chasms of understanding today (as always) between Jewish groups performing *mitzvot* differently. So the ultimate question can be formulated as, what is centrally Jewish? How does any Jew "know" that observed changes to ritual or liturgy are legitimately Jewish? Jewish groups have always disagreed on this very question, and their disagreements have been explained as being rooted in differing ontological hierarchies of revelation:

- The Torah is the true word of God given over to and recorded by Moses.
- The Torah is the word of God written and interpreted by human beings.
- The Torah is the work of wise human beings.

It is my view that the roots of disagreement are far deeper. Jewish legal systems function from the "top down": specifications for *mitzvot* are made by scholars who fight among themselves for the adherence of "catholic Israel." Even Reform Judaism, which is theoretically based on individual autonomy, functions today identically in this regard as do more traditional denominations. How do the rabbis of our time "know" what constitutes the most convincing answer to a particular *halakhic* or ethical problem? On what basis do Jewish communities decide which answers to incorporate and which to reject as "heretical" or not authentically "Jewish"?

Despite vocal claims to the contrary, these decisions are rarely intellectually straightforward. A given community generally accepts those customs and *mitzvot* that "feel" right—practices must conform to what that community accepts as conforming to their own religious tradition. That determination is governed in part by the hermeneutical experience of the community. Hence, an Orthodox community might retain a *halakhah* even though its abandonment can be justified for ethical reasons; in a Reform community, a doctrine must make ethical sense to be followed. To a great extent, however, such decisions are made according to unarticulated criteria such as customary practice. A cogent example of this is the burgeoning of rituals that mark female life-cycle events. Though the vast majority of such new rituals violate no *halakhic* norms, they are often branded in more traditional communities as not "authentically" Jewish, or even as violating Jewish law. Several classic *halakhic* divergences between modern Conservative and Orthodox rabbis also fall into this category. The decision about whether to allow electricity on Shabbat, for example, hinges on a relatively subjective determination of the definition of "fire." Orthodox prohibitions against eating cheese made with the curdling agent rennet are based on rennet's origin in the stomach lining of an improperly slaughtered animal. Conservative rabbis permit its use because, by the time it's used to make cheese, it has been transformed into a new, nonedible, chemical substance.

These examples of legitimate *halakhic* disagreement have been adjudicated less on intellectual grounds than on what felt right to each community. The intellectual argument dresses up the *a priori* rejection of such rulings by both the elite and the masses in each community. This, perhaps, is why custom without the force of law occupies such a prominent place in Jewish observance; non-*halakhic* custom reflects and sustains the monistic mode of being Jewish. The importance of customary practice suggests why rabbinic rulings are not universally accepted by all communities of Jews. Such rulings are traditionally comfortable to some communities while, in other communities, they are seen as dangerous tradition-busters.

The consequence of this decentralized monism is that Judaism defeats all attempts to precisely define it. Judaism makes the transmission of its knowledge—understood as diffused throughout one's entire being—impossible to those who do not engage in similar behaviors both repetitively and predictably. Perhaps this is the main reason why the Rabbis of antiquity were so uninterested in speculative theology.

Implications

It should not be surprising that the Hebrew Bible and the Rabbis of antiquity shared a monistic anthropology. Both the Israelite religion and rabbinic Judaism are at heart monistic enterprises. The Rabbis in particular assert that there is a single God, a single Torah, and a single legitimate Temple dedicated to serving the omnipresent God. This insistence on monistic singularity and unity has generated theological problems: how, for example, is evil to be accounted for? Like everything else in this world, evil must derive from God, who is, despite being the source of evil, essentially good and just:

> "I am the Lord and there is none else, I form light and create darkness, I make peace and *create evil*, I the Lord do all those things."[43]

More recently, the Holocaust has rekindled this problem of good and evil, and modern Jewish theologians have offered a variety of responses. The responses include denying God's omnipotence (God could not stop the Holocaust) or God's immanence (God is too far removed from human concerns to get involved). Yet there remains a stubborn resistance to recognizing an independent status for "evil." Even when confronted with the horror of Auschwitz, the central monistic tendency holds firm.

Judaic monism is a well-suited basis for looking at the relationship between religion and life science. Any understanding of Judaism that reduces it either to a set of rational, cognitive propositions *or* to a required set of *halakhic* behaviors must fail. Several years ago Jonathan Z. Smith drew upon theories of biological classification to propose a "polythetic" model of Judaism. His concept is that Judaism has no single essence but, rather, manifestations exhibiting family resemblances. Scholars of religion have found the model of polythetic classification appealing for understanding religion, although its potential usefulness has only recently been realized. Rather than seeing Judaism as a single unified organism with a definable essence, it would be more accurate to see it as a loose family of religious communities held together by overlapping but not identical characteristics. It is not "Judaism" itself that adapts to changing conditions so much as the historical communities falling within this family of Jewish communities.

The rabbinic resistance to dualism and its insistence on a monistic approach to human nature should warn against easy acceptance of the dualism that continues to pervade most Western thinking. I have attempted in this chapter to illuminate issues of Judaism using a monistic lens. Jewish monism can serve well as a model for proper investigation of complex human behaviors. What remains to be done is to utilize rabbinic monism and the monism of biological psychology/anthropology as models for reframing the more general intellectual issues. What might the epistemological divides between the sciences and humanities look like in a monistic framework? How can we better understand the human condition when the evolved body is taken fully into account? Such a reframing requires breaking down, or at least weakening, the recent division between "culture" and "nature," as well as "mind" and "body," in a forthright attempt to understand humans as integrated biological organisms. The social sciences cannot be seen as distinct from the biological sciences; humans, first and foremost, are living organisms, a claim all Judaic sources have affirmed.

The ramifications of this project extend far beyond abstruse speculation because there are practical implications of "embodied knowledge." Most Western educational philosophy is premised on the mind/body dichotomy. A monistic approach can force us to grapple with how we might better understand the "learning" process. Unitary thinking, which emphasizes learning as a whole-body experience, opens fresh paths for inquiry.

Personally, I do not find Saadia's answer to the conflict between "revelation" and "reason" compelling. For all its excesses, postmodernism has taught us that truth can frequently be a matter of perspective. The Rabbis are comfortable with the idea that God's true revelation is so full and rich that it could not be reduced to simple truths; *midrash* (rabbinic interpretations of the Bible) frequently assert multiple, mutually exclusive interpretations while refusing to judge which ones might be the most correct! So while I cannot subscribe to Saadia's simpler understanding of true "beliefs," I nevertheless think he is on to something. Religion and science, as traditionally construed, represent different intellectual approaches, but only dualistic assumptions would plot them on the opposite ends of a spectrum. Scientific method can help us better explain religious behavior, and one need not believe that religion is "true" in order to think its wisdom offers us opportunities to scrutinize human beings in new ways.

This chapter is a heavily revised and expanded version of an essay with a similar title that appeared in *Judaism* 45/4 (Fall 1996): 483–489. My thanks to *Judaism* and its editor, Prof. Murray Baumgarten, for granting permission for me to reprint and expand it. Unless noted, translations are mine or the editor's. Citations from the Bible are from, or based upon, *Tanakh: A New Translation of the Holy Scriptures According to the Traditional Hebrew Text* (Jewish Publication Society, 1985).

Notes

1. Hirsch, Rabbi S. R. 1966. *Hirsch Commentary on the Torah*, Vol. 2. Brooklyn: Judaica Press, p. 637 (commenting on Ex. 33:13).
2. Ibid., pp. 646–648 (commenting on Ex. 43:6–7).
3. Saadia Gaon, p. 29.
4. Ibid., p. 45.
5. Remember his classic expression, *"Cogito, ergo sum"* ("I think, therefore I am").
6. Ridley, p. 196.
7. In the S.S.S.M. "human nature," the evolved architecture of the human mind, cannot be a major cause of mental organization, social systems, culture or historic change. According to the S.S.S.M., cross-cultural variability demonstrates that human behavior, uncontaminated by biological influence, is the product solely of "culture" and "social processes" (Tooby and Cosmides, pp. 25–26, and 46).
8. Ca. 70–640 C.E.
9. Satlow, M., "Defining Judaism: Accounting for 'Religions' in the Study of Religion," *Journal of the American Academy of Religion* 74 (2006):837–860.
10. Gen. 1:27.
11. Cf. Schweizer 1992.
12. Gen. 2:7.
13. Cf. Deut. 6:10–25.
14. Exod. 34:6–7.
15. Jer. 31:30.
16. 70–640 C.E. (A.D.).
17. Cf. Boyarin 1993.
18. Lev. 4:2.
19. Lev. Rabbah 4:5.
20. Talmud Niddah 31a.
21. Eccl. Rabbah 5:10, translation by Urbach 1975, pp. 218–219.
22. Schofer 2005.
23. Cf. *Republic* 442A-B.
24. Ca. 30 B.C.E. (B.C.)–30 C.E. (A.D.).
25. Fraade 1986.
26. The chapter "Judaism's *Yetzer* as a Biological Construct" provides a full treatment of the topic.
27. Jewish War 2, p. 163.
28. Mishnah San. 10:1.

29. For a more detailed discussion, see the chapter "Traditionalism and Human Evolutionary Success."
30. Cf. Weber and Depew 2003.
31. Exod. 33:13. Also see Ned. 38a3.
32. Exod. 33:19–20.
33. Kaufmann 1972, pp. 13–20.
34. Exod. 32.
35. Ps. 115:5–8.
36. Gen. 11:1–7.
37. Exod. 24:7.
38. Rosenzweig 1961.
39. Heschel 1955, pp. 293–313.
40. Cf. Borowitz 1983, pp. 180–183.
41. See the chapter "Why Are Synagogue Services So Long?"
42. Cf. Douglas 1966.
43. Isa. 45:6–7; interestingly, Isaiah's claim has been sanitized in the traditional morning liturgy to read "who makes peace and *creates the all.*"

References

Bloom, Paul, 2005, "Is God an Accident?" *The Atlantic Monthly* 296/5 (December), pp. 105–112.

Borowitz, Eugene B., 1983, *Choices in Modern Jewish Thought* (Springfield, NJ: Behrman House).

Boyarin, Daniel, 1993, *Carnal Israel: Reading Sex in Talmudic Culture* (Berkeley: University of California Press).

Buber, Martin, 1970, *I and Thou* (New York: Charles Scribner's Sons).

Douglas, Mary, 1966, *Purity and Danger: An Analysis of Concepts of Pollution and Taboo* (New York: Routledge).

Fraade, Steven D., 1986, "Ascetical Aspects of Ancient Judaism," in *Jewish Spirituality: from the Bible through the Middle Ages,* Arthur Green, ed., (New York: Crossroads), pp. 253–288.

Heschel, Abraham Joshua, 1955, *God in Search of Man* (New York: Farrar, Straus and Giroux).

Kaufmann, Yehezkel, 1972, *The Religion of Israel,* trans. Moshe Greenberg (New York: Schocken).

Pinker, Steven, 2002, *The Modern Blank Slate: The Denial of Human Nature and Intellectual Life* (New York: Viking).

Ridley, Matt, 2003, *Nature via Nurture* (New York: HarperCollins).

Rosenzweig, Franz, 1961, "Teaching and Law," in *Franz Rosenzweig: His Life and Thought,* Nahum N. Glazer, ed. (New York: Schocken), pp. 234–242.

Saadia Gaon, 1985, "Book of Doctrines and Beliefs," Alexander Altmann, ed., in *Three Jewish Philosophers,* Hans Lewy, Alexander Altmann, and Isaak Heinemann, eds. (New York: Atheneum).

Satlow, Michael L., 2006, *Creating Judaism: History, Tradition, Practice* (New York: Columbia University Press).

Schofer, Jonathan, 2005. "The Beastly Body in Rabbinic Self-Formation," in *Religion and the Self in Antiquity,* David Brakke, Michael L. Satlow, and Steven Weitzman, eds. (Bloomington: Indiana University Press), pp. 197–221.

Schweizer, R. Eduard, 1992, "Body," *The Anchor Bible Dictionary* vol. 1, (New York: Doubleday), p. 768.

Smith, Jonathan Z., 1982, "Fences and Neighbors: Some Contours of Early Judaism," in *Imagining Religion: From Babylon to Jonestown* (Chicago: University of Chicago Press), pp. 1–18.

Sullivan, Lawrence E., 1998, "Coming to our Senses: Religious Studies in the Academy," *Journal of the American Academy of Religion* 66, pp. 1–11.

Tooby, John, and Leda Cosmides, 1992, "The Psychological Foundations of Culture," in *The Adapted Mind,* Jerome Barkow, Leda Cosmides, and John Tooby, eds. (Cambridge: Oxford University Press).

Urbach, Ephraim E., 1975, *The Sages: Their Concepts and Beliefs,* translated Israel Abrahams (Jerusalem: Magnes Press).

Weber, Bruce, and David Depew, eds., 2003, *Evolution and Learning: The Baldwin Effect Reconsidered* (Cambridge: MIT Press).

Biblical Lore and Biological Theory

Chapter 3

The Fertility of Prominent Men in the Bible and Ancient Middle East

Laura Betzig

Editor's Introduction

Throughout natural history, competition for the most valuable reproductive resources has been the hallmark of living organisms. Our species has been no exception: the creation of reproducing descendants has been a driving force for individual humans. Each of us alive today is the product of successful reproductive exertion by many generations of ancestors.

The Torah of Moses unambiguously defines a key element of religious success as the leaving of plentiful descendants. But a formula regarding exactly which Israelites will do the reproducing is not part of the mandate to "be fruitful and multiply." Within the biblical narrative, it is taken for granted that elite men should achieve disproportionate reproductive success through God's blessing.

In this chapter, replete with information from biblical and other ancient sources, Betzig astounds us with her conclusion: men of great prestige were able to father and provision the vast majority of the overall pool of descendants who, in turn, lived well enough themselves to successfully reproduce. Among the Jewish people, reproduction became more egalitarian only when postbiblical measures requiring monogamy that restricted extramarital sex came into the Tradition during the rabbinic period.

The Need for Men to Breed

Six days after creating the heavens and earth, and separating day from night; five days after putting up the firmament; four days after gathering together the seas and land, and bringing forth vegetation; three days after placing lights in the firmament; two days after bringing forth sea monsters and winged birds; and one day after making cattle and creeping things, God created Adam in His own image, and said, "be fruitful and multiply, and fill the earth and subdue it."[1]

Millennia after the Genesis account, Darwin's *On the Origin of Species* was published. In that book, Darwin suggests that wherever more individuals are produced than can possibly survive, a "struggle for existence" should follow. "Can we doubt," Darwin asked, "that individuals having any advantage, however slight, over others, would have the best chance of surviving and of procreating their kind? On the other hand, we may feel sure that any variation in the least degree injurious would be rigorously destroyed." In short, maladaptive traits should quickly die out, but adaptive traits promoting fertility should spread.[2] "Variations, however slight," he wrote, "if they be of any degree profitable to the individuals of a species, in their infinitely complex relations to other organic beings and to their physical conditions of life, will tend to the preservation of such individuals, and be generally inherited by their offspring." In other words, traits that make it easier for individuals to survive and reproduce should spread disproportionately into future generations.[3]

A dozen years later, Darwin elaborated on that theory in his next book, *On the Descent of Man and Selection in Relation to Sex*: "Amongst almost all animals there is a struggle between the males for the possession of the females," he asserted. Darwin filled chapter after chapter with woodcuts and written examples: from the "musical apparatus" of certain male insects competing for females' attention, to competing antelope males locking horns to gain prominence and thus monopolize the available females. And *H. sapiens* was no exception. As Darwin put it, "The strongest and most vigorous men—those who can best defend and hunt for their families, who were provided with the best weapons and possessed the most property, such as a large number of dogs or other animals—would succeed in rearing a greater than average number of offspring"; weaker men would rear less. Individuals should evolve to compete—for habitats, food, and mates.[4] Biological theory labels this sex drive "polygyny," the reproductive arrangement in which a male may, over his reproductive life, have relationships with more than one female. While we may prefer to think that humans are naturally monogamous, two-party marriage is a legal institution whose purpose is to control our drive that is instinctually polygamous.[5]

In 1948, nearly a century after Darwin, A. J. Bateman did experiments with the common fruit fly. He put five virgin males and five virgin females in a bottle; then he used genetic markers on the resulting offspring to determine their mothers and fathers. Bateman found all females almost always bred, but that males did not, and the best predictor of male reproductive success was their number of mates. A fifth of the males failed to breed at all; but a few did spectacularly well, producing almost three times as many offspring as the most prolific of the females. In other words, some males were big winners, some males were big losers, and most of the females were somewhere in between. As it turns out, male reproductive variance is greater than female reproductive variance—in fruit flies as well as most other species.

A generation after Bateman, in 1972, Robert Trivers generalized these polygyny-related findings, attributing the difference between male and female parenting to differing requirements of "parental investment." For the offspring of most species, mothers usually invest more than fathers.[6] Females invest more in a limited number of very large gametes (eggs), each of which travels down a fallopian tube for possible fertilization only periodically and precariously. In addition, females invest much more in the feeding and caring of young. In some species parental investment is small—in sea urchins, for example, eggs are fertilized externally and progeny are left to raise themselves. In other species, like most mammals, sex differences in parental investment are huge. Mothers will spend months, or even years, gestating; then they'll spend months, or even years, nursing. Fathers, on the other hand, may spend only a few minutes donating the sperm. Mathematically speaking, when a male invests less than 1 percent of what the female invests in their common offspring, his "resource budget" can afford one hundred mates instead of just one! The effect is a polygynous breeding system—some males will produce with more than one female, and other males will not produce at all. Where gender differences in offspring investment are small, the result is monogamous breeding—each female will usually mate with one male. But a polygynous breeding system will result when the minimum gender differences in investment are substantial. The effect of differential investment in offspring development is that most species, include all primates, have polygynous reproductive habits. As Trivers put it bluntly, "competition for mates usually characterizes males, because males of many species invest almost nothing in their offspring."[7]

Hundreds of studies have since borne out that conclusion. Across taxonomic groups—from insects to amphibians, to fish, birds, and mammals (including most monkeys and apes)—males most successful in competing for access to females also enjoy the most reproductive success. Dominant males have more sex, they have sex with more females, they father more offspring, and more of those offspring survive to reproductive age. Bigger, better fed, better armed, and better ornamented males outreproduce their competitors—from fruit flies to red deer.[8]

Inevitably, many males die, or don't reproduce at all. For every male with 100 mates, 99 others will do without; and for every male with 100 offspring, 99 other males will be lucky to create even one. The reason for this is that in stable, sexually reproducing populations, parents on average replace only themselves (the average number of surviving offspring per pair is two). So for every set of parents with more than two viable offspring, another set of parents will have one or none. Since in most stable populations the number of males roughly equals the number of females, for every male with more than one female, another male will fail to leave descendants.[9]

And these issues are also reflected in the behavior of our species. The female's egg is four orders of magnitude larger than a male's sperm, an asymmetry known as *anisogamy*. Other differences in parental investment follow from that fact: women gestate for nine months and nurse their children for many months or years. In traditional societies, weaning stops after three or four years only due to a new pregnancy. Men have the *opportunity* to contribute a great deal also—most men feed, house, protect, and otherwise care for their children. But while fathers have the *option* to contribute more than just sperm, they are not biologically *required* to do so. While many fathers have always been monogamous, in almost every human society some men have been polygynous (or extremely polygynous) if and when the opportunities present themselves.[10]

Like other species whose male parental investment is small, human males compete vigorously for females. Sometimes, they fight each other for sexual access, or as Darwin put it (remembering his Horace), they "went to war for a girl in Troy." Of course, men also fight to gain access to other resources such as habitats and meat; but the rewards of victory also include sexual access to fertile women. But interestingly, like other social species of animals, men have contrived the strategy of getting other men—often nonbreeders—to help feed, house, protect, and otherwise care for their children. In other words, dominant men fight also for access to other men's labor. So men compete for food, territory, women, and, in addition, control of other men.[11]

Recorded history bears out this pattern. For hundreds of thousands of years, small family groups of *Homo sapiens* moved around, hunting and gathering for a living. We lived in small family groups, and men who defended the best habitats, brought home the most meat, and won the most mates fathered, on average, the most children. Even now—from the armadillo-hunting Aché of Paraguay, to the dik dik–hunting Hadza of Tanzania, to the turtle-hunting Meriam Islanders of Northern Australia, to the whale-hunting Lamalera of Indonesia—good hunters achieve the highest reproductive success.[12]

The Need for Men to Breed in the Bible

Long before the ancient empires, the Hebrew people were blessed by a mandate to reproduce, which they did their best to fulfill. From Lamech the patriarch to Zedekiah the last king of Judah, they tried to "be fruitful and multiply, and fill the earth and subdue it." But some filled the earth better than others. Throughout the Hebrew Bible, men with means—more status, abundant food, and better habitats—outreproduced men without these advantages. A handful of men filled their households with women and children; but many more died young, without producing children.

The Hebrew Bible is a reflection of its historical context.[13] Powerful patriarchs, judges, and kings had sex with many women and fathered many children. Powerless men did not. It is uncertain whether Genesis 6:2 refers to powerful sons-of-gods or just powerful, mortal men; what is clear is that they were powerfully interested in reproducing with mortal females:

the sons of gods saw that the daughters of men were attractive, and took them as women (or wives) according to their choice.[14]

When God told Adam to "be fruitful and multiply" he said it just once. But nine generations after Adam, just after the Flood, Noah was commanded three times to fill the earth, to multiply in it, and to breed abundantly—along with every creeping thing.[15] Eleven generations after Noah, *YHVH* foretold the future to Abram in six ways: his descendants would be "as the dirt of this earth," as the "stars, if you are able to count them," and "as the sand on the seashore." Abram's destiny as successful ancestor was revealed in his newly given name: when *YHVH* made the covenant with Abram, his name changed to Abraham, "for I have made you the *father of a multitude* of nations."[16]

YHVH said the same thing to Abraham's wife, his wife's servant Hagar, two sons, and a grandson. At the advanced age of seventy-six, Abraham's wife Sarah was childless. So following Sarah's suggestion, Abraham tried to reproduce with Hagar. "Go in to my maid; it may be that I shall obtain children by her," said Sarah; and Ishmael, Abraham's "wild ass" of a son, was born. Ishmael turned out to be the father of twelve nations, as *YHVH* had promised. Soon thereafter, Sarah bore Isaac and obtained the same promise. She would be a mother of nations; her son would multiply like the stars of heaven. And Israel (Jacob), her grandson—having "struggled with God and with men"—would father another great nation, a company of tribes that spread out "to the west and to the east and to the north and to the south."[17]

Within the rest of the Torah, Moses repeated that prediction seven times. He told his people they'd be "a thousand times as many" as they were already; they'd "multiply greatly" in a land flowing with milk and honey; there'd be "not a male or female barren" among them, or among their cattle; they'd "abound in prosperity," in the fruits of their bodies, in the fruits of their herds, and in the fruits of their land. But Israel's predestination came with one condition. In Moses' words: "By loving the Lord your God, by walking in his ways, and by keeping his commandments and his statutes and his ordinances, then you shall live and multiply and the Lord your God will bless you in the land which you are entering to take possession of."[18]

But the covenant-breakers were cursed. As *YHVH* warned Moses, "You shall sow your seed in vain, for your enemies will eat it." There would be terror, consumption, fever, plagues, wild beasts, and pestilence. "You shall eat the flesh of your sons, and you shall eat the flesh of your daughters." Their land would lay desolate; their cities would lay waste. "And you shall perish among the nations, and the hand of your enemies shall eat you up."[19]

YHVH was as good as His word. The faithful brought home women as spoils. East of the Jordan, at Midian, Moses ordered his army to kill men, children, and older women, "but all the young girls who have not known man by lying with him, keep alive for yourselves." As a result, 32,000 virgins got Israelite husbands. Then Gideon at Peneul "slew the men of the city," but apparently left the women unharmed. David's commander, Joab, "slew every male" when he set up garrisons in Edom. There were more female spoils at Jabeshgilead, where the Israelite army killed men and defiled women, but found "four hundred young virgins who had not known man by lying with him; and they brought them to camp at Shiloh, which is in the land of Canaan."[20]

Israelite apostates, on the other hand, lost women and children. Even kings of Israel and of Judah were left without descendants. Within a generation after Solomon, Rehoboam lost the cities of Judah to Shishak of Egypt, who "took away the treasures of the house of the Lord and the treasures of the king's house; he took away everything." He made Jerusalem's inhabitants his "servants" *because*, as Shemaiah the prophet said, Rehoboam had "abandoned" the Lord. In Israel, Jeroboam's house was wiped out by a usurper, Baasha, *because*, as Iddo the prophet put it, he'd "made Israel to sin." Subsequently, "all the house of Baasha" was done in by another usurper, Zimri, *because*, said Abijah and Jehu, they'd "provoked" the Lord. Half a century later, in Israel, all seventy of Ahab's sons were slaughtered, along with "every male, bonded or free." In Judah, Jehoram, who'd married Ahab's daughter, lost his sons and his wives in an Arab raid, *because*, as Elijah pointed out, they'd "abominably" gone after idols. When the Assyrian Sennacherib set siege to Jerusalem in 701 B.C., he locked up King Hezekiah "like a bird in a cage," and took away "his daughters, his harem, his male and female musicians." Esarhaddon, who was Sennacherib's son, took Hezekiah's son Manasseh off with a hook in his nose and a bit in his mouth *because*, as Isaiah was aware, he'd "raged" against his Creator. The twenty-sixth dynasty pharaoh, Necho II, put an arrow in Josiah at Megiddo in 609 B.C. He then brought Josiah's son, Jehoahaz, back to Egypt to die *because*, in the words of Jeremiah's scribe, he'd done "evil in the sight of the Lord." Nebuchadnezzar II sent men to Jerusalem in 597 B.C., captured Jehoiachin, and brought "the king's mother, the king's wives, his officials, and the chief men of the land" back to Babylon *because*, as Ezekiel knew, they were "a nation of rebels." In 587 B.C., Nebuchadnezzar's men came again, "slew the sons of Zedekiah before his eyes," and led his women away *because*, as Jeremiah said again, he'd done "evil in the sight of the Lord."[21]

Winners and Losers: Polygynous Men Breeding in the Ancient Near East

Around 12,000 years ago in the Near East's fertile crescent, humans started herding animals and farming crops. Nomadic pastoralists and planters settled down for at least part of the year, and clan leaders with the biggest flocks, most abundant harvests, and the most servants produced the most children. Even today—from the Yomut Turkmen of Iran, to the Kipsigis and Gabbra of Kenya, to Yanomamo of Venezuela, to the Datoga of Tanzania—the most prolific gardeners and shepherds are the most prolific fathers.[22]

Just 5,000 years ago, in the space between the Tigris and Euphrates Rivers, the first empires were built. Since that time until nearly the present, emperors have lorded over their subjects, in part by collecting thousands of women and fathering hundreds of children. But the subjugated fared quite differently. For every emperor with 100 children, 99 subjects were lucky to raise even one to adulthood; and for every emperor with 1,000 women, 999 male subjects had none.[23] In every empire, millions of men worked as soldiers, slaves, or in sterile castes.

The mandate to breed and the punishment of lawbreakers didn't start with Genesis. All over the ancient Near East, the seed of the noncompliant was cursed. As early as the eighteenth century B.C., Hammurabi of Babylon, who by biblical chronology would have been Abraham's contemporary, threatened lawbreakers with "rebellion ... obliteration ... famine ... death; the spilling of his life force like water." In Egypt half a millennium later (around the time Moses was born), Jacob's descendants worked hard, building cities at Pithom and Raamses. And Seti I, who was Ramesses's father, warned violators of his decrees that (the falcon god) Horus and (the female Horus) Isis would go after their women and children. In Assyria, five hundred years later, Esarhaddon's vassal treaties cursed rebels with leprosy, locusts, floods, and infertility: "just as a mule has no offspring, may your name, offspring and descendants disappear from the land." But the Persian Darius the Great, who conquered Babylon, was most succinct: "Whosoever helped my house, him I favored; he who was hostile, him I destroyed."[24]

On the other hand, most emperors had legendary reproductive success. Nebuchadnezzar prayed to his Babylonian god, Marduk: "May I pull your yoke 'till I am sated with progeny?" Esarhaddon's Assyrian exorcist congratulated him on his production of numerous sons: "May they spread like seeds of grass and rule over all countries!" The Egyptian god Min, "Bull of the Great Phallus, the Great Male, Owner of All Females," presided when pharaohs were crowned. And for thousands of years, the Mesopotamian New Year's festival began with a fertility rite. The sitting king played the role of the shepherd god, Dumuzi (a.k.a. Tammuz), opposite an anonymous Inanna (a.k.a. Ishtar), the first Venus. Upon finishing her song of arousal, they had sex in a temple and thereby made the king's land fertile.[25]

Strong kings stole women and children from weak kings. In New Kingdom Egypt, pharaohs raided the families of hill country sheiks in Retenu (Canaan), bringing home 323 "female children of princes," 270 "favorite" women of princes, plus various "paraphernalia for entertaining the heart." The Assyrian Esarhaddon plundered women from a pharaoh's palace; Ashurbanipal, his son, brought home kings' wives, sisters, daughters, brothers' daughters, and concubines when he made war on Babylon, Tyre, and Elam. When Nebuchadnezzar II's father, Nabopolassar, left Ashurbanipal's son dead after his Nineveh siege, he turned the city into a "ruined heap" and hauled plunder and exiles to Babylon. When the Persians invaded the Aegean, they had "the most beautiful girls dragged from their homes and sent to Darius' court."[26]

Eighteen generations after Adam, Abraham made his way to Canaan from his home at Ur beyond the Euphrates. Upriver from Ur at Mari, and by biblical chronology at the same time, Hammurabi's friend Zimri-Lim kept 232 women in his harem. He once sent a letter to his wife Shibtu asking for thirty weavers, "or however many are choice and attractive, who from their toenails to the hair of their heads have no blemish."[27]

In New Kingdom Egypt around a millennium later, Amenhotep III got 317 girls ("marvels brought to his majesty") from Mitanni. Three hundred eighty-two women were requisitioned in the Amarna letters, according to the surviving clay tablets first deposited at the "House of the Correspondence of Pharaoh." As one letter writer said: "I heed all orders of the king, my lord, and herewith send on ten women." Others offered ten servants and ten maidservants, or promised twenty girls and five hundred oxen. Some were advised to send their daughters along: "Prepare your daughter for the king, your lord, and prepare the contributions." Others gave up their wives. A vassal wrote from Shechem: "If the king wrote for my wife, how could I hold her back? If the king ordered me to 'put a bronze dagger into your heart and die,' how could I not execute the order of the king?" A century after the Amarna letters, Ramesses II, possibly the pharaoh at the time of the Exodus, fathered forty-nine sons. He remembered the day his father gave him the crown: "I was a child between his arms ... his love of me was so great in his bowels, he equipped me with household women, a royal harem."[28]

In Assyria, hundreds of "women of the palace" (*sa ekalli*, or bearers of heirs) and "enclosed women" (*sekretu*, or bearers of bastards) waited on emperors at court. Esarhaddon made his son an emperor in "the royal harem," which Ashurbanipal would rebuild "on a magnificent scale." At Nineveh, in his twenty thousand–plus clay tablet library, Ashurbanipal kept a copy of the *Gilgamesh* epic—whose king took "the daughter of the warrior, the bride of the young man," and did what he wanted with her. Other tablets list "Harem Governesses and Weavers" and "Female Singers," counting thirty-six governesses, 145 weavers, fifty-two maids, and 194 miscellaneous women. Some tablets have sexual potency incantations written on them. They prescribe seeds, roots, leaves, twigs, the hearts of male ravens, the thumbs of bats, the penises of male partridges, the saliva of bulls with erections, and say: "Let the wind blow! Let the mountains quake! Wild bull, get an erection! Stag, get an erection! Potency! Potency! Bed! Bed! Copulate!"[29]

There was a "House of the Palace Women" in Nebuchadnezzar II's Babylon with its own provisioners and overseers of the slave girls. The famous hanging gardens, on vaults and arches, were put up for a Median wife. A generation later, Belshazzar entertained a thousand men, using the gold and silver vessels taken from the Temple in Jerusalem, so that "his wives and his concubines might drink from them."[30]

There were more harems in Persia. When Darius III went to war with Alexander the Great, he took along 365 female companions, one for each day of the year, his children, their governesses, and a "herd of eunuchs." After Alexander beat Darius at Issus, he "went some distance in the direction of Eastern arrogance" by recruiting women "of outstanding beauty" from all over Asia. A century earlier, Artaxerxes II fathered 115 illegitimate sons and three legitimate ones. His grandfather, Ahasuerus, or Xerxes I, sent out an order that "beautiful young virgins be sought out for the king." In the Scroll of Esther, she and the other "candidates" were bathed for six months in myrrh, for another six months in spices, after which they were brought into the palace. "In the evening [Esther] went, and in the morning she came back to the second harem in the custody of Sha-ash'gaz, the king's eunuch in charge of the concubines." Esther was told never to go in to Xerxes again, "unless the king delighted in her and she was summoned by name."[31]

Prestigious Men Breeding in the Bible

Most of the Hebrew patriarchs counted their women in the single digits (see Appendix). When Lamech, Adam's great-great-great-great-great grandson, "took two wives," he became Genesis' first named polygynist. Abraham's father, Terah, had children by at least two women, as did Abraham's younger brother, Nahor. Abraham had a son by Hagar, his wife's maid, another by his wife and half-sister, Sarah, and six more by Keturah, his second wife. Isaac and Rebecca's firstborn, Esau, had boys by all three of his wives; Isaac's secondborn, Jacob (Israel), had twelve sons by four women. Six of those sons (Reuben, Simeon, Levi, Judah, Issachar, and Zebulun) came from Leah, while two (Gad and Asher) came from Leah's maid, Zilpah. Two others (Joseph and Benjamin) came from Rachel, his second wife, and two more (Dan and Naphtali) were from Bilhah, who waited on Rachel.[32]

Judges produced more children by an order of magnitude. Gideon had seventy sons, "for he had many wives," and at least one boy by a concubine. Jair's thirty sons rode around on thirty asses; Ibzan fathered thirty sons "and thirty daughters." Abdon had forty sons and thirty grandsons, and Samson was "blessed"—though numbers are not reported.[33]

Kings were even more successful. Even before he became king, David took a few wives. There were Ahinoam, Abigail, and Michal daughter of Saul, Israel's first king. Then there were Haggith, Abital Eglah, and Maacah, daughter of the king of Geshur. After he became king, David took a few more. He "took more concubines and wives from Jerusalem, after he came from Hebron." The text does not recount how many. When Maacah's son Absalom made a bid for the throne, David went away and left ten concubines behind.[34]

David was reported to have fathered at least twenty sons. The Bible names Amnon, Chileab (or Daniel), Absalom, Adonijah, Shephatiah, Ithream, Shammua (or Shimea), Shobab, Nathan, Solomon, Ibhar, Elishua (or Elishama), Eliphelet (or Elpelet), Nogah, Nepheg, Japhia, Elishama, Eliadah (or Beeliada), another Eliphelet, Jerimot—and Tamar, reportedly his only known daughter. The "sons of his concubines" were undoubtedly also numerous. David lived in an ivory palace, wrapped in cassia-scented robes, surrounded by "ladies of honor" and their "virgin companions"—he was provided girls until the day he died. When he was on his deathbed at age seventy, his servants showed up with Abishag, an untouched Shunammite companion, but "the king knew her not."[35] Solomon did even better than his father David. He put up a bronze and cedar palace, on a hewn stone foundation, and filled it with seven hundred wives ("far more precious than jewels") and three hundred concubines ("man's delight") who "turned away his heart."[36] After Solomon's reign, the united kingdom fell apart. When Israel (in the north) and Judah (in the south) were left with fewer subjects, royal households shrank. In Judah, Solomon's son Rehoboam had just eighteen wives and sixty concubines, sixty daughters and twenty-eight sons. Rehoboam's son Abijah had just fourteen wives, sixteen daughters, and twenty-two sons. A century later Ahab made Jezebel of Tyre his queen, and fathered seventy sons "in Samaria" alone.[37]

Having a harem has always been characteristic of kingship. *YHVH* made that perfectly clear to David when He put these words in the prophet's mouth: "I anointed you king over Israel, and I delivered you out of the hand of Saul; and I gave you your master's house, *and your master's wives.*" Solomon's brother Absalom revolted against his father and made himself "odious" to David by consorting with his concubines. When Solomon's brother Adonijah wanted to take Solomon's place, he pursued David's Shunammite virgin and was put to death. Even Israel's oldest son, Reuben, lost his birthright "*because* he polluted his father's couch" by having relations with Bilhah, his father's maid.[38]

Moses understood that men in positions of power would steal weaker men's women. On their way into Canaan, he warned the patriarchs against future kings. The future king, he said, "must not multiply horses for himself," or "greatly multiply for himself silver and gold." Most of all, "he shall not multiply wives for himself, lest his heart turn away."

Gideon's son Jotham warned the judges, recounting a parable in which the trees tried to find a king of their own, but had trouble finding a good one. First they asked the olive, "by which gods and men are honored," but it turned the job down. Then they asked the fig, whose fruit was sustaining, but it too said no. Next they asked the grape vine, whose wine was uplifting, but it had better things to do. Last they asked the bramble, which offered its shade—it agreed, if they were asking in good faith, "but if not, let fire come out of the bramble and devour the cedars of Lebanon." Samuel, the last judge of Israel, warned his people again:

> These will be the ways of the king who will reign over you. He will take your sons and appoint them to his chariots and to be his horsemen, and to run before his chariots; and he will appoint for himself commanders of thousands and commanders of fifties, and some to plow his ground and to reap his harvest, and to make his implements of war and the equipment of his chariots. He will take your daughters to be perfumers and cooks and bakers. He will take the best of your fields and vineyards and olive orchards and give them to his servants. He will take the tenth of your grain and of your vineyards and give it to his officers and servants. He will take your menservants and maidservants, and the best of your cattle and your asses, and put them to do his work. He will take the tenth of your flocks, and you shall be his slaves. And in that day you will cry out because of your king, whom you have chosen for yourselves; but the Lord will not answer you in that day.

Though full of reservations, Samuel nonetheless did as he was told, and anointed King Saul.[39]

Men Unable to Breed in the Bible

Of the thirty-nine polygynous patriarchs, judges, and kings named in the Bible, all were men of prestige (see Appendix). It should be remembered, however, that for every prestigious man with a harem, many other men went without women. Some were turned into eunuchs, some died on the battlefield, and some became slaves. But most men simply were unable to acquire the basic resources to obtain women and successfully raise children.

Armies were composed mostly of young, unmarried men, millions of whom, according to Scripture, died in battle and failed to successfully reproduce. On his way out of Ur toward Canaan, Abraham took 318 slaves born in his house and routed the king of Elam. He then brought Lot "with his good women" back to Sodom. Later, on their way out of Egypt, and back toward Canaan, Joshua slaughtered the Amalekite warriors. Then he brought down the walls of Jericho with seven rams' horns, taking out men and women, young and old, "with the edge of the sword." He exterminated thirty-one kings west of the Jordan, with twelve thousand of their subjects at Ai: at Makkedah, at Libnah, at Lachish, at Eglon, at Hebron, at Debir, at Hazor, and so on, he "utterly destroyed all that breathed."[40]

Even before they made Othniel the first of their judges, the Judahites killed ten thousand at a battle in Canaan. Ehud, who came after Othniel, eliminated ten thousand in Moab; then Gideon used trumpets and broken pots to defeat one hundred thirty thousand Midianites. Shamgar leveled six hundred Philistines with an ox goad, Samson crushed a thousand with an ass's jawbone, then three thousand more when he pulled down the building to which he was chained. When Samuel was a boy, the Philistines eliminated thirty-four thousand Israelites.[41]

But Saul slew thousands of Philistines, and David ten thousand. David went on to slaughter twenty-two thousand Syrians at Zobah, eighteen thousand Edomites in the Valley of Salt, and another forty-seven thousand Syrians across the Jordan. Judah's king Asa put one million three hundred Ethiopians to death. When Israel's king Ahab went to war with Ben-hadad, one hundred thousand Syrians died on the battlefield, while another twenty-seven thousand died under a collapsed wall. Amaziah took out another twenty thousand Edomites, and when Sennacherib set siege to Jerusalem under "strong, proud" Hezekiah, one hundred eighty-five thousand Assyrians were left dead by "the angel of the Lord." Even after the exile, Esther's uncle Mordecai put an end to Amalek's descendant, Haman, along with all ten of his sons, five hundred others at Susa, and seventy-five thousand in the provinces of Persia.[42]

Many more died in civil wars. Just after Moses descends from Mt. Sinai, his fellow Levites put three thousand of their brothers and sons to death on account of their golden calf. One of the judges, Jephthah, had forty-two thousand insubordinate Ephraimites wiped out. Another judge, Abimelech, set fire to another thousand disobedient Ephraimites in a tower, after he'd already razed Shechem, killing seventy more. The Benjaminites took out 40,030 Israelites; then the Israelites took out 25,100 Benjaminites. David slew at least 360 in Saul's army, and had another twenty thousand slain when his son Absalom rebelled. Solomon's grandson Abijah, the king of

Judah, put away half a million picked men in Israel's army; then Israel's king Pekah slaughtered one hundred twenty thousand of Judah's men of valor "because they had forsaken the Lord."[43]

Thousands more men in the Bible worked at forced labor, making reproduction difficult or next to impossible. Under the judges, most slaves were captured in wars. Whenever a city accepted Israel's offer of peace, "then all the people who are found in it shall do forced labor for you and shall serve you," ordered Moses. On those terms, Joshua turned the people of Gibeon into wood hewers and water drawers. The descendants of Zebulun, Naphtali, and Joseph put the Canaanites to forced labor; Dan's descendants made the Amorites slaves. Then the descendants of Reuben, Gad, and Manasseh made war on the Hagarites, descendants of Ishmael, and carried off one hundred thousand men alive, who "dwelt in their place until the exile."[44]

Kings brought in servants as tribute. After David beat the Moabites, they became "servants to David." Once David defeated the Syrians, they "became servants to David"; after David put garrisons in Edom, "all the Edomites became David's servants"; after David had the Ammonites overthrown, "he set them to labor with saws and iron picks and axes." When Solomon triumphed over the Amorites, Hittites, Perizzites, Hivites, and Jebusites, he "made a forced levy of slaves, and so they are to this day." David had an officer, Adoram, who was in charge of forced labor. But Solomon mastered the art of conscription. He sent thirty thousand men to Lebanon to bring cedars; then he conscripted another seventy thousand to serve as burden bearers, along with eighty thousand to work as stone hewers on his palace and the Temple. But the conscripted resisted. Solomon's labor officer, Jeroboam, revolted against Solomon's son, Rehoboam: "Your father made our yoke heavy," he complained. But Rehoboam failed to console them: "My father chastised you with whips, but I will chastise you with scorpions."[45]

Others were turned into eunuchs. When Samuel, the last judge, warned his people about Saul, he predicted that kings would give tithes to their eunuchs—a prophecy borne out before long. On the day David brought people together and made Solomon his successor, his mighty men came along with his eunuchs, or *sarisim*. Ahab used eunuch messengers; Ahab's son, Jehoram, trusted a eunuch with control of his fields and produce. Jezebel, Ahab's widow, along with Jehoram's mother, was thrown out of a window by "two or three eunuch guards" and eaten by dogs. Josiah's chamberlain was another castrated man; when Josiah's son, Jehoiachim, got dragged off to Nebuchadnezzar's Babylon, his eunuchs came with him. Josiah's last son, Zedekiah, stayed behind in Jerusalem, with his Ethiopian eunuch, and a *saris* who commanded his army. The "women, children, and eunuchs" would remain, even after Zedekiah was gone.[46]

The Bible as History and Natural History

In the Bible, *YHVH* commanded His people to be fruitful, and it has been the purpose of this chapter to show that some were much more fruitful than others.

Patriarchs like Abraham counted their women and legitimate children in single digits; judges like Gideon counted offspring an order of magnitude more. Kings like Solomon kept hundreds of women, and probably fathered dozens of children. But hundreds of thousands of men were killed, enslaved, or otherwise prevented from breeding. In Darwinian terms, "The strongest and most vigorous men" raised "a greater average number of offspring."

The same polygynous patterns reported in the Bible were consistent with reports from other sources. The unassailable pattern in societies where wealth could be stored manifests a wide variance in male descendant-leaving success, an outcome enabled by prestigious men accumulating as many women as possible.[47] Pursuit of this reproductive strategy required not only the polygynous siring of many offspring, but also the acquisition of additional men, such as eunuchs, and channeling their parental care to benefit their master's offspring.

Finally, in matters of highly skewed polygyny, the ancient Near East was not unique. In empires from China to Mexico to Peru, strong men had many more women and children than others. While emperors had access to hundreds, thousands, or tens of thousands of women, millions of male subjects failed to reproduce as a result of early death, working as slaves, or filling sterile servant castes.

Appendix

Name	Wives	Concubines	Sons	Daughters	Source
Lamech (P)	2	—	3	1	Gen. 4:19–22
Terah (P)	1?	1?	3	1	Gen. 11:26–29; 12:13; 20:12; 22:20–24
Abraham (P)	2	1	8	—	Gen. 14:14; 16:4–15; 21:2–3; 25:1–2
Nahor (P)	1	1	12	—	Gen. 22:20–24; 28:5, 29:5
Ishmael (P)	—	—	12	—	Gen. 25:13–15
Lot (P)	1	2	2	2	Gen. 19:8, 36–38
Esau (P)	4?	—	5	—	Gen. 26:34; 28:9; 35:2–14
Jacob (P)	2	2	12	1	Gen. 35:22–26; 46:8–27
Eliphaz (P)	1	1	7	—	Gen. 36:11–15
Simeon (P)	2	—	6-8	—	Gen. 46:10; Ex 6:15; 1 Ch. 4:24
Judah (P)	1	1	5	—	Gen. 38:2–5, 24–30; 1 Ch. 2:3–4
Moses (P)	2	—	2?	—	Ex. 18:1–4; Num. 12:1
Hezron (P)	2?	—	4?	—	Gen. 46:12; 1 Ch. 2:9–21
Caleb (P)	3	—	4	—	1 Ch. 2:18–24, 46–50
Jerahmeel (P)	2	—	6	—	1 Ch. 2:25–26, 42
Asshur (P)	2?	—	8	—	1 Ch. 2:24; 4:5–7
Manasseh (P)	1?	1	7	—	Gen. 46:20; Jos. 17:1–6; 1 Ch. 7:14
Machir (P)	2?	—	2?	2?	1 Ch. 7:14–19
Mered (P)	2	—	6	—	1 Ch. 4:17–18
Shimei (P)	—	—	16	6	1 Ch. 4:27
Shaharaim (P)	3	—	9	—	1 Ch. 8:8–9
Gideon (J)	—	—	72	—	Jdg. 6:35; 8:30–31
Jair (J)	—	—	30	—	Num. 32:41; Jdg 10:4
Gilead (J)	1	1	6	—	Num. 26:30–32; Jdg 11:1–2
Ibzan (J)	—	—	30	30	Jdg. 12:8–9
Abdon (J)	—	—	40	—	Jdg. 12:13–14; 1 Ch 8:23

Samson (J)	2?	2	—	—	Jdg. 14:2; 15:2; 16:1,4
Elkanah (J)	2	—	5?	2	1 Sam. 1:1–2; 2:12–21
Saul (K)	Ws	1	7?	2	1 Sam. 14:49; 2 Sa 3:7; 21:8; 1 Ch 8:33; 9:39
David (K)	8	10?	19	1	1 Sam. 8:27; 2 Sa 3:2–5; 5:13–16; 1 Ch 3:1–9; 14:4–7
Solomon (K)	700	300	1	2	1 Kings 4:11–14; 11:3; 1 Ch 3:10–24
Rehoboam (K)	18	60	27	60	2 Ch. 11:21
Abijah (K)	14	—	22	16	2 Ch. 13:21
Ahab (K)	Ws	—	70?	—	1 Kings 20:3; 2 Kings 10:1
Jehroam (K)	Ws	—	22	16	2 Ch. 21:14, 17
Joash (K)	2	—	—	—	2 Ch. 24:3
Josiah (K)	2	—	2	—	2 Kings 23:30–36
Jehoiachin (K)	Ws	—	7	—	2 Kings 24:15
Zedekiah (K)	Ws	—	Ss	—	Jer. 38:23

Notes

Permission to reproduce portions from "Politics as Sex: The Old Testament Case," from *Evolutionary Psychology* 3: 326–346, kindly granted by Todd Shackelford, editor.

1. Genesis 1:28. All biblical translations are from the Revised Standard Version.
2. Darwin 1859:63–64.
3. Darwin 1859:51–52.
4. Darwin 1871:571, 631, 826, 899.
5. See comment on human polygyny in Fox, p. 204.
6. See an elaboration of anisogamy in the chapter "Judaism's *Yetzer* as a Biological Construct."
7. Bateman 1948; Trivers 1972. Darwin had anticipated these conclusions in *Descent of Man*: "The female has to spend much organic matter in the formation of her ova, whereas the male expends much force in fierce contests with his rivals, in wandering about in search of the female, in exerting his voice, pouring out odoriferous secretions, &c" (1871: 581).
8. See Clutton-Brock 1988 and Ellis 1995 for reviews of the animal evidence.
9. See, e.g., Pinaka 2000 on population replacement; see Fisher 1958 on sex ratio selection.
10. See Potts and Short 1999 on human reproductive physiology; see Murdock 1967 and Betzig 1986, 1988, 1993 on human polygyny.
11. See Darwin 1871: 871, quoting Horace, *Satires*, i.3. On female vs. resource defense polygyny, see Emlen and Oring 1977; on reproductive "skew" in animal societies, see Vehrencamp 1983 and Reeve 2006.
12. Reviewed in Smith 2004.
13. See Lemche 1998; Finkelstein and Silberman 2001, 2006; and Kitchen 2003 on the Bible as history.
14. These were "divine beings" of exalted rank who, when a girl was being adorned to enter the wedding canopy, would enter and have intercourse with her first (Rashi commenting on Bereshit Rabbah 26:5). A classic case of a powerful class of males subjugating a weaker class of females (Leibowitz, p. 55).
15. Genesis 8:17; 9:1, 7.

16. Genesis 12:2; 13:16; 15:5; 17:2–6; 18:18; 22:17 (emphasis added).
17. Genesis 16:2, 10; 17:20; 21:18; 26:4, 24; 28:14; 32:28; 35:11; 46:3.
18. Leviticus 26:9; Deuteronomy 1:11; 6:3; 7:14; 8:1; 28:11; 30:16.
19. Leviticus 26:16–38; Deuteronomy 28.
20. See Joshua 11:16–20, 12:7–24 on wars west of the Jordan, where they "utterly destroyed all that breathed," and compare Judges 4:16 on the Canaanite army, and 1 Samuel 15:4–8, 33 on Amalek. See Numbers 31:17–18, 35; Judges 8:14–17, 21:12–23, and 1 Kings 11:15 on wars east of the Jordan; and compare Deuteronomy 3:1–6 on Heshbon and Bashan. In Deuteronomy 20:13–16, Moses laid down two rules of war: "in the cities of those peoples that the Lord your God gives you for an inheritance, you shall save alive nothing that breathes"; but in cities far away, "you shall put all its males to the sword, but the women and the little ones, the cattle, and everything else in the city, all its spoil, you shall take as booty for yourselves." See also the discussion of *cherem* and "laying waste" the land and its inhabitants, found in "Making Biological Sense of Judaic Sacrificing".
21. 1 Kings 14:22–28; 2 Chronicles 12:1–2 [Rehoboam]; 1 Kings 15:26–30; 2 Chronicles 9:29, 13:22 [Jeroboam]; 1 Kings 16:11–13 [Baasha]; 1 Kings 21:21–25; 2 Kings 10:7; 2 Chronicles 21:10–18 [Ahab and Jehoram]; Sennacherib, *Annals,* Third Campaign; 2 Kings 18:3–7, 19:28, 20:18; 2 Chronicles 33:11; Isaiah 37:29, 39:7 [Hezekiah and Manasseh]; 2 Kings 23:31–35; 2 Chronicles 35:20–24, 36:1–4 [Josiah]; *Assyrian and Babylonian Chronicles,* 5, Year 7; 2 Kings 24:15; Ezekiel 2:3 [Jehoiachin]; 2 Kings 25:7; Jeremiah 38:23, 52:2, 10 [Zedekiah]. See Friedman 1987 on Jeremiah's scribe, Baruch, as an editor of Kings.
22. Reviewed in Betzig 1997, Irons 2006.
23. In stable, sexually reproducing populations, most parents will replace themselves: average number of offspring is two; Fisher 1958 explained why, in most populations, a 50:50 sex ratio holds.
24. For Old Babylon: Hammurabi, *Laws,* epilogue; compare Lipit-Ishtar's epilogue of two centuries before. For Egypt: Exodus 1:11; Seti I, *Wadi Abbad Temple Decree.* For Assyria: Esarhaddon, *Vassal Treaty,* 66. For Persia: Darius I, *Behistun Inscription,* 63. See van Rooy 1986 on curses in the ancient Near East.
25. Nebuchadnezzar II, *Wadi-Brisa Inscription,* 10.38–40; Adad-sumu-usur, *Letter* to Esarhaddon; *Hymn to Min* and Isaiah 65:4; *Courtship of Inanna and Dumuzi* and Ezekiel 8:14.
26. Amenhotep II, *Elephantine Stele,* Year 3, and Memphis *and Karnak Stele,* Year 7; Esarhaddon, *Dog River Stele* and *Senjili Stele,* Ashurbanipal, *Rassam Cylinder,* Third, Sixth–Eighth Campaigns; *Assyrian and Babylonian Chronicles,* 3, Year 14, and Nahum 1–3 on Nabopolassar; Herodotus, *Histories,* 4.32, on Persia.
27. See Genesis, 11:31 and Joshua 24:2–3 on Abram's itinerary; see Zimri-Lim, *Letter to Shibtu* and Dalley 2002 on Mari.
28. Amenhotep III, *Marriage with Kirgipa; Amarna Letters,* 64, 254, 301, 309, 369; Ramesses II, *Great Abydos Inscription,* 43–48; Fisher 2001 for Ramesses II's sons.
29. See Dalley and Postgate 1984 for *sa ekalli* and *sekretu*; Ashurbanipal, *Rassam Cylinder,* on his harem; *Imperial Administrative Records,* 23–26 for harem inventories; *Gilgamesh,* Tablet 1; Biggs 1967:13 for potency incantation.
30. Nebuchadnezzar II, *The Court,* 4; Strabo, *Geography,* xvi.1.5; Daniel 5:1–3.
31. Esther 2:2–14; Quintus Curtius, *History of Alexander,* iii.3, vi.6, x.5; Arrian, *Anabasis,*

vii.29; Diodorus Siculus, *Historical Library*, xvii.77; Plutarch, *Artaxerxes*, 27. Overall, see Patai 1959 and Parpola and Whiting 2002 on sex in the ancient Near East.

32. Genesis 4:19 [Lamech]; Genesis 20:12; 22:20–24 [Terah and Nahor]; Genesis 25:1–2 [Abraham]; Betzig 2005 on house slaves as possible bastards. On Isaac: Genesis 24:61, 27:37. On Jacob: Genesis 29:17, 35:22–26, 36:2–4, 29:17.

33. Judges 8:30–31; 10:4; 12: 9, 14; 13:24.

34. 1 Samuel 25:42–43; 2 Samuel 3:2–5; 5:13; 15:16.

35. 2 Samuel 5:13–16; 13; 1 Kings 1:1–4; 1 Chronicles 3:5–9; 14:3–7; 2 Chronicles 11:18; Psalms 45:9, 14.

36. 1 Kings 11:1–3; Proverbs 31:10; Ecclesiastes 2:8.

37. 2 Kings 10:1, 7; 2 Chronicles 11:21–23, 13:21; Amos 6:4.

38. Genesis 35:22, 49:4; 2 Samuel 12:7–8, 11; 14–18; 1 Kings 2:15–23; 1 Chronicles 5:1 (emphasis added).

39. See Deuteronomy 17:16–17 for Moses' warning; Judges 9:8–15 for Jotham's; 1 Samuel 8:10–18 for Samuel's.

40. Genesis 14:1–16 [Abraham and Lot]; Exodus 17:8–13 [Amalekites]; Joshua 6 [Jericho]; 8:25 [Ai]; Joshua 10:28–11:10 [Makkedah-Hazor].

41. Judges 1:4 [Canaan]; Judges 3:29 [Ehud]; Judges 7:20, 8:10 [Gideon]; Judges 3:31 [ox goad]; Judges 15:16 [jawbone]; Judges 16:27–30 [house down]; 1 Samuel 4:2, 10 [34,000].

42. 1 Samuel 18:7 [Saul and David]; 1 Chronicles 18:5–12, 19:18 [Zobah, Valley of Salt, 47,000]; 2 Chronicles 14:9–13 [Asa]; 1 Kings 20:29–30 [Ahab]; 2 Kings 14:7; 2 Chronicles 25:11–12 [Amaziah]; 2 Kings 19:35; Isaiah 37:36; Sennacherib, *Annals*, Sixth Campaign [Hezekiah]; Esther 9:5–16 [Mordecai].

43. Exodus 32:19–28 [calf]; Judges 9:45–49 [Shechem]; Judges 12:6 [Ephraimites]; Judges 20:21–46 [Benjaminites]; 2 Samuel 2:31 [360]; 2 Samuel 18:7 [Absalom]; 2 Chronicles 13:17 [Abijah]; 2 Chronicles 25:13 [3000]; 2 Chronicles 28:6 [Pekah].

44. Deuteronomy 20:11 [Moses]; Joshua 9:23–27 [Gibeon]; Joshua 16:10, 17:10 and Judges 1:28–35 [Canaanites and Amorites]; 1 Chronicles 5:18–22 [Hagrites].

45. 2 Samuel 8:2–14; 1 Chronicles 18:2–13, 20:1–3 [Moabites-Ammonites]; 1 Kings 9:20–21 [Amorites-Jebusites]; 2 Samuel 20:24 [Adoram]; 1 Kings 5:13–16, 9:20–20, 12:4–11; 2 Chronicles 10:11 [Solomon's levy]. Sometimes, of course, the tables turned: Mesha of Moab fought against the "House of David" in Hauranen, and threw off Israel's yoke, after Omri and his son had "oppressed Moab for many days"; then Hazael of Aram Damascus claimed to have killed the "king of Israel," killed another king from the "House of David," and imposed "tribute on their people"—says the *Tel Dan Stele*. Both these sources are hotly disputed.

46. 1 Samuel 8:15 [Saul]; 1 Chronicles 28:1 [David]; 1 Kings 22:9; 2 Kings 8:6, 9:32; 2 Chronicles 18:8 [Ahab and Jehoram]; 2 Kings 23:11, 24:12–15, 25:19; Jeremiah 29:2, 34:19, 38:7, 41:16, 52:25 [Josiah, Jehoiachin, Zedekiah, and Gedaliah]. The RSV translates most *saris* as "officers, but the Hebrew word *sarisim* means eunuch, used in the Bible as such forty-two times.

47. The Talmud reports that Rav and Rav Nachman, both famous rabbis, sent out emissaries seven days before visiting a town to search for women willing to marry them "for a day," even though the rabbis had families at home. The understanding that these "arrangements" would produce children is assumed (Yev. 37b1, incl. f.n. 7 and 8).

References

Adad-sumu-usur. *Letter* to Esarhaddon, translated in S. Parpola, *Letters from Assyrian and Babylonian Scholars,* 185. Helsinki: University of Helsinki Press, 1993.
Amarna Letters, translated by W. L. Moran. Baltimore: Johns Hopkins University Press, 1992.
Amenhotep II. *Elephantine Stele,* translated in J. H. Breasted, *Ancient Records of Egypt.* Chicago: University of Illinois Press, 2001.
Amenhotep II. *Great Sphenix Stele,* translated in B. Cumming, *Egyptian Historical Records of the Later Eighteenth Dynasty.* Warminster: Aris & Phillips, 1982.
Amenhotep II. *Memphis and Karnak Stele,* translated in J. B. Pritchard, *Ancient Near Eastern Texts.* Princeton: Princeton University Press, 1969.
Amenhotep III. *Marriage with Kirgipa,* translated in J. H. Breasted, *Ancient Records of Egypt.* Chicago: University of Illinois Press, 2001.
Arrian, Flavius Xenophon. *Anabasis of Alexander,* translated by E. I. Robson. London: Heinemann, 1933.
Ashoka. *Rock Edicts,* translated in Romila Thapar, *Ashoka and the Decline of the Mauryas.* Bombay: Oxford University Press, 1997.
Ashurbanipal. *Rassam Cylinder,* translated in D. D. Luckenbill, *Ancient Records of Assyria and Babylon.* London: Histories & Mysteries of Man, 1989.
Assyrian and Babylonian Chronicles, trans. by A. K. Grayson. New York: J. J. Augustin, 1975.
Betanzos, Juan de. 1557. *Narrative of the Incas,* translated by Roland Hamilton and Dana Buchanan. Austin: University of Texas Press, 1996.
Betzig, Laura. 1986. *Despotism and Differential Reproduction: A Darwinian View of History.* New York: Aldine de Gruyter.
———. 1993. Sex, succession, and stratification in the first six civilizations. In L. Ellis, ed., *Social Stratification and Socioeconomic Inequality,* pp. 37–74. New York: Praeger.
———. 1997. People are animals. In L. Betzig, ed., *Human Nature: A Critical Reader,* pp. 1–13. New York: Oxford University Press.
Biggs, Robert. 1967. *Ancient Mesopotamian Potency Incantions.* New York: J. J. Augustin.
Clutton-Brock, Timothy. 1988. *Reproductive Success.* Cambridge: Cambridge University Press.
Cobo, Bernabé. 1653. *History of the Inca Empire,* translated by Roland Hamilton. Austin: University of Texas Press, 1979.
Courtship of Inanna and Dumuzi, translated in D. Wolkenstein and S. N. Kramer, *Inanna,* pp. 29–49. San Francisco: Harper, 1993.
Cyrus the Great. 1969. *Cylinder,* translated in J. B. Pritchard, *Ancient Near Eastern Texts.* Princeton: Princeton University Press.
Dalley, Stephanie. 2002. *Mari and Karana: Two Old Babylonian Cities,* 2nd edition. Piscataway NJ: Gorgias Press.
Dalley, Stephenie and J. N. Postgate. 1984. *Tablets from Fort Shalmaneser.* London: British School of Archaeology in Iraq.
Darius I. *Behistun Inscription,* translated by Henry Rawlinson, L. W. King and R. C. Thompson. London: Harrison and Sons, 1907.
Darwin, Charles. 1859. *On the Origin of Species.* New York: Modern Library Reprint.
———. 1871. *The Descent of Man and Selection in Relation to Sex.* New York: Modern Library Reprint.

Diodorus Siculus. *Historical Library,* translated by C. H. Oldfather. London: Heinemann, 1970.
Ellis, Lee. 1995. Dominance and reproductive success among nonhuman animals: A cross-species comparison. *Ethology and Sociobiology, 16:* 257–333.
Esarhaddon. *Dog River Stele,* translated in D. D. Luckenbill, *Ancient Records of Assyria and Babylon.* London: Histories & Mysteries of Man, 1989.
———. *Senjirli Stele,* translated in D. D. Luckenbill, *Ancient Records of Assyria and Babylon.* London: Histories & Mysteries of Man, 1989.
———. *Vassal Treaty,* translated in S. Parpola and K. Watanabe, *Neoassyrian Treaties and Loyalty Oaths.* Helsinki: State Archives of Assyria, 1988.
Finkelstein, Israel and Neil Asher Silberman. 2001. *The Bible Unearthed.* New York: Touchstone.
———. 2006. *David and Solomon.* New York: Free Press.
Fisher, Marjorie. 2001. *The Sons of Ramesses II. Aegypten und altes testament, band 53.* Wiesbaden: Harrassowitz.
Fisher, Ronald. 1958. *The Genetical Theory of Natural Selection.* New York: Dover.
Fox, Robin. 1983. *The Red Lamp of Incest.* Notre Dame, IN: University of Notre Dame Press.
Friedman, Richard Elliot. 1987. *Who Wrote the Bible?* San Francisco: HarperCollins.
Garcilaso de la Vega. 1609. *Royal Commentaries of the Incas,* translated by Harold Livermore. Austin: University of Texas Press, 1966.
Gilgamesh, translated by M. G. Kovacs. Stanford: Stanford University Press, 1989.
Grayson, Albert Kirk. 1995. Eunuchs in power: Their role in the Assyrian bureaucracy, in M. Dietrich and O. Loretz, *Festschrift für Wolfram Freiherrn,* pp. 85–98. Neukirchen: Alter Orient und Altes Testament.
Hammurabi. *Laws,* translated in M. T. Roth, *Law Collections from Mesopotamia and Asia Minor.* Atlanta: Scholars Press, 1995.
Hazael. *Tel Dan Stela,* translated by A. Biran and J. Naveh, *Israel Exploration Journal, 43:* 81–98, 1993.
Herodotus. *Histories,* translated by Aubrey de Selincort. Harmondsworth: Penguin, 1996.
Hymn to Min, translated in Miriam Lichtheim, *Ancient Egyptian Literature.* Berkeley: University of California Press, 1983.
Imperial Administrative Records: Palace and Temple Administration, translated by F. M. Fales and J. N. Postgate. Helsinki: State Archives of Assyria, 1992.
Ixtlilxochitl, Fernando de Alva. 1640. *Obras históricas.* Mexico City: Universidad Nacional, 1977.
Irons, William. 2006. Cultural and reproductive success: a metaanalysis. Manuscript.
Josephus, Flavius. *Jewish Antiquities,* translated by H. S. Thackeray. Cambridge: Harvard University Press, 1998.
Kadish, Gerald. 1967. Eunuchs in ancient Egypt?, in *Studies in Honor of John A. Wilson.* Chicago: Oriental Institute.
Kautilya. *The Arthashastra,* translated by R. Shamasastry. Bombay: University of Bombay, 1951.
Kitchen, Kenneth. 2003. *On the Reliability of the Old Testament.* Grand Rapids: Eerdmans.
Ktesias. *Persika,* translated by J. W. McCrindle. Delhi: Manohar, 1973.
Leibowitz, Nehama. 1974. *Studies in Bereshit (Genesis).* World Zionist Organization, Department for Torah Education and Culture, Jerusalem.

Lemche, Niels Peter. 1998. *The Israelites in History and Tradition*. London: SPCK.
Lipit-Ishtar. *Laws,* translated in M. T. Roth, *Law Collections from Mesopotamia and Asia Minor.* Atlanta: Scholars Press, 1995.
Llewellyn-Jones, Lloyd. 2002. Eunuchs and the royal harem in Achaemenid Persia. In S. Tougher, *Eunuchs in Antiquity and Beyond,* pp. 19–49. London: Duckworth.
Manetho. *Aegyptiaca,* translated by W. G. Waddell. London: Heinemann, 1940.
Mattila, Raija. 2000. *The King's Magnates: A Study of the Highest Officials of the Neo-Assyrian Empire.* Helsinki: Neo-Assyrian Corpus Project.
Mesha. *Moabite Stone,* translated by Andre Lemaire in *Biblical Archaeology Review,* May/June:30–37, 1994.
Middle Assyrian Decrees, translated in M. T. Roth, *Law Collections from Mesopotamia and Asia Minor.* Atlanta: Scholars Press, 1995.
Nebuchadnezzar II. *The Court,* translated in J. B. Pritchard, *Ancient Near Eastern Texts,* pp. 307–08. Princeton: Princeton University Press, 1969.
———. *Wadi-Brisa Inscription,* translated in J. B. Pritchard, *Ancient Near Eastern Texts,* p. 307. Princeton: Princeton University Press, 1969.
Parpola, Simo and R. M. Whiting, eds. 2002. *Sex and Gender in the Ancient Near East.* Helsinki: State Archives of Assyria.
Patai, Raphael. 1959. *Sex and the Family in the Bible and Middle East.* New York: Doubleday.
Philo of Alexandria. *On Joseph,* translated by C. D. Younge. London: Bohn, 1890.
Plutarch. *Life of Artaxerxes,* translated by B. Perrin. Cambridge: Harvard University Press, 1994.
Quintus Curtius. *History of Alexander,* translated by J. C. Rolfe. London: Heinemann, 1971.
Rameses II. *Great Abydos Inscription,* translated in James Breasted, *Ancient Records of Egypt.* Chicago: University of Illinois reprint, 2001.
Sargon II. *Annals,* translated in D. D. Luckenbill, *Ancient Records of Assyria and Babylon.* London: Histories and Mysteries of Man, 1989.
Sennacherib. *Annals,* translated in D. D. Luckenbill, *Ancient Records of Assyria and Babylon.* London: Histories and Mysteries of Man, 1989.
Seti I. *Wadi Abbad Temple Decree,* translated in J. B. Pritchard, *Ancient Near Eastern Texts.* Princeton: Princeton University Press, 1969.
Sima Qian. *Shi ji,* translated by Burton Watson. New York: Columbia University Press, 1993.
Smith, Eric Alden. 2004. Why do good hunters have higher reproductive success? *Human Nature,* 15: 343–364.
Strabo. *Geography,* translated by J. Sterrett. Cambridge: Harvard University Press, 1966.
Thutmose III. *Gebel Stela,* translated in B. Cumming, *Egyptian Historical Records of the Eighteenth Dynasty.* Warminster: Aris & Phillips, 1982.
———. *Memphis and Karnak Stele,* translated in J. B. Pritchard, *Ancient Near Eastern Texts.* Princeton: Princeton University Press, 1969.
Tiglathpileser III. *Annals,* translated in J. B. Pritchard, *Ancient Near Eastern Texts.* Princeton: Princeton University Press, 1969.
Tougher, Shaun. 2002. *Eunuchs in Antiquity and Beyond.* London: Duckworth.
Tsai, Shih-shan Henry. 1996. *Eunuchs of the Ming Dynasty.* Albany: SUNY Press.
van Rooy, H. F. 1986. Fertility as blessing and infertility as curse in the ancient Near East

and the Old Testament. In Anthony Bonanno, ed., *Archaeology and Fertility Cult in the Ancient Mediterranean*, pp. 225–235. Amsterdam: B. R. Grüner.

Vatsayana. *Kamasutra*, translated by Richard Burton. Harmondsworth: Penguin, 1964.

Xenophon. *Cyropaedia*, translated by Wayne Ambler. Ithaca: Cornell University Press, 2001.

Zimri-Lim. *Letter to His Wife Shibtu*, translated in B. F. Batto, *Studies of Women at Mari*, p. 26. Baltimore: Johns Hopkins University Press, 1965.

Chapter 4

Intrafamily Conflict in the Bible and Biological Theory

David Barash

Editor's Introduction

Conflict between members of the same family is, of course, much older than the Bible. Reading or listening to accounts of family discord is poignant because, especially among close kin, we expect the opposite. This chapter explores many of the intrafamily feuds and rivalries chronicled in the Bible in an attempt to show why they can make sense biologically. Making biological sense, it should be pointed out, does not mean that family conflict is appropriate, acceptable, or inevitable. Barash's intention here is not to trivialize or degrade these biblical characters based on their behavior. To the contrary, the Bible remains vital and theologically accessible after so many centuries due to its honest, three-dimensional portraits of venerated individuals and families.

Whatever the Bible might be as a source of religious instruction, it is unquestionably a trove of memorable stories. Although many are sublime and inspiring, suffused with good feelings and peace, others are deeply disturbing, even violent. A strictly evolutionary approach to these narratives might be expected to predict two alternatives: first, when the characters are unrelated to one another, war and other forms of brutal tribal conflict should result and, second, when the interaction is between members of the same family, love and harmony should prevail.

Surprisingly, however, the Torah's tales of great pain, violence, betrayal, and even murder often occur among family members. Less surprisingly, such tales do not contradict current knowledge about the biologically based human nature that underlies the day-to-day activities of *Homo sapiens*—on the contrary, they reinforce it. In *A Midsummer Night's Dream*, Puck declares that "the course of true love never did run smooth." Although his remark is directed to romantic love between adults, this observation also applies to parents and offspring, as well as to close genetic relatives such as siblings. Family interactions are often bumpy, not just in the Bible, but even in modern life. And thanks to recent insights from sociobiology (more commonly known today as evolutionary psychology), we are beginning to understand why.

Perhaps the mere existence of intense within-family conflict is surprising. From an evolutionary perspective, we can readily predict conflict between men over dominance or money, both of which translate ultimately into reproductive opportunities and success with women. So male-male competition is to be expected, as is similar conflict among women, although usually with less bluster and violence. There is an evolutionary rationale for battles between the sexes, since men and women are different genetically as well as regarding their reproductive strategies, despite the fact that their interests converge for reproduction. But the evolutionary interests of parents and their offspring would seem to coincide perfectly, since parents profit genetically when their children succeed, as do the children themselves.

From a cold-eyed biological perspective, children are merely vehicles enabling parental genes to replicate themselves. This viewpoint suggests that children are the primary means by which parental genes can achieve their goals. As a result, little or no conflict might be expected between parents and offspring or among close relatives who, by definition, have a high level of genes that are partially related by descent. "Close" relatives have a higher probability of gene sharing, while distant relatives are those with a lower probability of sharing genes by descent. For example, Sotah 49a3 states that a grandfather, though a close relative, should not be expected to be as altruistic toward his grandson as the father.

It is widely anticipated—at least among those not versed in recent developments in evolutionary theory—that parent and offspring are the epitome of shared goals and perfect amiability. After all, mother-and-child is often considered the archetype of mutual contentment and satisfaction. Moreover, reproductive success has long been thought the sine qua non of evolutionary fitness. This supposition changed dramatically, however, with the recognition that evolution proceeds by differential success at the level of genes, not that of individuals. Accordingly, personal reproduction is only a specific case of the more general phenomenon whereby genes joust with one another for projection into the future. This fact makes it especially surprising that biblical accounts of conflict are so prominent in situations where it might be *least* expected—between parents and offspring, as well as among siblings.

I began by noting that biblical depictions of intrafamily conflict seem *unnaturally* frequent and violent. As we shall see, however, these problems in "real life" are both *frequent* and *natural*, remarkably consistent with both the biblical and evolutionary "take" on such events. The significance of such parallelism and consistency is open for debate, since the Bible was not intended to convey scientifically accurate claims or narratives. But the Bible has shown itself to have a remarkably long shelf life and, as a general rule, the longevity of stories (whether novels, plays, poems, epics, or scripture) is due in part to a large measure of "believability," depicting actions consistent with a universal, intuitive sense of "human nature." And this is certainly true with respect to the within-family conflict described in the Bible, similar to what we see today in our own lives. A basic argument of this chapter, therefore, is that some of the most striking depictions in the Bible, those associated with conflict between parents and offspring, as well as among siblings, turn out to be both explicable by and compatible with our current knowledge of evolutionary biology.

The nonevolutionary view is often, by contrast, closer to a naive misrepresentation of ideal images of families inevitably loving and cooperative, rather than those grittier, more honest, biologically genuine biblical families. We might say that developmental psychologists, anthropologists, and professionals specializing in family sociology have traditionally treated the child as an appendage to the parent, rather than as a separate individual with his or her own strengths and weaknesses and, even more importantly, his or her own separate *agenda*. In the case of parent-offspring conflict, long-standing social science wisdom has been that, if conflict emerges, the culprit must be a lack of bilateral "understanding," with its attendant "failures of communication." Everyone is supposed to mean well, but in the course of conveying heartfelt parental assistance, advice, and information to the child, sometimes there can be problems because the young, inexperienced, and headstrong child is "uninformed" about where his or her true interests lie. According to this view, the well-socialized and more mature child eventually recognizes that his or her best interests lie in going along with parental inclinations, at which point conflict ceases and "socialization" is finally achieved. Conflict between parents and offspring, being undesired, is typically underplayed. But when its resiliency can no longer be denied, Western social science attributes it to the fact that children are primitive, even barbaric, little creatures who need time to become incorporated into the society of responsible adults.

The view from evolutionary biology is quite different and somewhat darker, although much more persuasive. Biblical accounts of intrafamily conflict do not contradict those derived from evolutionary theory; if anything, the latter reinforce the former. Offering a rich collection of examples, biblical accounts are in concert with more recent scientific observations of the natural world, seen afresh through the lens of evolution by natural selection. To appreciate the correspondence, we must first review how this lens functions and what it permits us to see.

To my knowledge, there are no biblical accounts in which intrafamily conflict is lauded. To the contrary, conflict within families is always painful and sometimes tragic. But there is a relentless recognition that, like it or not, these behaviors are real. Ditto for the biological perspective on intrafamily conflict, for which we owe much to theorist Robert L. Trivers. He demonstrated that the conventional wisdom regarding parent-offspring relations needs major revision. As we shall see, his approach, derived entirely from theoretical genetics, buttressed by examples from animals, dramatically illuminates the family conflicts that are so characteristic of individuals in the Bible.

Trivers took as his starting point the simple fact that among sexually reproducing species, the evolutionary interests of parents and their offspring do not completely overlap, as they do in cases of asexual reproduction, where individuals produce "daughters" that are genetically identical to themselves. Sexual reproduction introduces genetic diversity between parents and offspring, since the process of meiosis—by which sperm and eggs are generated—involves a "reduction division" as a result of which diploid parents (each with a double set of genes) produce haploid gametes (each with a single set). This is adaptive, since it ensures that after fertilization, the newly formed zygote contains a restored diploid genome, comparable to that of each original parent. If that were not the case, fertilization would result in an unsustainable doubling of genes with each generation.

But one cost of this process is that parent-offspring genetic commonality is substantially diluted, since there is only a 50 percent probability that any gene present in a parent is also present in his or her child. Indeed, it is precisely this overlap that generates the gene-promulgating, biological payoff of producing children. But an unavoidable consequence of meiosis and sexual reproduction is that the parent-offspring genetic differential is ensured. If a 50 percent probability of shared genes is the driving force of reproduction itself, this "glass half-full" is accompanied by an evolutionary "glass half-empty," a 50 percent probability that parent and offspring will *not* share a given gene. When it comes to parent-child relations, biologists and laypersons alike have been focused on the former (that shared between parent and offspring),[1] all the while ignoring the other, empty half, those elements of child-parent genetic identity that do *not* exist.

Consider a newborn human infant. Initially, the interests of the infant and its mother coincide: the infant needs various resources from its parents, milk from its mother in particular. And the mother is prepared—physiologically, as well as behaviorally—to meet these needs. In the short term, her hormones as well as her anatomy predispose her to lactate; in the long run, her evolutionary interests are also served by helping to raise a healthy, successful child. Everything is just fine; mother and child are expected to be on the same page and, at first, they overwhelmingly are.

But gradually, the infant grows older, larger, and less needy of its mother's milk. As time goes on, the mother becomes inclined to stop nursing, a change that is not coincidentally tied to the reduced need on the part of her offspring. Milk is energetically costly to produce, and at some point the mother will do better in terms of her own fitness if she stops investing in her current child and prepares to keep precious resources for herself or save up for another child.[2] (In most mammals, lactating females are inhibited from ovulating, so the nourishing of one offspring precludes making another.) This in itself need not lead to conflict: if the infant agrees with the mother, then weaning would be as unconflicted as the early stages of nursing. Unfortunately, that early agreement may become quite strained.

Perhaps *the* key concept of evolutionary psychology is that living things are disposed to act in a manner that maximizes their own fitness; more precisely, they are the products of genes that have been selected for success in projecting copies of themselves into future generations. Thus, even a good Jewish mother is ultimately interested in making the most of *her* fitness at some cost to that of her offspring (as much as she might protest otherwise).³ This parent-child asymmetry is the key to Trivers's stunningly simple yet predictive biological insight—the infant is ultimately interested in making the most of *his or her* own fitness and not necessarily that of the mother. Another way of looking at it: the infant is 100 percent related to itself but only 50 percent related to its mother. (And vice versa for the mother.⁴) As a result, the infant devalues his or her mother's interests, and also the interest of the infant's father, by a factor of one-half. When the mother reaches the point where the balance of costs and benefits favors an end to nursing, her analysis is conducted by and for *herself* and not necessarily with her child's interests "in mind."⁵ The biological basis of her evaluation is simple: genes within reproductive females that induced their bodies to behave in this way left more copies in the bodies of descendants than did those who behaved otherwise. But the infant should be expected to see things differently. After all, the baby human is only one-half as concerned for its mother's cost/benefit considerations as is the mother herself. Using the cliché "I can really feel your pain," the infant should be expected to feel only half the mother's pain. And vice versa should be expected of the mother.

So at certain stages of the weaning process, genes within offspring who successfully resisted a mother's attempts to discontinue nursing would have been more fit than would alternative alleles that were more accommodating to the parent, but less contributory to their own success.⁶ Through most of human history and prehistory, the key limiting nutritional factor for infant survival was the quantity and quality of its mother's milk. Modern human beings might well give insufficient weight to lactation as seminally important. Certainly there must have been great significance to the battle between mother and nursing child for food resources during times of scarcity. Indeed, the Bible is replete with actual and metaphorical references to breasts, less for their erotic role than related to infant nutrition. Not surprisingly, breasts and suckling are intimately linked, not only in physiology but in the evolutionary psychology of the ancient Israelites. For them, as for every mammalian infant, milk was an absolute requirement for developmental fitness.

The biblical prohibition of cooking an animal in the milk of its mother, subsequently elaborated by the Rabbis into the restriction of mixing meat and milk as part of the laws of *kashrut,* could be considered an inchoate reflection of the necessity for lactation. Rabbinic authors undoubtedly recognized that survival of the next generation depends on bestowing critical resources from the older one. Since milk is integral to making the meat of which we are all constructed, perhaps the perception arose that to mix milk and meat in a meal is to pollute the deep interconnecting but separate significance of the two.

Returning to the conflict of interest in maternal lactation, mother and infant may find themselves locked in a battle of evolutionary wills, with the infant selected to demand more than the mother is selected to give. But there is light at the end of this biologically generated tunnel. For the mother the cost of nursing continues to mount, while for the infant the benefit of nursing begins to decline. At some point, therefore, their interests once again coincide. The time will arrive when it is also in the infant's interest for the mother to stop giving so much and start taking better care of herself. For one thing, the infant wants the mother to bring forth additional, closely related humans (siblings) and to invest appropriately in them. For another thing, a healthier mother can better invest in her offspring than if she were diseased or malnourished. The mother, for her part, is only too happy to oblige, so the two parties "agree" at last to discontinue nursing.

The evolutionary genetics of parent-offspring conflict provides a coherent way to look at many of the biblical conflicts between parents and offspring. Bear in mind that weaning is only a special case of a more widespread phenomenon in which conflict is not limited to milk or even to the straightforward provisioning of offspring by parents. Various patterns of conflict characterize virtually all mammals, human beings not the least. Something similar even takes place among birds. Large nestlings—big enough to fly, hence known as fledglings—can often be found pursuing their harried parents, importuning them for food. In late spring throughout North America, it is common to see these fledglings quivering their wings and uttering incessant "begging" calls, while the parents back away, look far into the distance (as though trying to ignore what is in front of them), after which they often literally take wing, pursued by their nearly grown but indefatigably demanding chicks.

Conflict over weaning does not exhaust the potential for parents and offspring to disagree. In this way of looking at parent-offspring relations, the bone of contention is the quality and quantity of "parental investment," defined as what parents provide to their offspring that contributes to the offspring's success. The other side of that coin is the concomitant lessening of the parent's ability to produce and invest in additional offspring. Parental investment—another concept elucidated by Trivers—is anything beneficial to the offspring but costly for the parents to provide, with both costs and benefits measured in units of fitness. Aside from milk, it includes other types of food, defense against predators, time spent giving instruction, keeping the children warm, and so forth. Among human beings, parental investment also includes the resource called money. Human investment in children goes on longer and is more intense than in any other species. Many a harried parent, struggling to provide for even the most rewarding child, will answer the question "What do you want your child to be?" with the immediate reply "Self supporting!"

The bar (bat) mitzvah provides a revealing example of this. There is a traditional blessing, which has fallen into disuse in modern Judaic ritual, in which parents thank God for absolving them of future responsibility for their child's discipline in observing the *mitzvot*. So bar mitzvah can be seen not only as a coming-of-age for the boy (or girl) but also as a traditional strategy for publicly announcing a *reduction* in the requirement for parental investment. The accompanying irony is that the bar mitzvah is also an occasion for abundant gift giving (resource provisioning) by others. Although in the past age thirteen might have been a suitable milestone for lessening parental provisioning, today investment is extended considerably longer, including the high school, college years, and sometimes even beyond, for postcollege young adults still needing to "find themselves."

Regardless of the investment details, worked out in each family, as children grow older some plan of transition is reached. Not surprisingly, children often expect more parental investment than parents are inclined to provide (not more intrusiveness in their lives, mind you, just more investment!). It would be interesting to see whether this pattern holds cross-culturally. The Bible provides numerous examples of parents and offspring in disagreement over the level of resources to be provided by parents to their children.

There are few, if any, biblical examples describing parental attempts to bestow resources upon their offspring, only to have the children oppose their generosity. Nonetheless, the image in literature of the overbearing Jewish parent (especially mother) persists and might even have evolutionary salience, since parental inclinations to "overinvest" in their offspring might be associated with parents having more than enough resources for themselves. This could possibly be part of an unconscious strategy to induce a pliant child to behave as though his or her interests coincided with those of the parent. Such manipulation has been attempted by appeal to guilt, long considered a Jewish specialty. Consider, for example, Philip Roth's masterful parental depiction in *Portnoy's Complaint*:

> So when are you going to get married already? In Newark and the surrounding suburbs this apparently is the question on everybody's lips: WHEN IS ALEXANDER PORTNOY GOING TO STOP BEING SELFISH AND GIVE HIS PARENTS, WHO ARE SUCH WONDERFUL PEOPLE, GRANDCHILDREN? "Well," says my father, the tears brimming up in his eyes, "well," he asks, *every single time I see him,* "is there a serious girl in the picture, Big Shot? Excuse me for asking, I'm only your father, but since I'm not going to be alive forever, and you (in case you forgot) carry the family name, I wonder if maybe you could let me in on the secret."[7]

When dealing with royal succession, including in the Bible, one might suppose that wealthy kings and queens would be especially generous to their offspring. However, since the most treasured investment a monarch can bestow on an offspring is to be crowned successor, royals are paradoxically limited in their capacity to meet their offspring's desires. Royal succession is, by definition, a "zero sum game" in which success for one child requires failure of all others. Thus, when parents have limitations on their ability to confer equal benefits to each of their offspring, the resulting conflict can be especially severe, even violent. A biblical example is the bloody rebellion led by King David's son Absalom against his father. Before this, Absalom had appropriated for sexual purposes his father's concubines[8] and, as a result, Absalom "became odious" to his father.[9] The story of David's woes continues: Adonijah, David's oldest son, eventually declared himself king when David grew too old to rule. But David had promised his wife Bathsheba that her son Solomon would succeed as king, resulting in Solomon being anointed. Adonijah then left in fear of retribution but was ultimately pardoned; he had to be content, alas, with less parental investment than he desired.

Evolutionary biology has developed a substantial body of theory and data based on the general phenomenon of male-male competition. Such competition can also extend to males within the same family. When it does, the outcome is liable to be worse than would be the case between unrelated competitors. In this respect, polygyny (mating of a man with multiple women) predisposes families to parent-offspring conflict, if only because some of the children will be half-siblings rather than full siblings.

What about sibling rivalry, which seems if anything too mild a phrase for the often murderous competition presented time and again in the Bible? As it happens, parent-offspring conflict theory has powerful implications here as well, going beyond "simple" disagreement over how much parents should invest in a child, or whether they should do so at all. Parent-offspring conflict may be predicted by disagreement over the child's behavior toward a third party. In the most frequent case, this third party is a brother or sister. For a parent, equally related to each child, every child should theoretically be of equal importance. This holds true if the parent judges that each child is both equally needy and equally likely to be successful: that every child is comparable in his or her ability to convert parental investment into fitness. Although this assumption is never true in the real world, it is essential to most basic models of family dynamics.

Parents benefit anytime one of their children acts benevolently toward a brother or sister. According to what is now known as "kin selection," or "inclusive fitness maximization," benevolence toward related others can be adaptive. Selection will occur at the level of genes when the benefit derived by the recipient multiplied by the coefficient of relatedness exceeds the cost incurred by the donor. In the case of full siblings, such altruism would be favored by a parent so long as the benefit to the recipient is greater than the cost to the altruist. Under such a circumstance, the parents come out ahead since they are equally related to each of their offspring.

Here is an example. Imagine little Chaim wants some of the food that his sister Malka is eating. If Chaim's need for the food is greater than the cost to Malka to give it up, then both Chaim and the parents are benefited by the gift because the net evolutionary payoff to the basket of parental fitness is thereby enhanced. But what about Malka's fitness?

Well-fed Malka, too, can benefit by giving food to hungry Chaim. After all, if Chaim is a full sibling, the two share a coefficient of genetic relatedness of 50 percent. But—and this is the crucial "but"—her calculation is different from that of her parents. Mom and Dad want Malka to help Chaim anytime his gain exceeds her loss. But Malka drives a harder bargain—she wants to help Chaim only when his gain is *twice* as large as her own loss. This is because Malka is genetically related to Chaim by a factor of 50 percent, but is 100 percent related to herself! In other words, she is expected to value her own needs twice as much as she values her brother's. The result may be conflict, not only between siblings, but also between parent and offspring. In this case, there can be a conflict between Malka and her parents over how Malka is expected to behave vis-à-vis Chaim. Evolutionary genetics thus provides a new way of understanding sibling rivalry, a phenomenon that, as we shall see, permeates many biblical narratives. Think of parents urging a child to play nicely with a brother or sister, often more cooperatively than the child is so inclined, or parents pressuring a child to share when the youngster wants to act selfishly. Part of the power of the evolutionary approach comes from its recognition that such cases are not due simply to childish stubbornness or sheer perversity; rather, children are inclined to act in response to *their own* biological interests rather than those of their siblings, their parents, or anyone else. The bottom line is that parents should be expected to exhort, extort, or otherwise induce their offspring to act more benevolently than the offspring would choose if left to their own devices.

According to the biblical account, Cain's murder of Abel was a consequence of rivalry, since God—the parental figure in this account—preferred the latter's offering to the former's. But isn't "siblicide"—the killing of one sibling by another—counter to evolutionary prediction, since it would seem maladaptive for an individual to kill another with whom he or she shares a 50 percent coefficient of genetic relationship? In fact, siblicide is rather common in the natural world, occurring—not surprisingly—when the payoff to the perpetrator exceeds his or her biological cost. There is no indication in the biblical text that Cain is aware, before he acts, of any cost or penalty for murdering his brother. When Cain responds to God, "Am I my brother's keeper?" perhaps our preferred answer from him would have been "yes." But if Cain thinks otherwise, an evolutionary perspective can help us understand why.

In one form or another, sibling rivalry is prominent in the Bible: in addition to Cain and Abel, consider Isaac and Ishmael, Jacob and Esau, Leah and Rachel, Joseph and his numerous brothers. According to Proverbs,[10] "A friend is devoted at all times, but a brother is born for adversity." This is widely supposed to mean that brothers can rely on one another more so than "mere" friends. As I have pointed out, evolutionary thinking would not dispute this idea, since siblings gain "automatically" by assisting each other. On the other hand, the sociobiology of friendship, reciprocal altruism, suggests that friendliness in the absence of shared genes must be predicated, eventually, on reciprocation. Parent-offspring conflict theory also suggests that siblings are "born for adversity" for reasons the interpreters of Proverbs may not have anticipated!

Of all the fraternal relationships in the Bible, only Moses and Aaron seem to have mostly gotten along, and it would be interesting to speculate why. Although Moses and Aaron are brothers, they were brought up in totally separate circumstances—Moses in Pharaoh's palace and Aaron among his fellow slaves. As a result, they had never had the opportunity during childhood to develop a sibling rivalry based on conflicts over parental investment. As adults, although Aaron was vested for high honor by God, Moses was clearly the one chosen to be "in charge." During the first part of their relationship, Moses (who stuttered) used Aaron mainly as a messenger and spokesman. Aaron, in turn, derived the power and prestige necessary for priestly lineage from his relationship with Moses. Thus, the two complementary siblings benefited each other more by cooperation than either would likely have gained by harmful competition.

Since Moses was in most ways the privileged brother, we might speculate that sibling rivalry is less likely when inequality among the siblings is sufficiently manifest. Rambam (Maimonides), commenting on the eventful meeting between Jacob and Esau,[11] says that Jacob's referring to himself as Esau's "servant"[12] should be interpreted as follows: in the Hebrew version of the commandment "Honor your father and your mother," the definite article is used before the word "father." This tells us that honor is also due to one's eldest brother, suggesting a submissive tactic that might apply, as well, in Aaron's behavior toward his older brother Moses; namely, an effort to avert potential sibling rivalry.[13] Similarly, consider Miriam, Moses' older sister. Indeed, she was so much older than Moses that when Pharaoh's daughter took Moses out of the water, it was Miriam who arranged for their biological mother, Yocheved, to nurse Moses and raise him until he was weaned.[14] Given the difference in their ages, it is not surprising that Moses and Miriam cooperated most of the time, as did Moses and Aaron. But even the well-functioning trio of Miriam, Moses, and Aaron was not always harmonious. At one point, for example, both Aaron and Miriam spoke out against Moses regarding an Ethiopian woman he had married.[15] Aaron and Miriam also objected to Moses' leadership, noting that he was not the only one capable of communicating with God.[16] And, like a parent angered by sibling rivalry, God reproaches Miriam and Aaron for questioning the authority of their brother, with Miriam subsequently punished for her behavior.[17] Finally, it is probably no coincidence that King David, whose difficult parent-offspring relationships were paralleled by the friction between his own children, had eighteen wives and numerous offspring. Therefore, many of David's children were half-siblings whose coefficient of genetic relationship would have been 25 percent, compared with 50 percent for full siblings. Evolutionary theory would accordingly predict that the relations between half-siblings would be more rivalrous than those of full siblings.

Judaism—as well as many other religious traditions—gives special status to the firstborn, suggesting the following speculation: perhaps primogeniture is adaptive, since legalizing preferential treatment among siblings can minimize the potentially divisive sibling strife that might otherwise occur. By exaggerating the asymmetries of the Miriam-Moses and Moses-Aaron relationships, Judaic preference for the *b'chor* (firstborn) might serve the purpose of intrafamily peacekeeping. The tradition of *pidyon ha-ben*—redeeming the eldest son from the responsibility of priestly service— may also emphasize the special status of the firstborn in Jewish families.[18]

In large families, there is commonly a disparity of power and status between the older and younger siblings. When one of the younger siblings somehow acquires a status higher than that of his older brothers, we would expect the ensuing rivalry to be explosive, since the payoff for vigorous competition could be great. Which brings us to the story of Joseph and his brothers: the patriarch Jacob fathered twelve sons, each a founder of a tribe of Israel: Reuben, Simeon, Levi, Judah, Zebulon, Issachar, Dan, Gad, Asher, Naphtali, Joseph, and Benjamin. Their intense rivalry was directed especially against Joseph, who was correctly perceived by his older siblings as being Jacob's favorite.[19] Jacob's favoritism was displayed unmistakably when he gave Joseph—and not his brothers—a coat of many colors. From that time forward, the ten half-brothers hated Joseph upon realizing that "their father loved [Joseph] more than all his brothers."[20] To make matters worse, Joseph then told his brothers of a dream in which they all bowed down to him—a behavior guaranteed to further fan the flames of sibling rivalry!

Unsurprisingly, Joseph's brothers then ganged up on him, thought about killing him, but ended up selling him to a caravan on its way to Egypt. Worth remembering is that Joseph's jealous and treacherous brothers felt constrained to lie to Jacob about Joseph's disappearance, further evidence (as if any were needed) that parents and offspring are prone to disagreements over the latter's treatment of each other. Joseph eventually achieved some measure of revenge on his own terms, but only after an especially emotional reunion with Benjamin, his only full sibling.

In his preferential disposition toward Joseph, Jacob was continuing his parents' tradition of showing preferences among their offspring. As we recall, Rebecca and Isaac "played favorites" with their sons: Rebecca favored Jacob, and Isaac preferred Esau. The matter of parental preference for these specific offspring warrants biological evaluation: the rivalry between Jacob and Esau is especially interesting since the two were fraternal twins. They clearly differed in proclivities, Jacob being the more scholarly, "at home in the tents," while Esau was a "rough man," accomplished as an outdoorsman and hunter. Although the text describes Jacob more favorably than his brother, there does not appear (like Cain and Abel, and unlike Moses and Aaron) to have been an inherently different status between them. But, as we know, parental interference produced and exacerbated the situation: Rebecca helped Jacob trick Isaac into giving her favorite the blessing Isaac had intended for Esau. Consequently, as Jacob was later to do regarding Joseph, she loaded the dice in favor of one of her offspring, and the outcome had plenty of consequences. Eventually, as with Joseph and his brothers, Jacob and Esau were at least partially reconciled as Isaac lay on his deathbed.

In many biblical encounters, "blood relatives" interact in a manner that is bloody indeed. Take the case of King David's sons: Amnon raped his half-sister, Tamar, whereupon Absalom, also David's son and Tamar's brother, killed Amnon. Absalom fled, but David could not stop longing for his presence. Eventually, David was persuaded to allow Absalom to return, only, as we have mentioned, to see him later on lead a revolt against his father.

By most interpretations, David's *tsuris* (trouble) derives in part from his earlier sin of lusting for Bathsheba and, to facilitate his liaison with her, arranging for her husband Uriah to be sent to the front lines of a battle to be killed. As God's punishment, the first child David conceived with Bathsheba died, and David was cursed with the promise of a rebellion from within his own house.[21] An evolutionary perspective of parent-offspring conflict can foreshadow this kind of "rebellion," although typically of quotidian rather than cosmic importance. It is testimony to its perspicacity that the Bible recognizes the fundamental importance of parent-offspring conflict and sibling rivalry long before evolutionary genetics comes along. After all, even in a post-Darwinian, post-Mendelian world, the best minds in modern biology were stymied by the phenomenon until Trivers connected the dots in 1974. In any event, do not let this discussion of parent-offspring conflict obscure the fact that the reason such conflict is so dramatic is that it is counterintuitive, occurring as it does amid expectations of parent-offspring love and benevolence, a behavior normally consistent with biological expectations.

Sometimes sibling rivalry of the most violent sort begins remarkably early in life, at least in the animal world. It is not uncommon, for example, for a newborn hyena to kill its brother or sister. Baby hyenas of both sexes are born with fearsome and fully developed teeth, as well as a disposition that makes the murderous Cain appear almost pacifistic. Young hyenas vie to literally tear one another apart, presumably to monopolize food from the mother. Since parent hyenas would rather their offspring behave respectfully to one another, hyena siblicide qualifies additionally as parent-offspring conflict.

There are other cases in which animal parents seem indifferent when their offspring kill one another. In fact, they sometimes appear to be indirect accomplices in the grisly business. The best-studied examples come from research by Douglas Mock and G. A. Parker. By studying great egrets and cattle egrets—long-legged wading birds of ponds and marshes—Mock documented that older siblings commonly kill the younger while the parents stand idly by. Even as nestlings, these birds are the avian equivalents of hyena cubs, outfitted with long, sharp beaks, which they use to engage in prolonged and lethal combat.

Just as a simplistic view of natural selection would suggest that parents and offspring should never be at odds, parental indifference to siblicide might seem to run counter to the evolutionary expectation. As we have seen, although it may occasionally be in the interest of an egret offspring to be nasty—even murderous—toward its sibling, such behavior should run counter to the interest of the parent and be prevented when possible. And yet, in nearly two decades of observing 3,000 battles among young egrets, Mock never saw a parent intervene. This stoic indifference occurred because the youngest is expendable and therefore usually killed by the eldest. An exception is made when food is especially abundant, in which case parents are able to rear additional offspring. Egrets produce "an heir and a spare," with the latter only surviving when conditions are extraordinarily favorable. Egret parents collaborate in the siblicide by endowing their first nestlings with a dose of testosterone up to twice the amount provided to the youngest. The juiced-up elder sibs employ their enhanced aggressiveness to the detriment of the youngest, but to the genetic benefit of themselves and their parents. By this means, potentially debilitating future competition is avoided. Siblicide is clearly more frequent in nature than previously thought. Embryonic sharks, for example, begin their predatory lives with an early burst of sibling-sibling competition, devouring each other *in utero* as they swim about before they are born. And pronghorn antelope fetuses kill each other in the womb, thereby increasing the amount of mother's milk the victor will obtain.

Egrets, sharks, and antelopes are extreme examples of parents loading the dice in favor of certain offspring. In some species, parents do just the opposite. Instead of playing favorites in the manner of Rebecca and Jacob, canaries provide the greatest share of testosterone to the youngest hatchlings, thereby leveling an otherwise lethal playing field. For every family of murderous little canaries, there may be hundreds or thousands composed of peaceable brothers and sisters. It remains to be seen whether the pattern of canaries or egrets is the more common, and which ecological factors have selected for one strategy instead of its alternative.

We can only speculate why Rebecca and Isaac differed in choosing favorites. Genesis gives us one reason, that Isaac appreciated the meat provided by Esau, the hunter.[22] But there is another possibility, one with evolutionary salience: Isaac preferred Esau perhaps because he more closely resembled his own father's appearance and, as a result, Isaac unconsciously valued him over Jacob. Evolutionary psychologists have documented that fathers, more so than mothers, are keen to perceive resemblances between themselves and "their" children. Moreover, the mother's family is especially eager to point out such resemblances, given that mothers do not need to be reassured about the genetic connection of offspring they carry for nine months and emerge from their own bodies. Fathers have no comparable guarantee, giving rise to the adage, "Mommy's babies, Daddy's maybes."[23]

The conflict between Cain and Abel may well be consistent with the most frequent pattern in the natural world in which competitive interactions are zero-sum games—success for one means defeat for the other. It is certainly possible that God could have valued the grain offering of Cain no less than the animal offering from Abel, or at least not made his preference abundantly clear.[24] God's decision to judge the offerings against each other can be considered a provocation stimulating Cain to murderous rivalry. But especially in the domain of male-male competition, zero-sum games are a frequent reality. This is because successful fertilization of a woman by a given man precludes shared success by another man. More generally, when resources are in short supply and genes are jousting with one another for relative success, zero-sum outcomes are in most cases unavoidable.

As of yet there is no evidence that human beings practice siblicide as a common evolutionary strategy, although brothers can compete violently. Sisters seem no less inclined toward competition, but such competition is typically more subtle and less violent. According to Scripture, Isaac's sons Jacob and Esau battled each other even before they were born, having struggled within Rebecca's womb (shades of those embryonic sharks and pronghorns).

Recent medical evidence suggests that Jacob and Esau may have been less antagonistic in their competition than are many other sibling pairs. Although *Homo sapiens* mothers normally give birth to one child at a time (thus spared the temptation of young egrets to kill their nest mates), human offspring remain dependent for many years, providing opportunities for selection to create subtle but potentially lethal strategies for sibling competition. For example, there is a phenomenon known as the *vanishing twin syndrome*, in which some pregnancies that begin with twins end up with a singleton child being born. Until recently, such early embryonic weeding-out has been attributed to spontaneous abortion. But nothing in nature is truly "spontaneous"—the word is simply a coverup for our ignorance of true causes. The possibility exists that human embryos, with or without the unconscious collusion of either parent, exert a nefarious evolutionary strategy to eliminate the other embryo.

Just as evolutionary theory predicts the existence of such conflict, it also anticipates that in most cases parents would be opposed. Since parents are equally related to each offspring, parents should prefer beneficence of one toward the other so long as the recipient gains more fitness than the donor loses. The offspring, as has been already described, can be expected to see things differently. They should favor cooperation only when the benefit derived by the recipient is more than twice the cost incurred by the donor.

When Esau and Jacob struggled in their mother's womb, this caused immense distress to Rebecca, who cried out in agony, "if so, why do I exist?"[25] She was answered, "Two peoples are in your belly; two nations shall branch off from each other [as they emerge] from your womb. One people shall prevail over the other; the elder shall serve the younger."[26] According to Maimonides, the descendants of Jacob and Esau were destined to become antagonists. The probability is that Jacob and Esau were fraternal twins rather than identical, since they looked so unlike (Jacob "smooth" and Esau "hairy"). These two genetically were brothers and not identical twins, who are *genetically* identical. So their conflict is well within the realm of evolutionary expectation, since it is more probable that brothers, unlike genetic twins, will have conflicting behavioral dispositions and, in many cases, be more competitive with one another.

A related subject is the possibility of intrauterine, parent-offspring conflict between parents and their embryonic children. At first blush, such conflict seems particularly unexpected, since embryos and fetuses appear altogether helpless and utterly dependent on maternal resources. Yet such conflict has been seriously suggested by biologist David Haig. Some of the complications that bedevil pregnancy, such as morning sickness, may be due to mother and fetus in disagreement over the genetic script. Although pregnancy is a cooperative endeavor, with the mother seeking to reproduce and the fetus facilitating its own production, the fetus can be expected to seek more maternal resources (oxygen and nutrients) than the mother may be able or inclined to provide.

High blood pressure and preeclampsia, for example, are two frequent complications of pregnancy suffered by the mother. They are primarily caused by fetal hormones attempting to increase blood flow to the unborn child at the expense of blood flow to the mother's body. Blood sugar is another possible battleground. During the last trimester of pregnancy, the placenta (a product of the fetus, incidentally, not the mother) secretes a hormone that interferes with the effect of the mother's insulin. At the same time, the mother is producing more and more insulin. Why this particular tug-of-war? Insulin suppresses blood sugar levels, so by making insulin, the mother can be trying to restrict the amount of *her* sugar made available to the fetus, who in turn responds by trying to get as much of *its* sugar as it can. In most cases, things work out all right. But sometimes the fetus "wins," and the result is gestational diabetes.[27] Although informative, the above speculations, based on recent medical discoveries, have no revealed corollaries in the biblical text.

But let's continue with examples of parent-offspring conflict regarding behavior toward third parties. Consider behavior between cousins: parents are more closely genetically related to their nieces and nephews than their cousins, the offspring of two siblings, are to each other. Remember that uncles and aunts have a genetic relationship to their nieces and nephews of 25 percent, whereas first cousins are only 12.5 percent related to each other. As a result, it is predictable that parents who are full siblings expect their children to be twice as nice to their first cousins as the first cousins are inclined to be toward each other! It is relatively common today for first cousins to interact often while young since their activities are largely controlled by their parents. As parents become less influential, however, the cousins grow older and become less subject to parental pressure. Evolutionary theory would predict, therefore, that, as time goes by, cousins will drift apart or at least become more distant now that cousins are more able to assert their own genetically related interests.

In parent-offspring conflict over behavior toward a third party, stepparenting is likely to take the cake because stepparents are totally unrelated to their stepchildren. If parents and their children can be expected to disagree over the latter's behavior toward siblings or cousins, at least in these cases the parents and offspring have a shared genetic interest. But when a stepparent enters the picture, conflict can be sky-high.[28] The genetic parent is in a bind, since he or she would like the child to behave benevolently toward the stepparent and the stepparent's children (if any), especially if the newly formed couple is young enough to contemplate producing their own children. The stepchild, however, sees his or her genetic interest in a different light. Even if the stepparent does not represent a threat, and even though the stepchild has a genuine interest in the happiness of the genetic parent, the truth is that the stepchild has relatively little *biological* interest in either the welfare of its stepparent or the stepparent's children from a previous union. Under these conditions, we can predict a virtual free-for-all of parent-offspring conflict, in which issues previously quiescent during courtship resurface as the new arrangements are negotiated. Anticipating this sort of conflict, the Mishnah reports (Ket. 101b3) that a woman with a daughter from a previous marriage can require in the new marriage agreement (*ketuba*) that her husband feed his step-daughter for five years.

Additionally, more than a little opportunity for conflict *between* the spouses may arise because each may favor dispensing resources preferentially toward its genetic children rather than stepchildren. Earlier, we mentioned Bathsheba's insistence that her child, Solomon, be David's successor rather than his son by another woman. But the paradigmatic biblical example of stepparenting and its conflicting consequences comes from the story of Isaac and Ishmael. Isaac was Abraham's son by Sarah. Prior to his birth, however, Sarah, thinking she was too old to bear Abraham a child, arranged for him to reproduce with her Egyptian handmaiden Hagar. Later, after giving birth to Isaac, Sarah became intolerant of her stepson and his mother, driving them both into the wilderness. Here, quite visible, is the double-edged sword of parent-offspring relations when some of the family members have no genetic relatedness. On the one hand, the family is characterized by genetically mediated beneficence and mutual caring and, on the other hand, by intolerance and selfish exclusivity.

Both the Bible and evolutionary theory resonate in agreement that childlessness is the greatest disaster that can befall a woman. It was Sarah's initial childlessness that led Abraham to impregnate Hagar. Later we are told that Rachel's childlessness with Jacob, compared to Leah's fecundity, generated consternation between the sisters and was instrumental in Jacob's taking two concubines. Sororal polygyny, sisters married to the same man, is widespread in the Bible. A cowife in the religious texts is *tsarah,* a word whose meaning implies that the relationship is inherently adversarial.[29] Evolutionary theory of genetic relatedness predicts this arrangement should diminish competition among the cowives, since each would also be an aunt to her sister's offspring. Although the total elimination of competition would not be expected, the enmity between the sisters Leah and Rachel pales in comparison to that between the unrelated Sarah and Hagar. Their rivalry was so severe it resulted in Hagar and Ishmael becoming outcasts.

As has been previously mentioned, it is obvious who should prevail in most conflicts of interest between parents and offspring. Parents are bigger, older, and more experienced in the ways of manipulating others. Offspring should not stand a chance. When Abraham was tested by God's command to sacrifice Isaac, one presumes he was sorely troubled. Had the command not been rescinded, the killing of Isaac would have been not only a clear case of parent-offspring conflict, but one that Isaac would certainly have lost. We can only presume that Isaac was at best ambivalent to the proceedings, or would have been had he understood what nearly transpired. In severe intrafamily conflicts it is unavoidable to leave indelible scars; Abraham's willingness to sacrifice Isaac italicizes the physical helplessness of offspring when confronting adult power. It is one thing when a grown child like Absalom engages in parent-offspring conflict. In such cases, the outcome may be in doubt due to the relatively equal distribution of power. But when it comes to young children such as Isaac, the parents hold all the cards.

The Bible describes a deity in the ancient Middle East named Moloch who was uncommonly fond of child sacrifices. These sacrifices are truly abominations but, from another perspective, can be seen as deriving from a lethal parent-offspring conflict. In times of severe stress, resources are so depleted that adults are faced with a kind of "Sophie's Choice." In these situations, the question is not which of two offspring to save, but, rather, whether to cease caring for one's own children in order to save oneself. There are many well-documented examples in the biological literature of adults terminating investment in offspring after living conditions have severely deteriorated. When offspring are very young and helpless, the amount of parental investment required over many years is at its highest level. The likelihood is that those children sacrificed to Moloch were the offspring of captives, slaves, and powerless Canaanites. It is most unlikely they were the children of Moloch's friends and relatives. Perhaps such sacrifices were a method for rulers to exercise control over the weak, in addition to reducing the number of hungry mouths to feed if conditions deteriorated. In any event, it is noteworthy that this practice among the Israelites was explicitly forbidden by Mosaic law: "You shall not give any of your children by donating them by fire to Moloch, and so profane the name of your God."[30]

Not only are young children relatively helpless when contending with their parents, they are also limited in what they can extract from parents who are unwilling donors. And yet, children are not entirely helpless because, ironically, their vulnerability provides them with a variety of strategies. Due to their physical subordination, biological selection provides children with techniques to win parents over. Young children especially have become experts at this kind of psychological warfare. Since offspring may know better than their parents what their needs are at any given moment, it is in the parents' interest to be attuned to offspring's indications of these needs and to respond appropriately. Biological theory predicts that when dealing with children, parents would be able to distinguish real needs from those that are exaggerated and dishonest. As the folktale advises, it is dangerous for the child to "cry wolf"—to insist on being needy when, in fact, he or she is merely being greedy. Parents can learn to see through such exaggerations, but are unlikely to discount them altogether. When in doubt, it may be best for parents to err on the side of leniency, caution, and generosity, especially if the cost to the parent is low and the outcome might be real distress or even endangerment if the child is truly in trouble.

Unless in the grip of extreme parent-offspring conflict (or their own pathology), parents will respond when offspring cry or give other indications of distress. Most any genetic tendency of parents to be indifferent to their offspring's requirements has likely been selected against. This, in turn, gives the offspring just the advantage he or she needs. The child can attempt to manipulate parental gullibility by sending false signals, pretending to be needier than he or she really is, to receive the additional parental investment the child desires that parents are otherwise reluctant to provide. At the same time, the opposite possibility also exists, that infants have been selected to send honest signals of need to their parents. When food is scarce or if they are in poor condition themselves, parents might be tempted to cut their losses (sacrifice to Moloch?) and cease investing in too costly children, especially if the parents are young enough to breed again at a later date. In this case, children would be under pressure to send reassuring signals to their parents, such as "I am healthy and strong. Therefore, I won't take much from you and, moreover, I might well provide you a good evolutionary return on your minimal investment." Given the choice, parents would likely favor offspring whose signals are likely to be honest, that could not readily be faked.[31] In short, selection should favor offspring signals that are expensive to produce and therefore reliable, since offspring in poor condition would be less able to send costly signals of well-being.

It is important to keep in mind that crying by human infants is quite costly, requiring an expenditure of calories about 11 percent higher than a quiet baby. Various illnesses and debilitating conditions produce consistent variations in "cry characteristics," variations to which parents respond. Crying, especially by healthy babies, may therefore be a way of proclaiming that he or she is "worthy" of parental investment. At the same time, children should be selected to carefully titrate the degree of annoyance generated by their crying. Although natural selection has seen to it that even sleep-deprived parents make allowances for a "cranky" or "colicky" baby, there are also abundant examples of child abuse and neglect under these conditions, which would be expected to set a biological outer limit to the crying strategies of infants and young children.

Of course, children do not only cry and complain. They also smile when they are happy and their needs are met. Not surprisingly, adults find this gratifying, to the point of performing all sorts of peculiar antics in the hope of generating a smile from a young child. Children, in response, can withhold their smile until their needs have been satisfied. The same strategies may be in play regarding sleep. For exhausted, sleep-deprived parents, sometimes the greatest reward their infant can provide is to go to sleep and let them do the same. The child is not saying to itself, "Don't go to sleep until all of your needs are met," any more than it is plotting "Hold off on that smile until you get some milk or a goofy look from Uncle Charley." But it would make biological sense if the child were to feel agitated and restless until his or her (unconsciously) desired outcome is achieved, and to act with that end in mind.

Child agitation and restlessness in extreme is the temper tantrum, with the child behaving in a way not only unpleasant for the parent but potentially injurious to the child. Picture a child beating his or her head against the wall unless or until getting his or her way—a game of Chicken played against its own parents. Temper tantrums are exclusive to the young of our species. Here are the words of Jane Goodall, recounting the tribulations of parent-offspring interactions among chimpanzees:

> Temper tantrums are a characteristic performance of the infant and young juvenile chimpanzee. The animal screaming loudly either leaps into the air with its arms above its head or hurls itself to the ground, writhing about and often hitting itself against surrounding objects. The first temper tantrum observed in one infant occurred when he was 11 months old. He looked around and was unable to see his mother. With a loud scream he flung himself to the ground and beat at it with his hands, and his mother at once rushed to gather him up. Two infants showed tantrums in connection with weaning and this has been recorded also in infant baboons and langurs.

Temper tantrums by juveniles as a means of manipulating their parents do not appear in the Bible, but there are frequent allusions to adults being "in great wrath." Biblical exhortations against excessive temper apply to adults and are not directed toward young children. This is consistent with the observation by historians that despite the biological importance of children, they generally had a much lower social profile in the ancient world than they do in modern times. The evolutionary salience of parent-offspring conflict allows speculation that the commandment "Honor your father and your mother" might be intended not only to induce obedience and mitigate parent-offspring conflict, but also to restrain excessive temper on the part of otherwise headstrong and self-serving children.

The Jewish Sages extol those who "keep their cool" by controlling their temper. Thus, talmudic tradition maintains that "a man should always be gentle like Hillel, and not impatient like Shammai."[32] A delightful story is told of two men, each wagering that he will succeed in making Hillel angry. After having been subjected to pestering and silly questions, however, the sage never lost his temper. The text makes the point that such restraint is worth much more to the community than whatever money either of the bettors might have won had Hillel become angry. There are numerous similar exhortations (e.g., "the Holy One, blessed be He, loves the one who does not display temper").[33] "He who loses his temper is exposed to all the torments of Gehenna";[34] "A bad tempered man gains nothing but [the ill effect of] his temper."[35] We might presume that holding one's temper with one's children would be considered at least as important as with unrelated other people.

Grossly losing one's temper with outsiders can have significant consequences for one's own family. Following the rape of Dina, the daughter of Jacob and Leah, Jacob's sons Simon and Levi proceed through a ruse to slaughter not only Shechem the rapist but all of his followers. As a result, Jacob condemned both Simon and Levi because their excessive temper led them to risky violence. Jacob's worry was that Simon and Levi had endangered the safety of his tribe by their intemperate actions; in consequence, Jacob's son Judah became leader of the family. From a biological perspective, Simon and Levi's belligerent actions and Jacob's reproaches illustrate that the interests of parents and their children do not necessarily coincide. Although it is unclear whose interests were served by Simon and Levi's bloody retribution for the rape of their sister, it is likely that Jacob's other children and their families were endangered in the process. Hot-headed Simon and Levi risked deadly consequences for kinsmen by their thoughtless aggression.

Trivers proposed that the well-known psychological phenomenon of "regression," adults behaving in ways that resemble children, may also have its roots in the parent-offspring tug-of-war. Accordingly, younger offspring are typically more in need and therefore less likely to be in conflict with the parent's self-interest. As a result, young children are most likely to send signals to induce positive responses from parents. When adults "regress," therefore, it might be seen as appealing to the universal human weakness for children who are strategically young, cute, vulnerable, and endearing. Since adults are especially receptive to signals of extreme youth and helplessness, it is to be expected they would have also evolved to send signals that mimic those same characteristics, such as the "baby-talk" that lovers adopt or "infantile regression" as a sign of vulnerability in the very elderly.

But parents also have psychological techniques at their disposal. Because of their greater age and experience, they have much of value to transmit to their offspring besides material resources. Offspring, in turn, are likely to be vulnerable to manipulative parents who exaggerate their wisdom, just as parents are vulnerable to offspring who exaggerate their neediness. As Trivers has ironically noted, it may be telling that the traditional view of parent-offspring relations, assuming that "father and mother know best," has been promulgated by adults! As a result, we can expect parents to justify their teaching, manipulating, and arm-twisting as "for your own good," accompanied by protestations that "this hurts me more than it hurts you."

On balance, Judaism supports this parental perspective, with Jewish tradition venerating the "wisdom of the fathers" and, at times less visibly, mothers as well. But perhaps as a cautionary tale against the younger generation being duped by the older, the Bible contains examples of parental figures cast in an unfavorable light. Consider Abraham's father Terach, who stubbornly remained an idol worshiper, ignoring his son's argument regarding the powerlessness of wooden statues. Or Laban's substitution of one daughter, Leah, for his other daughter, Rachel, thereby manipulating both his daughters. Laban also, for the time being, trumped Jacob, requiring him to work an additional seven years to earn the right to marry Rachel. In this case, Laban abuses his position as Jacob's "trusted" uncle to mask his deceitfulness, a conflict-of-interest-driven trickery that can characterize older-younger kinship relations. By giving away his less marriageable daughter first, Laban served his own reproductive interest with no mention in the text of his concern for Leah's or Rachel's desires, much less those of his kinsman Jacob.

Childhood sexuality, a mainstay of psychoanalytic theory, may, like the human conscience, owe its existence to parent-offspring conflict. When young children display an intense (but not erotic) interest in the opposite-sex parent, this could be to induce greater investment by that parent. It is only "human nature" to enjoy being flattered by one's child and to respond by providing the child with an extra-large portion of love and attention. If so, selection then could favor such actions by children, counteracting what might otherwise be a parental inclination to discontinue or diminish investment. At the same time, it would be in the interest of the child not to be too "over the top" in his or her demands to the opposite-sex parent, if only because this might arouse the ire of the same-sex parent.

The story of Lot's daughters is a lurid tale of incest, seen as yet another manifestation of the sins of Sodom and Gomorrah. After departing the doomed cities, Lot and his two daughters lived in a cave, whereupon the young women got their father drunk, took advantage of him, and conceived children by him. However one interprets this story, it certainly demonstrates biblical recognition of parent-offspring sexual attraction (à la Electra rather than Oedipus). It is certainly significant that included in the narrative is the fact that Lot's daughters believed that their father was the only male survivor; hence, they seduced him in response to their biological urge to reproduce. As has been previously mentioned, children can be more effective in getting their way, if not sexually, then in obtaining material resources, when the authority of parents is divided. This may be even truer if one of the parents is deceased, as was the case with Lot's wife.

In conclusion, it is fascinating and deeply significant that so many insights from modern evolutionary biology had been prefigured and played out at the behavioral level in the biblical texts thousands of years ago. When the Psalmist laments, "my father and mother have left me,"[36] both intrafamily dependence and conflict are painfully displayed. The universal patterns of family discord depicted in the Bible remain remarkably "true to life" even to this day.

Notes

I especially want to thank Rick Goldberg for his many helpful suggestions throughout this chapter that made the final product feel almost like coauthorship rather than collaboration between author and editor.

1. For example, the Talmud assumes that, if his daughter were held captive, the father (who is 50 percent related to her) would be more likely to pay her ransom than would her husband (who is genetically unrelated to her) (Ket. 47a2).

2. Acknowledging the conflict, the Talmud calls a developing fetus a *rodef,* or dangerous pursuer, of its mother.

3. In Ket. 94b3 there is a potent example of conflict of interest between a mother and her sons regarding the inheritance of property.

4. There is an important principle of rabbinic law that coincides perfectly with biological theory: "A person is closest [most closely related] to himself."

5. See this reflected in Ket. 59b3–60a1. The expected time for a mother to nurse her child is twenty-four months. A widow who is nursing must wait at least twenty-four months before remarrying and weaning the child (Ket. 60b1).

6. Bear in mind that this example, continued below, takes nursing for a specific case. As we shall see, its implications are much broader, however, including expenditures of time, energy, resources, willingness to run risks, and so forth. The crucial consideration is simply that the parent is providing something—anything—to its offspring that enhances the success and, ultimately, the fitness of that offspring, but which occurs at some cost to the parent's ability to invest in him- or herself or in other individuals, and thus to enhance his or her fitness via other carriers of those parental genes.

7. New York: Vintage, 1969.

8. 2 Sam. 16:21.

9. Biblical names can express rich irony: Absalom, which means "father of peace," was anything but a peaceful son.

10. Prov. 17:17.

11. Gen. 33:3.

12. Gen. 33:5.

13. Exod. 4:27; also, Rambam does not comment on the definite article used before the word "mother." Perhaps the need to honor an older sister is a given, unlike the requirement to honor (by not competing with) an older brother.

14. Exod. 2:7–9.

15. Zipporah, or possibly a second wife (Num. 12:1).

16. Num. 12:2.

17. Num. 12:5–10.

18. Exod. 34:20.

19. These sons were the offspring of three different women—Leah, Bilhah, and Zilpah—and were thus half-siblings of Joseph, whose only full sibling, Benjamin, was from Rachel, Jacob's primary focus.

20. Gen. 37:4.

21. Bathsheba and David nonetheless conceived a second son, Solomon.

22. Gen. 25:28.

23. See the discussion on paternity uncertainty in the chapter "Biosocial Regulation of Husband and Wife." Jewish law recognizes the potential problem of paternity uncertainty: a woman who was a captive but had been freed must wait at least three months before marrying, presumably to reassure the husband that any child she bears will be his (Ket. 37a1–37a2).

24. See further discussion in the chapter "Making Biological Sense of Judaic Sacrificing."

25. Gen. 25:22.

26. Gen. 25:23.

27. Is it a coincidence that the gene responsible for producing placental lactogen, the fetus's anti-insulin hormone, is provided by the *father*?

28. Ket. 102b5 recognizes the precarious, even dangerous, position of stepchildren. For that reason, the Rabbis are mindful to help stepdaughters continue to receive daily support from stepfathers both during the new marriage and even in the event that the mothers should later become divorced from the stepfathers. It is understood that a man's natural daughters are less likely to find themselves in such a precarious circumstance (see the Mishnah and Gemara in Ket. 101b3–102b4).

29. See 1 Sam. 1:6; Lev. 18:18 uses the verb form *litsror* (2 × "ר") instead of *latsor* (1 × "ר") to show that having sisters as cowives is "double trouble" (Yev. 3b2, n. 15). Yev. 120a2 uses the word צרה (*tsarah*, or cowife) to mean "rival."

30. Lev. 18:21.

31. See the discussion by Zahavi in Chapter 8 on "reliability components" in signaling.

32. Shab. 31a.
33. Pes. 113b.
34. Ned. 22a.
35. Kid. 41a.
36. Ps. 27:10.

References

Haig, D. 1993. Genetic conflicts in human pregnancy. *Quarterly Review of Biology* 68: 495–531.
Mock, D. W., and Parker, G. A. 1997. *The Evolution of Sibling Rivalry.* New York: Oxford University Press.
Trivers, R. L. 1974. Parent-offspring conflict. *American Zoologist* 14:249–264.
van Lawick-Goodall, J.. 1968. The behavior of free-living chimpanzees in the Gombe Stream Reserve. *Animal Behaviour Monographs* 1:161–311.

Chapter 5

Toward a Sociobiology of the Jews

Sexual Selection, Circumcision, and the Centrality of Texts in a Coevolutionary Framework

Melvin Konner

Editor's Introduction

During the Greco-Roman period, Jewish proselytism was fervently practiced and achieved much success. After the Hadrianic period, Jewish law actively discouraged conversion, and circumcision provided an effective barrier to Gentile men who might otherwise wish to convert. But, since circumcision applied only to males, it never impeded the conversion of females who wanted to marry Jewish men and rear Jewish children. As a result, the requirement of circumcision helped account for the far greater number of female than male converts to Judaism in the ancient world.

In recent centuries, Jewish communities have characteristically insisted on marriages within the religion and antipathy toward proselytizing.

The persistence of Jewish populations throughout history in the face of relentless, repeated exiles and occasional mass murder has challenged historians and religious Jews, who explain it by reference to divine intervention. In scientific terms, Jewish survival is a coevolutionary puzzle, requiring reference to the influence of religious beliefs and practices not only on cultural evolution but on mating systems.[1] The establishment of Jewish peoplehood in ancient times has been shown by archaeologists to have preceded Judaism, and Jewish (or Hebrew) residence in what is now Israel has been continuous ever since.[2] There is considerable evidence that thousands of inhabitants of Canaan, including Hebrew-speaking people, were captured in wars and carried away into slavery in Egypt (by the Egyptians' own description) during the second millennium B.C.E. Although Egypt ruled that same region with an iron fist for centuries, there is no evidence of a mass exodus from Egypt or of a conquest of Canaan by an outside force and replacement culture at any time.[3]

In fact, there is clear evidence of cultural continuity and gradual cultural evolution in what is now Israel throughout the Bronze Age and into the Iron Age. This corresponds to the time of the Five Books of Moses and the books of Joshua, Judges, Samuel, Kings, and Chronicles, up to the first mass conquests with large-scale population movements, that by the Assyrians of the northern kingdom of Israel (722 B.C.E.) and that by the Babylonians of the southern kingdom of Judah and its capital in Jerusalem (586 B.C.E.). Although it may indeed have involved a partial and gradual emergence from Egypt's harsh rule, the establishment of the Israelite kingdom, with its associated First Temple religion, was a cultural-evolutionary, not a revolutionary, development.[4]

Why was this process successful? No doubt part of the explanation was geopolitical and military. Egypt found in Israel a natural buffer zone in its more or less constant wars with powerful Middle Eastern neighbors, the Hittites (Hatti) and Philistines, later the Assyrians and Babylonians, and ultimately the Persians, Greeks, and Romans. This may have worked better for Egypt when Israel was somewhat independent than when it was being occupied but, in any case, both strategies were tried. During the second millennium, Egyptian armies conquered, suppressed, and reconquered the tribal peoples of Israel (Canaan). The Merneptah stele, dated to 1207 B.C.E., described the pacification and/or destruction of Libya, Hatti, Gaza, Ashkelon, Gezer, Yanoam, and Hurru. Of Israel it says, "Israel is stripped bare, wholly lacking seed."[5] This is the first mention of Israel in any form known to history or archaeology, and it is an announcement of the demise of the people, with vivid and specific reference to the apparatus of reproduction for both agricultural produce and, presumably, people. The demise in question turned out to be exaggerated and premature.

Mating Patterns in the Bible

Hypotheses arising from evolutionary theory immediately suggest a look at the mating system. Unreliable although it may be as a source of political information, the Bible is nevertheless a document that can be informative if its biases are understood. It may be more accurate as an anthropological document than as a national history,[6] since the way of life of biblical characters is plausibly similar to what has been observed for recent agricultural and pastoral cultures of anthropological interest. More importantly for our purposes, there is likely to be significant validity in the descriptions of the kinship and mating systems of the ancient Hebrews.

Jews in recent centuries have been known for their endogamy.[7] However, in the last millennium B.C.E., Jewish mating was not endogamous, as it later became, but expansionist. The biblical descriptions, referring to the first centuries of the second millennium, probably provide clues as to why. First, this was an aggressively polygynous society, at least for successful men.[8] Abraham initially has two sons, one by his wife and one by his wife's handmaid, but he later takes another wife who bears him six more children, while he is also described as having "sons by concubines." His brother Nahor has eight children by his wife (one of whom marries Abraham's son Isaac) and four by his concubine. Isaac has only two sons, but Jacob, the next patriarch, has twelve by two wives and two handmaids (in addition to several daughters), while Esau has five sons by three wives (daughters are not mentioned). In keeping with accepted evolutionary theory,[9] sons are favored by wealthy and powerful families, and investment in sons by adult kin is emphasized. Since males have higher variance in reproductive success than females, parents of either sex in rich environments will prefer to have sons so as to maximize their number of grandchildren. This process has often been seen to be important in human evolution and history.[10] Among the Kipsigis of Kenya, whose way of life bears considerable resemblance to that described in Genesis, polygyny is a great advantage for men and only a small disadvantage if any for women, in terms of reproductive success.[11] At least in the biblical account, this appears to have the desired results: each of the seventeen grandsons of Isaac is described as giving rise to a tribe or clan.

Second, it was a culture or group of cultures in which not only unmarried women but other men's wives could be taken by violent capture. Both Abraham and Isaac are described as having beautiful wives and as fearing that they will be killed for them. In fact, each finds himself in a situation where he lies about his relationship with his wife, saying that she is his sister. Through his servant Eliezer, Abraham transfers bride-wealth to Rebecca and her family so that she will leave home and marry Isaac. This act suggests that high-quality women of reproductive age were at a premium, a conclusion strongly underscored by Jacob's fourteen years of service-for-bride(s), the price he paid to acquire each of his two wives. This pattern too is reminiscent of recently studied agropastoralist societies.[12] (Scarcity of marriageable women need not be a consequence of female infanticide or even disadvantageous treatment of girls; polygyny alone creates such a scarcity.) Later, through treachery and violence, Jacob's sons first kill the men of Shechem and then capture their wives and daughters. Then as well as now, sufficient quantities of high-quality young women were hard to find.

Third, the biblical prohibition against adultery is without relevance to sexual intercourse between married men and unmarried women.[13] A married woman who has sex with a man other than her husband is an adulterer and so is the man in question, but the married man who has sex with an unmarried woman has not committed a breach of this commandment. Various rules applied to the protection of unmarried girls (or, more properly, to protection of the fathers' property rights), but such rules would not apply to non-Jewish girls. As a matter of fact, men who mated with women captured in war were generally unconcerned with the prior marital status of their booty. As a result, the commandment against adultery could not be applied to men in this circumstance.

Finally, while the theme of endogamy is struck in the marriages of Isaac and Jacob, the latter, like his grandfather, has numerous children by handmaids unrelated to his family. As the biblical narrative unfolds, each of these sons became the ancestor of a tribe of Israel. Joseph, although continuing the patriarchal lineage and the covenant of Abraham, had two sons in Egypt by "Asenath daughter of Potiphera priest of On." These two sons, Ephraim and Manasseh, receive Jacob's dying blessing. The blessing concludes, "By you shall Israel invoke blessings, saying: God make you like Ephraim and Manasseh."[14] To this day Jewish fathers bless their sons on *erev Shabbat* (Friday evenings), "God make you like Ephraim and Manasseh," evoking the memory of two boys born to and suckled by the daughter of an Egyptian priest. This theme continues. Moses marries the daughter of a priest of Midian and is reprimanded for it by his brother and sister. But they in turn are reprimanded by God, and Moses does not disown his sons.[15] Joshua does warn the people against intermarriage,[16] but this stricture apparently does not apply to everyone.

Ruth is a Moabite woman who marries two Jewish men in succession; first, one of the sons of Naomi and, after his death, the prominent and wealthy landowner Boaz. Between the two marriages, Ruth's pronouncement to Naomi is interpreted by the Rabbis as a conversion to Judaism: "Where you go I will go, your people shall be my people, and your God my God." Ruth's statement goes on to curse herself should she ever be disloyal. As a Moabite, intermarriage with Ruth would appear to be forbidden,[17] her good heart, noble nature, and commitment to the Jews and their God notwithstanding. Yet Ruth becomes the great-grandmother of King David and therefore the ancestor of the Jewish Messiah. This despite the Torah's declaration that "an Ammonite or Moabite shall not enter into the congregation of the Lord; to their tenth generation shall they not enter into the congregation of the Lord forever."[18] So on its surface, the ten-generation rule would delegitimize Kings David and Solomon and their Messianic future lineage. The Talmud came to remove the difficulty by explaining that the prohibition applies to Moabite and Ammonite *men* but not *women*. The women of these particular ancestries were fully accepted into the community as converts and able to marry Jewish men immediately.[19]

Solomon, for his part, married some 700 women, many of them outsiders, and his 300 concubines were unlikely to have been Hebrew women:

> King Solomon loved many foreign women in addition to Pharaoh's daughter—Moabite, Ammonite, Edomite, Phoenician, and Hittite women, from the nations of which the Lord had said to the Israelites, "None of you shall join them and none of them shall join you, lest they turn your heart away to follow their gods." Such Solomon clung to and loved.[20]

In his old age they did indeed turn his heart away, but presumably not before he had sired thousands of children with these thousand women. One of them, Rehoboam, the son of an Ammonite woman,[21] becomes king in Jerusalem after Solomon.

To be sure, wives and concubines by the hundreds are part of the privilege of empire, but as has been clearly shown,[22] evolutionary theory predicts such uses (or abuses) of power; they have been widespread in authoritarian regimes, including some of recent memory. Y-chromosome haplotype analysis has decisively confirmed this theory; a haplotype traceable to Genghis Khan is exceedingly widespread in Asia[23]—millions of men have it—and a similar though less dramatic pattern has been noted in the Irish descendants of an early chieftain. How many descendants of Solomon are there in the world today? How many of them are Jewish? Neither question is answerable at the present time. What we do know is that biblical injunctions against intermarriage did not stop powerful Hebrew men from taking women of other cultures and religions as wives and concubines, nor did it stop the offspring of these unions from being incorporated into what would become the Jewish fold.

Railing against these exogamous unions did, however, continue. Indeed, the text attributes the breakup of the kingdom into Judea and Israel to Solomon's turning away after other gods. Also implicated in the Land's division, however, was David's illicit acquisition of Solomon's mother, Bathsheba, as his wife. The rabbinic explanation is that, by committing adultery with her, David caused the death of Bathsheba's Hittite husband. The frequent violation of norms of marriage, described explicitly in the Bible, typically increased the reproductive success of powerful men and created a continual tension between the powerful, the prophets and the priests, who were both in and behind the text. In a sort of spiritual insurance policy, David conquered the holy city of Jerusalem and dedicated it to the one God of Israel. Solomon rendered his insurance premium by constructing the Holy Temple and establishing the Temple religion, which benefited the hereditary priesthood for many centuries.

Genetic and cultural evolution was pulling Jewish behavior in opposite directions during this historical period. To put it another way, the priests who were the guardians of cultural evolution had different reproductive interests than did the men of wealth and military power, and these differences led the priests to ally themselves with average men in using cultural evolution as a weapon. Men at the top of the social hierarchy maximized reproductive success by amassing mates and children, including non-Jewish women imported by incentive or by force.

However, in Darwinian perspective, it is not mainly women who are oppressed by polygyny (although they may suffer a decline in reproductive success). Men at the bottom of the social hierarchy end up having as a result no mates and no offspring. Throughout the social hierarchy one would expect the quantity and quality of women available to average men to decline as a result of polygynous hording by the higher social strata.[24] Priests and prophets (never required to be celibate in Jewish tradition) perhaps represented the interests of the fathers of Jewish girls by warning of the consequences of taking foreign women. Their defense of monotheism against idolatrous influence took the form of setting limits on how many foreign women could be imported because large numbers of imports could undermine their cultural tradition. Yet polygyny could not be controlled simply by sequestering Hebrew women, which would have taken even more potential mates away from ordinary men, most of whom did not have the means to acquire foreign wives and concubines. The result is that Darwinian and cultural evolution can be seen as severely at odds, even to the point of crisis.

One such crisis was during and after the Babylonian exile, perhaps around 550 B.C.E. Ezra, whose lineage is carefully traced back to Aaron,[25] is the first leader described as both priest and scribe. Unable to practice sacrificing in Babylon after the destruction of the First Temple, Ezra becomes in effect a new kind of priest, "a scribe expert in the Teaching of Moses."[26] After the Second Temple is built and operating, he conducts what looks like the first synagogue service on the first day of Rosh Hashana, the Jewish New Year, while animal sacrifices must have been ongoing in the Temple a few hundred yards away. He reads and teaches from the Torah scroll, raising it up before a moved and attentive congregation, praising the Torah and God.[27]

But Ezra, returning with many exiles, finds that the Israelites who remained behind have thoroughly mingled with Canaanites, Hittites, Perizzites, Jebusites, Ammonites, Moabites, Egyptians, and Amorites. His officers report, "They have taken their daughters as wives for themselves and for their sons"—again, the reference to intermarriage is unidirectional—"so that the holy seed has become intermingled with the peoples of the land; and it is the officers and prefects who have taken the lead in this trespass."[28] Those returning from Babylon soon propose "a covenant with our God to expel all these women and those who have been born to them, in accordance with the bidding of the Lord ... [despite] many people being involved ... nor is this the work of a day or two."[29]

Ezra, acting according to the model established by the priests and prophets of the David-Solomon era, invokes God's anger against these exogamous men; they are named, and their names make up a long and "distinguished" list. They pledge to rid themselves of their foreign wives, but we are not told how this works out. The last line of the book of Ezra reads, "All these had married foreign women, among whom were some women who had borne children."

Intermarriage continued to be discouraged in noncanonical writings such as the book of Jubilees and later in the Talmud, but there is reason to believe the strictures were honored as much in the breach as in the observance. When John, the nephew of Judah the Maccabee, became king in Jerusalem, he mounted wars of conquest that entailed both mass forced conversions to Judaism and the acquisition of foreign women for the dynasty. John's son crucified eight hundred Pharisees, in effect the cultural descendants of Ezra, while he himself feasted with his concubines; according to Josephus,[30] he had the throats of their wives and children cut before their eyes as they died on the cross.[31] Another who disregarded endogamy was Herod, a scion of one of the forced-convert families, who thoroughly brutalized the Jewish people on behalf of Rome.[32] In summary, the conflict between genetic particularity and cultural evolution did not abate, nor did it benefit the Jewish population as a whole.

Circumcision, Matrilineal "Endogamy," and Sexual Selection

We have seen that the most successful men of ancient Israel were not really restricted in their choice of wives and other sex partners. It was clearly in their interest to import rather than export women, wombs always being the rate-limiting factor in a male's reproduction. With the notable exception of Esther, whose intermarriage saves the Jews of Persia, we hear much less about Jewish women marrying non-Jewish men than the reverse. Powerful Jewish men can gather uteruses as they may, but Jewish women must be sequestered until they are mated properly with Jewish men. Could circumcision have played a role in this one-sided endogamy?

The biblical mandate of circumcision, the religious marker of covenantal obligation and the Jews' unique relationship to God, along with comparative anthropological evidence, has clear implications for fertility. Indeed, the covenant, on its human side, is *about* fertility. You circumcise yourself, God says to Abraham, as well as the males of all your future generations, and I will make you the genitor of nations. "[T]he Lord appeared to Abram, and said to him, 'I am God Almighty; walk before Me and be whole-hearted. And I will make My Covenant between Me and you, and you will multiply prodigiously.'"[33] Abram falls on his face and God communicates with him further, mentioning the Covenant again, changing Abram's name to Abraham, and saying (twice) that he will be "the father of a multitude of nations." Again: "'I will make you immensely fruitful, and I will make nations of you, and kings shall come out of you.'" God says "Covenant" twice more before promising Abraham and his descendants the Land of Canaan as an everlasting possession. But like any agreement, this one has two sides:

> And as for you, you shall keep My Covenant, you and your seed after you throughout their generations. This is My Covenant which you shall keep, between you and Me and your seed after you: every male among you shall be circumcised. And you shall be circumcised in the flesh of your foreskin; and it shall be a token of a Covenant between Me and you. And he that is eight days old shall be circumcised among you, every male throughout your generations ... and My Covenant shall be in your flesh for an everlasting Covenant. And the uncircumcised male who is not circumcised in the flesh of his foreskin, that soul shall be cut off from his people, for he has broken My Covenant.[34]

This repetitive litany is as ominous as the first one is full of promise. Ostracism was not just psychologically but physically deadly in that time and place, yet such is the fate of the man who has not had his foreskin ritually removed. And, since circumcision is a biblical condition for fertility, the uncircumcised Jewish man will be childless, cut off from the future as well as the present of his people.

According to a *midrash*,[35] Abram is somewhat reluctant, but God explains that circumcision will perfect him and complete the creation; that, indeed, "If you refuse this *mitzvah*, I shall return the world to nothingness."[36] This rabbinical interpretation conveys the pivotal importance accorded this ritual in Jewish tradition.[37] For millennia, Jews have risked their lives and the lives of their sons in observance of this practice.[38] Assyrian tyrants, clients of the Greek empire, punished circumcision by death, and are said in the book of Maccabees to have thrown Jewish mothers off cliffs with their newly circumcised sons dangling from ropes around their necks. Enemies of the Jews in many historical epochs have used circumcision as an identifying, indelible physical feature on which to base segregation and persecution. As a result, the circumcised Jew found himself the unwilling target of separation and discrimination. The apostate philosopher Spinoza believed circumcision was so important that it alone would preserve the Jewish nation forever.

According to Jewish tradition, the penis is not being mutilated, but sculpted, completed, and made perfect. This is consistent with other uses of the word ערל (*arel*), meaning "uncircumcised," in Jewish scripture.[39] For example, one who defies God's laws is said to have an "uncircumcised heart." One who lacks verbal dexterity, like Moses, is described as having "uncircumcised lips." Circumcising in agriculture refers to the pruning of juvenile fruit trees, without which the fruit is considered inedible. In addition, grafting of one species onto another is a horticultural technique that allows directed and successful breeding, and also uses the root word for "circumcision." References to fruit trees help answer the question: how and why does circumcision lead to the birth of multitudes? According to the Judaic view, the "perfected" organ has now become an instrument of God. Eilberg-Schwartz called circumcision "the fruitful cut" by characterizing its practice as symbolically linked to fertility not only for the ancient Hebrews but for other circumcising cultures.[40]

We know now that male circumcision to some extent protects the male genitalia and their female counterparts from infection. Studies show that circumcised boys are markedly less likely than uncircumcised boys to develop urinary tract infections (UTIs) in infancy and childhood[41] and sexually transmitted infections (STIs)[42] or penile cancer in adulthood.[43] At first glance this seems a compelling argument in favor of a hygienic interpretation of the original practice, but there are still three problems with the argument.

First, until modern times, circumcision itself carried a risk of hemorrhage or infection, and some male infants bled profusely or developed systemic sepsis and died. Recent studies of traditional circumcision done between ages three days and four years showed complications including hemorrhage (especially in newborns), infection, blockage or fistula of the urethra, and penile amputation.[44] In ancient times the connection between circumcision and these relatively few deaths from bacterial sepsis would have been more obvious than any connection between the practice and protection from UTIs or STIs. Jewish parents did understand this immediate, potentially fatal consequence of the practice, yet even those who had lost their sons to it went on to circumcise later sons in accordance with Jewish law. Second, the elevation in the rate of UTIs in the uncircumcised only brings males up to the level of normal females. Finally, careful foreskin hygiene has been shown to prevent infections and penile cancer.

Studies also show that the wives and other female partners of circumcised men are significantly less likely to contract cervical cancer. The vast majority of cervical cancers are caused by the human papilloma virus (HPV), today an extremely common sexually transmitted infection. Uncircumcised men are more likely to become infected with HPV than those who are circumcised, although here again, proper hygiene is protective. Also, if a relationship is monogamous, the advantage for a woman with a circumcised partner in terms of protection from cervical cancer disappears. It is only a significant risk factor if she is having sex with multiple uncircumcised partners or if her one uncircumcised partner is having sex with other women. In other words, circumcision is only protective in the context of nonmonogamy by either of the partners.

In ancient Israel, as in other ancient cultures, there was little restriction on male sexual activity with unmarried women, particularly in times of war. So while most women may have remained monogamous, perhaps most women's men had mated with multiple partners. Given the limitations on sanitation in that era, the advantage for a woman who chose a circumcised man could have been considerable and could have outweighed the disadvantage imposed on her infant sons through infectious risk resulting from the circumcision itself. Another possible reason for female preference for circumcised men is suggested by the handicap principle.[45] If a man successfully survived this surgery—either in infancy or, more so, in adulthood as a convert—his circumcised status would confirm his general health and strength, an honest signal of quality. Since circumcision has been a religious tradition, there would be no confusion about whether the handicap represented a genetic defect. Like all scars of initiation, circumcision would be well known as a deliberate cultural intervention communicating, among other things, overall male quality.[46]

But why the symbolic connection with fertility? Howard Eilberg-Schwartz has made great contributions in answering this question,[47] in part by contextualizing the Jewish practice among those of other circumcising cultures. What follows is an outline touching on some of these practices, relying on Eilberg-Schwartz and Silverman.[48] Muslims circumcise their sons, derived essentially by the same authority cited by Jews: Muslims believe they inherited God's covenant with Abraham through his first son, Ishmael. Traditional Islamic communities have often circumcised at puberty or a few years earlier. Modern Muslims do it on the seventh day of life (a day earlier than specified by Jewish law), but consider the ritual permissible to perform at any time during early childhood.

A number of Australian aboriginal cultures had a pubertal ceremony in which they not only circumcised but in some groups *sub*incised their boys. Subincision involves slitting the underside of the penis lengthwise from base to tip; the resulting scar was said to increase female sexual enjoyment. Circumcision was more common and was done at an age similar to the Jewish practice. Among the Ngatatjara of the Gibson Desert, the boy was laid across the backs of a row of friends on their hands and knees, making a living table. The foreskin was then cut off using a stone blade, in the midst of a dance around a great bonfire dedicated to the sacred Kangaroo. The ceremony was a test of the boy's willingness to suffer pain calmly, thus proving he was becoming a man.

For the South African Thonga, circumcision was the key event in a months-long pubertal initiation. Boys ran a gauntlet between two rows of men who stripped them, cut off their hair, and beat them with clubs. Intimidating men draped in lions' manes grabbed each boy's foreskin and severed it. During a three-month recovery period boys were indoctrinated into male secrets, remained mostly naked, and could not be seen by women. The Ndembu of Zambia circumcised at age eight to ten, with a ritual dance that imitated lions. As with the Thonga, the circumciser had to seem lion-like in order to cut the boy's tie to his mother. The ritual period of healing and teaching continued for months. The Merina of Madagascar circumcised much earlier, at one or two years of age, in a quiet, dignified ritual evoking continuity with their ancestors, thereby ensuring the toddler's eventual potency and fertility.

Fertility is a common and often explicit cross-cultural theme.[49] African circumcision rites in particular often entail explicit potency and fertility symbolism. Dances may mimic copulation. In some cultures, medicine made from the hard wood of fruit trees was applied to the wound, symbolizing both the hardness and the fruitfulness of a properly functioning male organ. In any case, the theme of making a boy into a man has always been crucial in pubertal or prepubertal circumcision ceremonies.

Since Jews circumcise at eight days rather than puberty, the transformation from boy to man is not part of the meaning, but the Torah does emphasize future fertility as I have previously discussed. When God tells elderly Sarah that she is to bear a son, she laughs. Abraham asks God to bless thirteen-year-old Ishmael, the son he already has. God complies, saying, "I will make him fertile and exceedingly numerous," after which Abraham circumcises himself, Ishmael, and his entire household. When Abraham is later visited by three strangers, described as messengers of God,[50] one of them repeats the promise that Sarah will have a son, and this time Sarah laughs. When God causes Sarah to conceive and give birth to Isaac, Abraham circumcises him also. God repeats His promise to Abraham of "descendants as numerous as the stars of heaven and the sands on the seashore; and your descendants shall seize the gates of your foes." Consequently, through both Ishmael and Isaac, Abraham becomes the most famously potent and fertile man in the Western tradition.

When God warns that if a man is not circumcised "his soul shall be cut off from his people," the implication is not just ostracism but *in*fertility, the converse of the promise made to Abraham. The childless man is cut off not just from the past and present but also the *future* of his people. Some biblical scholars have concluded that the circumcision part of Genesis was composed by the priestly author—probably much later than the rest of the book, in First Temple times. However old circumcision was, the Israelite priesthood wanted to reconfirm its importance. It could not be a mere pagan fertility rite; rather, it had to be the mark of the Covenant with the one true God, who assures an endless line of descendants for his people, provided that they maintain themselves as physically (i.e., sexually) distinct.

Circumcision and Intermarriage

Soon after its introduction in the Torah text, circumcision is used as a weapon by Jacob's sons to avenge their sister's rape. To the Bible-naïve reader, the story seems astounding, incapable of any sort of positive spin. Dinah goes out "to visit the daughters of the land," but is raped by a chieftain's son named Shechem, who tries to redeem himself: "Being drawn to Dinah daughter of Jacob, and in love with the maiden, he spoke to the maiden tenderly." He also speaks to his powerful father:

"Get me this girl as a wife." The father visits Jacob, bearing a fortune in gifts, but Dinah's numerous brothers are not impressed: Shechem "had committed an outrage in Israel by lying with Jacob's daughter—a thing not to be done."

The brothers then completely mask their intentions for retribution. "Speaking with guile because he had defiled their sister Dinah," they pretend exceptional magnanimity. "Only on this condition will we agree with you; that you will become like us in that every male among you is circumcised. Then we will give our daughters to you and take your daughters to ourselves; and we will dwell among you and become as one kindred."

Shechem and his father are pleased: "And the youth lost no time in doing the thing, for he wanted Jacob's daughter." He and his father go to a public place in their town and repeat to all the townsmen the conciliatory words of peace and friendship they had heard from Dinah's brothers. So to bring about Shechem's marriage to Dinah and a historic reconciliation and merger between two neighboring peoples, all the men of the town are circumcised.

This leads to their downfall. "On the third day, when they were in pain, Simeon and Levi, two of Jacob's sons, brothers of Dinah, each took his sword, came upon the city unmolested, and slew all the males." Included among the slain are both Shechem and his father; Simeon and Levi then take Dinah out of their house. "The other sons of Jacob came upon the slain and plundered the town, because their sister had been defiled. They seized their flocks and herds and asses ... all their wealth, all their children, and their wives, all that was in the houses, they took as captives and booty."[51]

In generic terms, this strategy of revenge was ubiquitous and ancient, easily explicable in sociobiological terms. The men of one tribe or town attack those of another, kill the males, and take the women, children, livestock, and other wealth as captives and spoil. It is not unusual that treachery would be involved; the siege of Troy (which begins with a captured woman) is a classic example, and there are many others. What is different here is that *brit milah,* Judaic circumcision, the sign of the Covenant itself, is used treacherously to weaken the enemy's males while plotting their slaughter and the seizure of their wives and daughters. Jacob himself is enraged at his sons: "You have brought trouble on me, making me odious among the inhabitants of the land ... my men are few in number, so that if they unite against me and attack me, I and my house will be destroyed." They reply, "Should our sister be treated like a whore?" By killing the men of a neighboring tribe who had circumcised and weakened themselves in response to the brothers' false promises, they make it clear that they will not allow *their* women to enhance the reproductive success of the males of other tribes.

Presumably this subterfuge could not have been used very often, any more than other enemies of the Greeks would have been fooled by a Trojan horse once its fame had spread. But even if this was not paradigmatic of ancient Jewish battles, it was symbolic, and holds three lessons: first, *your* women may be for *us,* but *our* women are not for *you;* second, you certainly have no access to our women unless you are circumcised; third, since you have violated lesson one, not even circumcision will save you.

Perhaps this story served as a warning against foreign men who might hope to join the Hebrew people legitimately, even while setting the precedent for importing foreign women, by force if necessary. Foreign women captured in combat were apparently common enough so that the Torah specifies how they should be treated:

> When you take the field against your enemies ... and you take some of them captive, and you see among the captives a beautiful woman and you desire her and would take her to wife, you shall bring her into your house, and she shall trim her hair, pare her nails, and discard her captive's garb. She shall spend a month's time in your house lamenting her father and mother; after that you may come to her and possess her, and she shall be your wife. Then, should you no longer want her, you must release her outright. You must not sell her for money: since you had your will of her, you must not enslave her.[52]

This is a humane and quite specific regime for the treatment of captive women and their later disposition as wives, but it does not cast the slightest aspersion on the man who may appropriate a woman by coercion. Indeed, humane though it may be in intent, a one-month pause before mating with a man who was among those who may have killed your husband or father seems to allow little time for grief. Rather, it seems mostly to allow the Jewish captor to ascertain that his captive is not pregnant and to seize a new reproductive opportunity in fairly short order. Since there was no prohibition against polygyny—indeed the very next passage of Deuteronomy begins, "If a man has two wives"—we may assume that such captive women were often added to households where one or more wives already lived.

We saw earlier the prohibition against bringing Ammonites or Moabites (men, but not women, says the Talmud) into "the congregation of the Lord." But the prohibition did not apply to Edomites or Egyptians, whom "you shall not abhor"; indeed, "children born to them may be admitted into the congregation of the Lord in the third generation."[53] All this follows the classic pattern of patriarchal accumulation of female partners. The importation of women also persisted in peacetime. Moses, as we noted, himself marries the daughter of a priest of Midian, and Ruth, a Moabite woman—a member of a tribe who were the Jews' bitter enemies—marries a prominent Jewish landowner and becomes the ancestor of King David and therefore of the Messiah. The symbolic power of these cultural icons must have influenced Jewish mating systems subsequently.

One way to deal with the status of all these foreign women's descendants was to circumcise their sons, decisively placing the male offspring within the Covenant and allowing those boys to grow up to take Hebrew wives. Perhaps the strangest episode in the life of Moses takes place in the fourth chapter of Exodus. As we have seen, the word *arel*—uncircumcised—occurs only a few times in Tanakh. One occurrence is in Exodus 6:12, where Moses describes himself as having *"arel s'fatayim,"* uncircumcised lips. The language is different in Exodus 4, but he makes the same point in his first argument with God, saying that he cannot speak to Pharaoh because he is slow of speech. God tells Moses that it is the Lord who gives man speech, and the suggestion is that God can and will circumcise (sculpt, perfect) his lips so he can be the spokesman for the Hebrew slaves. But within a few verses God instructs Moses: "'Go back to Egypt, for all the men who were seeking your life are dead.' So Moses took his wife and his sons and mounted them on a donkey, and returned to the land of Egypt."[54]

God reminds Moses that he must go to Pharaoh with signs and wonders, and God will harden Pharaoh's heart, but that Moses must persevere. Immediately following this straightforward set of instructions, we are told of God's intention to kill Moses, followed by his wife's very odd response:

> Now it came about at the lodging place on the way that the Lord met him and sought to put him to death. Then Zipporah took a flint and cut off her son's foreskin and struck it against Moses' leg, and she said, "You are indeed a bridegroom of blood to me." So He let him alone. At that time she said, "You are a bridegroom of blood"—because of the circumcision.[55]

The reason God seeks to kill Moses is the subject of much debate, but the response suggests that it was necessary for him and his foreign wife to prove their membership in the Covenant by doing something they should have done long since: circumcise their son. The peculiar phrase "a bridegroom of blood" suggests that this act consecrates for the first time their marriage in the Covenant. The fact that Zipporah does the circumcision herself suggests that she has something to prove, and the whole act has an air of resentment about it. Perhaps Zipporah's dramatic initiative is proof of her having left her father's home and abandoned his religion.

Much later, Aaron and Miriam publicly criticize Moses for intermarrying with a Cushite woman, after which they are severely chastised by God.[56] This begins a millennial tradition of criticism by the Israelite priests and prophets of marriage by influential Hebrew men to foreign women, a critique that resulted in permanent tension. Despite God's attitude about Moses and his siblings, in this matter it is the priests who appear to have had God on their side.

The agonistic use of circumcision is also clearly alluded to in 1 Samuel 18, where it is also linked to marriage, but in a very different way. David, a rising rival to King Saul, wants to marry the king's daughter, but Saul demands as a bride-price the foreskins of one hundred Philistines killed in battle. David brings him two hundred, becomes the king's son-in-law, and goes on to replace the king. In a strange symbolic inversion that echoes the treachery at Shechem, the enemies of Israel are circumcised in death and their foreskins become the bride-price for the daughter of an Israelite king.[57] This bride-price might be viewed as a sort of supercircumcision in which David must prove himself a hundred times more worthy of being a husband than the average circumcised man, and then proves himself twice as worthy as that.

Fertility Advantages of Circumcision?

Clearly Jewish women (and their fathers) wanted circumcised husbands, and it was in the interest of successful Jewish men to be able to appropriate non-Jewish women despite the protests of the priests and less powerful men. But why might some Gentile women, or more likely their fathers, have chosen marriage to Jewish men?[58] Worldly success was no doubt essential, and the relative literacy of the Jews and the centrality of texts in Judaism may have been another factor. It is likely that women whose families volunteered to join their lives and fortunes to the Jewish people were themselves select and self-selected.

But circumcision may also have played a role. Growing evidence points to a role for circumcision in protecting against sexually transmitted genitourinary infections and genital cancers.[59] The circumcised penis is easier to keep clean and free of infection,[60] and this was undoubtedly more the case in ancient times. An ancient Egyptian medical papyrus mentions a treatment for urethral purulence,[61] and a bas relief depicting circumcision of adolescent boys in Egypt dates from about 6,000 years ago; whether the two were connected is not known. Clearly urinary tract infections are reduced by circumcision in some populations, although in modern populations proper foreskin hygiene abolishes the increased risk. High levels of exposure to *Schistosoma hematobium* (blood flukes) in the Nile River frequently caused morbidity and mortality, and it has been suggested that, in part because of the prominent symptom of hematuria, it may have been the purpose of ancient Egyptian circumcision to reduce this risk,[62] although this linkage has been challenged.[63]

However, it is extremely unlikely that schistosomal disease was the only genital infection threatening male urinary function and fertility. Trichomonal infestation (*Trichomonas vaginalis*) is a cause of male infertility due to inflammation of the epididymis.[64] Among patients with tuberculosis, 4 to 8 percent have genitourinary complications, which can cause male infertility through tuberculous scarring of the epididymal and ejaculatory ducts.[65] However, the extent of male infertility due to infection remains an open question regarding most infectious agents.[66]

The same cannot be said of women, who for anatomical and physiological reasons are more vulnerable than men to STIs.[67] Infections acquired from sexual intercourse are a major cause of infertility in women. One-third to two-thirds of women presenting for infertility treatment globally show signs of prior infection.[68] Bacterial STIs such as gonorrhea (*Neisseria gonorrheae*) and especially chlamydia (*Chlamydia trachomatis*) are among the leading causes of female infertility due to infection of the fallopian tubes and/or subsequent autoimmune reactions,[69] chlamydia being most insidious because it is often symptomatically silent. An acute phase of pelvic inflammatory disease (PID) is often followed by chronic asymptomatic infection and tubal obliteration. The risk of laparoscopically demonstrated tubal infertility is estimated to be about 25 percent after one episode of chlamydial PID and 75 percent after three or more episodes; severity of the episode is also predictive. Nongonococcal urethritis due to *Mycobacterium genitalium* can also cause tubal infertility.[70] Bacterial vaginosis, overgrowth of anaerobes at the expense of lactobacilli, is associated with endometritis and second-trimester miscarriage; it too can be influenced by sexual partners. Among viral infections, genital herpes (herpes simplex virus, HSV) is associated with poor pregnancy outcomes,[71] and the protozoan *T. vaginalis* is associated with both tubal infertility and poor pregnancy outcomes.[72] Both HSV and gonorrhea can infect neonates during delivery.

As I have already noted, male foreskin removal affects disease risk in female partners. Circumcision protects women from human papilloma virus, the cause of cervical cancer, and from other sexually transmitted diseases.[73] When penile hygiene and monogamy do not obtain, there is evidence that severe problems can occur. In one meta-analysis, the risk of both chancroid and syphilis (and to a lesser extent HSV-2) was lower in circumcised than in uncircumcised men.[74] As a disease that evolved in the New World, syphilis could not have been present in ancient Israel or Egypt,[75] but chancroid (genital ulcers due to *Haemophilus ducreyi*, which was present) increases the likelihood of transmission of other sexually transmitted infections, as do HSV-1 and HSV-2, both of which were probably present.

The current evidence is strongest for HIV transmission,[76] which did not exist in the ancient world, and for genital ulcers, which did, and which increase the likelihood of transmitting other STIs. Overall, although there is some controversy over the protective effect of circumcision, this disagreement does not occur among investigators working in the developing world,[77] especially in Africa,[78] where offering circumcision to men at risk for HIV may soon become standard policy.[79] The explanations offered for the greater risk of infecting female sexual partners from an intact penis include the difficulty of keeping the foreskin clean. Also, risk may result from the foreskin being less keratinized than other parts of the penile skin surface and therefore more subject to microabrasions during intercourse. The foreskin encloses a warm, moist, smegma-filled space that can incubate bacteria.[80]

Above and beyond the protective effect of circumcision (especially in cultures of questionable hygiene) in relation to UTIs in general,[81] it reduces the likelihood of transmission of at least some STIs. This is especially true of the developing world and may have been true in the ancient world as well. If so, the connection between circumcision and fertility would have been far more than symbolic. However, it would have been mainly through women that the protection against infertility was achieved. Consequently, all else being equal, there would have been both natural and cultural selection favoring women who married or otherwise mated with circumcised rather than uncircumcised men. This would have had the double effect of keeping Jewish women, for whom the cultural selection would have been strongest, from leaving the Jewish fold, and attracting foreign women to Jewish men. If so, it might help explain the archaeologically documented, rapid expansion of Jewish populations in Israel leading up to the eighth century B.C.E., when Israel was the most densely populated area in the Levant.[82]

On the other side of the ledger, circumcision can have significant adverse effects,[83] and some of these, such as infection of the wound and sepsis, would have been greater and potentially fatal before modern times. Finally, there is some evidence that women's enjoyment of sexual intercourse is greater with uncircumcised men,[84] which could presumably also influence female choice and intercourse frequency, although family and cultural pressures would have limited both personal choice and number of sexual partners. Ongoing research, especially with randomized clinical trials, should throw more light on the costs and benefits of circumcision. At present, both the hypothesis of a link between circumcision, fertility, and female choice (in the expanded sense of choice by women and their families) remains viable.

Diaspora, Rabbinical Judaism, and Endogamy

Beginning at least by 586 B.C.E., the year of the Babylonian conquest of Judah and Jerusalem, Jewish populations dispersed westward to Babylon (Iraq), Persia (Iran), Central Asia, and India; thereafter, south to Egypt and west from there through North Africa; then north to Turkey, and eventually all of Europe. The exile after the Babylonian war was partial and brief. The exquisite Psalm 137—"By the rivers of Babylon, there we sat down, yea, we wept, when we remembered Zion"—paints a devastating literary portrait of grief and anger, one that has stood the test of time as the quintessential poetic account of displacement and slavery. Yet both archaeology and the Bible itself suggest that this pain was short-lived.

Many Jewish exiles became tenants of the landed aristocracy of Babylon. In time they were able to engage in commerce and to accumulate some wealth. Jeremiah gives some programmatic advice to the exiles that provides a stunning contrast to the despairing account in Psalm 137:

> Build yourselves houses, and dwell in them; and plant gardens, and eat the fruit of them; Take yourselves wives, and beget sons and daughters; and take wives for your sons, and give your daughters to husbands, that they may bear sons and daughters; that ye may be increased there, and not diminished.[85]

A Darwinian piece of advice if there ever was one. Then Jeremiah goes on to say, "And seek the peace of the city where I have caused you to be carried away captives, and pray to the Lord for it: for in the peace there shall you have peace."[86] This speech became the model strategy for every Jewish diaspora since, and it comprises a feature of culture that may have interacted synergistically with genetic evolution.

Another cultural feature whose foundation was laid in the Babylonian exile was the requirement to study religious texts in the absence of the Temple and its opportunities for sacrifice. The Jewish communities of Babylon in time became the leading centers of rabbinic Judaism for the first millennium of the Common Era. But prior to that time, Ezra, the priest and scribe we encountered as the champion of endogamy, placed those texts on a par with Temple ceremonies even after the Temple was rebuilt in Jerusalem. Throughout the Second Temple period, there were large, thriving Jewish communities in Egypt (Alexandria), Syria (Damascus), and several Persian cities, as well as Babylonia. In addition, there were many smaller academies for textual study that we know less about. In the city of Rome, there were an estimated 50,000 Jews and thirteen synagogues by the end of the first century C.E.; these Jews were mostly poor and had given up polygyny in accordance with Roman law.

Some historians believe that large conversions to Judaism in response to Jewish proselytizing occurred in the two centuries bracketing the start of the Common Era. The larger numbers claimed have been seriously challenged,[87] but there was significant proselytizing activity, and Roman writers such as Juvenal and Tacitus express grave concern about Judaizing among Romans.[88] Probably most of these converts were women, for two reasons: women were prominent among the early converts to the Christian branch of Judaism, suggesting that the position of women in the Roman world made them amenable to alternative religious opportunities; second, while the cost of conversion for a man included circumcision, for women there was no comparable requirement. The visible circumcisions of Jewish men set them clearly apart, especially in the Greek world of public baths and naked sports competitions. This served as a deterrent to intermarriage by Jewish women throughout the history of the Diaspora.

In Israel, however, the two unsuccessful rebellions against Roman rule (in 70 and 135 C.E., respectively) had dire consequences. Some hundreds of thousands of Jews are believed to have been killed; the Second Temple, along with the Jewish community in Jerusalem, was largely destroyed. Although there remained a small Jewish presence in the Galilee, the remaining population dispersed to join Diaspora communities at points all over the map;[89] Jewish population history would unfold in those places for two millennia.

During this period, as clearly demonstrated by current molecular genetic evidence, substantial amounts of genetic material were imported by all Jewish Diaspora populations from neighboring non-Jewish ones. Consequently, the assessment by modern Jews of their own past endogamy must have been greatly exaggerated. The issue of the extent of Diaspora admixture is largely settled—a considerable amount—but the question of when it occurred remains unanswered. We do know that at some point during the development of rabbinic Judaism, perhaps as early as the establishment of the first academy in Yavneh (Israel) after the destruction of the Second Temple (but perhaps as late as the fourth century), descent by parental status changed from patrilineal to matrilineal.[90] Although the change may have occurred gradually, this legal modification constituted a stark change from biblical practice, and its origins are obscure.

The explanation most plausible in Darwinian terms is also the most commonly offered one by Jewish scholars: Rome's two wars against the Jews of Israel included so many rapes of Jewish women that to have failed to trace Jewish identity through the mother would have further reduced an already decimated community. This does not explain why the complementary other half of the descent issue was not adopted: why should offspring of Jewish men and Gentile women, contrary to all prior Jewish and Israelite history, not be considered Jewish? The fact remains that conversion by men required immersion in a ritual bath and circumcision, while conversion by women only required immersion. Thus patrilineal descent was in effect preserved with a relatively minor obstacle to be overcome, while the obstacle to matrilineal descent was completely removed. The result would have been a net gain in reproductive success *given* the new requirement of monogamy under Roman law.

Modern DNA technology has traced the genetic history of Jews and confirmed much of what historians believe.[91] All Jewish populations in the world, with the possible exception of the Jews of Ethiopia, have in common a substantial genetic resemblance to the non-Jewish Semitic peoples of the Middle East, especially the Levant. But Jews also depart substantially from this central Semitic tendency in the direction of the surrounding people's genes.[92] So the genetic data confirm what the eye suggests: Moroccan Jews often look more or less Moroccan, Indian Jews, Indian, and Russian Jews, Russian. We do not know the extent to which proper conversion was involved; these may have been conversions of prospective spouses or just of interested members of the non-Jewish community. Since we know genes were imported, we know people must have been also.

The conversion process that was relatively informal in ancient Israel was made rigorous and formalized in rabbinic Judaism. Despite initial discouragement, anyone can convert to Judaism, and converts ("Jews by choice") are fully Jewish according to Jewish law. But the conversion process and subsequent religious responsibilities are not without difficulty, even for women. Consider not only anti-Semitism as a deterrent to conversion, but also the assumption of obligations: Sabbath and kosher laws, laws of menstrual purity,[93] and, for males, circumcision. As a result, conversion has not been common for more than a millennium. This means that while Judaism is neither a racial category nor a biological characteristic, its practice has historically overlapped with a population that can, to some extent, be genetically defined.

During most of the period of the Jewish Diaspora, the focus was on quality rather than quantity of offspring, although maximizing quantity within the confines of monogamy was considered meritorious. Within Jewish communities, talmudic academies served as magnets for the brightest young men living in small communities scattered over thousands of square miles. Regardless of the content of the texts being studied, these intensely competitive learning centers served, from a biological perspective, as leks[94] in which the display of intellectual prowess was the equivalent of the peacock seeking prominence by displaying its tail. Because of the centrality of texts in Jewish life and high literacy rates dating back to the Babylonian exile, Jewish culture became preadapted to generate sexual selection for intelligence in the Diaspora. The wealthiest merchants in town competed for the brightest young rabbinical students to make matches for their daughters, and the common practice of housing or at least feeding the students in local homes must have enhanced the students' mating opportunities and the centrality of female choice. According to the description given by one historian, there were instances in which something resembling a ceremonial reproductive display by young Torah scholars occurred:

> Just as in the Bible wives were won by bold feats on the battlefield, so in the Middle Ages the way to a maiden's heart was often made by the brilliant exploits of a young, budding Talmudist on the field of rabbinic controversy. The youths would often display intellectual prowess under the gaze of their future wives. In the Talmud, public opportunities for courtship [of this type] were already a popular institution.[95]

The resulting marriages put the best genes in the best possible environments.

This reproductive effect should have operated in all three major branches of the Jewish population historically: that of the Middle East and North Africa, that of Iberia (Sepharad), and that of Northern, Central, and later Eastern Europe (Ashkenaz). In demographic terms, however, the first two were eclipsed by the third.[96]

The medieval expansion of the Jewish population of Spain and Portugal was halted by forced conversion and exile in the fifteenth century, and a large proportion of the exile's descendants were eliminated by mass murder during the 1940s. However, 30 percent of the current Jewish population of the State of Israel is Sephardic. We know little about the descendants of the converts to Catholicism and their reproductive success, but some Spanish Catholic groups certainly carry a disproportionate amount of Jewish genes.[97] In any case, their conversion put an end to the coevolution of Jewish genes and Jewish culture in that branch of the population. Some of the exile's descendants thrived in the Netherlands and joined with Dutch traders in settling the Western Hemisphere. The indigenous Jews of North Africa and the Middle East fled persecution during the twentieth century, with most going to Israel where they make up 23 percent of the Jewish population. In Israel today, all three population branches appear to be demographically expanding.

Founder Effect, Genetic Drift, and Endogamy in Ashkenazic Jewry

The Jews of Ashkenaz (Central and Eastern European descent) are a special case, because they began as a small founder population and now represent about 80 percent of the world's Jews.[98] It has long been understood that Ashkenazic Jews manifest certain genetic diseases in prevalence rates much higher than that for other Jewish or neighboring non-Jewish populations.[99] At least forty genetic disorders are either confined to or more likely to occur in Ashkenazic Jews than in non-Jews, including some diseases that also occur in other groups but through different mutations. The particular genetic defect has been characterized for almost all of the forty diseases; the metabolic pathways from genes to diseases are many.

Tay-Sachs disease (TSD), for example, is a devastating form of mental retardation, now largely prevented through genetic testing and counseling. It is an autosomal recessive disorder with a defect in the lysosome hydrolase enzyme beta-hexosaminidase A, which normally removes the toxic GM2 ganglioside (TSD is one of several lysosomal storage diseases characteristic of Ashkenazic Jews, a point to which we will have to return). The ganglioside builds to toxic levels in brain neurons, deforming the dendrites and stripping them of spines needed for incoming synaptic connections, which results in progressive muscular and mental retardation and death before age five.

In torsion dystonia, an autosomal dominant that causes symptoms at seven to ten years of age, intelligence is (at least) normal, but involuntary, sustained, dystonic muscle contractions result in contorted postures, beginning in the legs, arms, or neck, and lead to progressive disability.[100] Due to incomplete penetrance, not every child who carries it develops symptoms, depending on interactions with other genes, but it occurs in one out of two thousand to six thousand Ashkenazic children, substantially above a plausible mutation rate. Other disproportionately Ashkenazic genetic conditions include Gaucher's disease,[101] now largely treatable,[102] Bloom syndrome, Fanconi's anemia, and certain forms of nonsyndromal genetic deafness. In addition, two genes predisposing women to breast and/or ovarian cancer[103] are far more common in Ashkenazic Jews than in other populations.

The perhaps unusual population-genetic history long suggested by these patterns has now been investigated using advanced techniques of molecular-genetic analysis. There is wide consensus that genetic drift and founder effects played an important role in the accumulation of distinctive Ashkenazic genetic diseases, but the questions remain:

1. Where and when did the effect(s) occur?
2. Did natural selection also play a role?

Both historical and the more persuasive genetic evidence strongly suggest that there was at least one and probably two population bottlenecks that made the Ashkenazic population subject to drift that resulted in founder effects.[104] The likely opportunities for the whole Ashkenazic population to have been small enough for drift would have occurred at the outset of Central European settlement, after the Black Death and the subsequent mass murders of Jews in the fourteenth century. Some of the data on the age of alleles are consistent with geographically specific bottlenecks that affected only some of the Ashkenazim.[105]

In addition to more general analysis of disease genes and autosomal genes, matrilineal and patrilineal genetic heritages have been examined through mitochondrial genetics (mtDNA) and Y-chromosome haplotypes, respectively. Studies have shown strong overrepresentation of two mtDNA haplo-groups, K and N1b. These findings suggest a matrilineal founding event and have been extended through specific analysis of haplo-group evolutionary trees.[106] The result is that four founding maternal lineages account for 40 percent of Ashkenazic Jews, roughly 3.5 million people, a dramatic example of the founder effect as classically defined.[107] These haplo-group distributions, compared with other populations, also strongly suggest a Middle Eastern/Levantine origin.

But, since Ashkenazic autosomal DNA diverges from the Middle Eastern pattern in the direction of European populations,[108] there must have been considerable admixture at some point in Ashkenazic history. Analyses of haplotypes of the nonrecombining portion of the Y chromosome (NRY), however, show descent from a highly varied ancient Middle Eastern population, with low levels of admixture on the male side after settlement in Europe. The remaining possibility seems to be that the 60 percent of Ashkenazim who are not descended from the four mtDNA founding lineages would have included substantial numbers of imported women. This is a logical possibility; while some men would have brought their wives with them to settle in regions of Central Europe far from Israel, many others would likely have been merchants traveling alone, and they may have taken non-Jewish European wives with or without conversion. This marriage pattern could, in effect, be considered a continuation of the biblical patrilineal pattern during a time when Judaic insistence on matrilineal descent was not yet fully formed and was remote from the realities of Jewish life in Central Europe.

Considerable attention of late has been given to Y-chromosome haplotypes that are specific to the descendants of priests (Kohanim) and, to a lesser extent, the assistants of priests (Levites). For our purposes, this finding is of interest because these groups of men were at the top of the hierarchy in ancient Israel, and because their status is inherited by strict patrilineality. Since celibacy was never a requirement for the Jewish priesthood, one might expect these privileged men to have had opportunities for descendant leaving that other men did not have. Despite the fact that no Temple has stood for almost two millennia, Kohanim and Levites perform specified functions and receive honors in synagogues today, and a significant minority of Jewish men still proudly identify themselves by family tradition as belonging to one of these two groups.

The claim that today's Kohanim are descended from Temple priests would strain credulity were it not for the genetic evidence. Distinctive NRY haplotypes found almost exclusively in Kohanim are estimated to be about 3,000 years old, consistent with a point of origin very early in the First Temple period.[109] These haplotypes are found in high frequency in both Sephardic and Ashkenazic men who identify themselves as Kohanim, confirming a point of origin before these groups geographically diverged. Men identifying themselves as Levites have a more diverse origin:[110] remarkably, about half of Ashkenazic Levites share a haplotype not found among other Jews, but found in substantial frequency among Central and Eastern European populations. This suggests that one or only a few non-Jewish men early in the European Jewish Diaspora became ancestors of a large proportion of today's Levites.

Remarkably, Kohanic haplotypes are not completely restricted to Jews; indeed, they also occur in at least one population that has claimed Jewish ties not accepted by other Jews. Men among the Lemba of South Africa[111] carry the Kohanic haplotype in much larger than expected frequency, especially men of the highest status. It is remotely conceivable that they acquired the haplotype from Arabian traders but, if that were the case, why would they have a long-standing Jewish religious tradition? This is indeed a fascinating dilemma that continues to be investigated. So are the genetic affinities of other populations in Africa that have expressed seemingly implausible claims to Jewish affiliation. Given the remarkable discovery that a significant minority of men in Asia today are direct descendants of Genghis Khan, it would be of great interest to know how many men—Jewish or not—living today are descendants of Temple priests. It is a classic sociobiological question.

Founder Effect, Selection, or Both?

The existence of Ashkenazic genetic diseases does not exclude the importation of other genes, only that there was significant genetic drift involved in the founding or in subsequent bottlenecks, followed by significant endogamy. Some, perhaps most, investigators are convinced that selection is not needed to explain Ashkenazic genetic diseases, only genetic drift.[112] But others continue to believe that heterozygote advantage may play a role, creating a balanced polymorphism for the disease genes similar to those well demonstrated for sickle cell anemia and the thalassemias. One proposal often discussed is that common fatal lung diseases such as pneumonia and tuberculosis may have a more difficult time colonizing individuals heterozygous for lysosomal storage disorders such as Tay-Sachs, Gaucher disease, and two other Ashkenazic syndromes.[113] This would help explain why the homozygotes for these conditions are more common than could be explained by the mutation rate, despite their being typically fatal before reproductive maturity. (It is puzzling that resistance to the Black Death itself, one of the possible Ashkenazic genetic bottlenecks, does not appear to be under active consideration as a possible selective force generating a balanced polymorphism.)

However, a very different explanation for heterozygote advantage has been fielded. Recent theorizing has suggested that Ashkenazic genetic diseases may have been inadvertently selected for because the heterozygotes are superior in intelligence.[114] It is well established that Ashkenazic Jews (but not other Jews) have an average IQ that is 0.75 to 1.00 standard deviations above the European mean, and that they are represented among Nobel Prize and other distinguished winners far beyond their proportion in the European or U.S. populations. The IQ difference does not apply equally across all subtests; Ashkenazic Jews are at an advantage in answering verbal and arithmetic questions but not spatial ones. Cultural influences on upbringing and education surely explain much of this advantage but perhaps not all of it.

Cochran et al. argue that Ashkenazic genetic diseases fall mainly into subgroups having in common a few metabolic shifts that in the heterozygotes might favorably influence brain development. They group the diseases into five categories in following a previous classification:[115] sphingolipid storage diseases like Tay-Sachs and Gaucher, glycogen storage defects, blood clotting disorders, adrenal enzyme defects, and DNA repair disorders. Some argue against the claim that these disorders can be explained by founder effect and drift[116] based on the improbability of achieving such clusters of metabolic impairment randomly. Regarding the sphingolipid storage defects, they cite evidence for a stimulation of axonal growth consistent with heterozygote levels or with homozygote levels in the case of Gaucher patients with low penetrance; the latter appear to have high-IQ occupations. Torsion dystonia does not fall into one of the five categories, but is itself associated with high IQ. The gene *BRCA1*, when defective in Ashkenazic women, confers a larger risk of breast cancer; it is also expressed in embryonic and adult neural stem cells, where it appears to down-regulate cell proliferation.

Cochran et al. posit a selective advantage for intelligence, attributable to the notion that most Ashkenazic Jews, or at least the most successful ones, were financiers or moneylenders. Some were, but most were merchants, craftsmen, managers hired by non-Jews, teachers, and minor religious officials.[117] Most importantly, many were rabbis and rabbinical students, including lifelong students supported by their wives and their wives' families. Indeed, many authors have criticized the Rabbis and their students for imposing a heavy burden of economically unproductive men on communities of Jews that could ill afford it. However, if, as indicated above, we can view rabbinic academies as venues of intensive sexual selection, they may well have served the purpose of individual selection for intelligence and verbal acuity. To recapitulate, the academies generated strenuous competition among boys and young men in the oral expression of analytic ability, and the wealthiest merchants competed for those young men as husbands for their daughters. Their families were able to provide higher-quality average resources, resulting in producing more and healthier surviving offspring than their less advantaged counterparts, especially under conditions of high infectious mortality. Their offspring, especially their sons, could then have exported genes for intelligence down the social hierarchy.

This argument, along with founder effect and drift, could help explain Ashkenazic intelligence irrespective of its relevance to genetic diseases. Intelligence would be selected for in all the common Jewish occupational roles, and female choice would favor intelligence in most marriages, not to mention the advantage of intelligence in standard natural selection. If one result was the rare individual born with a devastating disease, this would be a small price to pay in evolutionary terms for the selective advantage of greater intelligence in the overall Jewish population. The cultural payoffs in Jewish communities of having intellectually gifted descendants were enormous.

Current and Future Prospects: Ongoing Selection?

The world's Jewish population was cut by a third due to mass murder between 1939 and 1945, a reduction greater than any since the Black Death and perhaps since the Roman-Jewish wars. The number of Jews worldwide is estimated today to be about the same as it was in 1939, between thirteen and fourteen million.[118] The only expanding major Jewish population is in Israel (about five million), and it will soon eclipse the size of the U.S. Jewish population, which is contracting, even when emigration out of Israel is included. If current trends continue, non-Ashkenazic Jews, who make up more than half of Israeli Jews, will become more numerous and make up a greater proportion of the world's Jewish population than they have in recent centuries. The distinctive coevolutionary coupling of intellectual prowess and reproductive success will wane among Ashkenazim as they rise in status, intermarry, and fail to replace themselves through births. But intellectual capability will still characterize a core group in each of the three branches of the Jewish population. Perhaps a new coevolutionary coupling, between self-defense and self-conscious pro-natalism in the service of demographic survival, will continue to expand the Israeli Jewish population and even feed the Jewish populations elsewhere, as it is now doing in the United States and parts of Western Europe. However, most emigrants from Israel are secular, and may within a few generations merge with the non-Jewish populations of their host countries as non-Orthodox U.S. Jews now appear to be doing. Future geneticists will certainly be able to trace formerly Jewish genes in non-Jewish populations, and this too can represent reproductive success, but the millennial coevolutionary coupling of intellect and reproductive success will no longer sustain most of the Jewish population. Whether a tradition-centered core of religious, endogamous Jews (perhaps a fourth to a third) with a high birthrate will provide a sufficiently high rate of increase to replace the Jewish population being lost remains to be seen, but the Orthodox are likely to maintain the time-honored, coevolutionary synergies.

Conclusions

The following tentative conclusions may be drawn from this overview:

1. Prestigious men among the ancient Hebrews were polygynous, married Hebrew as well as other women, kept concubines, and took foreign women in war. Some of these men had many children by multiple wives and other mates.
2. Circumcision almost certainly reduced the risk of sexually transmitted infection and the consequent female infertility often caused by such infections. Circumcised men were probably attractive to marriageable women and their families for this reason, and perhaps also because it was a culturally sanctioned, self-inflicted handicap that honestly advertised male quality.
3. Circumcision probably biased the import of non-Hebrew (and later non-Jewish) mates toward women. There are many biblical examples of Jewish men bringing in foreign women, but few of the reverse. Thus, circumcision may have helped the Jewish population sequester women at the expense of the men of surrounding peoples.
4. Jewish legal status based on matrilineal descent arose with rabbinic Judaism, which also formalized the conversion process and made it intellectually challenging. The instigation of matrilineal descent may have been a response to wars that the Jews lost, which leave behind substantial numbers of Jewish women who had become pregnant through rape. This paralleled a shift in the Jewish reproductive strategy from quantity toward quality of offspring.
5. Rabbinical academies in most Jewish populations drew the boys and young men with the highest verbal and analytical intelligence from many miles around, put them in competition with one another, and ranked them. This process allowed the wealthiest fathers as well as prestigious families distinguished by learning to choose the most brilliant young men for their daughters. Children of these matches were raised in the most protected and richest environments.
6. Under Christianity and, to a lesser extent under Islam, Jews were pushed into occupations such as craftsmen or the merchant middleman class. These discriminatory policies favored high Jewish intelligence as well. Both dominant religions prohibited Jews from importing non-Jewish or converted spouses, often on pain of death.
7. Ancient Jewish populations of the Middle East, North Africa, and the

northern Mediterranean (Italy, the Balkans, Greece, and Turkey) lasted for at least two millennia, until most were dispersed as refugees, mainly to Israel in the mid-twentieth century.

8. Jews of Sepharad lived on the Iberian peninsula from ancient times until 1492 (1497 for Portugal), when the roughly half who had not been forcibly converted to Catholicism (several hundred thousand) were exiled. Many of their descendants (mostly in the Balkans and Greece) were murdered in the Holocaust.

9. Jews of Ashkenaz arose from a very small founder population, perhaps a millennium ago, and may have gone through one or more population bottlenecks. This population was largely endogamous and culturally selected for high intelligence. Its remarkable expansion was halted by the Holocaust, but it still makes up 80 percent of the world's Jewish population.

10. Except in Israel, Jewish populations are not reproducing at replacement levels, and most are no longer markedly endogamous. Except among the Orthodox, it seems likely that the world's self-identified Jewish population will experience negative population growth. The population expansions characteristic of ancient times and before 1939 are no more, and Jewish numbers may decline well into the foreseeable future.

11. The one expanding Jewish population is in Israel, and it has a new and different coevolutionary process, coupling self-defense with self-conscious pro-natalism. It is likely that the ancient and modern synergy between Jewish cultural and genetic evolution will continue to be maintained long-term by a core population of Orthodox Jews both within and outside of Israel.

Notes

I thank Molly Zuckerman and Rick Goldberg for comments that greatly improved this chapter.

1. Durham, 1991.
2. Finkelstein and Silberman, 2001; Konner, 2003.
3. Finkelstein and Silberman, 2001.
4. Coote, 1990.
5. Ibid.
6. Matthews and Benjamin, 1993.
7. "Endogamy" refers to marrying within the group, based on the biblical injunction of Exod. 34:16.
8. See the chapter "The Fertility of Prominent Men in the Bible and Ancient Middle East."
9. Trivers and Willard, 1973; Gould and Gould, 1989.
10. Betzig, 1986, 1997; Miller, 1998.
11. Borgerhoff Mulder, 1988.
12. Ibid.
13. Hauptman, 1998.

14. Gen. 48:20.
15. We will take up the odd circumcision of one of his sons in the section "Inheritance for Inter-Generational Success."
16. Josh. 23:13.
17. Deut. 23:4–7.
18. Deut. 23:4.
19. See the parsing of these distinctions on Yev. 76b2–b4.
20. 1 Kings 11:1–2.
21. 1 Kings 14:21.
22. Betzig, 1986.
23. Zerjal, Xue et al., 2003.
24. See Betzig's elaboration in the chapter "The Fertility of Prominent Men."
25. Male lineage reflects the need for patrilineal continuity and explains the double standard for adultery.
26. Ezra 7:6.
27. Neh. 8.
28. Ezra 9:2.
29. Ezra 10:13.
30. *Antiquities* 13:380.
31. Whiston, 1987.
32. Stern, 1976.
33. Gen. 17:1–2.
34. Gen. 17:9–14.
35. A rabbinic commentary focusing on a biblical passage.
36. Weissman, 1980, p. 153.
37. Rabbi Ishmael said, "Great is the precept of circumcision, for 'covenant' is mentioned thirteen times in Genesis 17" (Ned. 31b).
38. Some do find Judaic circumcision biologically "very perplexing." See Reynolds and Tanner, 1995, p. 125.
39. Gen. 17:14; see also 1 Sam. 17:26, 36, 14:6, 31:4; Jer. 6:10; Lev. 26:41; Ezek. 44:9.
40. Eilberg-Schwartz, 1990.
41. American Academy of Pediatrics, 1999; Singh-Grewal, Macdessi, et al., 2005.
42. Alanis and Lucidi, 2004.
43. Daling, Madeleine, et al., 2005; Micali, Nasca, et al., 2006.
44. Ahmed, Mbibi, et al., 1999; Mogotlane, Ntlangulela, et al., 2004.
45. Zahavi, 1975, 1991; see also the chapters in the section "Costly Signaling (Handicap) Theory and Jewish Life."
46. See Sosis, Kress, et al., 2007.
47. Eilberg-Schwartz, 1990.
48. Eilberg-Schwartz, 1990; Silverman, 2004.
49. Eilberg-Schwartz, 1990.
50. Gen. 18.
51. Gen. 34:27–29.
52. Deut. 21:10–14.
53. Deut. 23:7–8.
54. Exod. 4:19–20.

55. Exod. 4:24–26.
56. Num. 12:1.
57. A kind of sexual scalping.
58. Not referring to those men who were spoils of war.
59. Moses, Bailey, et al., 1998; Weiss, Thomas, et al., 2006.
60. O'Farrell, Quigley, et al., 2005.
61. Alanis and Lucidi, 2004.
62. Weiss, 1997.
63. Van Howe, 1998.
64. Martinez-Garcia, Regadera, et al., 1996; Soper, 2004.
65. Lenk and Schroeder, 2001.
66. Ness, Markovic, et al., 1997; Keck, Gerber-Schafer, et al., 1998.
67. Gerbase, Rowley, et al., 1998; Shafii and Burstein, 2004.
68. Sciarra, 1993.
69. Mardh, 2004.
70. Taylor-Robinson, 2002.
71. Workowski, Levine, et al., 2002.
72. Soper, 2004.
73. Lerman and Liao, 2001; Alanis and Lucidi, 2004.
74. Weiss, Thomas, et al., 2006.
75. Rothschild, 2005.
76. Szabo and Short, 2000; Weiss, Quigley, et al., 2000.
77. Drain, Smith, et al., 2004.
78. Langeni, 2005.
79. Krieger, Bailey, et al., 2005.
80. Alanis and Lucidi, 2004.
81. Singh-Grewal, Macdessi, et al., 2005.
82. Finkelstein and Silberman, 2001.
83. Benatar and Benatar, 2003.
84. O'Hara and O'Hara, 1999.
85. Jer. 29:5–6.
86. Jer. 29:7.
87. McGing, 2002.
88. Barclay, 1996.
89. In an attempt to assimilate the conquered Jews, the Romans issued an edict forbidding Jews from Torah study, keeping the Sabbath and *circumcising their sons,* all distinguishing behaviors (Taanit 18a1).
90. Cohen, 1985.
91. Ostrer, 2001.
92. Bonne-Tamir and Adam, 1992.
93. See the chapter on menstruation-based conjugal separation, "Biosocial Regulation of Husband and Wife."
94. *Lek* refers to the seasonal gathering of males of some bird species to display reproductive value to onlookers, both male competitors and fertile females.
95. Abrahams, 1896, pp. 171–172.
96. Ostrer, 2001.
97. Picornell, Castro, et al., 1997.

98. Ostrer, 2001.
99. Goodman, 1979; Behar, Thomas, et al., 2003; Charrow, 2004.
100. Bressman, 1998.
101. Cox, 2001.
102. Grabowski, 2005.
103. *BRCA1* and *BRCA2*.
104. Risch, Tang, et al., 2003; Slatkin, 2004.
105. Risch, Tang, et al., 2003.
106. Behar, Metspalu, et al., 2006.
107. Mayr, 1963.
108. Bonne-Tamir and Adam, 1992; Amar, Kwon, et al., 1999.
109. Skorecki, Selig, et al., 1997; Thomas, Skorecki, et al., 1998.
110. Behar, Thomas, et al., 2003.
111. Thomas, Parfitt, et al., 2000.
112. Risch, Tang, et al., 2003; Slatkin, 2004.
113. Zlotogora, Zeigler, et al., 1988.
114. Cochran, Hardy, et al., 2006.
115. Ostrer, 2001.
116. Risch, Tang, et al., 2003.
117. Goldscheider and Zuckerman, 1986.
118. Della Pergola, 2004.

References

Abrahams, I. 1896. *Jewish Life in the Middle Ages*. New York: Macmillan.
Ahmed, A., Mbibi, N. H., et al. 1999. Complications of traditional male circumcision. *Annals of Tropical Paediatrics* 19(1):113–117.
Alanis, M. C., and Lucidi, R. S. 2004. Neonatal circumcision: a review of the world's oldest and most controversial operation. *Obstetrical and Gynecological Survey* 59(5):379–395.
Amar, A., Kwon, O. J., et al. 1999. Molecular analysis of HLA class II polymorphisms among different ethnic groups in Israel. *Human Immunology* 60(8):723–730.
American Academy of Pediatrics. 1999. Circumcision policy statement. American Academy of Pediatrics. Task Force on Circumcision [see comment]. *Pediatrics* 103(3):686–693.
Barclay, J. M. G. 1996. *Jews in the Mediterranean Diaspora: from Alexander to Trajan (323 B.C.E.–117 C.E.)*. Berkeley: University of California Press.
Behar, D. M., Metspalu, E., et al. 2006. The matrilineal ancestry of Ashkenazi Jewry: portrait of a recent founder event. *American Journal of Human Genetics* 78(3):487–497.
Behar, D. M., Thomas, M. G., et al. 2003. Multiple origins of Ashkenazi Levites: Y chromosome evidence for both Near Eastern and European ancestries. *American Journal of Human Genetics* 73(4):768–779.
Benatar, M., and Benatar, D. 2003. Between prophylaxis and child abuse: the ethics of neonatal male circumcision [see comment]. *American Journal of Bioethics* 3(2):35–48.
Betzig, L. 1986. *Despotism and Differential Reproduction: A Darwinian View of History*. New York: Aldine.

———. 1997. Roman polygyny. In L. Betzig, ed., *Human Nature: A Critical Reader* (pp. 375–398). New York: Oxford University Press.

Bonne-Tamir, B., and Adam, A. 1992. *Genetic Diversity among Jews.* Oxford, UK: Oxford University Press.

Borgerhoff Mulder, M. 1988. Kipsigis bridewealth payments. In L. Betzig, M. B. Mulder, and P. Turke, eds. (pp. 65–82). *Human Reproductive Behavior: A Darwinian Perspective.* New York: Cambridge University Press.

Bressman, S. B. 1998. Dystonia. *Current Opinion in Neurology* 11(4):363–372.

Charrow, J. 2004. Ashkenazi Jewish genetic disorders. *Familial Cancer* 3(3–4):201–206.

Cochran, G., Hardy, J., et al. 2006. Natural history of Ashkenazi intelligence. *Journal of Biosocial Science* 38(5):659–693.

Cohen, S. J. D. 1985. The origins of the matrilineal principle in rabbinic law. *AJS Review* 10(1):19–53.

Coote, R. B. 1990. *Early Israel: A New Horizon.* Minneapolis: Fortress Press.

Cox, T. M. 2001. Gaucher disease: understanding the molecular pathogenesis of sphingolipidoses. *Journal of Inherited Metabolic Disease* 24(Suppl 2):106–121; discussion, 87–88.

Daling, J. R., Madeleine, M. M., et al. 2005. Penile cancer: importance of circumcision, human papillomavirus and smoking in in situ and invasive disease. *International Journal of Cancer* 116(4):606–616.

Della Pergola, S. 2004. World Jewish population, 2004. *American Jewish Year Book* 104:489–521.

Drain, P. K., Smith, J. S., et al. 2004. Correlates of national HIV seroprevalence: an ecologic analysis of 122 developing countries. *Journal of Acquired Immune Deficiency Syndromes* 35(4):407–420.

Durham, W. H. 1991. *Coevolution: Genes, Culture, and Human Diversity.* Stanford, CA: Stanford University Press.

Eilberg-Schwartz, H. 1990. *The Savage in Judaism: An Anthropology of Israelite Religion and Ancient Judaism.* Bloomington: Indiana University Press.

Finkelstein, I., and Silberman, N. A. 2001. *The Bible Unearthed: Archeology's new Vision of Ancient Israel and the Origin of Its Sacred Texts.* New York: Free Press.

Gerbase, A. C., Rowley, J. T., et al. 1998. Global prevalence and incidence estimates of selected curable STDs. *Sexually Transmitted Infections* 74(Suppl 1):S12–S16.

Goldscheider, C., and Zuckerman, A. S. 1986. *The Transformation of the Jews.* Chicago: University of Chicago Press.

Goodman, R. M. 1979. *Genetic Disorders among the Jewish People.* Baltimore: Johns Hopkins University Press.

Gould, J. L., and Gould, C. G. 1989. *Sexual Selection.* New York: Scientific American Library.

Grabowski, G. A. 2005. Recent clinical progress in Gaucher disease [see comment]. *Current Opinion in Pediatrics* 17(4):519–524.

Hauptman, J. 1998. *Rereading the Rabbis: A Woman's Voice.* Boulder, CO: Westview Press.

Keck, C., Gerber-Schafer, C., et al. 1998. Seminal tract infections: impact on male fertility and treatment options. *Human Reproduction Update* 4(6):891–903.

Konner, M. 2003. *Unsettled: An Anthropology of the Jews.* New York: Viking Penguin.

Krieger, J. N., Bailey, R. C., et al. 2005. Adult male circumcision: results of a standardized procedure in Kisumu District, Kenya. *BJU International* 96(7):1109–1113.

Langeni, T. 2005. Male circumcision and sexually transmitted infections in Botswana. *Journal of Biosocial Science* 37(1):75–88.

Lenk, S., and Schroeder, J. 2001. Genitourinary tuberculosis. *Current Opinion in Urology* 11(1):93–98.

Lerman, S. E., and Liao, J. C. 2001. Neonatal circumcision. *Pediatric Clinics of North America* 48(6):1539–1557.

Mardh, P.-A. 2004. Tubal factor infertility, with special regard to chlamydial salpingitis. *Current Opinion in Infectious Diseases* 17(1):49–52.

Martinez-Garcia, F., Regadera, J., et al. 1996. Protozoan infections in the male genital tract. *Journal of Urology* 156(2 Pt 1):340–349.

Matthews, V. H., and Benjamin, D. C. 1993. *Social World of Ancient Israel 1250–587 BCE*. Peabody, MA: Hendrickson.

Mayr, E. 1963. *Animal species and evolution*. Cambridge, MA: Harvard University Press.

McGing, B. 2002. Population and proselytism: how many Jews were there in the ancient world? In J. R. Bartlett, ed., *Jews in the Hellenistic and Roman Cities* (pp. 88–106). London, UK: Routledge.

Micali, G., Nasca, M. R., et al. 2006. Penile cancer. *Journal of the American Academy of Dermatology* 54(3):369–391; quiz, 391–394.

Miller, G. F. 1998. How mate choice shaped human nature: a review of sexual selection and human evolution. In C. Crawford and D. L. Krebs, eds. *Handbook of Evolutionary Psychology* (pp. 87–129). Mahwah, NJ: Lawrence Erlbaum.

Mogotlane, S. M., Ntlangulela, J. T., et al. 2004. Mortality and morbidity among traditionally circumcised Xhosa boys in the Eastern Cape Province, South Africa. *Curationis* 27(2):57–62.

Moses, S., Bailey, R. C., et al. 1998. Male circumcision: assessment of health benefits and risks [see comment]. *Sexually Transmitted Infections* 74(5):368–373.

Ness, R. B., Markovic, N., et al. 1997. Do men become infertile after having sexually transmitted urethritis? An epidemiologic examination. *Fertility and Sterility* 68(2):205–213.

O'Farrell, N., Quigley, M., et al. 2005. Association between the intact foreskin and inferior standards of male genital hygiene behaviour: a cross-sectional study. *International Journal of STD and AIDS* 16(8):556–559.

O'Hara, K., and O'Hara, J. 1999. The effect of male circumcision on the sexual enjoyment of the female partner. *BJU International* 83(Suppl 1):79–84.

Ostrer, H. 2001. A genetic profile of contemporary Jewish populations. *Nature Reviews Genetics* 2(11):891–898.

Picornell, A., Castro, J. A., et al. 1997. Genetics of the Chuetas (Majorcan Jews): a comparative study. *Human Biology* 69(3):313–328.

Reynolds, V., and Tanner, R. 1995. *The Social Ecology of Religion*. New York: Oxford University Press.

Risch, N., Tang, H., et al. 2003. Geographic distribution of disease mutations in the Ashkenazi Jewish population supports genetic drift over selection [see comment]. *American Journal of Human Genetics* 72(4):812–822.

Rothschild, B. M. 2005. History of syphilis [see comment]. *Clinical Infectious Diseases* 40(10):1454–1463.

Sciarra, J. J. 1993. Reproductive health: a global perspective. *American Journal of Obstetrics and Gynecology* 168(6 Pt 1):1649–1654.
Shafii, T., and Burstein, G. R. 2004. An overview of sexually transmitted infections among adolescents. *Adolescent Medicine Clinics* 15(2):201–214.
Silverman, E. K. 2004. Anthropology and circumcision. *Annual Review of Anthropology* 33(1):419–445.
Singh-Grewal, D., Macdessi, J., et al. 2005. Circumcision for the prevention of urinary tract infection in boys: a systematic review of randomised trials and observational studies [see comment]. *Archives of Disease in Childhood* 90(8):853–858.
Skorecki, K., Selig, S., et al. 1997. Y chromosomes of Jewish priests. *Nature* 385(6611):32.
Slatkin, M. 2004. A population-genetic test of founder effects and implications for Ashkenazi Jewish diseases. *American Journal of Human Genetics* 75(2):282–293.
Soper, D. 2004. Trichomoniasis: under control or undercontrolled? *American Journal of Obstetrics and Gynecology* 190(1):281–290.
Sosis, R., Kress, H., et al. 2007. Scars for war: evaluating alternative signaling explanations for cross-cultural variance in ritual costs. *Evolution and Human Behavior* 28:234–247.
Stern, M. 1976. The political and social history of Judea under Roman rule. In H. H. Ben-Sasson, ed. *A History of the Jewish People* (p. 239). Cambridge: Harvard University Press.
Szabo, R., and Short, R. V. 2000. How does male circumcision protect against HIV infection? [see comment]. *British Medical Journal* 320(7249):1592–1594.
Taylor-Robinson, D. 2002. Mycoplasma genitalium—an up-date. *International Journal of STD and AIDS* 13(3):145–151.
Thomas, M. G., Parfitt, T., et al. 2000. Y chromosomes traveling south: the cohen modal haplotype and the origins of the Lemba—the "Black Jews of Southern Africa." *American Journal of Human Genetics* 66(2):674–686.
Thomas, M. G., Skorecki, K., et al. 1998. Origins of Old Testament priests. *Nature* 394(6689):138–140.
Trivers, R. L., and Willard, D. E. 1973. Natural selection of parental ability to vary the sex ratio of offspring. *Science* 179:90–92.
Van Howe, R. S. 1998. Circumcision and infectious diseases revisited [see comment]. *Pediatric Infectious Disease Journal* 17(1):1–6.
Weiss, G. N. 1997. Prophylactic neonatal surgery and infectious diseases [see comment]. *Pediatric Infectious Disease Journal* 16(8):727–734.
Weiss, H. A., Quigley, M. A., et al. 2000. Male circumcision and risk of HIV infection in sub-Saharan Africa: a systematic review and meta-analysis. *AIDS* 14(15):2361–2370.
Weiss, H. A., Thomas, S. L., et al. 2006. Male circumcision and risk of syphilis, chancroid, and genital herpes: a systematic review and meta-analysis. *Sexually Transmitted Infections* 82(2):101–109; discussion, 110.
Weissman, M. 1980. *The Midrash Says: The Narrative of the Weekly Torah-Portion in the Perspective of Our Sages.* Brooklyn: Benei Yakov Publications.
Whiston, W. 1987. *The Works of Josephus.* Peabody, MA: Hendrickson.
Workowski, K. A., Levine, W. C., et al. 2002. U.S. Centers for Disease Control and Prevention guidelines for the treatment of sexually transmitted diseases: an opportunity to unify clinical and public health practice. *Annals of Internal Medicine* 137(4):255–262.

Zahavi, A. 1975. Mate selection—a selection for a handicap. *Journal of Theoretical Biology* 53:205–214.

———. 1991. On the definition of sexual selection, Fisher's model, and the evolution of waste and of signals in general. *Animal Behavior* 42(3):501–503.

Zerjal, T., Xue, Y., et al. 2003. The genetic legacy of the Mongols. *American Journal of Human Genetics* 72(3):717–721.

Zlotogora, J., Zeigler, M., et al. 1988. Selection in favor of lysosomal storage disorders? *American Journal of Human Genetics* 42(2):271–273.

Inheritance for Intergenerational Success

Chapter 6

Biosocial Regulation of Husband and Wife

The Requirement for Periodic Conjugal Separation and Reunion

Rick Goldberg

Introduction

Polygyny—one man mating simultaneously with more than one woman—has evolved to be the preferred sexual pattern in over 83 percent of the world's cultures.[1] Although both biblical and rabbinic Judaism acknowledged and accepted polygamy, polyandry[2] is nowhere to be found.[3] Regardless of the father-mother marital arrangement, children come into the world incapable of taking care of themselves, so they will rely on others for many years to provide food, protection, and learning opportunities. Given the differing and competing reproductive strategies of men and women,[4] one would expect polygynous behavior and other sources of marital instability to be less likely when communal standards are imposed to support stability of marriages and investment in children.[5]

Dealing in part with the biological reality of child dependency, postbiblical Judaism has sanctified long-term coupling, married *and* monogamous, as the single most religiously consequential social relationship.[6] In the marriage ceremony, the bond between bride and groom is sanctified "according to the law of Moses and Israel." The vows exchanged form the heart of the wedding ceremony and create an ongoing communal interest in the welfare of the married couple and its offspring. To that end, the marriage contract adopts a set of publicly enforced, mutual obligations for the spouses. It is made clear in Jewish law that the performance of marital duties is obligatory and consequential for the marriage partners and their families, in addition to a higher authority. For that purpose, biblical and rabbinic law has explicitly developed the rights and responsibilities of wives and husbands as conjugal partners.

This chapter describes a portion of the *halakhic* (Judaic legal) framework for regulating family relations, called *taharat ha-mishpakhah*,[7] whose purpose is in part to overcome the biological enemy of family relations (i.e., the inherent conflicts of interest between husbands, wives, and children).[8] A biosocial construction of marriage and sexuality can furnish insight into the potentially adaptive function of Judaic conjugal separation. My hypothesis is that this cycle of sexual activity and abstinence can increase paternity certainty, reduce jealous antagonisms, and increase paternal investment in children. As a corollary, the sex/abstinence cycle may manipulate the husband's testosterone to conform to his wife's cycle of fertility. If my analysis is correct, long-term family well-being and reproductive success should result from increased paternity certainty and the couple's improved hormonal compatibility.

Sexual relations in general and marital relations in particular have always been considered matters of great religious importance. Unregulated sexual activity has been recognized as potentially disruptive to stable reproductive families.[9] Many religions encourage sexual relations within the framework of marriage and during the wife's fertile period by forbidding or restricting them during menstruation. When religious norms promote intercourse during the wife's fertile phase, they can be expected to improve the reproductive success of the couple.[10] This chapter proposes a novel characterization of *niddah-tvilah*, conjugal separation and reunion of spouses, as a biosocial regulator of family relationships whose purpose is to enhance reproduction, reduce destructive behaviors, and increase the likelihood of paternal investment. This biological rendering does not imply that married Jewish men and women would otherwise be engaging in behaviors deleterious to their marriages and families. But, since Jewish couples can experience the same marital conflicts as other couples, Jewish marriages are subject to the same evolved pressures found elsewhere.

Judaic Regulation of Marital Sexuality

Since biblical times, Judaism has both circumscribed and encouraged the sexual bond between husband and wife. The biblical text enumerates the basic rules regulating the cycle of marital sexual relations.[11] Although the Bible gives no justifications for this set of rules, there is ample rabbinic discourse regarding *ta'amei mitzvot*, the reasoning that justifies the rules.[12]

In Middle Eastern antiquity, menstruation was seen in many cultures as a period of specialized female demonic activity, particularly dangerous to men.[13] A twelfth-century French document describes women refraining from entering the synagogue and touching Hebrew books while ritually impure.[14] During the Second Temple period,[15] laws of sexual forbearance required menstruating women to be segregated by residing in special "houses of impurity." Throughout their menses, women could not adorn themselves with jewelry or perfume and were forbidden from performing household duties in their own homes. From the destruction of the Second Temple onward, however, these laws were fundamentally transformed from mostly Temple-centered ritual impurities to marital sexual relations. As a result, conjugal relations, but not living arrangements, were restricted. By the Middle Ages, women in most Jewish communities were allowed to function normally at home, except that spousal intimacy was disallowed.[16]

Within the body of *halakha* (Judaic law), *niddah-tvilah* is the name given to the legal framework for married couples governing required sexual abstinence followed by renewed sexual activity. *Niddah* refers to the period of abstinence when the wife is considered sexually unavailable to her husband. It begins with the first evidence of menstrual flow[17] and ends when flow ceases plus seven "white" days. Accordingly, husbands are forbidden sexual intimacy with their wives for the period corresponding to just before, during, and after menstruation.[18]

Niddah is concluded by *tvilah,* the wife's ritual immersion that must precede the resumption of intimate relations: after having counted seven days from her last visual evidence of menstrual flow, the wife goes privately to the *mikvah*,[19] a body of "living" water.[20] The *mikvah* is usually a small, communally managed indoor pool used by observant women to ritually transition from one sexual status to the other. A female attendant is there to help prepare and assist the woman with the ritual. Before immersion, the woman removes all foreign objects from her body such as wigs, jewelry, makeup, and so forth. Once prepared, she totally immerses herself twice, after which she is considered transformed and ready to resume relations with her husband. Performing *tvilah,* ritualized self-immersion, she physically and emotionally prepares herself for renewed conjugal relations.[21]

Upon returning home, the sexual reunion on "*mikvah* night" is elevated in the minds of the spouses to a sacred, community-sanctioned event. Complementing sexual abstinence during *niddah* are talmudic requirements for the husband to "satisfy" his wife sexually during the permitted time of her cycle, especially on those days when she is most likely to be ovulating. Sexual intimacy is considered the wife's legal right independent of the probability of procreation. Accordingly, the law assures every married woman the right to regular sexual relations with her husband;[22] intercourse on Shabbat is considered especially meritorious. Throughout the *niddah-tvilah* cycle the wife is in control, because she is the sole arbiter of her sexual status.[23] Although biblical distinctions were made for different sources of vaginal bleeding,[24] the Rabbis collapsed all distinctions due to their concern that women would not be able to distinguish menses from other types of vaginal emissions. It is for this reason that rabbinic injunction also prohibits relations for seven "white" days that commence once flows have completely ceased. Depending on the individual woman's cycle, the period of *niddah* abstinence usually lasts twelve days.[25]

As a preventative measure, during *niddah* husbands and wives do not come in physical contact or even close proximity to one another. If, for example, a husband wants to hand something to his wife while she is a *niddah,* he will avoid touching her by first putting it down before she will pick it up. At the dinner table, some obvious deviation from the norm (such as changing seats or place settings) is often made to remind the couple of the wife's condition. At bedtime, the wife will "cover up" more than usual—she may wear pajamas instead of a nightgown.[26] The couple will not share a bed or even sit beside one another without some object interposed between them.[27]

At least theoretically, the *niddah*'s interaction with other family members and the community at large was not curtailed. In practice, however, it became the custom in many communities to limit the activities of the *niddah* in public. In modern observant communities this is much less the case, perhaps due to a lessening of the perceived need for communal concern about adultery. But surveillance by the community was often quite stringent. The Mishnah requires divorce for a couple who have intercourse while the wife is menstruating. The Gemara asks, how could an outsider determine if the wife is a *niddah*? Rav Judah answers that her neighbors would know.[28] Commentators inform us that women wore different clothes in public during menstruating, and, as a result, their *niddah* status was publicly discernable. So community involvement in what would today be a private family matter was probably common in Jewish history.

Stemming from the biblical obligation to "be fruitful and multiply,"[29] the purpose of *niddah-tvilah* is explicitly to avoid "wasting the husband's seed" during the time of his wife's infertility. Although knowledge of human physiology in the ancient world was far less than today's, the biblical authors clearly understood the link between male ejaculate and the window of opportunity during which a woman is capable of conception. That understanding of human procreation was canonized in the Bible and embellished during the rabbinic period to add "life" to the marriage and maximize childbearing. This is not to say Jewish law sought to prohibit marital sexual activity not leading to procreation: intercourse, for example, is not prohibited after menopause or during pregnancy. Likewise, mutually pleasurable nonintercourse sexual contact is not excluded to the married couple. Additionally, one should not assume that the *niddah* prohibition has anything to do with either abhorrence for blood or female hygiene. Menstruation was classified by the Rabbis as a type of ritual impurity because the flow of blood evidenced a "loss of potential life," not because the woman herself was impure.[30] Maimonides, twelfth-century talmudist and physician, forcefully rejected the beliefs of certain Eastern peoples demonizing menstrual flow.[31] Especially as modernity arrived, it would not be accurate to view *hilchot niddah* (laws of conjugal separation) as a strategy to marginalize women. Rather, as I will show, they may be seen from a contemporary biological perspective as spousal behavior standards promoting marital stability, fertility, and investment in children.

Basic Theory—Parental Reproductive Choices

According to evolutionary theory, behaviors can be called adaptive if they ultimately confer relative descendant-leaving success. From the time modern humans first appeared 100,000 years ago, our children have been comparatively dependent and costly to raise. A concurrent adaptation to this reproductive demand has been significant investment in youngsters over many years by parents and extended families. The nine-month gestation plus the period of lactation require great dedication by the mother and cannot be accomplished without the assistance of those who help support her. Infant mortality and underdeveloped children result most often when kinfolk, especially fathers, provide less than sufficient resources and attention. Although their initial investments in children are far less than mothers', fathers do have a considerable stake in the survival of their children. The conflict within each father between polygynous desires and monogamous traditions has been historically of epic proportions. In human history, polygyny made more sense biologically when mating with multiple partners produced, on average, a larger quantity of *viable* children. On the other hand, monogamy is a more successful strategy when fewer, better-provisioned children end up leaving the father with a greater number of descendants.[32]

The degree of discord in family life often hinges on the husband's ability and willingness to provide for his whole family according to the standards of his wife and community. Over the millennia, Jewish law and custom have weighed in on the side of strict monogamy and high paternal investment, thereby suppressing the husband's creation of extramarital children and emphasizing his investment in the survivability of the children within his marriage.[33] In the next two parts of this chapter, we will look at the gender-specific, biosexual patterns that give us clues about the impact of *niddah-tvilah*. First, focusing on men, might shifts in testosterone correlate with sexual desire and, if so, how might the observance of *niddah-tvilah* be implicated in the testosterone fluctuations? Second, focusing on women, is sexual desire affected by the ovulatory cycle phase and, if so, in what way? What is meant by the biological term *concealed ovulation,* and what might result from a married woman's ovulation being "revealed" by her observance of *niddah-tvilah*?

Hormonal Variation Associated with Men's Sexual Desire

Within the past fifteen years, increased attention has been paid by researchers to the patterns of testosterone production in single men, fathers, and husbands. In a study published in 1993, it was demonstrated that higher levels of testosterone in men positively correlated with being single and, if married, marital instability. The study found that high male testosterone "has a consistently negative relationship with every aspect of marital quality."[34] Later research found lower morning and higher evening levels of testosterone in both unmarried and married men (with or without children), but lower afternoon and evening measurements were found among married men.[35] These results could reflect the decreased willingness or ability of married men to seek mating opportunities at night when philandering is usually easiest to conceal. In other words, staying at home at night with the family seems to be positively associated with lower testosterone.

In another study, a biosocial model of the relationship between testosterone and stable marriage was tested. The issue under study was whether the relatively lower testosterone of married men is a *cause* or an *effect* of secure marriages. The resulting data demonstrated that both may be true (i.e., that the relationship between testosterone levels and marital relations/fatherhood is mutually reinforcing).[36] In another recent study, the testosterone levels of unmarried men, self-reported in romantic and committed relationships, revealed that these men have 21 percent lower testosterone than the uncommitted control group.[37] Thus, the testosterone level of pair-bonded men, married or not, was shown to be reduced in comparison with men not involved in a stable relationship.

Newer research produced a result that corroborates and extends that of previous studies: men (married and unmarried) in long-term relationships had lower testosterone than those whose relationships were less than six months old.[38] Apparently, the age of committed relationships also affects testosterone levels. Over an extended period of courtship and marriage, testosterone is reduced as men become habituated to the consortship of their partners and remove themselves from competition with other men for new sexual partners.[39] When married men seek sexual opportunities with new women by dedicating time to extra-pair mating effort, testosterone rises to the level of those men without long-term partners.[40]

Complementary studies have added other ingredients to the stew. One study looked at testosterone variation in expectant fathers. A sample of expectant Canadian fathers demonstrated lower testosterone than uncommitted men; immediately following birth of the child, their testosterone levels became even further reduced.[41] Similarly, fathers with lower testosterone have been judged more responsive to infant crying.[42] In a Chinese study, fathers had significantly lower testosterone levels than nonfathers.[43] Looking at all these data, a plausible interpretation is that cues for monogamy and fatherhood depress testosterone release and promote investing behaviors. Male testosterone levels can have a consequential effect on family relationships. Monogamy and fatherhood seem to function as testosterone suppressors, especially at night. If staying at home in the evenings lowers a man's testosterone, perhaps the (untested) corollary may also be true: spending time away from the family may raise testosterone due to a stronger potential for extra-pair imaginings and encounters.

Although empirical work has yet to be undertaken, I would hypothesize that the *niddah-tvilah* cycle impulses the conjugal entrainment of the husband to his wife's cyclical variations through testosterone manipulation. Without the discipline of *niddah-tvilah*, there would be no reason to expect the daily sexual needs of a husband to be in harmony with those of his wife. We have seen how factors inside and outside of marriage are associated with testosterone variations in men. By imposing a conjugal rhythm, cycle- and gender-based hormonal discrepancies might be mutually adjustable in the short and long term. Lower testosterone should result in both diminished extra-pair interest and desire to masturbate during his wife's *niddah* period. Sexual restraint based on the wife's reproductive cycle is required of *both* partners; the husband is thereby influenced to synchronize to his wife's rhythm, effectively modifying his natural pattern of desires. Although perhaps not always observed, religious law leaves him no choice but to entrain his desire to his wife's availability.

Hormonal Variations Associated with Women's Sexual Desire

Recently, attention has begun to focus on the sexual motivations and behaviors of women across the menstrual cycle. As is the case with men,[44] women have evolved to follow a dual-mating strategy: in pursuit of the first strategy, investment for herself and her children is obtained through a long-term partner. Pursuing the second, "good genes" for higher-quality children, may be obtained from a short-term partner. Throughout human history, women would have received the greatest fitness benefits by securing long-term monogamous relationships with men who display cues for investment potential and genetic quality (attractiveness). However, the most sexually attractive men are not typically the most reliable long-term investors. Attractive men are in great demand and are presented by women with many more opportunities for short-term sex. Consequently, these men may seek "quickie" sexual encounters requiring none of the long-term investment essential in marriage and parenting. Since their short-term strategic behavior is discernable by potential female partners, "fast living" makes these men more attractive to women seeking high-quality sperm donors and less attractive to women seeking long-term partners.[45]

Depending on environmental factors, women who have already secured long-term investors may also seek short-term mating opportunities. In this scenario, the risk of engaging in extramarital sex can be catastrophic to the long-term relationship. But genetic benefits to children sired by "Mr. Good Genes" can also be huge.[46] So there are circumstances in which women in committed relationships may opportunistically seek extra-pair partners to help create higher-quality children.[47] This short-term mating strategy, when pursued by married women, is known as cuckoldry.[48] If her long-term investor husband remains unaware that the child is not his, he will continue to invest as if he were the father.[49] Although this game can be explosive for the marriage, if the woman succeeds in fooling her husband, she can have for her child the best of both worlds: higher-quality genes *and* long-term investment. As a default strategy, if women sense a scarcity of long-term investors in their environment, their only reproductive recourse is sex with noninvesting, short-term partners. In these circumstances, pregnant women may be able to receive much-needed investment for themselves and their children from family, friends, or the state.

Since a woman's ability to conceive is restricted to a small portion of her menstrual cycle, it is not surprising that a recent study reported women having increased desire during the time of high fertility.[50] One should then expect women's biological and emotional rhythms to covary, depending on cycle phase. Biologically speaking, design features of female sexual desire linked to the ovulation cycle are associated with shifts in the intensity and object of desire.[51] This complex association of hormones and sexual/reproductive desire has been called the ovulatory effect.[52] Given the association between a woman's sexual motivations and her ovulatory cycle phase, *niddah-tvilah* makes good biological sense. As high fertility and enhanced desire approach, women may increasingly engage in public reproductive display, evidenced, for example, by wearing more appealing clothes and body ornamentation.[53]

The Existence and Implications of Concealed Ovulation and Menstruation

Although it might make biological "sense" for human males to be able to detect female ovulation and consider ovulating females the most sexually attractive (as do other primate males),[54] the evidence so far is that no such adaptation exists in humans.[55] We currently have no data showing that ovulation is readily apparent to either women or men; consequently, there are likely to have been strong selection pressures on men to detect it and women to keep it hidden. Many cultures resolve this conflict of interest with a variety of menstrual taboos that, in effect, advertise women's reproductive status.[56]

In humans, as in the majority of mammals, the most significant mating decisions are a matter of female choice. Our process of sexual selection can be seen as antagonistic reproductive coevolution, a gender-based conflict expressing the strategies of monogamy, polyandry, and polygyny. In pursuit of their interests, women have a relatively hidden reproductive cycle; men do not *naturally* cycle at all. Female loss of estrus,[57] accompanied by highly concealed ovulation, may have been a selected trait because it enhances women's control over their reproductive options at the expense of men.[58] For example, a study of upwardly mobile women of Syrian Jewish extraction reported that practicing *niddah-tvilah* gives wives "authority and collective strength in shaping male sexuality."[59]

Although women are cyclically sensitive to the likelihood of conception, their sexual partners, especially of the short-term variety, are usually "unaware and don't care." Long-term partners may "care" about conception (because, at minimum, they will be called upon to invest resources if a birth occurs), but they remain "unaware" of their partner's time of ovulation unless informed of such.

When a woman is malnourished or in bad health, it will be in her interest to conceal her menstrual cycle. Since menstrual capability is a reliable signal of good physical condition and fertility,[60] it will be in her interest, if not currently cycling, to conceal that fact from others to prevent lowering of her perceived reproductive value. When in ill health, a woman's period may cease or become otherwise disordered.[61] Accordingly, menstrual flow will reliably communicate sufficiency of strength for childbearing, demonstrated by the amount of blood and tissue she can afford to "waste" during each menstruation.[62]

Women's brief period of highest fertility comprises the five days preceding ovulation. Since *tvilah* is not allowed until twelve or thirteen days after menstruation begins, we can compute how its timing correlates with the fertile period of most women. First, there is more variability in women's follicular (preovulation) than luteal (postovulation) phase. As a result, counting backward to predict fertility is more reliable because ovulation occurs reliably fifteen days before the onset of menstruation. For women with thirty-day cycles, high fertility is from ten to fifteen days after menstruation began. But for those with more regular thirty-five-day cycles, the most fertile days will be about fifteen to twenty days after onset of menses. We can calculate that *niddah* ends and *tvilah* can occur within the range of peak fertility for most women.

By concealing menstrual fitness, women may have also evolved, as I have speculated, to conceal their phase of high fertility. This concealment could serve their long-term reproductive strategy (monogamy) by hiding ovulation from men other than their husbands. Men in positions of dominance could use their knowledge of women's fertility and their power over them to sexually supplant their preferred mates.[63] So fertility concealed from extra-pair men could serve as an anticuckoldry mechanism.[64] While a *niddah*, the wife's interaction with family members other than her husband, in addition to the community at large, is, at least theoretically, not modified. In practice, however, it became the custom in many communities to curtail her activities in the public sphere.[65] In modern, observant communities this is much less the case, perhaps due to a lessened perceived need for communal mate guarding. A husband's actions may give further confidence of fidelity; it has also been shown that when men pay more sexual attention to their partner (as is required after *tvilah*, when fertility is highest), cuckoldry is much less likely.[66]

In ancestral mating environments, hidden ovulation could also have functioned as a selection pressure, forcing greater sperm competition among males. The comparatively large size of human testes, relative to body size, could be evidence of the need for higher sperm counts and ejaculate volumes. In addition, the development of testes housed in the scrotum could have developed to extend the shelf life of sperm through cooler, external storage. By that means, males would be prepared to ejaculate and inseminate repeatedly to compete with the similar capability of other males. Since ovulation is concealed, males must be prepared to take advantage of every sexual opportunity to increase the odds of sending their genes into the next generation. In the male-male competition to breed, timing is everything, and survival of the fastest can often result in evolutionary success.[67]

The Suspicion of Female Adultery and Paternity Uncertainty

As I have mentioned, a man may confront the bewildering problem that, although he has had regular relations with his wife, when she is expecting a baby he cannot be certain the child is his.[68] This lingering doubt has been called "paternity uncertainty," a destructive force in spousal relations that can result in male jealousy and unwillingness to invest in his wife's child.[69] Most researchers of male jealousy have ignored gender-related instigators, including those related to the ovulatory cycle. David Buss, however, has written extensively about male jealousy arising from the zeal to protect paternity.[70] Male jealousy can trigger a series of mate retention tactics, one of which is male vigilance or "mate guarding." Mate guarding occurs in pair-bonded species when the male or female "guards" sexual access to the partner in an attempt to stifle mate poaching. It is in a husband's interest to monitor his wife's extramarital opportunities to ensure that his future parental investment will not be squandered on the children of other men. When men are assured of their mate's faithfulness, they will increase investment in what they believe to be their own children.[71] But when jealousy is aroused by suspected infidelity, men exhibit less willingness to invest in children due to paternity uncertainty. For this reason, the treatment of adopted, unrelated children is often far less than ideal; stepchildren sometimes have a hard time of it.[72] But even if a husband should have unconscious fears of his wife's infidelity during *niddah*, they should be allayed if her receptivity at the post-*tvilah* reunion is genuinely favorable. To ensure paternal certainty, the rabbis require a widow or divorcee to wait at least three months before remarrying so that a pregnancy will be seen as from the new and not the old husband.[73] In this way, the Rabbis ensured that paternal uncertainty would not undermine the new marriage.[74]

Ritual Impurity and Female Adultery

The laws that define *niddah* are based on both sexual relations and the more general state called *tumah*, usually translated as "impurity." In addition to *niddah*, the Bible labels various conditions as *tumah*, including:

> An accused adulteress, a woman who recently gave birth, a man who had sex with a menstruant, a man who experienced nocturnal emissions, a woman who had non-menstrual emissions, coming in contact with a dead body (in some circumstances), touching a non-kosher animal or the corpse of any dead animal, any dead animal itself, any non-kosher animal itself, persons with certain skin diseases, a vessel left uncovered, land in adverse possession, a stutterer, worshipers of other gods, human nature itself polluted, the morally debased and those of infamous reputation.[75]

Although there are many ways of becoming *tameh*, for purposes of this chapter I focus on only two of them: a woman experiencing *niddah* and a wife accused of adultery (*sotah*). In and of themselves, neither of these circumstances is considered a sin or transgression. The conditions of *sotah* and *niddah* related to *tameh* are both temporary and alterable by prescribed formulas. For example, R. Yehuda compares the destroyed city of Jerusalem to a *niddah* in that, just as a menstruant is temporarily *tameh* before sexual reunion, so Jerusalem will be subject to renewal (rebuilding) after her temporary destruction.[76]

Another definition of *tameh* is one who is "unfit" for a particular purpose, a translation that resonates with biological implications. A menstruating wife is (temporarily) "unfit" to conceive, and an accused adulteress is (at least temporarily) "unfit" as a proper wife. By rousing her husband's jealousy, the accused adulteress threatens the stability of her marriage, the welfare of her children, and communal integrity.[77] The *sotah* is considered so dangerous that, like the *niddah,* an entire talmudic tractate carries that name. There are several elements of the biblical *sotah* that are instructive for our analysis. First, the wife is not necessarily an adulteress, but only *accused* of such by her husband. While she is designated a *sotah* she is sexually unavailable to her husband, the accuser,[78] who is required to make the accusation if the *spirit* of jealousy comes upon him.[79] Parallel to the meaning of "spirit" (*ruach*) found in other biblical contexts, here the explosive power of male jealousy is treated as a quasi-external force that may control husbands involuntarily. After an elaborate and enigmatic procedure, the wife's guilt or innocence is determined by God functioning as mate guard. Formulaic remediation of the *sotah* seems designed more to assuage the husband's jealousy than to judge his wife's guilt.

When the *sotah* accusation is made, it is not the charge of adultery that is of immediate concern to the community; rather, it is the potentially lethal anxiety of the husband possessed by jealousy. Judaism considers male jealousy to be a major destabilizing force, as evidenced by the admonition not to "covet" the wives of neighbors.[80] When Israel is accused of idolatry, her faithlessness to God is compared to the faithlessness of the *sotah* to her husband.[81] The murdering of wives suspected of infidelity has been all too common in human history; the *sotah* formulation may be seen as taking the matter out of the husband's hands. Judgment of the *sotah* is rendered by God alone—both husband and community are restrained from taking physical action against her.

Judaic Promotion of Family and Communal Certainty

Since observance of *niddah* effectively exposes his wife's fertility status, the husband's paternity certainty should be fortified. Mate cycle recognition enables him to relax his mate focus during *niddah* and intensify it during her time of fertility. Along these lines, studies have shown that, in general, men are more attentive to (and jealous of) their partners when conception is more likely.[82] When fertility is hidden from them, men are forced to mate guard unnecessarily even at times conception cannot occur. The benefits of private fertility revelation also inure to the community, since it has an abiding interest in lowering the male-male competitive violence that often originates in spousal jealousy.

The Jewish wife does not have to justify to her husband her sexual unavailability—Torah law does it for her. As a result, the *niddah* need not worry about having to rebuff her husband's advances during that time when, not coincidentally, her sexual desire is lessened. Since both spouses submit to her status as *niddah,* her periodic inaccessibility will not in itself rouse his jealous urges; neither spouse will suspect infidelity or disinterest as the motive for spatial separation. By "guarding" against the suspicion of spousal infidelity, *niddah* can reduce the husband's anxiety and promote *shalom ba-bayit* (peace at home).[83]

Besides disarming the husband's jealousy, structured periodic abstinence can also be eroticizing.[84] No voluntary sexual separation could be as effective in achieving this effect because *taharat ha-mishpakha* is mutually recognized as binding. From the wife's perspective, periodic abstinence, coupled with her upcoming ovulation, can increase receptiveness to her husband's sexual advances, along with the likelihood of orgasm and conception. From the husband's perspective, periodic abstinence should boost sperm count in preparation for sexual renewal, especially since masturbation and extramarital sex during the prohibited period (as well as at other times) are forbidden.

Long-term effects of *niddah-tvilah* may also be biologically beneficial. Having grown accustomed to periods of physical separation over the years, the couple may be better able to adjust to the age effect of waning sexual interest. Predictable abstinence could also help redirect the spouses' interest from sexual interest to family economic matters and parental investment.[85] To this purpose, diverting the sexual urge (*yetzer*) to other productive outlets is the subject of much rabbinic discourse.[86] As *niddah-tvilah* disciplines sexual behavior, an ancillary effect might be the stimulation of resource acquisition by the family during sexual abstinence. The couple's dwelling on money-related issues may be less divisive when the wife is a *niddah*, since the tension of sexual relations does not loom large in the background.

Niddah-tvilah demonstrates a communal interest by circumscribing social relations. Since reproductive display can have a disruptive effect on the life of an inward-looking community, Jewish women in public are expected to cover their hair, dress with decorum, and, in general, follow the communal customs of *tsniut* (modesty). A woman must avoid going into a room where she would be alone with a man other than her husband or close relative, regardless of the circumstances.[87] Long ago, the Talmud suggested a need for mate guarding, as the following story reveals. A man returns to his house in the company of two other men. His wife greets him outside dressed up nicely and wearing her jewelry. Why, the Talmud asks, did the husband let his wife reenter the house before both him and the other two men? Commenting on this passage, Rashi advises that a husband should never take for granted the good character [of other men] when alone with his wife even for a moment.[88] Generally, when women go anywhere alone it is noticed and frowned upon. When a married couple is less affectionate in public than usual, family and friends will assume that they are within their days of abstinence. Rules of family behavior, along with normal vigilance and gossip, reflect the life of an involved and interdependent community.[89] As I noted earlier, these rules can be characterized biologically as communal mate guarding with the goal of protecting communal integrity by reducing potential spousal conflict. It must be remembered that the community, not just the individual family, has a stake in the husband provisioning resources to his wife and children. If the husband shirks his responsibilities, the extended family and the community (as a last resort) will have no choice but to support the wife and children.[90]

Communal mate guarding can also be used before betrothal to limit or eliminate a girl's choice of marriage partner. In many traditional societies, cultural norms require fathers and mothers to arrange marriages or at least choose a pool of acceptable suitors for their daughters or sons.[91] The presumption is that close adult kin are more likely to choose long-term "investors" than if the girl alone were doing the choosing. On average, Romeo and Juliet romances lack the staying power of marriages endorsed by family and community. Therefore, marriage arranging can be seen biologically as a premarital mate-guarding tactic complemented by rules such as *niddah* that take effect once married life begins. Restricted dating and semi-arranged marriages help assure the extended family that its resources will not be called upon to support the wife and children if the husband becomes delinquent. Once betrothal has occurred, extended families will enthusiastically "guard" both mates from relationships with adulterous potential because even the faintest suspicion of "illegitimacy" could dissuade relatives from providing resources to grandchildren, nieces, or nephews.

Summary

Monogamous behaviors make family life more stable, increasing parental willingness to invest resources in children. The closer family proximity found in monogamous couples is associated with an overall reduction in the man's testosterone. With *niddah-tvilah* as part of the family environment, male testosterone may be routinely manipulated. Cyclically diminished male testosterone can benefit the

- monogamous pair, by decreasing the potential for male sexual jealousy;
- existing offspring, by enhancing the willingness for male investment;
- odds of future offspring being created, since the sexual "expectations" of both spouses culminate in the post-*tvilah* reunion.

Paternity uncertainty has been an important cause of men abandoning wives and children. From the female strategic perspective, *niddah* as a religious stricture should reduce the intensity and consequences of her spouse's sexual jealousy. From a male strategic perspective, observance of these laws functions as a surrogate mate guard that helps him monopolize his spouse's reproductive availability. In biotheological terms, God and community function as additional mate guards, protecting the woman from her own mate's advances during menstruation (when her sexual receptivity is lessened), and limiting her involvement with competing males. In Jewish life, adultery is a concern for the community as well as the affected family.[92] As Baskin relates, "[the community experiences] an anxiety regarding women's potential for sexual misconduct in contacts with men outside the family circle."[93] Although a wife becomes a *niddah* only during her period of infertility, observance of these rules may also ameliorate threats to the matrimony during ovulation by eliminating extramarital temptations occurring during the *niddah* period. The adaptive advantage of dual-purpose mate guarding enhances paternity certainty and renews the spouses' sexual interest at the time for resumption of their physical relationship.

Conclusions

Orthodox Judaism increasingly and emphatically identifies *niddah-tvilah* as the backbone of Jewish family life and a mainstay of Jewish communal life. As a biblical/rabbinic construction, these laws are based exclusively on a religious, not a biological, mandate. But a biosocial analysis can shed light on how and why this traditional practice can succeed in achieving religious goals. Although *niddah-tvilah* was not created to be "biologically correct," that this *mitzvah* can make scientific sense as a mating strategy is not coincidental. Regardless of the original purpose, the unambiguous function of these rules of conjugal separation is to avoid wasting sexual resources that influence the productive vitality and stability of Jewish marriages. As Rabbi Lamm writes, when a couple adheres to *niddah-tvilah,* "periodic replenishment occurs of both libido and semen ... this cycle of abstinence and fulfillment provides a recovery period for both husband and wife, one which establishes a much needed [synchronization] of male and female sexual rhythms."[94]

The hypotheses of this chapter are twofold: in benefiting husbands, *niddah-tvilah* can reduce both marital costs and suspicion of cuckoldry. In benefiting wives, the polygynous potential of husbands is more controllable. By manipulating testosterone production, *niddah-tvilah* may influence the husband's sexual desires, entraining his hormonal fluctuations more closely with his wife's menstruation, fertility, and desire. A more cooperative environment between husband and wife should produce more children, more child-directed investment, and less sexual conflict.

At first glance the practice of *niddah-tvilah* might appear to be an unwelcome imposition on the husband-wife relationship, since sexual abstinence is required for what amounts to about 40 percent of their married lives. A closer look, however, demonstrates its clear reproductive advantage as a *halakhic* (legal) structure regulating the distance between the spouses. Ejaculatory abstinence for a few days has been shown to increase sperm count; as a consequence, upon resuming sexual relations, reproductive success should likely improve.[95] In a study by Baker and Bellis, it was found that sperm count depended not only on elapsed time since the last ejaculation but also on elapsed time since the pair saw each other. Since during *niddah* the couple continues to live together within visual contact, the application of their study here is in question. But it is plausible that their results would have been replicated had the sample consisted of *niddah*-observant partners instead of couples separated in space for a period of time. For centuries, Jewish communities have taken pride in the comparative stability of family life, seen as stemming from the discipline imposed by Judaic family law. Lamm describes the laws of family purity as "protecting the marital bond from one of its universal enemies ... the tendency for sex to become routinized.... And it is abstinence [*niddah*] that helps keep that attraction and longing fresh and youthful."[96] In common parlance, the wife plays "hard to get" for a time whose length she alone measures; her husband must wait with anticipation until she informs him sexual relations are again permitted. By this method, Judaic law places the wife's menstruation-ovulation cycle "front and center" in the marriage relationship. The couple's right to sexual intimacy is made sacred and placed in both a personal and communal context. Talmudic discourse candidly announces the value of separation and reunion: "Because a man may become overly acquainted with [his wife] and thus repelled by her, the Torah said she is [for a time] considered a *niddah* so she might become as beloved of her husband on the day of her [renewed sexual availability] as on her wedding day."[97]

Interestingly, the laws of *niddah-tvilah* are virtually unknown among less traditional Jews, but observant Jews not only know but also strictly practice them. As a result, observance of *niddah-tvilah* has been described as "a dividing line between Orthodox Jews and [other Jews]."[98]

Further research will be necessary to flesh out the hypotheses of this chapter. The testosterone research cited here has typically not measured male variations within monthly cycles, so applicability of these data to our object of study may prove to be inappropriate. Lacking at this time is direct empirical evidence of testosterone fluctuations in observant husbands relative to their wives' menstrual cycle. Testosterone levels of observant husbands could be measured daily and compared with menstrual cycle phases of their respective wives. If my hypothesis is correct, each husband's testosterone should be suppressed during his wife's follicular phase (*niddah*), and increased as he anticipates her renewed availability.

Notes

I gratefully acknowledge Elizabeth Pillsworth for her helpful comments that informed the preparation of this chapter.

1. Marlowe, 2000; Murdock, 1967; Ven den Berghe, 1979.
2. One woman married to more than one man at the same time.
3. Deut. 24 states that a woman may take a second husband, but only after having received a divorce from the first one. Nowhere else in the Judaic religious texts is a cohusband mentioned.
4. For additional discussion of the short-term male mating strategy, see the chapter "Judaism's *Yetzer* as a Biotheological Construct."
5. To the extent that husbands and wives support their own children, the community's responsibility to be the support of last resort is proportionally reduced or eliminated.
6. The Talmud infers that marriage and children are the *essence*, indeed the *business*, of Judaism and the Jewish people (Ket. 7b1–2).
7. This phrase refers to a portion of the family laws of ritualized "purity."
8. For examples of conflicting interests in biblical families, see the chapter "Intrafamily Conflict in the Bible and Biological Theory."
9. Tiger, 2000, p. 159.
10. Reynolds and Tanner, 1995, p. 61.
11. Lev. 15:19–28.
12. Literally, "taste" of the *mitzvot*; rabbinic discourse is predicated on a "taste" (predilection) for reasoning.
13. Sumner, 1906, p. 511.
14. From Cohen, cited in Baskin, 2001, p. 134.

15. Prior to the second century C.E.
16. Wasserfall, 1999, p. 5.
17. Jewish law assumes menstruation to be regularly occurring, based on a pattern established for at least three straight months (*veset*). So even if a wife fails to examine herself or see evidence of flow, her *niddah* restriction begins according to her customary *veset* (see Yev. 65a1 and n1.
18. Biologically speaking, all physical contact is prohibited during the follicular phase of her menstrual cycle when, not coincidentally, she is unlikely to conceive. Violating her period of sexual unavailability causes the man to incur a fine (Ket. 29a2 and n. 15).
19. Modesty requires that the wife go to the *mikvah* at night and without telling anyone (Wex, 2006, p. 254).
20. "Living" water means naturally flowing. In a pool *mikvah,* a minimum volumetric water exchange is required. Interestingly, *mikvah* immersion is also the final step in the process of conversion to Judaism.
21. To give the reader a "flavor" of the *mikvah* experience, the following is a seventeenth- to eighteenth-century devotional Yiddish prayer recited by the woman before immersion: "God, my Lord, may it be your will that my cleanness, washing and immersion be accounted before You like the purity of all the pious women of Israel who purify themselves ... at the proper time." After immersion, the woman recites an additional prayer expressing a desire for pious offspring (quoted in Weissler, 1992, p. 109).
22. *Mitzvat onah* (Ket. 47b3) interpreting Exod. 21:10; also see Biale, 1992, p. 54).
23. Hartman and Marmon, 2004, p. 399. Although enforcement of most Jewish law requires *two* witnesses, the wife's renewed status as available to her husband requires only *one,* the wife herself. A woman who determines her sexual status is believed (is the authority) (Ket. 72a3).
24. Lev. 15:25–33.
25. See Forst, 1997, for details.
26. Hartman and Marmon, 2004, p. 393.
27. Steinberg, 2006, p. 9.
28. Ket. 72a.
29. Gen. 1:28.
30. Wasserfall, 1999, p. 7.
31. Maimonides, *Mikvaot* 11:12; Guide, Part III, Ch. 47.
32. Marlowe, 2000, 2001, 2003.
33. True at least *post*-biblically; see the chapter "The Fertility of Prominent Men in the Bible and Ancient Middle East."
34. Booth and Dabbs, 1993, p. 468.
35. Gray, Kahlenberg, et al., 2002; Gray, Campbell, et al., 2004.
36. Mazur and Michalek, 1998, p. 326.
37. Burnham, Chapman, et al., 2003.
38. Gray, Chapman, et al., 2004.
39. Mazur and Michalek, 1998, p. 327.
40. McIntyre, Gangestad, et al., 2006.
41. Berg and Wynne-Edwards, 2001.
42. Fleming, Corder, et al., 2002.
43. Gray, Chi-Fu, et al., 2006.
44. See the chapter "Judaism's *Yetzer* as a Biotheological Construct."
45. Pillsworth and Haselton, 2006(2).

46. Pillsworth and Haselton, 2002.

47. Hrdy, 1999, p. 246.

48. The Talmud acknowledges that if a woman's husband is "short as an ant," has a degrading job, or has a "tainted lineage," she will "commit adultery and ascribe the resulting children to her husband" (Yev. 118b6).

49. Women who dote on their undesirable husbands "all commit adultery and ascribe the resulting children to their husbands" (a Baraisa and Rashi's comment, Ket. 75a2 and n. 17).

50. Pillsworth and Haselton, 2006.

51. Pillsworth, Haselton, et al., 2004.

52. A woman may also seek extra-pair encounters based on the perception of inadequate provisioning by her long-term mate; that is, she may seek a "sugar daddy" investor for herself and her children. Women's pursuit of extra-pair investors, however, has not yet been shown to fluctuate with ovulatory cycle phase.

53. Haselton, 2006, p. 15.

54. Note, for example, the increased interest by male chimps during the visible, sexual swellings of females.

55. Barkow, Cosmides, et al., 1992, p. 144, referencing Doty.

56. Cronk, 2006, p. 172.

57. In most mammals (but not humans), females are receptive to male advances only during this period of detectable fertility. Olfactory cues (odor) given off by men may provide women even greater control than loss of estrus in mate-choice (see Grammer). For a nice summary of estrus loss in humans, see Fisher, 1992, pp. 186–188.

58. The Talmud recognizes that a woman may use her status as *niddah* to manipulate her husband (Ket. 22a4).

59. Quoted from the Ginsburg study by Kaufman, 1991, p. 84.

60. The Rabbis recognized the correlation between menstrual flow and fertility (Ket. 10b1).

61. It was also understood that low menstrual flow is a reliable sign of malnutrition (Ket. 10b2).

62. Zahavi and Zahavi, 1997, pp. 214, 215.

63. Women possess a "defensive weapon" (sexual access) to stay alive when powerful men (like highway robbers) would otherwise kill them along with the men at their mercy (Yev. 115a2).

64. Barkow, Cosmides, et al., 1992, p. 299.

65. Biale, quoted in Kaufman, 1991, p. 74.

66. Pillsworth and Haselton, 2006.

67. See Hong, 1984.

68. Tiger, 2000, p. 143.

69. As is the case in many cultures, Judaism is adamantly involved even at the beginning of a marriage with the wife's sexual status. At the time of their first relations, there is a community interest in the husband (or his agents) verifying his bride's claim of virginity (Ket. 5a2).

70. See, for example, David M. Buss's *The Dangerous Passion*, 2001. London: Bloomsbury Publishing.

71. Birkhead, 2000, pp. 33–34, 50. The Talmud explicitly recognizes the propensity of a husband to guard his wife, especially during her time of high fertility (Sotah 27a2).

72. The Talmud recognizes that a stepfather may not be as careful in copulating with his pregnant wife when the pregnancy is from a previous husband. In addition, the mother

might be more likely to provide abundant resources to this child than the stepfather might allow (Yev. 42a5–42b1). A widow nursing a child from her deceased husband must wait twenty-four months before remarrying to make sure the interests of the new husband do not come in conflict with those of her child (Yev. 43a3).

73. Yev. 34b3 and 35a1. See the full talmudic discussion at Yev. 37a2 and 41a3. There are many reasons why Jewish law requires that paternity be discovered (Yev. 42a2). Paternity must be ascertained even in the case where the former and present husbands are brothers (Yev. 42a1).

74. Regarding *havchana,* from Rambam, Geirushin 11:20; see also the case in Yev. 69b2–b3. Also, the Talmud includes a leniency that, if birth has not occurred within nine months, the fetus is considered "lingering" in the womb (for up to three additional months). Since a husband is urged to have relations with his wife just before beginning an extended trip (Yev. 62b5), he may not challenge his pregnant wife even if the child is born up to *twelve months* after his departure (unless witnesses saw her behaving promiscuously during his absence).

75. Respectively, Num. 11–31; Lev. 12:2, 15:32–33 (Meg. 20a2), 15:25; Num. 9:6 and 13, Lev. 5:2 and Hag. 2:13; Lev. 11:4, 13:11; Num. 9:15; Josh. 22:19; Isa. 6:15; Jer. 19:13; Job 14:4; Isa. 64:16 and Lam. 4:15; Ezek. 22:5.

76. Taanit 20a2.

77. A woman who is reported to be an adulteress may be given a divorce without monetary compensation (Ket. 101a5).

78. Yev. 95a5.

79. Num. 5:14. See the rabbinic debate regarding the type of spirit that comes over the husband in Sotah 2b5-3a3.

80. Exod. 20:17; Deut. 5:21.

81. See Isa. 30:22; Ezek. 16:23–39, 20:31, 22:3–4, 23:7, 36:18, 37:23; Hosea 4:10–15, 5:3, 9:1; Jer. 3:1–9, 5:7. The Talmud compares adultery in a house like a worm in a sesame seed, which eats the seed from within and leaves no trace of its destruction on the outside. Similarly, an adulterous wife dissipates her husband's money to support her infidelity and the husband remains unaware until his money is gone (Sotah 3b2).

82. Haselton and Gangestad, 2006; Pillsworth and Haselton, 2006.

83. Interestingly, the Hebrew language has an indigenous word for "cuckold" (*ba'al karnayim*), but Yiddish does not. Perhaps this is an indicator of the historical rarity of female adultery among Ashkenazic Jews (or perhaps not).

84. Biale summarizing Lamm, 1992, p. 213.

85. Supporting the continued investment by nursing mothers in existing children, the Talmud understands that a new pregnancy will cause lactation to cease (Yev. 34b1). Additionally the Sages allow the mother to use a contraceptive device to prevent a new pregnancy that would cease lactation (Yev. 12b1).

86. The chapter "Judaism's *Yetzer* as a Biotheological Construct" includes a discussion of this rabbinic principle.

87. When this does occur, the door to the room is to be left open. See this concern expressed in Yev. 11a3.

88. Taanit 23b1, including n. 9.

89. For example: "When she came back from the *mikvah* everybody who met her on the street would wish her to conceive a nice son that night" (a witness's testimony from Zborowski and Herzog, 1995, p. 286). There were communities in which a woman would signal her status as *niddah* by wearing old clothes (Ket. 65a1 and 72a3).

90. Fathers must support their children so the responsibility does not fall to the community (Ket. 48a2). Unsupportive fathers are shamed into providing for their children.

Rav Yehuda said to the "deadbeat" father: "a jackal gave birth then threw the needs of its offspring upon the people of the town." Rav Chisda has the father stand on a pedestal in a public place and announces, "Even a raven wants its children, and *that* man [the father himself] does not want his children" (Ket. 49b1–49b2).

91. See Apostolou for recent research on sexual selection by parental choice. Actually, the Talmud claims that Fate arranges marriage partners as life begins, forty days before formation of the embryo (Sotah 2a3).

92. For a father of priestly lineage (כהן), paternity uncertainty can be an even greater problem. If there is uncertainty about the boy being his biological son, the father's treatment of the boy may change since the son might therefore not be considered a כהן.

93. Baskin, 2001, p. 137.
94. Lamm, 1987, p. 46.
95. Gallup and Burch, 2002.
96. Lamm, 1987, pp. 55, 58.
97. Talmud Nid. 31b.
98. Meacham, 1999, p. 35. See this distinction reflected in Sotah 27a2.

References

Apostolou, M. 2007. Sexual selection under parental choice: The role of parents in the evolution of human mating. *Evolution and Human Behavior* 28:403–409.

Baker, R. R., and Bellis, M. A. 1989. Number of sperm in human ejaculates varies in accordance with sperm competition theory. *Animal Behavior* 37:867–869.

Barkow, J. H., Cosmides, L., et al. 1992. *The Adapted Mind*. New York: Oxford University Press.

Baskin, J. 2001. Women and ritual immersion in medieval Ashkenaz: the sexual politics of piety. In L. Fine, ed., *Judaism in Practice*. Princeton, NJ: Princeton University Press.

Berg, S. J., and Wynne-Edwards, K. E. 2001. Changes in testosterone, cortisol, and estradiol levels in men becoming fathers. *Mayo Clinic Proceedings* 76:582–592.

Biale, D. 1992. *Eros and the Jews*. New York: Basic Books.

Birkhead, T. 2000. *Promiscuity*. Cambridge: Harvard University Press.

Booth, A., and Dabbs, J. M., Jr. 1993. Testosterone and men's marriages. *Social Forces* 72(2):463–477.

Burnham, T. C., J. Flynn Chapman, et al. 2003. Men in committed romantic relationships have lower testosterone. *Hormones and Behavior* 44(2):119–122.

Buss, D. M. September 1988. From vigilance to violence: tactics of mate retention in American undergraduates. *Ethology and Sociobiology* 9:291–317.

Cronk, L. 2006. Behavioral ecology and the social sciences. In J. H. Barkow, ed., *Missing the Revolution* (pp. 167–185). New York: Oxford University Press.

Fisher, H. 1992. *Anatomy of Love*. New York: Fawcett Columbine/Ballantine Books.

Fleming, A. S., Carl Corder, et al. 2002. Testosterone and prolactin are associated with emotional responses to infant cries in new fathers. *Hormones and Behavior* 42(4):399–413.

Forst, B. 1997. *The Laws of Niddah*. Brooklyn: Mesorah Publications.

Gallup, G., and Burch, R. 2002. Male sexual behavior varies following separation from female partner. Paper presented at Human Behavior and Evolution Society Conference, Rutgers University.

Grammer, K. 1993. 5-A-androst-16en-3A-on: a male pheromone? A brief report. *Ethology and Sociobiology* 14:201–208.

Gray, P. B., Campbell, B. C., et al. 2004. Social variables predict between-subject but not day-to-day variation in the testosterone of U.S. men. *Psychoneuroendocrinology* 29(9):1153–1162.

Gray, P. B., Chapman, J. F., et al. 2004. Human male pair bonding and testosterone. *Human Nature* 15(2):119–131.

Gray, P. B., Chi-Fu Jeffrey Yang, et al. 2006. Fathers have lower salivary testosterone levels than unmarried men and married non-fathers in Beijing, China. *Proceedings of the Royal Society B* 273:333–339.

Gray, P., Kahlenberg, Sonya, et al. 2002. Marriage and fatherhood are associated with lower testosterone in males. *Evolution and Human Behavior* 23(3):193–201.

Hartman, T., and Marmon, N. 2004. Lived regulations, systematic attributions—menstrual separation and ritual immersion in the experience of Orthodox Jewish women. *Gender and Society* 18(3):389–408.

Haselton, M. G. 2006. Best dressed women have babies on their mind. *New Scientist*, January 13.

Haselton, M. G., and Gangestad, S. W. 2006. Conditional expression of women's desires and men's mate guarding across the ovulatory cycle. *Hormones and Behavior* 49(4):509–518.

Hong, L. K. 1984. Survival of the fastest: on the origin of premature ejaculation. *Journal of Sex Research* 20:109–122.

Hrdy, S. B. 1999. *Mother Nature*. New York: Ballantine.

Kaufman, D. R. 1991. *Rachel's Daughters—Newly Orthodox Jewish Women*. New Brunswick, NJ: Rutgers University Press.

Lamm, Rabbi N. 1987. *A Hedge of Roses*. New York: Feldheim Publishers.

Maimonides. 2007. *Guide for the Perplexed*. BN Publishing, www.bnpublishing.com.

———. 1989. *Mishne Torah, Hilchot Yesodei Hatorah—Laws of Mikvaot*. Moznaim Publishing.

Marlowe, F. 2003. A critical period for provisioning by Hazda men: Implications for pair bonding. *Evolution and Human Behavior* 24:217–229.

———. 2001. Male contribution to diet and female reproductive success among foragers. *Current Anthropology* 42(5):755–760.

———. 2000. Paternal investment and the human mating system. *Behavioural Processes* 51:45–61.

Mazur, A., and Michalek, J. 1998. Marriage, divorce and male testosterone. *Social Forces* 77(1):315–330.

McIntyre, M. H., Gangestad, S., et al. 2006. Romantic involvement often reduces men's testosterone levels—but not always: the moderating role of extra-pair sexual interest." *Journal of Personality and Social Psychology* 91(4):642–651.

Meacham, T. 1999. An abbreviated history of the development of the Jewish menstrual laws. In R. Wasserfall, ed., *Women and Water* (pp. 23–39). Waltham, MA: Brandeis University Press.

Murdock, G. P. 1967. *Ethnographic Atlas*. Pittsburgh: University of Pittsburgh Press.

Pillsworth, E. G., and Haselton, M. G. 2006. Male sexual attractiveness predicts differential ovulatory shifts in female extra-pair attraction and male mate-retention. *Evolution and Human Behavior* 27(4):247–258.

———. 2006. Women's sexual strategies: the evolution of long-term and extra-pair sex. *Annual Review of Sex Research* 17(2):59–100.

———. 2002. What women know and men don't: changes in women's sexual behavior found as a function of fertility. Paper presented at Human Behavior and Evolution Society Conference, Rutgers University.

Pillsworth, E. G., Haselton, M., et al. 2004. Ovulatory shifts in female sexual desire. *Journal of Sex Research* 41(1):55–65.

Reynolds, V., and Tanner, R. 1995. *The Social Ecology of Religion.* New York: Oxford University Press.

Steinberg, J. 2006. From a "pot of filth" to a "hedge of roses" (and back): changing theorizations of menstruation in Judaism. *Journal of Feminist Studies* 13(2):5–27.

Sumner, W. G. 1906. *Folkways.* Boston: Ginn.

Telushkin, J. 1991. *Jewish Literacy* (pp. 617–619). New York: William Morrow.

Tiger, L. 2000. *The Pursuit of Pleasure.* New Brunswick: Transaction.

Ven den Berghe, P. 1979. *Human Family Systems: An Evolutionary View.* New York: Elsevier.

Wasserfall, R. 1999. Menstrual blood into Jewish blood. In R. Wasserfall, ed., *Women and Water* (pp. 1–18). Waltham, MA: Brandeis University Press.

Weissler, C. 1992. *Mitzvot* built into the body: Tkines for Niddah, pregnancy, and childbirth. In H. Eilberg-Schwartz, ed., *People of the Body* (pp. 101–111). New York: State University of New York Press.

Wex, M. 2006. *Born to Kvetch.* New York: HarperPerennial.

Zahavi, A., and Zahavi, A. 1997. *The Handicap Principle.* New York: Oxford University Press.

Zborowski, M., and Herzog, E. 1995. *Life Is with People.* New York: Schocken.

Chapter 7

Traditionalism and Human Evolutionary Success

The Example of Judaism

Craig Palmer, Lyle Steadman, and Rick Goldberg

> The past does appear in the present and it does so against the obstacles of death and birth.... The succession of generations is the moving biological ground over which the past endures into the present.
> —*sociologist Edward Shils*[1]

Introduction: The Generalized Proposition

Darwin's theory of evolution by natural and sexual selection attempts to explain why living things are the way they are. In this chapter we will use the example of Judaism to demonstrate why understanding traditions, cultural behaviors transmitted from one generation to the next via offspring copying the behavior of their parents, answers many questions about our evolved nature. In this chapter we assert that cultural traditions have been an integral part of human biological evolution. Our large brains and the extreme helplessness of our children were favored in our history because parental transmission of traditions to offspring well served our survival needs for thousands of generations. As William Graham Sumner observed: "Custom regulates the whole of men's actions [which] imitate what they see others do; they accomplish this imitation more easily [if] their forefathers practiced the same act.... From his cradle to his grave, he is the slave of ancient usage."[2] Sumner's brief characterization of traditions is as much a description of our evolved nature as is the observation that we walk on two legs.

Before proceeding further, we must clarify that our use of the term *tradition* contains no sense of inferiority as it did among nineteenth-century anthropologists like Sir James Frazer, who wrote, the "poor savage" was "hidebound by custom and tradition."[3] Our view is that traditional behaviors were passed down for many generations and, far from being the chains of slavery Frazer describes, were actually elemental to human survival and reproduction. In that spirit, we acknowledge the profoundly traditional nature of past and present human cultures and avoid all negative assessments of traditionalism itself. Neutrality is crucial to an accurate evaluation of both human culture and human evolution because, although at least minimal changes have occurred in all cultures over time, many traditions remain unchanged for impressive periods of time.[4] Traditions can also be maintained by subcultures within *non*traditional societies, as demonstrated by the Hutterites who "have retained their medieval speech patterns for over four centuries."[5] For this to occur there must be almost total overlap between an individual's biological and cultural descendants. The same linguistic pattern developed among the two major sets of codescendants in the subordinated Jewish world. Eastern European Jews (Ashkenazim) used Yiddish (mostly old German mixed with Hebrew) as their secular language for centuries. The same is true for Jews of Spanish-Portuguese descent (Sephardim) who spoke Ladino (old Spanish flavored with Hebrew) for many generations.

In the first part of this chapter we present our model of how traditions fit into current understandings of evolution, culture, and human development. In the second part, we illustrate this model by investigating Judaic traditionalism.

Tradition and Darwinian Selection

The most powerful, identifiable influences on all organisms, including humans, are their living and dead ancestors. All living organisms are influenced profoundly by their ancestors' genes and, additionally, many animals acquire and are influenced by the behavior of their ancestors, which becomes tradition.[6] The evolutionary significance of traditions is best expressed by the interactionist theory of development: "every visible attribute of every organism is the product of a marvelously complex and all-pervasive interaction between genes and environment."[7] Aside from individual differences, all behavior is the result of genes interacting with myriad environmental factors. Traditions, however, are the only behaviors that require an ancestor to perform the behavior and a descendant to observe and then copy it or follow its instruction. As such, traditions are a subset of cultural behavior, defined as behavior copied from or influenced by another individual, ancestor or otherwise. When tradition is properly considered as a phenotypic phenomenon caused by both genetic and environmental factors, it is clear that traditional behavior is inherited the same way as every other aspect of the phenotype—by inheriting the genetic and environmental factors that interact to produce the phenotype.[8] Traditions are thus a necessary part of "biologically sophisticated models" of human ontogeny.[9]

Traditions are especially necessary in sophisticated models of human evolution because the influence of traditions has been overwhelmingly powerful in our social species. Both Alexander and Trivers have stressed that parents can increase their own reproductive success by influencing the behavior of offspring. Alexander observed that "the potential significance of parental manipulation may assume remarkable proportions."[10] However, the full force of parental influence is transmitted not only while parents and grandparents are still living, but also indirectly by influencing yet unborn distant descendants. The Jewish religion has exhibited that descendants can be strongly influenced by traditions handed down from *very distant* ancestors. An appreciation of how traditions work multigenerationally is crucial. The ability of traditional behavior to have profound effects on even very distant generations demonstrates why "classical fitness is an inadequate measure of an individual's total reproductive (genetic) contribution."[11] What we are suggesting is that the descendant-leaving success of parental (and grandparental) behavior is best judged not by the number of children in a particular generation, or even the number of living grandchildren, but, rather, by the "number of descendants alive after some very large number of generations."[12] It is important to understand that parents may not behave in particular ways because they consciously want to influence their children to leave more descendants. Indeed, parents need not be consciously aware of influencing their children in any manner whatsoever. Just as desiring sex does not imply a conscious desire to reproduce, so parental investment that hands down traditions does not require a conscious desire to do so. This explains why, as children grow up and have children of their own, they tend to mimic the parental behaviors they experienced as children without consciously choosing to do so.

Recognizing the relationship between ancestral influence and success in leaving descendants has enormous consequences for understanding human behavior. All ancestors are distinguished in at least one activity, namely, the ability to leave descendants. Since the continuance of all life has occurred by lineages, not a single one of our own ancestors, perhaps back to the beginning of life, failed to reproduce. This is no mean achievement, for in every living population many individuals do fail to reproduce. Although all organisms are descendants of ancestors who successfully left descendants, only some became ancestors themselves. Thus, although our individual existence proves our own *ancestral* success, it does not imply our future *descendant-leaving* success. The failure of organisms to leave descendants does not challenge the fact that we are all products of generations of reproductive success.

It is axiomatic that anything replicable (acquired from ancestors) is subject to Darwinian selection. Although in the popular press "selection" has come to refer only to genetic selection, our use of the term *Darwinian selection* is consistent with how Darwin used the term to describe the processes he discovered a century and a half ago. Darwin's grand conclusion was that anything heritable and replicable can influence its own frequency in later generations. Such a process, we argue, must include traditions, since they are both heritable and replicable. Anything heritable *and* replicable that promotes the leaving of descendants tends to increase in frequency in succeeding generations; any gene or cultural trait that reduces such success tends to disappear.[13] Like all living organisms, individual humans are continuously being fashioned out of the combinations of genes and traditions received from ancestors. Traditions are distinctive neither because they are learned behavior nor because they are learned behavior acquired from others (i.e., culture). Rather, they are distinctive because they are learned behavior acquired from generations of ancestors and thus subject to selection.

Because of the process of Darwinian selection,[14] it is human ancestors who have been selected to care the most for their descendants' welfare. This is true because their descendants directly represent an ancestor's proprietary stake in future generations. It is for this reason that parents and grandparents are the ones who most encourage offspring to acquire and perform the traditions that constitute, for example, their religious behavior. Humans leave descendants not just by physiological reproduction but by investing efforts over a long period directed toward their living descendants. To state bluntly the value of traditions, those individuals who do not transmit, or support the transmission of, traditions to their descendants end up leaving fewer descendants than those who do. *The most consequential effect of traditions is that they not only increase the number of descendants, but they also induce those descendants to cooperate with one another.* As classical economist F. A. Hayek tells us:

> [I]n social evolution the decisive factor is ... the selection by imitation of successful institutions and habits.... [Our] cultural heritage is passed on by learning and imitation..., and we often find it necessary to be guided by habit rather than reflection. This evolutionary view is based on the insightful experimentation of many generations ... [that causes] conformity to unconscious patterns of conduct..., firmly established habits and traditions. The general observance of these conventions is a necessary condition of the orderliness of the world in which we live.[15]

Traditions and Kinship Cooperation

Until recently, all humans lived in traditional societies where cultural behaviors tended to be copied from or influenced by ancestors. Even today, societies referred to as "traditional" strongly exhibit this behavior that has for so long been characteristic of all societies. Individuals in such societies typically identify one another as kin by referencing their descent from common ancestors. Although some traditional societies are small, the tradition of passing descent names from ancestors to descendants *over many generations* can lead to the identification of a great number of codescendants. As Fox informs us, each generation's continuing inheritance of descent names enables "large lineages or clans ... [to] grow up over time as the descendants of the original ancestor/ancestress."[16] So, with time, some traditional societies became very large. As van den Berghe and Barash explain, unilineal descent "can be seen as a cultural adaptation enabling up to millions of people to organize."[17] Among the Tiv, for example, "the whole population of some 800,000 traces descent by traditional genealogical links from a single, founding ancestor."[18] The phenomenon of tens of thousands of individuals recognizing the same unilineal descent name can *only* occur if such traditional names are transmitted without change to descendants over many generations.[19]

Although traditions such as descent names enable large numbers of individuals to be identified as kin, there are other traditions that also help produce the cooperative social relationships that form these individual kin into a society.[20] For example, the Lugbara of Africa claim that "the rules of social behavior are 'the words of our Ancestors'."[21] Keen found that Australian aboriginal peoples use the terms *ancestral law* and *the proper way* to connect the words of ancestors with cooperation among their descendants. As he writes, "Networks of regional cooperation underpin the sharing of ancestral law."[22] Additionally, Hiatt claims that "'traditional values and expectations' include 'the ethic of generosity'."[23] Specific examples of aboriginal parents telling their offspring traditional stories that "taught them to share" with one another can be found in Ilyatjari.[24]

Our intention here is not to endorse traditions as wonderful or just admirable, terrible or just objectionable. As there are traditions for proper conduct, there are also traditional consequences for conduct contrary to the wishes of ancestors. Folkloric stories told to children scare them into avoiding bad behavior ("the bogeyman will get you" if you do that!). Spirits of ancestors may rise from the dead and punish those who ignore ancestral instructions (for example, so-and-so will "turn over in his grave" to avenge what his grandson did!). Whether traditions take the form of behavior to be copied or warnings to be heeded, their evolutionary value lies in the encouragement of cooperation among codescendants, including *distant* codescendants. As a central feature of human sociality, religion has been engaged in such encouragement. When individuals behave traditionally, the frequency of religious behaviors should covary according to its descendant-leaving influence.

Religion as a Descendant-Leaving Strategy

The propensity for religious behavior to be traditional, especially until recent times, has been noted by many scholars. For example, Boyer says that religion is often strongly influenced by ancestors.[25] Thompson pointedly asks, "Why, if we are believers, is the one and only true god the god of our parents and grandparents?"[26] Religious myths are a major part of religion and obviously a form of traditional stories;[27] religious rituals are characterized by repetition and stereotyping and, for that reason, can never be merely created. The vast majority of rituals reported in anthropological studies have been repeated, relatively unchanged, over many generations. Rituals are based on and encourage cooperative social behavior,[28] a truth demonstrated by the familiar phrases "rites of intensification" and "rites of solidarity." The very nature of ritual facilitates interactions "in which performers can simultaneously make and keep promises to each other simply by coordinating their action."[29]

Religious rituals explicitly encourage people to accept the influence of ancestors by encouraging them to respect their ancestors' ritual "style." Indeed, "ancestor worship" may be a universal element found in traditional, localized religions.[30] The ubiquity of ancestor veneration, spread across the globe from the Kalahari to Easter Island, confirms the antiquity and persistence of ancestor-focused religion in human society.[31] Taboos, sacrificial offerings, and inflicted pain during initiation ceremonies are some of the best-known traditional rituals found worldwide.[32] The voluntary acceptance of socially encouraged suffering communicates a willingness to accept the guidance of others to fulfill a traditional obligation. Cooperation implies a willingness to accept the influence of others, a condition that may subject one *intentionally* to distress or even agony.[33] So engaging in sacrificial behavior in socially sanctioned ceremonies fosters bonding between codescendants. Developing and maintaining tight social bonds encourages loyalty and a readiness to sacrifice under stressful conditions, shown by the expression "we're all in this together." Proof of the (biological) value of socially encouraged suffering is evidenced by its persistence in many places over many generations.

Taboos present an excellent example of traditional "trials and tribulations." Why should the imposition of seemingly pointless hardships that benefit no one materially become traditional? Social relationships are distinguished by enduring cooperation that may not at a given moment be to everyone's advantage. Accepting a taboo communicates to those encouraging it one's willingness to be disciplined and should influence the encourager to behave reciprocally. Breaking or defying a taboo, of course, communicates the opposite. But it is more than this. *To show a willingness to suffer for others not only influences individuals to reciprocate, it also influences them to exhibit such behavior toward others.* Some psychological studies have shown that witnessing "helping" actions influences observers to themselves help others: "exposure to others who act in a generous or helpful manner has been found to increase subjects' tendency to offer aid to [other] persons in need of assistance. Further, exposure to selfish[ness] has been shown to sharply reduce helping and generosity by observers."[34] Sacrificial parental behavior has as its most important consequence not reciprocity but, rather, a model for their children to *willingly sacrifice, in turn, for their own children.* As the adage goes, enjoyment of grandchildren is the reward given to parents who refrain from killing their children as teenagers. The effect of traditional taboos that accounts for their persistence is the promotion of inter- and intragenerational selflessness.

We now undertake to apply our descendant-leaving model to Judaic traditionalism, which has successfully promoted cooperative social relationships among Jews over many generations.

Jewish Traditionalism

Here are the words of Tevye the Milkman from the opening scene of *Fiddler on the Roof*:

> Because of our traditions, we've kept our balance for many, many years. Here in Anatevka we have traditions for everything ... how to eat, how to sleep, even how to wear clothes. For instance, we always keep our heads covered and always wear a little prayer shawl. This shows our constant devotion to God. You may ask, how did these traditions start? I'll tell you, I don't know ... but it's a tradition! Because of our traditions everyone knows who he is and what God expects him to do.

Why has a reverence for ancestors and their practices been found in so many societies investigated by anthropologists? Just as the song "Tradition" sets the stage for *Fiddler*, so the song brings to stage center the traditionalism of the Jewish religion. In fact, among observant Jewish communities, the entirety of Judaism may be referred to simply as "the Tradition."[35]

Traditions, generated social products based on kinship and metaphorical kinship, are seldom mentioned in recent scientific analyses of religion. Although today's social science has sought to make "tradition" an antiquated phenomenon, among observant Jews and many others traditions retain the power of national anthems. In Judaism, the values and behaviors of venerated ancestors are unmistakably considered worthy of the highest respect and emulation. This is because access to God's assistance in every generation is based on the merit (*z'khut*) of those ancestors with whom God is claimed to have established a covenant.[36] Generally speaking, traditional Jewish life can be characterized as living vicariously through commonly recognized ancestors. In Talmudic discourse, referencing the opinions of specific authorities exemplifies their venerated, ancestral status.

Tribal-traditionalist religions are organized around social arrangements inherited from those who came before.[37] In Judaism, God is revealed as man's primary, metaphorical Ancestor who seeks, deserves, and requires influence over mankind, in general, and Jews in particular. Humans were formed from the beginning "in the image of God," evidencing the claim of metaphorical kinship with the Creator. Additionally, in the Judaic texts God is often referred to as Father (*Av*), Source of Influence for humankind, His "children." As an expression of God's covenantal relationship with the Jewish people, the identity of each Jew is based on a genealogical lineage of biological kinsmen.[38] Implicit in this claim of homology is the assumption that defying the traditions passed down by biological ancestors is tantamount to defying the instruction of the First Ancestor Himself, God.[39]

In every culture, tradition is *intrinsically* authoritative, by which we mean it is received and revered nonskeptically. As both *relived* behavior and fear-generating *restrictions* on behavior, tradition has compelling, stand-alone value to its inheritors.[40] Behaving traditionally is not premeditated; rather, it is unthinkingly copied from those from whom one learns, usually kin and extended kin. Far from proof of its irrationality, acting without thinking surely paid dividends in human evolutionary history. Although some may perceive premodern peoples as "culturally backward" because they are tradition based, the viability of traditions is as much a part of human nature as are other inherited traits. As Sumner observed, "If asked why they act in a certain way... [traditional] people always answer it is because they and their ancestors always have done so."[41] If an observant Jew were asked why he or she keeps kosher, "it's my family's tradition" would be considered a sufficient answer. A similar, tradition-based response could be given to almost any pattern of premodern religious practice, Judaic or otherwise. Although modern social science often assumes that tradition and rationality are mutually exclusive,[42] within the Jewish texts (and their ongoing study), tradition and rationality not only coexist but most often fortify each other.

There is a story told about a synagogue in which every person ducked his head at a certain point in the Torah procession.[43] A visitor who observed this unusual behavior asked one of the younger congregants what the "ducking" was all about. He was told, "We duck our heads at that place because it's traditional." The visitor had never heard of this Jewish tradition, so he asked a much older member of the congregation about it. He was told that, in the congregation's prior location, there had been a low-hanging chandelier in that place that required ducking. Although there was no such chandelier in the new building, the ducking continued because it had by then become integral to the ceremony practiced by synagogue members.

This story illustrates that, for a tradition to have value in a given generation, it need not be in any manner functional. For example, traditional Jews study scrupulously the laws of Temple sacrificing, although these practices were suspended almost 2,000 years ago when the Romans destroyed the Second Temple. Knowledge of the intricacies of Temple sacrificing remains widespread among traditional Jews up to the present day, despite the absence of a functioning Temple in Jerusalem.

In commenting on the inheritance of land, Rabbi Akiva compares the bequeathing ancestor[44] to a flowing stream that will, in the future, benefit descendants.[45] The inheritance of land is thereby comparable to the inheritance of tradition. As successful reproducers, ancestors have a large stake in the ongoing welfare of their descendants. As Rav Soloveitchik explains, "God endowed man with [the power] to learn from someone else: the ability to be influenced... like clay in the hands of the potter.... Every human being is master and disciple, influencer and influenced, receiver and bestowerr."[46]

Although traditionalism is omnipresent in the Judaic landscape, the Tradition neither reproduces nor constrains behavior *for its own sake*. Rather, the transmission of knowledge is commanding due to its multigenerational social effect. Tradition is the device by which ancestors empower and control their descendants: Judaism requires each succeeding generation to accept ancestral ways as authoritative inheritance. For instance, in each generation every Jew must regard himself as if he were part of the generation that went out from slavery in Egypt.[47] Consequently, this mandatory, collective memory instills in every generation a strong identification with the Exodus, considered one of the seminal events in Jewish history.[48]

With fealty to the texts of revelation, Jewish Diaspora communities have retained in common the traditions most essential to the core values of Judaism. But just as core patterns of the Tradition became relatively fixed in the Jewish world, each community developed its own legal interpretations and practiced its own customs.[49] Since Torah law is more ancient than rabbinic law, it is considered everywhere to have more authority. As a result, communities experience less variation over time in Torah law than in rabbinic law and customs. The Tradition also includes a tenet known as the "decline of generations," a doctrine that gives greater authority to earlier rabbinic commentators than latter ones.[50] This assumption of declension in rabbinic quality over the centuries can be labeled hypertraditionalism, an interpretation that venerates earlier traditionalists over later ones. As such, the most ancient traditions are considered the most authoritative, giving latter generations less authority to tamper with them.

This cross-culturally common notion that "things were better in times past" reflects the honorific perception of ancestral ways. Although there is great devotion to inherited arrangements per se, traditional societies are also spared the problem of "reinventing the wheels" that have functioned adequately in previous generations. As Barkow describes this process biologically, "When a species becomes capable of a sufficient degree of social learning ... local populations may develop pools of shared information that is communicated both within and across generations."[51] Examples of religious "speciation," in which "new" religious movements branch off old ones, can be found everywhere, including the Israelite religion, earliest Christianity, Islam, and many others.

As we have just suggested, like the evolution of all life forms, the development of "new" traditions first begins by borrowing from already established ones. When "new" religions emerge, the founders incorporate as their point of departure those traditions familiar to them and their base of potential converts. By coopting the authentic flavor of preexisting traditions, the founders' "message" is made more persuasive to the core religious community.[52] The "new" community will have achieved success (stability) when, at least three generations later, the modified traditions are perceived as having existed "from time immemorial."[53] The longer traditions are practiced, the more commanding is their authority for codescendants. For recipients of religious traditions, the historical importation of traditions remains an insignificant issue, shrouded in the mists of their ancestral past. In the biocultural world, where everything derives from something else, traditions are no exception.

The former notwithstanding, in every generation rabbinic authorities must be perceived as steeped in tradition; if not, their judgments risk nonacceptance by their communities. In the history of Judaism, all persistent laws and customs achieved the status of "traditional." In its incipiency, the Israelite religion adapted (at least in part) traditions from neighboring peoples.[54] In time, Jewish longevity resulted in many of those "borrowed" traditions being associated uniquely with Judaism. For example, the traditional language associated with Judaism is Hebrew. But, as is the case with every language, Hebrew developed within the context of the other Semitic languages spoken in the ancient Middle East. In time, using Hebrew[55] became traditional exclusively in religious matters and ceremonies. A much newer development was the revival of Hebrew as the modern language for the State of Israel. The "father" of this secular project, a crusader named Eliezer Ben-Yehuda, was successful in no small part because of Hebrew's traditional status as Judaism's holy tongue. Although most of Israel's founders were militantly secular, they bowed to the weight of tradition and accepted Hebrew, even though from a purely practical perspective, Yiddish or English would have been a better choice at the time.

As an intrinsic part of the human biological dynamic, the observance of tradition provides intergenerational continuity.[56] In constructing the Tradition, the rabbis argue from principles to praxis and vice versa. Judaic behavioral requirements (*mitzvot*), from the Bible onward, are multigenerational by design. Likewise, rewards and punishments pertain to lineages as well as individuals and are stated as such. Every Jew's ability to perform *mitzvot* requires substantial traditional knowledge, although *knowledge* of traditions, while laudable, is not enough. Inherited knowledge attains value only if it leads to the *performance* of obligations.[57] Traditional behavior provides a standard by which coreligionists appraise one another.[58] The Hebrew Prophets disparaged the evil conduct of the people by claiming their behavior was at variance with God's traditional requirements. In addition, Judaism is parsimonious—no "extra credit" is given to those who perform *beyond* their obligations—in fact, the highest reward is reserved for Jews who comply with traditional obligations strictly and without unauthorized embellishment.[59]

In Judaic liturgy, a frequently found term is *generation to generation* (*dor l'dor*), an indication that Judaism transmits its traditional knowledge through ancestor-descendant lineages. Although Jews venerate a well-defined set of distant ancestors,[60] immediate ancestors like fathers and mothers must also be honored.[61] The Book of Proverbs gives ample instruction on the importance of learning from fathers and mothers.[62] Newborns are named after ancestors who are either deceased (Ashkenazim) or living (Sephardim) as a strategy of placing the child "under the influence" of his or her namesake. When parents bless their children on Sabbath eve, they invoke the names of venerated ancestors with qualities they hope their children will emulate.[63]

Because traditions are behaviors copied and prohibitions received from ancestors, the Jews realized early on that successful tradition-leaving was greatly enhanced by writing things down.[64] Historically, before writing was used, preserving knowledge required memorization of commentaries to the Five Books of the Hebrew Bible that failed to pass down their precise complexity. At one time Judaism had both a written and an oral Torah. But about the year 200 C.E. the Oral Law was formatted in writing, because its ever-increasing length rendered it difficult to be properly memorized. Also, the redaction project was rationalized because parts of the Oral Law might otherwise have been forgotten and abrogated,[65] although prior to its redaction, the oral tradition was considered fully authoritative.[66] The Masoritic scholars, from the sixth to the tenth centuries C.E., assumed the task of shaping the biblical text into its final form. With the development of written texts, traditional knowledge became more fixed, a development that made the comparison of different texts possible.[67]

Texts that are many centuries old remain unaltered to this day, because all Jewish religious movements would consider changing even one letter to be sacrilegious.[68] As soon as there were Jews, there were sacred writings—the Jews belonged as much to the texts as the texts belonged to them.[69] Until books were mass produced, Judaic texts were, like the Tradition they conveyed, literally "handed down" from one generation to the next and successively studied (by those who could obtain them). But it should be kept in mind that reducing ancient traditions to writing does not preclude reasoned interpretation of the corpus of those texts in every generation. To the contrary, the texts *themselves* most often take the form of a multigenerational disputation, a living tradition in which the deliberation process itself is expressed in traditional modes. Tradition-based social learning is accomplished, therefore, by incorporating the intellectual influence of both the living *and* the dead.

But the question remains, how did the Jews progress historically to the status of a hyperliterate people? The primary means for transmitting traditions has been through study of sacred written texts by the method of *close reading*. Knowledge of the Tradition is incumbent on every Jewish man, not just highly educated rabbis. Merit is the basis for entrance into the educated elite by deserving young scholars. Although *yichus* (prestigious lineage) certainly could help a brilliant student, the demonstration of traditional knowledge and personal demeanor were the keys to impressing both teachers and the community at large. But *all* literate Jewish males must achieve a religiously significant life through, in part, the regular study of sacred texts, including the Bible and an extensive canon of exegetic commentaries compiled over the past 1,600 years. The purpose of this enormous personal investment in learning was to thoroughly understand (hence, know how to observe) the traditional obligations. Additionally, scholars who had no intention or requirement to observe the Tradition found these voluminous texts useful as anthropological documents of the first order.[70]

Over the centuries, the legal framework continued to develop in scope and complexity. To keep people from coming too close to violations, the Sages "protected" the Law from abrogation by creating sets of restrictions, or "fences around the Law."[71] Although "fences" were cautionary in origin, they quickly attained the weight of established law. The Rabbis interpreted Ecclesiastes 10:8, "Whoever breaks through a fence will be bitten by a snake," to mean that one who "breaks through a fence" that surrounds the law is guilty of a transgression. The phenomenon of widespread commentary began with interpretations of biblical language and the application of biblical requirements to daily life in various communities of Jews. What ensued thereafter were interpretations on the codified commentaries, a multicentury dynamic that continues until the present day. As conditions change in diverse Jewish communities, new rulings take their place alongside the old ones in the traditional canon.[72] Theologically speaking, novel insights based on new fact situations are issued by prominent rabbis and, if they achieve consensus, are considered implicit in the Torah given to Moses at Sinai. As Sholem relates: "The biblical scholar perceives revelation not as unique and clearly delineated occurrences, but rather as phenomena of eternal fruitfulness to be unearthed and examined: 'Turn it and turn it again, for everything is in it.'... The achievement of every generation, its contribution to tradition, is projected back into the eternal present of the revelation at Sinai."[73]

Over the centuries, command of the Tradition has become more difficult because, in addition to the *written* "older" Tradition, the ongoing addition of written commentaries caused learning to be increasingly complex.[74] The Talmud relates a story of King Ptolemy, who summoned seventy-two scholars of Israel and isolated them in seventy-two separate dwellings. Without telling them why they were convened, he requested each one to write a Greek translation of the Torah. Since each scholar knew there were elements in the Torah that would offend the king, they received divine guidance enabling them to identically *mistranslate* the potentially dangerous verses![75] What this story never questions is that if the scholars had wanted to write the Torah identically, they could have all done so from memory! Their presumed accuracy was considered the result of the Torah having been passed down through the generations in written rather than oral form.

In Jewish history, the most reliable means of upward mobility has been the intellectual mastery of traditional texts, a process demanding a prodigious aptitude for abstract thinking.[76] Keenness of mind, sharpened by lifelong study, allowed a student to penetrate and untangle the most complicated textual knots.[77] Formal learning began when a boy was very young and his family sent him to a school (or a tutor) for daily study.[78] His early education required absorbing traditions from family and teachers, an endeavor that forms the center of his young life. Boys typically started at the age of three, spending most of their waking hours in school for the next few years. The boy was no longer free to run and play, except during the brief time he was not at school or in his home.

From eight to six, five days a week, plus half a day on Friday he sat in a small, poorly furnished room in the teacher's home, crowded with fifteen or twenty other boys of assorted ages.[79] The students left home every morning in the dark and returned in the dark, often carrying paper lanterns to light their way. Boys of ten or eleven began studying the principal codes of Jewish legal discourse. Here the student displayed the quality of his memory while spending long hours explicating a difficult problem with aptness and insight.[80] This school of higher learning was (and is) called a *yeshiva*. Testifying to their importance, the various towns and cities assumed the burden of supporting not only the *yeshiva* academy itself, but each individual student as well. Additionally, families in the community undertook the responsibility of feeding one or more students for as many days a week as they could afford.[81]

But even a boy who left school at ten, before the *yeshiva* years, had at least received seven years (of twelve-hour days) of learning.[82] The brightest students parlayed their scholarly reputations into financially supported marriages, a strategy enabling them to continue their regimen of intensive daily study.[83] Those greatest in Torah knowledge are said to have earned great prestige,[84] reflected by the deference they received from lesser scholars.[85] But, on the other side of things, since scholarly competition between students can be intense, those who do not achieve splendidly suffer the indignity of intellectual mediocrity, no small matter in Jewish culture.[86]

To be poorly educated in the Tradition has the consequence of diminished quality of marital success, as the Talmud warns:

> Rabbi Meir used to say, "Anyone who marries his daughter to an unlearned and unobservant man can be said to have tied her up and set her down in front of a lion. For just as a lion steps on its prey, then eats it and has no shame, so does an unlearned and unobservant man hit his wife, then lie with her and feel no shame."[87]

Keeping Them Sharp: A *Drash* (Interpretation) on the Maintenance of Tradition

The *Shema*, a principal prayer in Hebrew liturgy, suggests a metaphor for maintaining tradition in Jewish life. In the first paragraph, we find the command *v'shinantam l'vanekha*, generally translated as "and you should teach them diligently to your children."[88] But the next paragraph of the *Shema* includes a command, which, in translation, is virtually identical: "and you shall teach them to your children" (*v'limad'tem otam et b'neikhem*).[89] Why would the *Shema* need to state this requirement twice? A possible answer is that each is, in fact, a different kind of requirement. Regarding the first case, when the root for *v'shinantam* is used in the Bible, it has nothing to do per se with "teaching."[90] In those passages, the root שׁ-נ-נ (*sh-n-n*) refers to a sharp object or the condition of sharpness.[91] A closely related root, שׁ-נ-ה (*sh-n-h*), means "to repeat."[92] So the more accurate translation of *v'shinantam l'vanekha*, "and you shall sharpen them repeatedly for your children," is one that invites further explication. Let me suggest that the object to be "sharpened" for children (descendants) is the Tradition itself in all its complexity. The "sharpening" process can be interpreted as "fortifying [the Judaic] will and stimulating the creativity to overcome"[93] challenges inherent in the maintenance of tradition. It can also mean that the Tradition should be guarded against "weakening compromises and subjective expediencies,"[94] such as politically driven innovations.

Picture a knife that, because it is in regular use, must be continually sharpened. If the blade is not whetted properly, dullness soon makes the knife less efficient. But since sharpness makes a knife not only more functional but also more dangerous, it must be handled with great care. So it is with Torah traditions: in every generation, they are best conveyed by personal example and the careful rendering of complex religious texts by highly skilled teachers to the sharpest students.[95] Just as friction is needed to sharpen the knife, so too the learning of tradition is undertaken in disputation-filled school environments characterized by competing interpretations within the text and between the students.[96] *Yeshiva* learning is often characterized as *pilpul*, a derivative of the root for "pepper." This connotes that Talmud study is meant to be sharp and spicy. Following is an accurate depiction of a *chevruta* relationship (a pair of traditional students who study together the majority of most every day):

After a couple of days Hershele couldn't take it anymore. He betook himself to Moyshele in all his glory, intent on teaching him a lesson. Choose your *Gemore*[97]—and they'd see who came out on top. The war between them was begun; each belabored the other with difficult questions. Hershele got worked up, threw himself about, twisting his limbs in every direction. Moyshele, on the other hand, wriggled out of everything, refuted all of Hershele's questions coolly and calmly, and the upshot was: they were friends.[98]

It is precisely the wealth of contradictory views, often expressed confrontationally, that is expressed and affirmed *within* the Tradition.[99] How lofty is the stature given to Torah study? Rav Shmuel bar Marsa proposes it to be more important than rebuilding the Temple or honoring parents. R. Yosef said it is even more important than saving lives (if the threat to life is not immediate).[100] The competitive "friction" between scholars, one of whom chooses to pursue wealth and the other a life of *yeshiva* learning, is found in the Talmudic tale of Ilfa and R. Yochanan.[101]

Although the religious identity of other peoples relied mainly on territory, Diaspora Jewish communities stressed intelligence demonstrated by the command of religious texts.[102] The man of outstanding learning enjoys high prestige in the community. At social gatherings, he is accorded the best place—the host will insist on seating him at the head of the table. At family feasts, he will be served first.[103] Promoting textual study and mastery meant Jewish literacy rates were substantially higher than those of non-Jews among whom they lived.[104] In addition, traditional skills that were costly to acquire have had the effect over time of enabling coreligionists all over the world to identify as codescendants. Persistence of the Tradition implies that acceptance of ancestral influence has occurred.[105] Familiarity has equipped Jews to identify their common ancestry and communicate a willingness to cooperate in common endeavors. For instance, Judaic "markers" have promoted the trust that has facilitated the internationalization of trade in which Jews have played so prominent a role.

Orthodox (traditional) Judaism assumes that scholarly innovations made by the most highly respected contemporary Rabbis were implicit in that which God delivered to Moses at Sinai. For traditional Jews, the religious texts constitute a redacted consensus, an inheritance derived "from time immemorial." Interestingly, due to a paucity of textual support in the Bible, some traditions are characterized as mountains "hanging by a hair." Despite minimal precedence, these traditions are considered just as authoritative and enforceable as those with much stronger textual support.[106]

When each generation "sharpens" the traditions,[107] the process is viewed as an intrinsic one, beyond the influence of non-Judaic, modernistic perspectives. Tradition-centered Judaism is text-centered, maintaining the authority and integrity of the text as revealed and interpreted.[108] The transmission of traditional, textual knowledge from one generation to another is called *masorah*. The less tradition-centered movements,[109] to varying degrees, modify or eliminate traditional elements in an effort to ameliorate contemporary needs and sensibilities. As a result, the "newer" movements are different from the more traditional Judaism of our focus because they allow nontraditional needs to heavily influence their theological decision making. Modernizing denominations view the traditional texts and obligations as less authoritative in their construction of Judaism, with congregants often accepting the "aroma" of tradition as religiously sufficient. But virtually all Judaic movements nevertheless consider at least portions of the Tradition authoritative—the difference between the movements lies in the interpretive latitude taken by their respective rabbis.

Religious ritual is one of the very best examples of traditional behavior. Barbara King describes the essential characteristic of ritual: "Ritual in humans cannot be performed in any old way, according to individual whim or desire; it unfolds according to precise rules devised by the community."[110] Ritual's formality precludes it from being essentially creative, although impromptu elements may be added according to traditional styles of innovation.[111] Ritual acquires its naturalistic force from the conscious choice of community members to submit their bodies and resources to its cooperative influence.[112] Thus traditions, by definition, can never be wholly new; communities will accept as authoritative only slight modifications of existing ones. In this particular, generating tradition is similar biologically to speciation, in which new species emerge by adaptation from existing ones. In Darwinian selection, the emergence of a species requires a number of antecedent phases.

In ritual's convergent display by a set of individuals, "making it up as you go along" would eliminate ritual's commanding presence coming from its predetermined content and style. In addition, a ritual's "truth" or "falsity" is irrelevant to practitioners; in communities where tradition is authoritative, ritual value is found in communal acceptance.[113] As is elaborated in the chapter on Judaic sacrificing, rituals may be malfunctional *by design* in the strictest sense when valuables are donated for deliberate and public wasting. And from what source comes the power of traditional rituals? From the forcefulness, we argue, of common ancestry—tradition is a constant reminder that blood (literally and metaphorically) is thicker than water. The claim of identity—we are *us* and not *them*—constitutes a communal oneness reinforced by unique traditions inherited from unique ancestors.

In Judaism, religious rituals are expressed in traditional garb, including learning, praying, and social relations. Like the performance of other *mitzvot,* ritual is never spontaneous or inventive; rather, its forms communicate the community's traditional ways. It is also true that the prayer services, especially the liturgical chants and melodies, have been much more amenable to alteration over the centuries than the traditional texts.[114] The "borrowing" of popular tunes from non-Judaic sources and incorporating them into the religious liturgy has been common in Jewish history. But, since the widespread availability of prayer books, the prayer texts and modalities of expression have reliably retained their traditional styling, because "wording" is given much heavier weight in the Tradition than melody.

Questioning the technical *usefulness* of tradition to a community is quite pointless—the existence of codescendants cooperating traditionally is a necessary precondition for *achieving* community in the first place. If an analogy were made comparing communities to brick houses, individual lineages make up the genealogical "bricks," and traditions are the socially constructed "mortar" holding them together across generations. Although its traditions are self-evidently justifiable to a *particular* community, outsiders may consider some of them inhumane from a *universalist* perspective, even though the majority of traditions would be considered morally innocuous. Additionally, whether a tradition conforms to a universal moral standard is of concern only to nonmembers who judge the tradition's "content" from a cultural distance. For example, whether Judaic circumcision is morally justifiable to non-Jews is irrelevant to Jewish parents who decide if their son will bear the physical mark of communal obligation. The transgenerational stability of traditional communities inevitably will run counter to modernity, in which individuality (freedom from traditional constraints) reigns supreme.

When thinking about religious tradition, although ritual is the first to come to mind, there are many other examples of living collective memory. Time-tested ways of combining and preparing foods are called recipes, so a suite of traditions can be thought of as a recipe for communal maintenance.[115] The Bible goes into great detail describing the "recipes" for preparing animals, bread, flour, oil, and spices as ingredients in Temple sacrificing. Etymologically (like a tradition), a "recipe" is a fixed order of knowledge *received* from previous generations. Recipes for holiday foods have achieved traditional status and, as a result, are touted as *authentic*. Although Jewish communities have a wide variety of traditional recipes, some, such as wine and *challah* (bread) on Shabbat, along with *matzah*, bitter herbs, and *charoset*, exhibited and eaten at the Passover *seder*, are religiously mandated. Other foods traditionally linked to holidays include apples (or bread) and honey on Rosh Hashanah, dairy dishes for *Shavuot*, fresh fruits for *Sukkot* and *Tu B'Shvat*, foods cooked in oil for Chanukah, "ear-shaped" cookies (*hamantashen*) for Purim, and roasted meat for Passover (most Jews of Spanish descent). But beyond specific traditional foods, there is a necessary ingredient that harmonizes flavors Judaically:

> Jews' food on [Sabbath and holidays] has a taste of its own. According to our holy sages, there is a spice in it called *Shabbes*. This spice, which grows nowhere in the world, which can't be bought for the finest gold and is unknown to all other peoples—every Friday holy angels bring this spice direct from the Garden of Eden to the house of every Jew, where they, as we say, help cook the *tsholent*.[116]

Comedian Jackie Mason says that when a Jew enters a Jewish delicatessen, he struts in like he owns the place. Eating an early breakfast recently in a well-known Houston deli, I casually asked the unoccupied owner, "So how's business?" Despite the fact that the owner did not know me from Adam, I nonetheless received a detailed analysis of his restaurant's cyclical operations, including a business forecast for the coming year. Why did the owner talk to me like a person of trust? The answer is that Jewish delicatessens are purveyors of traditional (Ashkenazic) food in a traditional deli ambience,[117] and the Jewish customer is assumed in some way to have a stake in the business! Deli owner and customer, each from his own side of the counter, participate in the "sharing" of traditional food and business information.[118] Overeating at the deli (and elsewhere) is also considered traditional—for that reason, portions are gargantuan. Who else but a traditional, metaphorical "partner" should merit an overstuffed pastrami sandwich that is too big to be eaten by a single person!

Modern Implications of Judaic Traditionalism

Living a modern life necessarily includes a concomitant "tradition deficiency." Modern lives are characterized by living among the fragments of past moralities combined with an unwillingness to be much influenced by ancestors. Where individualism dominates the *zeitgeist* (spirit of the age), tradition is often seen as an irksome burden whose force should be escaped whenever possible. It is supposed that rationalism-progressivism stands on one side opposed by traditionalism-superstition on the other. Being "true to oneself" seems to imply the discovery of a "self" uncontaminated by the influence of ancestors. Yet our predecessors who lived traditionally were not fundamentally different from us as human beings, their living descendants. Although over the years circumstances of life have changed and individualism has become attractive and pervasive, is there necessarily a net gain when modernity devalues traditional obligations, thereby justifying "throwing out the baby with the bath water"? This chapter does not seek to answer this transcendent question. But it is our intention to convey the potential evolutionary benefit of adhering to the traditional wisdom of those who came before, a value that has been central to Jewish life over the millennia. Biologically speaking, we propose that traditionalism has been selected for in human history because of its track record in relative descendant-leaving success.

The many Jewish traditions practiced in diverse communities did not, of course, remain unchanged over the generations. When change occurs it is, of necessity, so slow as to be imperceptible to the self-selected "guardians" of the Tradition. By perceiving constancy, the authenticity of every generation's religious consensus remains intact. Even the recent, non-Orthodox movements like Conservative and Reform Judaism select for observance elements from that same Tradition to ensure Judaic authenticity. When a particular practice is perceived as having gone too far, it faces rejection by traditional Jews and its sustainability is placed in question. Today, for example, the movement to promote full egalitarianism of rabbis in ritual leadership is a point of major disagreement between traditional and modernized Jews. Another deviation, Messianic Judaism (that accepts Jesus as Messiah), is considered unacceptable by all Jews even if many messianic practices conform to traditional Judaic standards. Rejection of Jesus has been one of the most stringently enforced Jewish traditions over the past 2,000 years.

In the Jewish religious world, Orthodox Judaism is considered the most tradition-infused environment for prayer, study, and celebrating holidays. As a recent multidenominational study reports:

> The traditionalism ... among the Orthodox is readily apparent. They join synagogues earlier in their adulthood ... than do members of other denominations. They score

higher than others on all conventional measures of Jewish engagement [such as] going to services, seeing being Jewish as very important and marrying a Jew. Being Jewishly involved for the Orthodox is more of a life-long and all-embracing commitment.[119]

As Modern Orthodox Rabbi Norman Lamm tells us about maintaining traditions in modernizing environments, "legitimate challenges to precedent and earlier authority must itself be authoritative ... [i.e.,] those accepted by generations of observant Jewry."[120] Arnold Eisen, head of a Conservative rabbinic seminary, acknowledges that a ritual will be embraced by the community only if "its roots are sunk into the tradition of our ancestors."[121] In its brief history, Reform Judaism has generally rejected the authority of traditional obligations in both theology and practice.[122]

Endemic to the nature of tradition is that each generation of elders waxes eloquent about the past and deprecates the present as morally adrift. Extolling the "good old days" reflects a claim that our traditional ethic is free from historical relativity. Even among those for whom youthfulness is a lifelong pursuit, there is a sense that some things like trees, antiques, and friends increase in value with age. Why, after all, should a well-preserved antique clock be worth so much more than a better-functioning, modern one? Why is "old-time religion" considered more authentic than religion of recent origin? "Time-honored" often modifies the word *tradition,* and *nostalgia* can mean the longing for tradition lost or forgotten. In an attempt to conjure up religiosity, "New Age" romantic primitivism uses pieces of tribal ethnographies and vivid imaginations to fill the void of tradition-starved lives. Needless to say, nontraditional religious claims and infrequently observed ritual practices seldom last more than a generation and, most often, are of much shorter duration. In our day, the idealized "traditional community" is noticed most often by those who are aware of its absence in their own lives.

Conclusion

Tradition is simply knowledge and behavior accepted on the authority of elders and ancestors, a cultural patrimony bequeathed to posterity. As such, tradition is *incorporated* knowledge that underpins social life. Included also are *restrictions* on behaviors, violations of which will incur the disfavor of coreligionists. The Jewish people are said to be besieged twenty-four hours a day by a variety of ancestral agents (spirits and demons) that take retribution against those who violate law and custom. As Rav Huna says, "Every one of us has a thousand of them to his left and ten thousand to his right,"[123] a condition that can be ameliorated by practices such as "pushing off" the evil eye.[124] Could the multigenerational Judaic system long endure if the generations based their relationship with one another only on fawning admiration?[125] Descendants who are *fearful* of transgressing their ancestors' ways are, in the end, less likely to do so.

Observant Jews not only *keep* the Tradition, but are also *kept together* by it. A well-known talmudic story depicts Judaism's multigenerational strategy. R. Yochanan relates an anecdote:

> One day while Choni was on the road he saw a certain man planting a carob tree. Choni asked him, "How many years does it take for this carob tree to bear fruit?" The man answered Choni, "Seventy years." Choni said to him, "Is it clear to you that you will live another seventy years?" He said to Choni, "I found a world with fully grown carob trees. Just as my ancestors planted those trees for me knowing they themselves would never live to see them fully grown, so I plant them for my descendants."[126]

As Wieseltier comments, "Over the generations, the saga of family is also the saga of tradition. Kinship is stewardship."[127]

"The chain of Torah tradition is an unbroken one. From generation to generation the Jewish people have kept the ancient teachings alive."[128] The phrase "chain of tradition," so well-known in Jewish circles, can be understood in two ways: first, generations keeping the Tradition can be compared to the links in a chain that hold together only if each individual link remains strong. Second, received tradition as a whole can be seen as an unbroken chain, binding each generation to its task of guarding (observing) the inherited set of obligations. Hoping to become an influential ancestor himself, each individual descendant strives to cooperate with codescendants so the traditions can be of benefit during his lifetime and long after his life is only a memory. The Talmud declares that when a deceased scholar's teaching is quoted in a succeeding generation, his lips move as if he were speaking. Thus intergenerational continuity can be characterized as "moving the lips of those who sleep."[129]

Due to the long period of dependence on caretakers, children require substantial investment by parents and others. As a result, a caregiver has the opportunity over many years to influence the knowledge and behavior of offspring and, eventually and indirectly, that of more distant descendants. The biologically successful ancestor's strategy is to influence his or her descendants in future generations to cooperate with one another. I would state the "golden rule" of human evolutionary achievement as follows: "Cooperate with kin and metaphorical kin as you would have them cooperate with you." The medium through which ongoing influence is spread is in the "guarding"[130] of ancestral traditions. But how does a tradition arise in the first place? Answer: by the same means as every biological fact—by descent with infrequent modification.

Like most traditional religions, Judaism is intended to be a complete *way* of life, not just a *slice* of it. For this reason, premodern tribes make no distinction between religious and nonreligious (secular) traditions. In tribal settings, freedom from traditional constraints, as well as individual autonomy in general, does not exist as it does in the modern West.[131] All aspects of life are woven together into a seamless tapestry of customs and mandated behaviors. Elegantly, novelist George Eliot calls traditional behavior our "sweet habits of the blood." Those who are "bursting with descent"[132] live fully linked lives as agents of their ancestors. What they *are to become* is, for the most part, determined by what they *inherit*. They have memories of ancestral ways that are self-actualizing, empowering them to better transmit the traditions to descendants. Tradition has muscle—it seeks to endure by conferring evolutionary advantages on successive generations. The Jewish religion appears to be a good example of traditionalism that actively enables descendant-leaving success.

Notes

1. *Tradition*. (Chicago: University of Chicago Press, 1981, p. 35).
2. Sumner, 2001, p. 5.
3. Frazer, 1979, p. 351.
4. See Coe, 2003; Coe, Palmer, et al., 2005; Palmer, Coe, et al. 2005; VanPool, Palmer, et al., 2008.
5. Hostettler and Huntington, 1996, p. 16.
6. See Avital and Jablonka, 2000.
7. Alcock, 2003, p. 44.
8. See Thornhill and Palmer, 2000, pp. 24–29.
9. Griffiths and Grey, 2001, p. 196; see also Sterelny, 2001, and Oyama, et al., 2001.
10. Alexander, 1974, p. 337.
11. West Eberhard, 1980, p. 186.
12. Dawkins, 1982, p. 184; see also West Eberhard, 1980, p. 186; Palmer and Steadman, 1997; and Palmer, Steadman, et al. 2006.
13. Aristocratic privileges are heritable and replicable; real property, although heritable, is not replicable.
14. Defined here as the influence of heritable, replicable elements on their own frequency in succeeding generations.
15. Hayek, 2007, pp. 59, 62, 66.
16. Fox, 1983, p. 122.
17. Van den Berghe and Barash, p. 404.
18. Keesing, 1975, pp. 32–33; see also Evans-Pritchard, 1940, p. 29.
19. Palmer and Steadman, 1997.
20. Palmer and Steadman, 1997; Palmer and Coe, 2006.
21. Middleton, 1960, p. 27.
22. Keen, p. 244.
23. Hiatt, 1982, p. 23; see also Elkin, 1964, p. 118.
24. Ilyatjari, p. 4.
25. Boyer, p. 23.
26. Thompson, p. 130.
27. Steadman and Palmer, 1997; Coe, Palmer, et al., 2005; Coe, Aiken, et al., 2006.
28. See Lavenda and Schultz, 2003, p. 72; Levinson, 1996, p. 194.
29. Watanabe and Smuts, 1999, p. 101; see also Palmer, 2005; Palmer and Pomianek, in press.
30. Steadman, Palmer, et al., 1996; see also Steadman and Palmer, 1994.
31. See entirety of Tylor, 1958, for wide-ranging examples.

32. Palmer, Steadman, et al., 2006.
33. See Sosis, Kress, et al., 2007.
34. Baron and Byrne, 1977, pp. 324–325.
35. In earlier times, the "*Gemara*"; in recent times, the "*Masora.*"
36. Initially, Abraham, Isaac, Jacob, Sarah, Rebecca, Rachel, and Leah.
37. Commenting on Jacob's embalming (Gen. 50:2, 10, 13), R' Yochanan suggests in Taanit 5b2 that Jacob does not die because, by his descendants following his tradition, he was redeemed from death. Thus, although we are told specifically that Jacob dies, becoming an influential ancestor saves him from "extinction."
38. Venerated ancestors are called "fathers" (*avot*), but also "ancients" (*kadmoniot*—1 Sam. 24:13 and Job 18:20).
39. In the *Yigdal* hymn, God is referred to as Ancestor (*kadmon l'khol davar*); the word for "ancestor" is *av kadmon*.
40. Obligations are divided into two types, positive and negative *mitzvot* (תעשה- *ta'aseh* and לא תעשה-*lo ta'aseh*).
41. Sumner, 1996, p. 3.
42. "Scientific" study of religion often excludes "tradition" and other "folkloric" (supposedly nonscientific) elements.
43. The Torah is carried on display through the aisles among the congregants before it is opened and read.
44. *Mitnahel.*
45. Referenced in Wieseltier, 1998, p. 257.
46. Soloveitchik, 2002, pp. 71–72.
47. Pes. 116b.
48. Hartman, 1976, p. 181. The other was the giving of the Torah at Sinai.
49. Wisse describes the decentralized nature of rabbinic authority: "[The Rabbis] traded opinions across countries and continents, with the locus of authority shifting according to the intellectual rise and decline of competing centers of learning" (p. 37). Also, see the applicable discussion in Yev. 14a2.
50. See Shabbat 112b, Er. 53a, Taanit 24a-b, Ber. 35b, M.K. 3b2, and Yev. 39b. The Tradition provides physiological evidence of "generational decline." Early on in the history of Talmud study, students were said to remain standing throughout the hours of learning to honor the Torah. But in later generations, Torah study is done while sitting since students are presumed to be weaker.
51. Barkow, 2006, p. 22.
52. "A new tradition: what enchanting words!... [but] what is new cannot survive except as what is old" (Wieseltier, 1998, p. 91).
53. Shils, 1981, p. 15.
54. And vociferously rejected a great many others.
55. *Lashon kadosh,* the holy tongue.
56. Blessed is God who gives [us] sons who can comprehend, delve into, and expound upon [Torah] (Chag. 14b1).
57. In the third paragraph of the Shema, Jews are told twice not only to *remember* them but to *do* them.
58. One with vast traditional knowledge, a *ba'al shmu'ot* ("master of what is heard") is accorded great prestige (Chag. 14a3, n. 35).
59. The pejorative term *ba'al toseph* ("master of excess") applies to one who adds unnecessarily to the *mitzvot*.

60. The progenitors Abraham, Sarah, Isaac, Rebecca, Jacob, Rachel, and Leah. Although the entire Torah was delivered to the Jews by the hand of Moses, he is not considered a venerated *ancestor* as such (B.B. 109b).

61. Statements of the "commandment" are found in Exod. 20:12, Lev. 19:3, and Deut. 5:16.

62. Prov. 1:8, 4:1–4, 4:10–13, 4:20–22, 6:20–22, 7:1–3, and 17:6.

63. For boys, Ephraim and Manasseh; for girls, Sarah, Rebecca, Rachel, and Leah.

64. The Bible relates that Moses *wrote down* the law to permanently measure the compliance of all succeeding generations (Deut. 31:24, 26).

65. Ps. 119:126, referenced by T'murah 14b, Gittin 60a and Taanit 28a.

66. See comment on the pronouncements of Ezekiel in Taanit 17b2. There is a category of Oral Law, used as precedence, called "halakha of Moses from Sinai." These unwritten traditions were nonetheless authoritative for the Talmudic Sages (see, for example, Nazir 56b2).

67. Nyiri, 1995, p. 13.

68. Jacobs, 1995, p. 339.

69. Konner, 2003, p. 1.

70. Ibid., p. 4.

71. Av. Zarah 27b; Yoma 30a, 73b, 84a; Yev. 90b; San. 46a; Nid. 3b, 4b, all referencing Eccl. 10:8 (Avot. I:1).

72. The actual Torah scroll is described as "black fire on white fire"; the "black" refers to the written letters, while the "white" refers to the spaces between them. Thus the "black" reflects the plain meaning of the script, while the "white" represents the available room for ideas that students in each generation bring into the text by interacting with it (Midrash Tan., Gen. 1).

73. Scholem, 1971, pp. 287, 289.

74. Thus a new Torah must be copied from a *kosher* (accurately written) text, not from memory (Meg. 18b3).

75. Meg. 9a2–9b1.

76. Barkow's conclusion, based on his study of the city of Maradi in Niger, does not seem applicable to the Jews: "Peoples who seek prestige primarily in terms of display or religious learning are less likely to prosper economically than those who seek prestige through the long-term accumulation of resources, including skills and education" (Barkow, 2006, p. 36).

77. Zborowski and Herzog, 1995, p. 81.

78. It is the parents' responsibility to educate their children; see Chag. 3a4 commenting on Deut. 31:13.

79. Zoborowski and Herzog, 1995, p. 89.

80. Ibid., p. 97.

81. Ibid., p. 99; for a fictionalized description of the European *yeshiva,* read the novel *Yeshiva* by Chaim Grade. That the *yeshiva* system existed in Jewish communities even at the time of compilation of the *Gemara* is confirmed in Gittin 6a2.

82. Wex, 2005, pp. 101, 102.

83. "[When a father] marries his daughter to a Torah scholar ... Scripture reckons his deed as if he were clinging to the Divine Presence" (Ket. 111b2). For further elaboration of this historical practice, see the chapter "Toward a Sociobiology of the Jews."

84. Those who know "how to thrust and parry in scholarly discussions" (Chag. 14a4).

85. M.K. 16b2–3; Exemplifying the competitive spirit, a mentor admonished his respected pupil by saying, "you have no brain" when the pupil made a particularly poor comment on an issue under discussion (Yev. 9a5, 10a2).

86. Also, a Torah scholar who forsakes his study to pursue trivial matters is held in the greatest disregard, considered like a bird that [foolishly] wanders from its nest (R. Yehudah ben Lakish in Chag. 9b3, commenting on Prov. 27:8).

87. Pes. 49b.
88. Deut. 6:7.
89. Deut. 11:19.
90. Hirsch, 1966, p. 98.
91. Deut. 32:41; Ps. 45:5, 64:3, 73:21, 120:4, 140:3; Prov. 25:18, Isa. 5:28; see Lamm, 2000, pp. 156–157.
92. For example, see Meg. 4a2, 21a3.
93. Soloveitchik, 2002, p. 24. The Rav analogizes *kotzim*, the small lines extending from the top of some letters in the Torah scroll. Since *kotzim* are "thorns" or "difficulties," the view of R. Akiba is that these (sharp) "thorns" are like imposed obstacles that must be overcome in the transmission of Torah knowledge.

94. Hirsch, 1966, p. 99.

95. A teacher calls his student or colleague שינא, (*shinana*-sharp-witted) due to his prodigious analytic ability (R.H. 24b3; Taanit 4a1; Chag. 15b3; Ket. 12b2, 14a1, 53a1).

96. Note R. Chanina referring to Prov. 27:17—students' minds are sharpened by debating each other (Taanit 7a2). He who excels in competitive scholarly pyrotechnics has been called *oker horim*, an "uprooter of mountains" (Zborowski and Herzog, 1995, p. 73).

97. A particular topic of discussion in the sacred text.

98. Abramovitsh, 2003, p. 66. One who is acute in this process is said to have *kharif*, or pungency. *Yeshiva* study is competitive by design (Nazir 49b2). Students who study Torah daily concomitantly acquire cunning (Sotah 21b1).

99. Scholem, 1971, p. 290.
100. Meg. 16b4.
101. Taanit 21a1.
102. "In any community that adheres strictly to the Tradition, some men are always engaged in fulfilling the divinely decreed obligation of study. If his occupation does not permit a Jew to devote himself entirely to learning, he may study in the morning before work, or in the evening, or devote at least one day a week—the Sabbath—to study. Not all of them do so, but those who do are recognized as living up to the traditional pattern" (Zborowski and Herzog, 1995, p. 72).

103. Ibid., p. 80.
104. Konner, 2003, p. 196.
105. Coe, 2003, p. 229.
106. Gemara (Chag. 10b2) elaborating on the Mishna (Chag. 10a1).
107. The Talmud compliments Rav Yosef, whose dexterity in deciding matters of law is "sharp as a knife" (Yev. 122a1).
108. Yiddish has an expression for deflating someone else's argument, "*A vue shtet geschreiber*" ("Who says so?"; literally, "Where is it *written*?").
109. Including Conservative, Reform, Reconstructionist, Renewal, and Post-Denominational.
110. King, 2007, p. 56.

111. Rappaport, 1979, p. 175. Also note Rabbi Kushner's comments in Feinstein, 2007, p. 137.
112. Burkert, 1996, p. 75.
113. Gruenwald, 2003, p. 195; Harris, 2005 refers to traditional rituals as "habits of the heart."
114. The wording of Judaism's liturgy should remain relatively fixed according to *matbea shel t'fila*. This principle conjures up the image of a series of coins (prayers) stamped uniformly with the same well-accepted image.
115. See Harris, 2005.
116. *The* traditional Ashkenazic Sabbath dish; from Abramovitsh, 2003, p. 68.
117. In strict compliance with traditional deli culture, the walls are lined with signed pictures and caricatures of Jewish show business icons, a pantheon of American Jewish demigods.
118. Retail businesses owned and run by Jews, delicatessens or otherwise, might all be considered a "traditional" living.
119. Cohen, 2006, p. 11.
120. Lamm, 1990, p. 98.
121. Eisen, 1998, pp. 259–261.
122. See Wisse's description of the back-and-forth early rejection followed by modern-day acceptance of some traditional Hebrew in Reform liturgical practice (p. 40).
123. Bra. 6a.
124. *Keynehore*, "no evil eye," an expression that must be uttered following any compliment.
125. Wieseltier, 1998, p. 325.
126. Taanit 23a3.
127. 1998, p. 144.
128. Kleiman, 2004, p. 141.
129. Yev. 97a1.
130. *Shmirah*.
131. Sandall, 2001, p. 103.
132. Wieseltier, 1998, p. 584.

References

Abromovitsh, S. Y. (Mendele Mokher Sforim). 2003. *The Wishing Ring*. Syracuse, NY: Syracuse University Press.
Alcock, J. 2003. *The Triumph of Sociobiology*. New York: Oxford University Press.
Alexander, R. D. 1974. The evolution of social behavior. *Annals of Ecology and Systematics Reviews* 5:325–384.
Avital, E., and Jablonka, E. 2000. *Animal Traditions: Behavioural Inheritance and Evolution*. Cambridge: Cambridge University Press.
Barkow, J. H. 2006. Introduction: sometimes the bus does wait. In J. H. Barkow, ed., *Missing the Revolution* (pp. 3–59). New York: Oxford University Press.
Baron, R. A., and Byrne, D. 1977. *Social Psychology*. New York: Allyn and Bacon.
Burkert, W. 1996. *Creation of the Sacred*. Cambridge: Harvard University Press.
Coe, K. 2003. *The Ancestress Hypothesis*. New Brunswick, NJ: Rutgers University Press.
Coe, K., Aiken, N., et al. 2006. Once upon a time: ancestors and the evolutionary significance of stories. *Anthropological Forum* 16(1):21–40.
Coe, K., and Palmer, C. T. 2007. The words of our ancestors: Kinship, tradition, and moral codes. *World Cultures* 16(1):2–27.

Coe, K., Palmer, C., et al. 2005. The role of traditional children's stories in human evolution. *Entelechy: Mind and Culture* 6.
Cohen, S. M. 2006. *S3K Report*. New York: Synagogue S3K Studies Institute.
Dawkins, R. 1982. *The Extended Phenotype*. New York: Oxford University Press.
Eisen, A. M. 1998. *Rethinking Modern Judaism*. Chicago: University of Chicago Press.
Elkin, A. P. 1964. *The Australian Aborigines*. New York: Doubleday.
Evans-Pritchard, E. E. 1940. *The Nuer*. New York: Clarendon.
Feinstein, E., ed. 2007. *Jews and Judaism in the 21st Century*. Woodstock, VT: Jewish Lights.
Fox, R. 1983. *The Red Lamp of Incest*. Notre Dame, IN: University of Notre Dame Press.
Frazer, J. 1979. Sympathetic magic. In W. Lessa and E. Z. Vogt, eds., *Reader in Comparative Religion: An Anthropological Approach*, 4th ed. New York: Harper & Row.
Grade, C. 1976. *Folkways*. Boston: Atheneum Press.
Griffiths, P. E., and Grey, R. D. 2001. Darwinism and developmental systems. In S. Oyama, P. E. Griffiths, et al., eds., *Cycles of Contingency: Developmental Systems and Evolution* (pp. 195–218). Cambridge, MA: MIT Press.
Gruenwald, I. 2003. *Rituals and Ritual Theory in Ancient Israel*. Boston: Brill.
Harris, L. 2005. The future of tradition. *Policy Review* 131.
Hartman, D. 1976. *Maimonides—Torah and Philosophic Quest*. Philadelphia: Jewish Publication Society of America.
Hayek, F. 2007. *The Road to Serfdom*. New York: Routledge.
Hiatt, L. R. 1982. Traditional attitudes to land resources. In R. M. Berndt, ed., *Aboriginal Sites, Rights and Resource Development* (pp. 13–26). Perth: University of Western Australia Press.
Hirsch, S. R. 1966. *Commentary on the Torah—Deuteronomy*, Vol. 6. New York: Judaica Press.
Hostetler, J., and Huntington, G. E. 1996. *The Hutterites of North America*. New York: Harcourt Brace.
Jacobs, L. 1995. *The Jewish Religion*. New York: Oxford University Press.
Keesing, R. M. 1975. *Kin Groups and Social Structure*. New York: Holt, Rinehart and Winston.
King, B. J. 2007. *Evolving God*. New York: Doubleday.
Kleiman, Y. 2004. *DNA and Tradition*. Englewood, NJ: Devora Publishing.
Konner, M. 2003. *Unsettled*. New York: Penguin.
Lamm, N. 1990. *Torah Umadda*. Lanham, Maryland: Jason Aronson.
———. 2000. *The Shema*. Philadelphia: Jewish Publication Society.
Lavenda, R. H., and Schultz, E. A. 2003. *Core Concepts in Cultural Anthropology*. New York: McGraw-Hill.
Levinson, D. 1996. *Religion: A Cross-cultural Dictionary*. New York: Oxford University Press.
Matsuzawa, T. 2008. "Chimpanzee Mind: Studies in the Field and the Laboratory." Kyoto: Plenary Presentation, Conference of the Human Behavior and Evolution Society.
Middleton, J. 1960. *Lugbara Religion*. New York: Oxford University Press.
Nyiri, C. J. 1995. Notes towards a theory of traditions. In C. J. Nyiri, ed., *Tradition, Proceedings of an International Research Workshop at IFK*. Wien.
Oyama, S., Griffiths, P. E., et al., eds. 2001. *Cycles of Contingency: Developmental Systems and Evolution*. Cambridge, MA: MIT Press.
Palmer, C. T. 2005. Mummers and moshers: a comparison of two rituals of trust in changing social environments. *Ethnology* 44(2):147–166.

Palmer, C. T., Coe, K., et al. 2005. Comment on "The large cutting tools from the South African Acheulean and the question of social traditions," by McNabb, J., F. Binyon, and L. Hazelwood. *Current Anthropology* 46(3):459–460.

Palmer, C. T., and Steadman, L. B. 1997. Human kinship as a descendant-leaving strategy: a solution to an evolutionary puzzle. *Journal of Social Evolutionary Systems* 20(1):39–51.

Palmer, C. T., Steadman, L., et al. 2005. Comment on "Restaging the Will to Believe: Religious Pluralism, Anti-Syncretism, and the Problem of Belief," by Thomas G. Kirsch. *American Anthropologist* 107(2):319.

Palmer, C. T., Steadman, L. B., et al. 2006. More kin: an effect of the tradition of marriage. *Structure and Dynamics* 1(2):1–16.

Rappaport, R. A. 1979. *Ecology, Meaning and Religion*. Berkeley: North Atlantic Books.

Sandall, R. 2001. *The Culture Cult*. Boulder, CO: Westview Press.

Scholem, G. 1971. *The Messianic Idea in Judaism*. New York: Schocken Books.

Shils, E. 1981. *Tradition*. Chicago: University of Chicago Press.

Soloveitchik, J. B. 2002. *The Rav Speaks*. New York: Judaica Press.

Sosis, R., Kress, H., et al. 2007. Scars for war: evaluating alternative signaling explanations for cross-cultural variance in ritual costs. *Evolution and Human Behavior* 28:234–247.

Steadman, L., and Palmer, C. T. 1994. Visiting dead ancestors: shamans as interpreters of religious traditions. *Zygon* 29:173–189.

Steadman, L., Palmer, C. T., et al. 1996. The universality of ancestor worship. *Ethnology* 35(1):63–76.

Sterelny, K. 2001. *The Evolution of Agency and Other Essays*. Cambridge: Cambridge University Press.

Sumner, W. G. 1996. *Folkways*. Boston: Ginn and Company.

Thornhill, R., and Palmer, C. T. 2000. *A Natural History of Rape*. Cambridge, MA: MIT Press.

Tylor, E. B. 1958. *Religion in Primitive Culture*. New York: HarperTorchbooks.

VanPool, T., Palmer, C. T., et al. 2008. Horned serpents, tradition, and the tapestry of culture. In M. O'Brien, ed. *Cultural Transmission in Archaeology* (pp. 77–90). Washington, DC: SAA Press.

Watanabe, J. M., and Smuts, B. B. 1999. Explaining religion without explaining it away: trust, truth, and the evolution of cooperation. In R. A. Rappaport, ed., *The Obvious Aspects of Ritual. Ecologies for Tomorrow: Reading Rappaport Today*. Contemporary Issues Forum. Ed. Aletta Biersack. *American Anthropologist* 101(1):98–112.

West Eberhard, M. J. 1975. The evolution of social behaviour by kin selection. *The Quarterly Review of Biology* 50(1), pp. 1–33.

Wex, M. 2005. *Born to Kvetch*. New York: St. Martin's Press.

Whitten, A., Horner, V., et al. 2003. Cultural panthropology. *Evolutionary Anthropology* 12:92–105.

Wieseltier, L. 1998. *Kaddish*. New York: Vintage Books.

Wisse, R R. 2007. *Jews and Power*. New York: Nextbook-Schocken.

Zborowski, M., and Herzog, E. 1995. *Life Is with People*. New York: Schocken.

Talmudic citations are from Artscroll, The Shottenstein Edition, Mesorah Publications, 2005.

Costly Signaling (Handicap) Theory and Jewish Life

Chapter 8

The Handicap Principle in Human Social Interaction

Amotz Zahavi

Editor's Introduction

The underlying assumption of Zahavi's theory of biological communication is that there are exceptional situations in which individual organisms can benefit by signaling one another. This is the case when the information exchange contains vital information helpful for the survival and/or reproduction of both the sender and receiver of signals. The theory's assumption is that the sender's signal will be perceived as reliable by the receiver only to the extent of the cost incurred to produce and send the signal. For example, a predator needs to know the condition of potential prey, and prey the immediate intentions of the predator. When males compete with other males, females with other females, or males and females for attention from the opposite sex, signals are sent that facilitate the ability of individuals to "size each other up."

Dr. Zahavi's use of the word handicap *does not refer to "disability" as we commonly understand the word. Rather, in biological context,* handicap *refers to an organism's bodily features and behaviors that appear at first to be wasteful or even dysfunctional. The message sent by an organism displaying its handicap is "I am of such high quality that I function really well despite my inherited or acquired impairments." Among competing individual organisms, higher quality is demonstrated by those who can survive and thrive by overcoming built-in obstacles (handicaps). This elemental communication has been called both "theory of handicaps" and "costly signaling theory."*

I first introduced the term *handicap principle* to explain why peahens prefer those peacocks with the heaviest, most elaborate, and most cumbersome tails. I proposed that the ability of a male to survive in spite of the burden imposed by its tail is a reliable demonstration of its high quality.[1] Therefore, when peahens are choosing mates, they show preference for males with the most extraordinary tails. In the competition between peacocks for access to females, those males with perceived inferior tails and/or functional impairment are judged as inferior in quality and, as a result, experience far fewer mating opportunities than their high-quality competitors. Later, experiments verified that males with the heaviest tails were chosen more often by females and produced more offspring.[2]

Social science has started using the handicap principle to explore the messages contained in human social interactions and, more specifically, to explain the evolution of rituals and other social displays.[3] I welcome the attempt in the present volume to apply the handicap principle to Judaic behaviors that reliably and mutually signal important information to participants in Jewish communal observances.

In this introductory chapter to this section, my goal is to describe the biological meaning of handicaps. Communication is a social act involving at least one signaler and one receiver. Additional individuals are often involved as potential signalers, competing for the attention of one or more receivers. In order to be biologically stable over successive generations, communication generally has to be advantageous to both signaler and receiver. An individual benefits from signaling if the signal influences the behavior of the receiver in a way that would benefit the interests of the signaler. A receiver may benefit from reacting to a signal if the signal contains useful information otherwise not apparent. However, since deception in signals would serve the signaler but not the receiver, evolution will predictably select receivers who pay attention only to reliable signals and ignore the unreliable (deceptive) ones. The mechanism by which a signaler can ensure the reliability of the encoded message is one in which the advertised signal itself handicaps the signaler. The investment in such handicaps should be affordable for honest signalers and unaffordable for cheaters. Thus, although the handicap principle was formulated to explain the evolution of extravagant signals of mate choice, it can just as easily ensure the reliability of any other system of biological communication.[4] Signalers may burden themselves with handicaps in order to increase their biological fitness relative to competitors who cannot sustain such handicaps. As such, an individual who takes on a reasonable handicap is like a businessperson investing in advertising: as a risky expenditure, the advertisement may lead to gain or loss, depending on whether the individual "sinks or swims" if the advertising expenditure proves ill-advised.

The costly investment in a signal may be accomplished by various means—wasting time, energy, or resources, or by enhancing body movements, voice, concentration, or physical appearance. However, the message of the signal must be encoded in the signal itself: wealth can be signaled by wasting money, and courage may be displayed by taking risks, but money wasting will not display courage nor risk taking display wealth.

The meaning of a signal may be deciphered according to the receiver's reaction: flexing muscles can be understood as a threat if the receiver retreats. For other receivers, however, the same show of muscles can attract a mate or a collaborator. Therefore, the meaning of a signal can be better comprehended by examining the handicap it entails. Flexing muscles can be a reliable message about the strength and aggressive intentions of the signaler. On the other hand, there are other ways to signal strength: one can display muscles with clothing or decoration ("muscle" shirts or arm bands), or perform a job that requires strength. The investment's costliness is the basic requirement of a biological handicap. Continuing with this example, if every signaler could signal strength under all circumstances, the signal would no longer serve to distinguish between signalers. A signal of the same magnitude should be easier for a higher-qualified individual than for a less qualified one. Having made a costly investment in musculature, a body builder is more credible signaling strength than a weakling attempting the same signal. In fact, if the weakling should attempt to copy the body builder's signal of strength, the weakling would only more explicitly demonstrate his weakness.

Rituals evolve out of the competition among individuals to display their own qualities and facilitate the evaluation process by other individuals.[5] Observers can better judge small but crucial differences among competitors if those competitors first "agree" to display their attributes in a standardized way. Strict display standards are therefore required for all competitions—uniforms are mandatory at sporting events and beauty contests, for example. Uniformity of dress makes it easier for observers to evaluate the quality of the teams or individual contestants. I would interpret ritualization as the process by which these standards for competition evolve.

Why do members of a social group wear a similar, but not identical, style of clothing? One interpretation given by others is that common dress evolved as signals of affiliation to the group, or conformity per se. However, the principle of handicaps suggests that collective modes of dress also evolved out of competition among group members. Their conforming dress reveals to the observer qualitative differences among individuals in body shape and movement. It is relatively easy to recognize the handicap in a cumbersome tail, a pair of heavy antlers, or the investment required to endure and perform well during a four-hour religious ritual. The investment required to execute well a ritual much smaller in scope is harder to perceive. Performing ritual movements in concert with similarly dressed others performing very similar movements serves to facilitate judgments about the observed quality of each participant.

Staring down an opponent, for example, displays threat because fixing one's eyes on the opponent communicates intensity and determination. But when attention is directed specifically at a target, the signaler greatly reduces his or her ability to collect any additional information about what else may be going on around the individual. So to fix gaze in such a situation is a risky tactic, or handicap, if the signaler has not yet decided to fight. If staring does not sufficiently intimidate the opponent and he or she does not submit, the signaler will need to remain aware of the surroundings in case another strategy must be improvised. Staring down an opponent is less risky if one has already decided to fight than if one is hesitating. As a result, vacillation serves to increase the handicap.

Thus, signaling honest and detailed information about one's quality requires handicaps. The same signals that display accurately the superiority of one signaler will display accurately the inferiority of others. So the purpose of the handicap is to help provide reliable information that the receiver needs that would otherwise not be available. Better-quality signalers are less hindered when displaying handicaps than are inferior individuals.

Testing the Social Bond

I explained above why individuals have to take on handicaps to prove the reliability of their signals. But I have discovered recently that individuals also *impose* handicaps on others to extract from them reliable information about themselves.[6] Since 1970 I have been studying the complex social system of the Arabian babbler, a bird species that cooperates in breeding and defending common territory. Babbler behavior in many ways resembles human behavior, including the religious behavior described in the following two chapters. These birds live permanently in small groups that often have fights with neighboring groups. During such fights, a single bird may be attacked by rivals from another group, thereby becoming dependent on members of its own group for help. For this and other reasons, every babbler has to assess daily its social standing; to that end, daily activities include displays that test its own prestige and the group's social bonds. Babblers impose other intragroup handicaps as well: they "encourage" others to clump, dance, play, and preen with them.[7] The response to these impositions varies—sometimes the other bird joins in, but, at other times, it moves away or even responds aggressively. It should be remembered that when accommodating its fellows, these birds "waste" time that might be otherwise spent eating or guarding against predators. Babblers nearly always invite the group to dance in the open, away from the tree canopy, where they are *more* exposed to predatory danger.

My conclusion is that many rituals of affection in animals, as well as humans, test social bonds by requiring mutually risky investments, or handicaps. The investment may be in resources, self-restrictions, and so forth. Social rituals, such as dancing, shaking hands, embracing, or kissing, provide reliable information about the relationship of the interacting parties because of the burden of "getting it right," however large or small, they impose.

Altruism as a Handicap

Perhaps the most important finding in our babbler research was that their altruistic acts are signals.[8] The altruistic act provides information about the quality of the altruist and may also advertise the interest of the altruist to other members of the group, a dynamic discussed by Sosis in the present volume. Babblers perform many complex altruistic behaviors, such as tending to offspring not their own, donating food to others, standing guard when the rest of the group is feeding, participating in fights with neighboring groups, or risking themselves to rescue group members from predators. Altruism is not equally performed by all group members. Dominant individuals may furnish food to subordinates, but subordinates very rarely are seen providing food to dominants. Interestingly, dominants will even interfere with subordinates trying to behave altruistically, such as serving as sentinels,[9] helping to fight rival groups,[10] joining in to mob predators,[11] or donating food.[12]

The competition among babblers to act as altruists and their suppression of the altruistic acts of other birds suggest that the altruist must be gaining directly from his altruism rather than indirectly through its group or kinship ties. If the benefit to the individual were to come by way of its group, there would be no reason for the birds to compete for altruistic opportunities since benefits would have been received anyway. In other words, if group-level selection were occurring, there would be no benefit to the effort required in stifling the altruism of others. My suggestion is that, in social species like babblers and humans, the successful altruist gains by increasing its social prestige. Social prestige, like an invisible peacock's tail, serves to deflate same-sex rivals and attract both same-sex collaborators and opposite-sex mates.[13] Other theories claiming to explain the evolution of altruism, such as group selection, kin selection, or reciprocal altruism, cannot explain why altruism among individuals is so transparently competitive.

Life in a cooperating group is a mixture of common and conflicting interests. Among babblers the *common interest* is the defense of territory against neighboring groups, but it should be remembered that the birds also *compete* over breeding opportunities. Despite the competition to breed, there is very little overt aggression among adult birds of the same group. Intragroup aggression is rendered more costly due to constant monitoring by other group members. Even the winner in a fight may end up wounded or tired, and therefore be vulnerable to aggression by a "fresh" bird poised to take advantage. As a result, conflicts have to be resolved by other means. In babblers as well as people, competitive altruism benefiting subordinate members of the group advertises the high quality of the altruist, replacing overt aggression as the means for resolving conflicts. However, conflicts are ever present, and when altruistic signaling does not resolve them, aggression may suddenly erupt. The result is that babblers that for many years have displayed affection toward one another will nonetheless fight violently until one is either killed or chased from the group.

It is proposed in the following two chapters that, like these birds, people exhibit altruistic religious behaviors because those behavioral traits benefit the individual's survival and descendant-leaving success. In our social species, we "naturally" want to be highly placed in the minds of other people. An effective tactic for judiciously increasing individual prestige, always a scarce commodity, is to take on the handicap of altruistic displays that enhance standing and, subsequently, reproductive success.

Notes

1. Zahavi, 1975.
2. Petrie, Halliday, et al., 1991.
3. Sosis, 2004; Hawkes, 1991; Hawkes and Bliege Bird, 2002; Kohn and Mithen, 1999; Miller, 2000.
4. Zahavi, 1977a; Zahavi and Zahavi, 1997.
5. Zahavi, 1980.
6. Zahavi, 1977b.
7. Ostreiher, 1995; Posis-Francois, Zahavi, et al., 2004; Dattner, 2005.
8. Zahavi, 1977a, 1995.
9. Zahavi and Zahavi, 1997, ch. 12.
10. Berger, 2002.
11. Anava, 1992.
12. Kalishov, Zahavi, et al., 2005.
13. Zahavi, 2003.

References

Anava, A. 1992. The value of mobbing behaviour for the individual babbler. Master's of science thesis, Ben-Gurion University, Negev (Hebrew with English summary).

Berger, H. 2002. Interference and competition while attacking intruder in groups of Arabian babblers. Master's of science thesis, Tel-Aviv University (Hebrew with English summary).

Dattner, A. 2005. Allopreening in the Arabian babbler. Master's of science thesis, Tel-Aviv University (Hebrew with English summary).

Hawkes, K. 1991. Showing off: tests of another hypothesis about men's foraging goals. *Ethology and Sociobiology* 12:29–54.

Hawkes, K., and Bliege Bird, R. 2002. Showing off, handicap signaling, and the evolution of men's work. *Evolutionary Anthropology* 11:58–67.

Kalishov, A. Zahavi, A., et al. 2005. Allofeeding in Arabian dabblers (*Turdoides squamiceps*). *Journal of Ornithology* 146:141–150.

Kohn, M., and Mithen, S. 1999. Handaxes: products of sexual selection? *Antiquity* 73:518–525.

Miller, G. F. 2000. *The Mating Mind*. New York: Doubleday.

Ostreiher, R. 1995. Influence of the observer on the frequency of the "morning dance" in the Arabian babbler. *Ethology* 100:320–330.

Petrie, M., Halliday, T., et al. 1991. Peahens prefer peacocks with elaborate trains. *Animal Behaviour* 41:323–331.

Pozis-Francois, O., Zahavi, A., et al. 2004. Social play in Arabian babblers. *Behaviour* 141:425–450.

Sosis, R. 2004. The adaptive value of religious ritual. *American Scientist* 92:166–172.

Zahavi, Amotz. 1975. Mate selection—selection for a handicap. *Journal of Theoretical Biology* 53:205–214.

———. 1977a. Reliability in communication systems and the evolution of altruism. In

C. M. Perrins and B. Stonehouse, eds. *Evolutionary Ecology* (pp. 253–259). London: Macmillan.
———. 1977b. The testing of a bond. *Animal Behaviour* 25:246–247.
———. 1980. Ritualization and the evolution of movement signals. *Behaviour* 72:77–81.
———. 1995. Altruism as a handicap—the limitations of kin selection and reciprocity. *Avian Biology* 26:1–3.
Zahavi, A., and Zahavi, A. 1997. *The Handicap Principle.* New York: Oxford University Press.
Zahavi, Avishag. 2003. Indirect selection and individual selection in sociobiology: my personal views on theories of social behaviour. *Animal Behaviour* 65:859–863.

Chapter 9

Making Biological Sense of Judaic Sacrificing

Rick Goldberg

> When we offer sacrifices to Him ... we ought first to pray for the welfare of all, and, after that, for our own selves [for we are made for fellowship with one another]. He who prefers the common good to his own private good is especially acceptable to God.
> —Flavius Josephus, *Against Apion*, circa C.E. 96

Introduction

When we hear the term *religious sacrifice* we typically associate the sacrificial act with ritualized offerings of appeasement to locally operating supernatural agents. It is the ceremony *itself*, with its donations of produce, animals, or even people, that we think of as "the sacrifice." A systematic study of religious sacrificing, done by Hubert and Mauss, provides a wide-ranging general description of what has been considered, since Victorian times, this primitive, seemingly incomprehensible phenomenon. The purpose of sacrifice, as they describe it, is "to affect the religious state of the [donor] or the object of sacrifice" and a "means of communication between sacred and profane worlds."[1] Although these generalizations may serve to describe sacrificing from a religious perspective, science is helpless to verify the existence or absence of "religious" states, "sacred" worlds, "consecrated" objects, or "religious characters."[2] Explaining sacrifices using terminology of the unverifiable relegates their study to scientific unintelligibility. Supernatural existence and agency, unverifiable by the senses, may be interesting as folklore or powerful from a religious perspective, but they cannot constitute the data for research purporting to be scientific.

Applying costly signaling (handicap) theory to sacrifices, on the other hand, frees us from seeing the costly valuable or the ritual *itself* as the sacrifice. In addition, the sacrificial method and the supernatural agent "receiving" the offering are moved from their position of central focus to the margin. Unlike other approaches, biological theory can suggest a sufficiently predictive, fully functional explanation of this universal activity. This chapter specifies that donations are "sacrificial" when a highly valued possession is publicly surrendered by its owner who, in turn, is rewarded with goodwill and possibly notoriety.[3] Hubert and Mauss do mention that, when sacrificing, an individual "nourishes social forces" by "renouncing property."[4] But, in their view, the effect benefits the social group rather than the individual who donates. Although "nourish" is too vague to qualify as a scientific term, the questions of *who* consecrates an object for sacrifice and *why* this is done are not typically elaborated in the literature on religious sacrificing. The closest social science has come to valuing a "donor-centered" interpretation of sacrifice was proposed in Tylor's abnegation theory, in which "the [sacrifice's] virtue lies in the worshiper's depriving himself of something prized."[5] But Tylor does not attempt a scientific explanation of why a donor would want to give away his possessions to be destroyed or eaten by others.

My claim in this chapter is that the increased status bestowed on the altruist (and, subsequently, his or her descendants) who donates valuable property for a public ritual explains why sacrificing is so common in human populations. That public sacrificing is a net loss to the donor is illusory; a formal donation of property for sacrifice is one way an individual displays his largesse and, thereby, enhances his communal standing. Ritual sacrificing should be considered part of the mix of traditional behaviors. Like all traditions, sacrificing must be copied from ancestors and is always formalized ritualistically. Giving away the wrong valuable at the wrong time and in the wrong (nontraditional) way will degrade rather than enhance one's prestige. When one donates a valuable according to the tradition, although one may do so with reluctance, one may be comforted by the approval of others that confirms one's elevated prestige. Donating inappropriately not only diminishes one's property but also brings derision to the donor.

Upon making the sacrifice, the donor may even markedly alter his physical appearance[6] and change his name[7] to display his enhanced status. Additionally, prestige achieved by the living will likely inure to the benefit of descendants, thereby qualifying sacrificing and other altruistic behavior as multigeneration descendant-leaving strategies. Other factors being equal, those with higher prestige, whether achieved or ascribed, have greater access to reproductive resources. In the historical record, those with prestige produce, on average, greater numbers of children and healthier children who are more likely themselves to reproduce successfully.

In discussing the phenomenon of religious sacrifice scientifically, I will address three issues in novel ways. First, who or what should the word *sacrifice* refer to (i.e., *who* is actually *doing* the sacrificing)? Second, why is it so often the case that the surrendered objects must be *destroyed* (wasted) during the sacrificial event? Finally, if the sacrificed object is not destroyed, why cross-culturally have individuals given up possession of valuable property to be eaten or used beneficially by *unrelated* others? The first task of this chapter is to investigate how the religious scheme called "sacrificing" got its name. To facilitate my approach, religious sacrifice is defined as the contribution of costly possessions by willing donors at culturally sanctioned times and places. A basic theory of biological communication, waste-based costly signaling (handicap) theory, will be used to explain why donors' willingness to furnish valuables for sacrificial rituals improves their prestige-enhanced access to reproductive resources.

Historical Overview of Religious Sacrificing

Human history is replete with sacrificial practices, identified as one of the three most essential elements of religion.[8] Although this chapter does not describe in depth the wide array of human sacrificial practices, a brief introduction to sacrificing as a universal category of social behavior should be helpful.

World folklore is replete with colorful descriptions of ritualized offerings. Sacrifices are performed according to established patterns of daily, monthly, or seasonal events, or on special life-cycle occasions, such as birth, puberty, marriage, and death. The sacrificial act may express homage and veneration or thanksgiving for realized or anticipated good fortune. Sacrifices of expiation are offered to publicly acknowledge and give recompense for transgressions of traditional personal or social arrangements. Humans have been known to sacrifice anything valuable; rituals have included the killing of living things, ruining by being left exposed, pouring out on[9] or burying in the ground, or burning up.

The Paleolithic evidence for sacrifice is unclear, but it has been observed in both pastoral and agricultural societies.[10] Ancient Greece used a variety of occasions for sacrificial ceremonies, including drought, weddings, and death. In Roman times, as a requirement of the agricultural cycle, offerings of newly harvested grain were dumped on the ground to rot as a "gift-exchange with the gods."[11] India's Vedic religion has a highly developed set of sacrificial rituals detailed in the Brahmanic texts. Child sacrifice, along with that of adolescent females in the form of sacred harlotry, was reported by Sumner.[12] The Maya and Aztec practiced a bloody version of ritualized human sacrifice.[13] According to Evans-Pritchard[14] the Nuer people made sacrificial offerings on many occasions to encourage successful outcomes. Afro-Caribbean Santería are known for ecstatic rituals that include animal sacrifice. In Christianity's New Testament, Jesus is described as the "sacrificial lamb"; Catholics refer to Mass as "the holy sacrifice" because its performance continues the sacrifice of Jesus at Calvary. In Shiite Islam, ceremonial male self-flagellation mourns the unjust death of the venerated Imam Hussein.

Judaic Sacrificing as Conspicuous Display

My effort to explore a biological approach to sacrificing will use examples from Judaic texts and *mitzvot* (obligated behaviors). The Israelite redemption from Egypt was merited, according to the Rabbis, by two sacrificial practices: the faithful adherence to circumcision of newborns during the servitude and the paschal lamb sacrificed before the Exodus. Ancient Judaism established an array of structured, obligatory sacrifices to be brought for many occasions, including seasonal gatherings at the Temple in Jerusalem. When the Temple was destroyed for the second time in 72 C.E., the ability to perform the sacrifices was terminated. Since rebuilding the Temple in Jerusalem would restore the sacrificial obligations for observant Jews, the reference to Temple sacrificing was removed from the liturgy by modernized Jewish denominations that reject having the sacrifices reinstituted (in a rebuilt Temple) as a central feature of Judaic observance.[15]

Ancient animal sacrificing was conspicuously displayed.[16] The priestly spectacle took place on a raised altar, where the owner gave over his animal for sacrifice by placing his hands on the animal's head *in full public view* so there would be no doubt about whose property was being consecrated for public purpose.[17] In dedicating his animal, the donor leaned with full force on the animal's head and either confessed his sin or praised God, depending on the reason for the offering.[18] The sight and smell of the cooked/burned animals, along with sprayed blood, were also plainly apparent to the community. Grain offerings, such as the springtime *omer* sacrifices, were also displayed to the onlookers by "elevating" the sheaves. Purposefully, the identity of the donors was demonstrably displayed as property was surrendered to the priests at the Temple for slaughter, cooking (and eating),[19] or burning up (immolating as wasting).[20]

The most common biblical term for "sacrifice" is *korban*, a word derived from the root meaning "near."[21] In what way, one might ask, could the root, ב-ר-ק (*k-r-b*), make sense biologically as *sacrifice*? The traditional etymology of *korban* is of a valuable object "brought *near* to God" (through the sacrificial act). Fortunately, for our purposes, the English meaning of *nearness* is similar to that of the Hebrew.[22] In accordance with the biological hermeneutic, a person enhances his prestige by relinquishing (sacrificing) that which is "closely held" and valuable (*near* and *dear* to him).[23] This interpretation may be seen by looking at the language of Leviticus 1:2: "A man who will sacrifice from among you a sacrifice." At first glance, the word structure of this verse appears cumbersome, even flawed. However, R. Schnuer Zalman of Liadi offered the following explanation of the phrase: it was not the sacrifice of the animal or grain itself that God cherished; rather, it was the sacrifice of the person himself ("from among you") that was important. When a person offered a sacrifice, he offered for conversion a part of his very self (of high value *to him*) to fulfill the sacrificial obligation.[24] What is considered sufficiently valuable will, according to public perception, vary from person to person. As a consequence, individuals are required to sacrifice according to their ability to do so.[25]

In the biblical commandments for sacrificing, a time limit for their consumption is often mandated. Those portions of the sacrifice not eaten by the deadline must be burned up on the altar (biologically speaking, wasted). Lest we assume these wasted leftovers were garbage, the Hebrew root י-ת-ר (y-t-r) can mean "valuable excess," "abundant," and "to excel," as well as the "remainder" from a sacrifice.[26] We can therefore infer that the prescribed wasting of useful food was an integral element of the sacrificial ritual. We shall see later how the formalized wasting of valuables can make sense biologically.

Vows and Oaths

Although descriptions of the categories of sacrifice are extensive in Judaic texts, the ceremonial language and/or liturgy performed during the rituals remains relatively unknown. As Gruenwald tells us: "Israelite forms of sacrifice are very sparing in their descriptions of what is actually said during the sacrifices.... Hardly any form of speech is reported in connection with [them]."[27] An exception is the vow, a public or private promissory sacrifice whose performance may depend on a qualifying stipulation.[28] Commenting on Numbers 30, Jacobs understands vows and oaths to be religious offerings: refraining from some enjoyment is a kind of sacrifice to God.[29] Also called votive offerings, vows are put into effect by declaring an object or a set of objects off limits to oneself.[30] In the case of a conditional vow, the potential donor is able to wait for the occurrence of a prespecified benefit before the sacrifice of valuables must be made.[31] Unlike communal rituals of sacrifice, vows are made by individuals at their own instigation,[32] as is the case with the Nazarite vow.[33] According to the Hebrew, he who vows deserves honor because he "separates himself [from others] wondrously by vowing."[34] In the Jewish religious texts vowing is taken very seriously—if one chooses to vow, there are ominous consequences for failure to perform.[35] Where there is any doubt about one's willingness to fulfill the vow, it would be better not to vow in the first place.[36] R' Meir acknowledges a man's great risk in failing to annul his wife's vow by using the simile "like putting a finger between the teeth." By this he refers to getting it bitten, the potentially dangerous sacrifice of one's finger.[37] The inability of a wife to fulfill her vow may sabotage her marriage, and she may be divorced without monetary compensation.[38] One does not have the latitude to subject all desirable outcomes to a vow—vowing in the wrong situations is considered illegal.[39] There is an instance in the Bible when a vow had disastrous consequences: a judge of Israel, Yiftakh, was forced to sacrifice his daughter due to his vow conditioned upon victory in war.[40] The need for forgiveness of incidental and unperformed vows is so grave a matter that it is the basis of the *kol nidrei* appeal to God that opens the *erev* Yom Kippur service.

From a costly signaling perspective, the prestige gained by vowing and completing the vow appropriately is like that of any sacrifice. Vows and oaths are self-imposed, custom-tailored social tests of one's willingness to fulfill the promise to sacrifice. They are individually generated, self-restricting encumbrances to display an individual's quality. When performing as promised, one gains prestige from the successful sacrifice. In a vow subject to condition, if the contingency does not obtain, the promise need not be kept, and the one who vowed neither gains nor loses face. But if the condition is met, prestige will grow only if one makes good on the vow; if the promise is not kept, the one who reneges is stigmatized.[41] The Talmud says when an oath is uttered out loud in front of a quorum of people, it is more enforceable. As such, the oath will be especially status-lowering if abrogated.[42] As a result, taking a vow or an oath is a risky business if, when the time comes, one is unable or unwilling to fulfill it.

The Competitive Sacrifices of Cain and Abel

Often overlooked in this story of fratricide is why each brother's offering competed with the other for God's favor. Was it necessary that God judge one sacrifice as preferable to the other? Neither ancient nor modern commentaries question the text's assumption that it was necessary for the brothers' gifts to compete with one another for God's approval. Yet the useful model brought by the text is that sacrificing, in fact, is often unsolicited and always competitive by nature.

In line with the biblical paradigm, this chapter applies costly signaling theory to explain why sacrificing is an *inherently* competitive phenomenon in which elevated prestige is the reward for value surrendered. Like all costly signals, sacrifices are made under watchful public (and divine) scrutiny. As was the case with Cain, the person offering comparatively less in value is judged harshly. Sacrificing as a contest suggests a different interpretation of Cain's famous rhetorical question, "Am I my brother's keeper?"[43] Since God had just told Cain that, whether he realized it or not, he had been in competition with his brother, why should God then expect him to watch out for Abel, his competitor? So Cain could have seen his murder of Abel as no more than a useful tactic in the adversarial framework previously established by God. In the Talmud, Cain is said to defend himself by arguing that God Himself had implanted the evil desire in him and thus gave him a competitive nature.[44] In Cain's subsequent banishment by God, perhaps the lesson is that, while competitive signaling between people is necessary, each competition has its limits, especially among kinsmen, and murder is outside the limit. Although sibling rivalry is neither unexpected nor immoral,[45] siblicide *is* judged to be punishable. The *midrash* suggests the Cain-Abel narrative is a paradigm for human conflict in general, the basis of violence in general, and of war in particular.[46]

Once God's choice of Abel is made, there are two textual clues as to why Abel's offering was of greater value than Cain's. Abel offered from the *choicest* of *his* flock, while Cain brought edible fruits from the ground.[47] The first important clue is that Abel's offering was a choice *animal*, while Cain's was from uncultivated *plants* growing in the ground. Meat offerings have been more highly valued in all cultures than offerings of plants or fruits.[48] By themselves, Cain and Abel are ideal representatives of the two classic Middle Eastern communities: pastoral nomads and sedentary agriculturalists.⁴⁹ The Midrash⁵⁰ reinforces this notion, when it describes Cain and Abel as dividing up the world between themselves, with Abel taking the movable property (animals) and Cain the immovable property (farmland). Although both ways of life produce necessary foodstuffs, the providers of meat, milk, skins, and wool have traditionally enjoyed higher prestige cross-culturally than those who tend crops. It is no coincidence that the patriarchs of the Jewish people were shepherds and not farmers.⁵¹

So the nomadic-sedentary contrast can provide a reasonable explanation for God's picking Abel's offering over Cain's. Due to its relative scarcity and abundant protein, meat has been the food of choice throughout human history. The preference for meat is common in anthropological literature,⁵² and when meat is on the menu, veggies come in a distant second. Throughout our history, vegetarian diets occur only by default when meat is unavailable. Celebratory feasts without abundant meat are unheard of. Paleoanthropologists now believe the rapid growth of brain size (encephalization) of protohumans and *Homo sapiens* over the past three million years would not have been possible without increasingly plentiful supplies of meat.⁵³

Since Abel was a herder of animals, he started out with a competitive advantage that Cain, a gatherer of edible plants, could not have overcome. Simply put, "choice" animals were more highly prized as sacrifices than grain, oil, or other produce.⁵⁴ As we are told later in the Bible, Esau was the beloved of Isaac because, as a hunter, he provided Isaac with meat.⁵⁵ In formulaically anthropomorphizing God's reaction, scripture repeatedly mentions the "pleasing odor" of meat burning on the sacrificial altar.⁵⁶

The second clue suggested by the text is that Abel's offering was his *own* possession; that of Cain, on the other hand, is not described as being his own. As costly signaling theory would predict, there is no prestige for bringing sacrificial items not one's own, like bringing Mom a bouquet of flowers plucked from a neighbor's garden. Sacrifice requires surrender of valuable property, hence offering ownerless property or property owned by someone else is fruitless.⁵⁷ Isaiah tells us that God "hates stolen goods" offered for sacrifice.⁵⁸ As a consequence, the Rabbis excluded all sacrificial offerings wrongfully obtained by theft or coercion. Insisting that an individual contribute willingly only from his own property, Judaic law intrinsically connects the sacrificial act with an opportunity for increased prestige. Donating one's own goods sends a costly, sacrificial signal that improves status; "donating" someone else's property sends a deceptive signal meriting status denigration.

Covenant "Between the Pieces"

As God promises the Land to Abraham and his descendants, Abraham asks God how his promise can be relied upon.⁵⁹ In modern law, a binding contract requires payment of "consideration," surrendering control of a valuable by one party to the other. Responding to Abraham, God details an enabling ceremony to serve as "consideration" for the Covenant of the Land. God instructs Abraham to bring five animals and cut four of the five into two pieces. Each half of the divided animals was then placed opposite the other corresponding half. It is then that God foretells to a dreaming Abraham the Israelite slavery in Egypt, the emancipation with riches, and the inheritance of the Land. Once darkness falls, Abraham sees a "smoking oven" and "flaming torch" moving between the separated pieces of animals to phenomenologically authenticate both God's future vision of and covenantal obligation with Israel.[60]

Why would God "demonstrate" the Covenant's portent with this substantiation ceremony called "between the pieces"? In the Bible, God's recurrent threat to those who transgress a commandment is to be "cut off from one's lineage."[61] The Hebrew root for "cut," כ-ר-ת (k-r-t), has a parallel etymology in English—an agreement is exe*cut*ed or, colloquially, a deal is *cut*.[62] To formalize this Covenant, exe*cut*ion (sacrificing) of these animals served as the legal consideration binding the two parties.[63]

From a biological point of view, the Covenant was validated by the sacrificial "wasting" of these animals. Having these valuable animals wastefully killed and displayed according to instruction helped to give weight to the agreement struck by God with Abraham and his descendants. As proof, Jeremiah says that God threatens to "waste" the Israelites just like the animals in this ceremony if covenantal obligations are transgressed.[64] Interestingly, the biblical text itself suggests these carcasses were to be wasted because a bird of prey descended to eat from them before darkness enabled the ceremony to take place.[65] There is no mention if, after the ceremony, the animal pieces were put to any beneficial human use. Perhaps the verse implies that, once the rite was over, the buzzards would again descend to "wastefully" scavenge the animals' remains.[66]

Beheading the Heifer for Communal Expiation

Deuteronomy 21 describes the prescriptive rite for expiation from murder when a dead body is found outside a city but nevertheless within the community's jurisdiction. The stated purpose for purchasing and sacrificing the heifer is the absolution of communal bloodguilt for the death due to the community's failure to provide sufficient security for the victim.[67] There are many explanations regarding the purpose of this ceremony, but my biological interpretation focuses on the "wasting" of both the heifer and the valuable land where the ritual was to take place.[68] Maimonides suggests that, to avoid the expense of wasting the animal and making the land unusable, the community should make a greater effort to find the person responsible for the killing. As such, the rite to absolve communal guilt would be unnecessary.[69]

Abraham's Obedient Preparation of Isaac for Sacrifice

Emblematic of sacrificing is that only items of the highest value, such as "first fruits" and "unblemished" animals, are considered appropriate. It should not therefore be incomprehensible that God tests Abraham's willingness to sacrifice Isaac, his "most beloved" and genealogically necessary son.[70] Isaac's lofty value to Abraham is based on both genetic relatedness (nearness) and degree of fatherly love (dearness). The binding of Isaac can be seen biologically as a test of Abraham's readiness to sacrificially waste his most valued possession. The Rabbis speculated that by taking away Isaac for sacrifice, Abraham also sacrificed his relationship with Sarah, his wife, who never forgave him.

In the most commonly accepted interpretation of this story, Maimonides proposes that the intended sacrifice of Isaac was a test of Abraham's love and fear of God. As a corollary, it could be suggested that the upper limit of allowable wastefulness was also delineated here. Although he who sacrifices the most attains the most social prestige (as God fearing), God "tests" Abraham to set the limit of sacrificial wastefulness not only for men but perhaps also for himself. God demonstrates self-limitation in sending a messenger to stay Abraham's knife, thereby allowing Israelite genealogy to continue. Therefore, Abrahamic descendant leaving is shown to be more valuable than sacrificial wasting. Today human sacrifice is regarded as immoral, but that judgment has not been historically self-evident. For thousands of years, in the Middle East and elsewhere, the wasting of captives in sacrificial rituals, including virgins and children, has been well documented.[71] Speaking moralistically (using biological terminology), the "binding of Isaac" teaches that costly signaling in pursuit of prestige for man has a morally restrictive upper limit. To that end, human sacrifice *by humans* is strictly prohibited in Judaic law.[72]

God's Surprising Sacrifice of the Priests Nadav and Avihu

Israel's priestly lineage was established as the patrilineal inheritance of Aaron's descendants. The first three verses of Leviticus 10 tell the brief account of Nadav and Avihu, Aaron's oldest two sons, who were "consumed by heavenly fire." The reason given by the text for their death is the inappropriate offering of "strange fire" while performing their priestly duties. As was apparent in the story of Cain and Abel, sacrificing can be dangerous and competitive and can have serious consequences. In performing to the standard set by God, the young priests' "fire" was judged so harshly that capital punishment resulted.[73]

Throughout the centuries, Jewish sages have expressed discomfort with the "lesson" of this story.[74] What, they ask, could Nadav and Avihu have done to deserve death? For our analysis here, however, the language at the end of Leviticus 10:3 is an insightful formulation for applying costly signaling theory to this incident. After the priests had been killed, Moses "justifies" God's action by repeating God's words: "By My sacrifice [of those *near* to Me] I become holy and before all the people I gain honor." As priestly functionaries, Nadav and Avihu can be seen as among the most valuable of God's human instruments.[75] Although Nadav and Avihu were of high value, their deaths by the hand of God did not bring an end to the Israelite (or the priestly) lineage, as would have been the case had Isaac been sacrificed.

Additionally, when Isaac was "bound" for sacrifice, God had the attention of only Abraham and his household, so a public display wasting Isaac would have had no audience. In contrast, by the time of Nadav and Avihu, public wasting of the two young priests was apparently needed to display God's holiness and honor before the entire people Israel.

As is the case for all sacrifices, only the most valuable possessions are appropriate for "wasting."[76] As the narrative implies, God's holiness and honor are demonstrated by His ability and willingness to waste, according to His judgment, those *nearest* (and dearest) to Him.[77] By this costly and wasteful sacrifice of Aaron's sons, God sends an unmistakably reliable signal to the people of His power and, consequently, His honor.[78]

Another instance of God's public and wasteful display of power takes place later when He visits the ten plagues on the Egyptians. The plagues can be seen as costly signals, communicating God's ability and willingness to "waste" Egyptian property and lives, including those of the Egyptians' firstborn sons.[79] God's momentous manipulation of Pharaoh, the Egyptian "competitor" god, is meant to convincingly demonstrate for all to see God's overwhelming might.[80]

The Yom Kippur "Scapegoat" Sacrifice

During the time of the Tabernacle and Temple, the Atonement Day ritual[81] required two goats to be brought before the priests. One goat was slaughtered and cooked on the altar, while the other had responsibility for the sins of Israel placed "on its head." Once the scapegoat had been burdened with sins, it was driven into the desert to perish.[82]

From a biological perspective, the functions of the two goats are instructive. Although the donor of the first goat sacrifices an animal to benefit the priests, who benefits from the death of the scapegoat? According to the biblical account, the scapegoat is an offering to Azazel, a desert demon.[83] Effectively, no one benefits from the scapegoat's destruction in the desert, and the goat's being "wasted" is exactly the point. The same can be said when, at various times in history, humans have become scapegoats to be blamed and wasted by the powerful. From a costly signaling perspective, sacrificial wasting is an end in itself, demonstrating the ability and willingness of the prestigious to act as wastefully as their prestige allows.

Sacrificing the "Red Heifer": Preparation of Ingredients to Reverse Defilement

In the Israelite camp, when a person came into proximity with a corpse, a state of ritual contamination resulted, and a process of purification was specified. The primary ingredient needed to concoct the mixture for purification was the ashes of an unblemished and never-yoked red heifer.[84] To produce the ashes, the whole animal was completely burned. The immaculate red heifer sacrificed for this purpose was such a rarity that, since biblical times, one has yet to be found and rabbinically authenticated.

This cow was of the highest value due to its flawlessly uniform color. Those who have never made a living in animal husbandry might wonder how a cow could be so highly valued based on appearance alone. Livestock breeders, however, value animals both functionally and aesthetically. The market value of this unique red heifer would not have been based on milk production; rather, like all especially attractive domesticated animals, its worth would reflect its desirability for breeding purposes.[85]

Strictly speaking, turning even a prized cow into ashes could not be considered on its face "wasteful," since the product (ashes) was for a specific use. But one wonders why only the most valuable cow would suffice as the sacrifice. From a costly signaling perspective, reducing to ashes a more ordinary cow would not have been "wasteful" enough. Said another way, wasting anything less than the most valuable of animals would have been, presumably, insufficiently costly.[86]

Judaic Circumcision (*Brit Milah*) as Sacrifice

The Judaic obligation of male circumcision is considered a "covenant in the flesh" between God and the descendants of Abraham. As I previously noted, the Israelite redemption from Egypt was merited, according to the Rabbis, by two sacrifices during their enslavement, one of which was faithful circumcision of newborn males. This embodied initiation is not usually categorized as a sacrifice, but it can make sense to interpret *brit milah* as sacrifice from a biological perspective. The Akedat Yitzhak tells us that *brit milah* served as a "uniform Divine distinctive marking" with the purpose of generating covenantal harmony among Jews.[87] This novel interpretation is that when sacrifice is shared equally, it may become a unifying force (the analysis below of the biblical *cherem* provides another example of the same phenomenon).

Being born of a Jewish mother by itself establishes the boy as Jewish. Judaic circumcision, on the other hand, is the permanent mark of covenantal obligation. Maimonides described the procedure as so difficult and disagreeable (i.e., *sacrificial*) that no parents would subject their son to it unless they sincerely wanted him bound by the Covenant. Removal of the foreskin may be seen as unnecessary, even "wasteful," if it is seen as serving no functional biological purpose. Philo, however, writes that circumcision should be practiced to limit sexual appetite, reminding Jews that intercourse is more for procreation than pleasure. As Bulka adds, Judaism marks this sacrifice convincingly by imprinting the covenantal reminder on the very organ that generates posterity.[88] The Gentiles, say some rabbis, are hypersexual not only because they lack Torah (to help keep desires under control), but also because they retain their foreskins.[89] Thus, as a consequence of circumcision, Jewish males are seen as sacrificing some degree of sexual pleasure to serve a religious purpose. Supporting the view that circumcision is sacrificial, Ehrenreich speculates that "circumcision may well be a remnant of a tradition of human sacrifice, with the foreskin serving as a substitute for the whole [man]."[90] But, like the *cherem* sacrificing of war spoils, the excision of foreskins can be viewed as a unifying influence because this "impairment" is obligatory for all males.

Warrior Reputation: The Costly Display of Male Reproductive Value

Fighting skills have been an important source of male prestige throughout human history. In our polygynous species, males compete with one another for female attention and favors by demonstrating physical prowess in one-on-one battles and as members of fighting units. The psalmist trumpets the warrior's high prestige when advising him, "Gird your sword on your thigh, and be mighty with glory and majesty."[91] A key element in the attainment of high status is the warrior's willingness to risk his well-being by sacrificing to benefit both his fighting comrades and his people. A soldier's reputation is strengthened by his individual performance against the enemy and his willingness to take risks for the sake of his comrades. With prominent warriors, individual display and acquiescence to group morale are bound together so seamlessly that it is difficult to tell where one stops and the other starts. Raids and wars have been most successful, other factors being equal, when camaraderie between fighters has been well established beforehand. A warfare ethic of "one for all and all for one" usually defeats one of "each man for himself." As Pinker writes: "A war party faces the problem of altruism par excellence. Every member has an incentive to cheat by keeping himself out of harm's way and exposing the others to greater risk." But, he concludes, "Bravery and discipline are the obsessions [of successful fighting units]."[92] As a result, a morale-building, risk-sharing attitude among the troops increases the likelihood of victory. Building a spirit of interdependence enhances an army's ability to prevail over less cohesive opponents.[93] When one side has the advantage in battle discipline, triumph is more likely for both high-status sacrificers and low-status cheaters. It is ironic that the descendant-leaving potential of a soldier depends not only on his skills at self-preservation, but also on his self-sacrificial readiness to risk death and contribute to a successful outcome. Why should this be the case?

Forging the Spoils of War: The Biblical *Cherem* Construct as Sacrificial

The prospect of appropriating war booty has always been a primary incentive for warriors to risk life and limb on the battlefield.[94] As Hobbes told us long ago, "[it is] in the nature of man ... [to use] Violence to make themselves Masters of other men's persons, wives, children and chattel."[95] In her study of the ancient Middle East, Lerner writes, "there is overwhelming historical evidence for ... the practice of killing or mutilating male prisoners and for the large scale enslavement and rape of female prisoners."⁹⁶ Veblen placed in cross-cultural context the desire for collecting females: "The accepted evidence of wealth [across cultures] is the possession of many women." He then refers to the practice by victorious warriors of "wife capture from hostile tribes."⁹⁷ According to Torah and *midrash,* the desire for fertile women as reproductive spoils is a basic cause of war.⁹⁸ This notwithstanding (and postbiblically), the talmudic commentary on the Scroll of Esther claims that whenever the Jews attacked their enemies in the king's empire, they did not take any war booty from them.⁹⁹

From an evolutionary perspective, therefore, war has been prosecuted to enhance the well-being of the victors through acquisition of valuable resources, especially women.¹⁰⁰ In our polygynous species, the short-term male reproductive strategy¹⁰¹ reflects the desire for the opportunistic copulations available to conquering armies. Even in modern environments, where polygamy is illegal, a study has shown that soldiers gaining high prestige, such as Medal of Honor winners, are more likely to get married and leave more children than a general sample of World War II veterans.¹⁰²

With the foregoing in mind, let me introduce a religious mandate in which war spoils acquired by the victorious were *required to be given up*. The biblical narration relates that, after having been freed from slavery in Egypt, the Israelite tribes spent forty years of nomadic existence in the Sinai desert. As they were preparing to conquer the Land, Moses receives a divine instruction of constraint: as the conquest proceeds from city to city, Moses selectively *precludes* the Israelite warriors from taking possession of the war spoils (ש-ל-ל or sh-l-l), which were to be reserved for the priests¹⁰³ or totally destroyed. This ban on the seizure of war spoils, called *cherem* (ח-ר-ם), renders them taboo for use by individuals.¹⁰⁴ In addition, prohibited things could not be redeemed by substituting other valuable things.¹⁰⁵ War spoils requiring sacred destruction include, in various instances, captured men, women, children, and domestic animals.¹⁰⁶ Items with precious metals and jewels also had to be surrendered and consigned for destruction.¹⁰⁷ At times a "scorched earth" policy was imposed, requiring destruction of every living thing and all property seized from the conquered.¹⁰⁸

The meaning conveyed by the word *cherem* is that of a sacred thing prohibited for human use.¹⁰⁹ The religious claim implicit in the *cherem* mandate is a war ideology in which the enemy is to be utterly destroyed as an offering to God who made victory possible.¹¹⁰ Before conquest of the Land, God assures Moses that the current inhabitants will be vanquished "because they are *toast*."¹¹¹ In imposing the *cherem,* God requires the Israelites to sacrifice future war spoils as a quid pro quo to ensure successful outcomes. In this sense, my characterizing *cherem* as a sacrifice provides a good fit with costly signaling theory.

The ancient Israelites have not been the only conquerors who surrendered or destroyed war booty. The history of warfare provides numerous examples of ritualistic wasting of valuable war spoils. The Celtic tribes, for example, "not only hanged all captured enemies as sacrificial offerings, but killed their horses, hacked them to pieces, and threw them into a river or lake, along with all the enemies' weapons and gold."[112] Since acquisition of resources like slaves, horses, and gold could significantly enhance fitness, what purpose is served by requiring soldiers to give up war spoils to which they feel entitled after having risked their lives in battle?

Judaic sages and scholars over the millennia have wrestled with the seemingly cruel and arbitrary imperatives of the biblical *cherem*, enforced often without explanation before each of the Land conquests. Why would the purposefully wasteful destruction of people, and, on occasion, crops and other valuables, be "reserved as God's portion"?[113] Ethical justification of *cherem* as a war ideology is outside the scope of this chapter. But a clue to *cherem*'s functional value is given by Niditch, who writes, "To disassociate the Israelite [*cherem*] from ... the concept of *sacrifice* is to ignore the obvious."[114] Another clue: Rav Soloveitchik discussed the *sacrifice* of young Jews who allocate time for Torah study, thereby resisting the temptation to devote their time to learning secular subjects that would lead to greater income.[115] To illustrate his point, he refers to Achan, who sinned by taking forbidden war booty for himself.[116] The Rav's teaching is that, in lands with great economic opportunity, those who immerse themselves in Torah learning *sacrifice* the opportunity for greater wealth, just as Achan should have *sacrificed* the opportunity to take valuable war spoils in compliance with the *cherem* injunction. Following the spirit of these insights, I now undertake to characterize *cherem* and other religious sacrifices as self-imposed, costly signals (handicaps) that reliably communicate a willingness to cooperate within the structure of the larger community.

Sacrifices as Costly Signals of Handicap Communicating Cooperation

Costly signaling theory postulates that the only way communication between living organisms can be reliable is if the signal is recognizably costly. Inherent within the theory is that individuals incur cost and communicate fitness by handicapping themselves in a variety of species-specific ways. The ability to withstand the handicap's cost demonstrates, through the apparent wastefulness of ontogenetic investment, the adaptive value of communicating fitness. Examples include the intricate plumage of peacocks, bright coloration in many poisonous species of reptiles and amphibians, and competitive stotting by individual antelopes in the presence of predators.[117]

Like most social species of animals, interdependent cooperation has always characterized human social behavior. Individual survival is put at risk when cooperative potential is taken for granted and squandered. As a result, each person's willingness to cooperate must be demonstrated often, publicly and repeatedly. Religious sacrificing should be seen as a competitive *and* cooperative activity functioning as altruistic display by individual donors.[118] In all societies, demonstrating altruism according to established cultural standards results in augmented status.[119] Valuables donated for sacrifice must always be the highest in value of their kind, such as animals "without blemish" and "first" fruits.[120] Unwillingness to display altruistically above one's "station" may be status sustaining at best, or stigmatizing at worst. Those who sacrifice reliably according to "the call of duty" accrue the most prestige; those who do so outside the limits of cultural approval are perceived as self-depleting and foolish. Competitive gift giving and ostentatious wasting have been widely practiced in human history; good examples would be rituals like the Native American potlatches. When the Israelite High Priest made an error in judgment, he was required to obtain and donate for his own expiation a bull, the costliest item in the array of Temple sacrifices.[121] Other factors being equal, high prestige enhances an individual's reproductive value and potential descendant-leaving success, the "gold standard" of natural and sexual selection.[122]

Some have suggested that within-group altruism diminishes or even displaces within-group competition, directing competitive urges toward outsiders. Girard, for example, thinks violence in sacrificial ritual takes the place of violent acts that would otherwise be committed against in-group members.[123] More plausible, I would argue, is that within-group altruistic acts, when understood as costly signals, are just as competitive as other forms of fitness display.[124] As a side note, sacrificing of resources to benefit close kin is routinely expected. Grandparents, for example, are much more likely to give nice gifts to their own grandchildren than to the neighbor's grandchildren. For my purposes, prestige-elevating altruistic sacrifice describes the seemingly uncompensated acts that benefit nonkin.

The Adaptive Value of Wasting as Costly Fitness Displays

Although researchers have treated ritualized sacrificing in a variety of ways, no one has placed the phenomenon squarely within the context of overarching biological theory. Social scientists most often define religious sacrifice by referencing the supernatural. By participating in religious sacrifice, according to Durkheim, the "worshipper communes with his god by taking in sacred food, and at the same time he makes an offering to this god."[125] Driver speculates that sacrificial ceremonies are undertaken purely for public performance value and without social function.[126]

Some also propose functional explanations for sacrifice. Burkert's perspective is that sacrificial gift giving in religious history is a transaction of reciprocity. Accordingly, sacrificial offerings are universally perceived as profitable investments, paying back to the donor over time greater returns than the value of the donation.[127] His prime example is that of the sacrificial feast celebrating a successful hunt, in which food sharing functions to reinforce social solidarity.[128] By using the term *acquisition by sacrifice,* Rav Soloveitchik makes the same point.[129] Commenting on the laws of tithing, the Talmud notices that the word *tithe* is doubled in Deuteronomy 14:22. R. Yochanan interprets this to mean that by tithing one becomes wealthy (more than compensated for his gift).[130] Knight reports the existence among many peoples of the "own-kill rule," by which hunters are proscribed from eating animals they themselves have killed. As a result, they are obligated to sacrifice their own needs by first sharing the meat with others. Knight refers to Evans-Pritchard's account of the Neur of Sudan, who "will not kill cattle in order to eat the meat themselves." In the Neur's "own-flesh rule," "an ox slain simply from desire for meat may ... take ghostly vengeance on its slayer."[131] Bataille gets closer to the biological heart of the matter when he concludes that "one sacrifices what is useful" precisely to lift the oblation out of the realm of utility and into the realm of "immanence."[132] Bataille's point can be made intelligible from the scientific perspective if we substitute the biologically loaded term *wastefulness* for his nonscientific term *immanence*.

Without denigrating the explanations by others for religious sacrificing, none are measured by the biological yardstick of potential adaptive value. Breaking or destroying characterizes ceremonial sacrifice, a process that may be simultaneously brutal and dispassionate, even when the objects destroyed are human beings. If sacrifice were focused on revenge or punishment, the rites of human sacrifice would maximize suffering, which they typically do not. Although ritually taking vengeance on enemies may be gratifying, the quick, pain-minimizing sacrificial act evokes a different mood, one of anger-free, sanctioned wasting.

Forfeiture of money as a penalty for mistake or bad judgment is not considered a prestige-enhancing sacrifice. Additionally, sacrifice cannot be seen as generating monetary or in-kind compensation; rather, it must be deliberately wasteful to the donor.[133] Property of the highest value is given for sacrifices precisely because its relinquishment is the most costly. Leviticus 22:24 makes the point explicitly: "You shall not offer to God that which is squeezed, crushed, torn or cut"; that is, mutilated animals are unacceptable as sacrificial offerings. While providing the *re'iyah* sacrifice, the donor expects to *be seen* giving this most valuable of sacrifices,[134] an animal offered to God entirely and completely burned up on the altar (wasted).[135] Throughout history, feasting requires the host to provide the most desirable foods *in excess*.[136] Serving second-rate or insufficient food to invited guests results in denigration rather than enhancement of the host's reputation.

If not for the social dominance value as the most costly and wasteful of signals, how else might one explain the horrific existence of child sacrifice described by historians and ethnographers? As Sumner notes, "[when] men sacrificed their children and other human beings ... those selected [were] the bravest or most beautiful."[137] Only abject wastefulness can explain why Mesha, king of the Moabites, offered his own son as a burnt offering to influence a beneficial war outcome.[138] In the game of competitive signal display, one is judged by the resources one is able and willing to squander, give away, or destroy.

In costly signaling theory, wasting makes biological sense for two reasons. First, by surrendering ownership of a valuable, one communicates the ability to survive and prosper *despite* its loss. Second, one sends a costly (and therefore reliable) signal of willingness to sacrifice one's own property to serve a communal purpose. From this perspective, Maimonides' hierarchy of charitable giving makes perfect sense: the highest credit is due to the benefactor who gives anonymously to an unknown recipient precisely because this type of altruistic sacrifice can accrue no prestige. Secret gifts are, from a biological point of view, the most wasteful because no targeted credit or gratitude can be attributed. That fact explains why publicly displayed philanthropy is so common and anonymous gift giving so rare (the exception proves the biology-based rule). The Maimonidean hierarchy of charitable giving can be seen as an attempt to contravene the natural desire of donors for prestige by limiting altruistic competition without reducing the overall level of the gifts. Consequently, anonymous charity is the most prestigious in the eyes of God because it cannot, by its nature, garner prestige in the eyes of peers.

Within sexual selection theory, it is the high cost of wasting that makes the advertising of one's fitness a reliable signal.[139] Among very high-ranking individuals, the ability to waste time, opportunity, talent, and money confers great respect on those who can lavishly afford to do so without reducing their overall fitness.[140] Extravagance within limits, cross-culturally a costly signal, awards prestige to those who are so able and inclined. Consider those who regularly use alcohol or drugs recreationally. Comrades may view the habit of getting "wasted" as a mark of geniality, and those who do so are held in high regard if the wasting is not seen as fitness reducing. Only those with the time, money, and reproductive value to waste can afford the extravagance of getting "wasted." When limits are exceeded, however, the signaler of wasteful habits risks being perceived as a pathetic drunkard instead of a genial drinker. The same is true of religious observance. Like overuse of alcohol or drugs, peers will perceive excessive pietism as strange. Wasting oneself moderately can increase status; "over-the-top" wasting drops one's status precipitously.

As was discussed regarding the biblical *cherem,* conquering armies, ancient and modern, have ravaged enemies by "laying waste" their land and people. This cost-ineffective, wasteful desolation sends costly signals regarding the infamous prestige of conquerors. Throughout the history of warfare, savagery has functioned as a costly display of power precisely *because* of its wasteful, vulgar destructiveness. The root ש-א-ה (sh-o-a) in biblical usage refers to the *wasting* of cultivated lands, cities, and the people inhabiting them.[141] Gruenwald explains that contained within the meaning of ש-א-ה is the notion that sins are transferred from one group of humans onto the objects they sacrifice.[142] Sad to say, "rape and pillage" as costly displays have, throughout human history, successfully communicated the unconstrained appetites and abilities of conquerors. As Betzig shows in her chapter in this volume and elsewhere, a despot ruling with an iron fist is the most able to operationalize the polygynous desires of human males. Like it or not, in human history the ruthlessly powerful invariably leave exponentially more descendants than everyone else.[143]

Conclusion

Social scientists have often mischaracterized religious rituals, including sacrificing, as irrational customs aimed at propitiating supernatural powers.[144] The truly *scientific* study of religion, however, should *never* reference them by theological association because beliefs about and relationships with supernaturals are not verifiable by the senses, and therefore cannot serve as scientific data. As I have asserted in this chapter, religious rituals must be extracted from their theological milieu by a nonideational method to generate scientific data.[145]

Since they require the consumption of valuable resources, sacrificial rites would appear to diminish an individual donor's reproductive fitness, exhibiting a tension between one's own welfare and one's dedication to communal religious practices. In ancient and modern civilizations, however, the word *sacrifice* never meant reluctance, deprivation, or impoverishment grimly accepted. Sacrificial acts were, to the contrary, occasions of great communal festivity. Sacrifices are typically as conspicuously excessive as can be afforded; the larger the festivity, the greater the required magnanimity[146] of the donor, appreciated fully by the noncontributing participants.[147]

Many with modern sensibilities may consider religious sacrifices (or rituals in general) to be a frivolous waste of time and resources. Ironically, from a costly signaling perspective, sacrificial wastefulness is exactly the point. As Zahavi and Zahavi point out, "We are vividly conscious of the costs, risks and dangers entailed by the handicap, and that's precisely why we are so impressed by [sacrificial] altruism."[148] Unlike reciprocity models for altruistic behavior, costly signaling theory rewards donations as sacrificial acts when individuals seek to increase their social standing relative to the less altruistic. Studies have found that altruists are the most inclined to punish the stingy.[149] Used to justify strong reciprocity theory, this conclusion can just as well support a theory of altruism as costly, competitive display. When self-imposing a sacrificial handicap, an individual accurately advertises his quality to potential rivals and mates. The message sent is one of high stature: "I am so well-endowed with resources that I can afford to waste a portion of them in communally sanctioned events that benefit others." In this way, religious sacrifices and vows can be seen as venues for altruistic competition within the costly signaling-based model of Darwinian sexual selection.

Altruism benefiting nonkin remains one of the most important phenomena seeking explanation from an evolutionary perspective.[150] Religious sacrifice can be seen as simultaneously competitive *and* cooperative, enhancing the status of the individual donor and rewarding the community with donated resources. Reciprocity models give unsatisfying and incomplete answers to the conundrum of why sacrificing valuable possessions using unreciprocated displays is so common in our social species. If altruism required reciprocity, religious sacrifices and feasts would not be characterized by such extravagant wasting. Use of costly signaling theory, however, allows us to classify sacrificial altruism as status competition in which individuals compete with their peers to demonstrate who is most able and willing to "give 'til it hurts."[151] Within the dynamic of Darwinian sexual selection, altruists are likely to acquire more prestige and, as a result, leave more descendants. In this way, altruism as a prestige booster has been selected for and spread in human populations. Colloquially speaking, altruistic behavior is sexy.

Prestige attainment can also be a multigenerational strategy, since the descendants of high-ranking ancestors typically inherit prestige. Sociological theory refers to this feature of social hierarchy as ascribed status, an example of which is European aristocracy. As has been evident among the aristocratic, inherited position allows descendants opportunities for wastefulness (idleness) not available to other classes. The accumulation of prestige and its conspicuous display by costly signaling can be seen as a strategy to increase one's own reproductive value and to accrue (save) prestige for the benefit of one's future lineage. Religious sacrificing, as a noticeable public exhibition of altruism, enables donors to demonstrate their ability and willingness to contribute valuables for conspicuous, wasteful use or destruction for the welfare of unrelated others.

Notes

1. Hubert and Mauss, 1981, pp. 51, 97.
2. Ibid., p. 9.
3. There are instances in which the Talmud uses the word *sacrifice* in this way. See, for example, the Mishnah and Gemara in Naz. 12b2–12b3.
4. Ibid., p. 102.
5. Tylor, 1958, p. 462.
6. Ibid., pp. 20–24.
7. Ibid., p. 63.
8. James, 1962, p. 503.
9. Tiger refers to the West African practice of pouring liquor out on the ground "for ancestors to enjoy" (2000, p. 197).
10. See James, 1962, pp. 20–25, for examples.
11. Epictetus, referenced in Burkert, 1996, p. 142.
12. Sumner, 1906, chap. 16.
13. Watson, 1995, p. 166. Mayan rituals, conducted at Chichén Itzá, included heaving live humans painted with a special blue pigment down the *cenote* (sacred sinkhole) as offerings to the rain god Chaak.
14. Evans-Pritchard, 1956, pp. 197–215.
15. Refers to the phrase *ishey Yisrael* ([sacrificial] fires of Israel) dropped from the Amida, the central set of liturgical prayers. "Sacrifice seems to be a ritual act which we would like to forget" (Scolnic, 1984, p. 28).
16. Interestingly, the word *bless* originated in *blessen,* to "redden" with sacrificial blood (Funk, 1998, p. 269).
17. Maimonides, Hil. Maaseh Ha-korbanot 3:13–15; Taanit 23a2, 26a2, 27a1; Sotah 8a1 (the donor must be present).
18. Chag. 16a4. Only the owner must lean; a nonowner cannot (Tosafot S.V. to Chag. 16b). The *s'michah* ritual demonstrates transference of the animal's ownership publicly (Mishnah Chag. 16a4). Could the owner be demonstrably and symbolically divesting ownership by forcefully pushing the animal away from himself?
19. *T'nufa* (waving in the air) was an important part of sacrificial display of ownership. The Talmud tells us that *t'nufa* was done with her *mincha* offering by the accused adulteress (Sotah 19a2-a3). Additionally, at their inauguration ritual, each Levite was bodily lifted and waived (Nazir 40a2). Expiation sacrifices given to the priests were deemed effective *after* they were consumed (Yev. 40a1).
20. An animal sacrifice (*olah*) and a flour offering (*kemitzah*) are examples of offerings wasted. There were other instances in which abject wasting was mandated. Consecrated animals unusable for an intended sacrifice were denied food and water and left to die (Nazir 24a1, 25a1-a2). When funds were donated for specific sacrifices, if those sacrifices could not

be performed, the funds were thrown into the Dead Sea (Nazir 24a2 and 24b2). As a side observation, what could demonstrate sacrificial wasting better than throwing good money into the Dead Sea, a "wasteland" body of water incapable of sustaining life!

21. In proclaiming that the Torah is "not in the Heavens" but rather "near to you," the same *k-r-b* root is found (Deut. 30:14); also in the *Ashrei* declaration recited in the daily liturgy (Ps. 145:18).

22. In Hebrew, one's relatives are קרובים (*krovim*).

23. For examples that the valuable offered needed to be *proportionately* valuable to the wealth of the donor, see Num. Mid. Rab. 14:11.

24. Sacrifices accepted at the Temple had to be maintained in a state of *tahara*, or ritual purity. This high standard of care imposed on donors made the objects given over to the priests inherently more valuable.

25. Chag. 10a2, referencing Exod. 35:5 (donate with *n'div lebow*, "a generous heart").

26. Exod. 36:7; Deut. 28:11, 30:9; Gen. 49:4; Exod. 12:10, 16:8, 29:34; Lev. 7:17, 19:6, respectively.

27. Gruenwald, 2003, p. 182.

28. See Lev. 22:21; Num. 15:3.

29. Jacobs, p. 581.

30. Bergman, 2000, p. 234, referencing Num. 33:3 and Ned. 2b. In addition, once an object has been consecrated by vow, one may not thereafter derive benefit from it (Ned. 35a).

31. In Hebrew called נדר על תנאי (*neder al tanai*).

32. Lev. 27:2.

33. Num. 6:2. The nazarite vow, due to its abstentions, is considered sacrificial (Naz. 11a1).

34. Ibid.

35. Deut. 23:21, 23; drought is caused by those who make pledges but do not pay them (Taanit 8b3).

36. Deut. 23:22.

37. Ket. 71a3.

38. Ket. 72a4.

39. Yev. 109b1 discusses an example.

40. Judg. 11:30–31.

41. See Exod. 20:7.

42. Ket. 75a1.

43. Gen. 4:9.

44. Kid. 30b–f.12.

45. See the chapter "Intrafamily Conflict in the Bible and Biological Theory."

46. Gen. Rabbah 22:7, explicated in Jacobs, 1995, p. 61.

47. From the "inferior," Leibowitz, 1974a, p. 40, quotes Rashi on Gen. 4:3–5.

48. Birds and cakes are less valuable as sacrifices than the meat from larger animals (Chag. 8b1, n. 2).

49. Swidler, 1973, p. 23.

50. On Exod. 31:17.

51. Tiger, 1999, p. 108.

52. See Konner, 2002, p. 12. See Ket. 98b2 regarding the high value of meat given to dinner guests.

53. Wilson, 2000, p. 548.

54. See Yev. 72a2.
55. Gen. 25:28.
56. Gen. 8:21; Exod. 29:18, 25; 29:41; Lev. 1:9, 13, 17, 2:2, 9, 12; 3:5, 16; 4:31; 6:15, 21; 8:21, 28; 17:6; 23:13, 18; 26:31; Num. 15:3, 7, 10, 13, 14, 24; 18:17; 28:2, 6, 13, 24, 27; 29:2, 6, 8, 13, 36.
57. Using the same reasoning, nondomesticated (wild) animals may also not be brought as sacrifices.
58. Isa. 61:8.
59. This sacrificial ceremony atoned for pre-Flood sins and gave Abraham's descendants the right to inherit the Land (Taanit 27b1). The satisfying odor of Noah's post-Flood sacrifices influenced God to never again be so disappointed with man's nature that he would destroy the biological world (Gen. 8:20–21).
60. Gen. 15:8–18.
61. For example, Gen. 17:14; Exod. 4:25, 12:15, 30:33, 31:14; Lev. 7:20–21.
62. For example, Gen. 15:18, 21:27, 26:28, 31:44; Exod. 34:10, 34:12; Deut. 7:2; Josh. 9:6–7.
63. See Meg. 31b2, n. 16 (Rashi on Gen. 15:9). Circumcision is the embodied mark of the Covenant.
64. Jer. 34:18.
65. Gen. 8:11.
66. Jer. 34:20 threatens the transgressors of his time with the same fate.
67. Deut. 21:7–9. Further explained in Sotah 38b3 and 46a1, n.4.
68. Deut. 21:4 requires the land where the sacrifice takes place remain unsown even after the ceremony. Farmland with an ever-flowing stream is the most valuable for crop cultivation and, when prohibited for cultivation, constitutes the biggest waste. Also see Rava's statement in Sotah 46b1.
69. Maimonides, 1963, chap. 40. See also Ket. 37b2 and n. 15.
70. Gen. 22:1–19; "Avraham ... came from a legal background where it was mandatory to seal a contract or covenant with an animal sacrifice. The covenant with God was of such transcendent enormity that it demanded something more: a sacrifice of the best-loved in the fullest sense" (Johnson, 1987, p. 18).
71. Telushkin, 1991, p. 36; Hubert and Mauss, 1981, p. 72; 2 Kings 3:27.
72. Lev. 18:21; Deut. 18:10. See the discussion of the child sacrifices of Yiftach and Meisha in Taanit 4a2.
73. See also 1 Sam. 4:11; Talmud Jer., Yoma, Gem. I, 1, 5.
74. For example, see Wiesel, 2003, p. 71.
75. In rabbinic commentary, the brothers were esteemed despite their fatal error; see, for example, R.H. 25a4.
76. Hirsch, 1966, p. 414, describes Nadav and Avihu as "the spiritual elite of the Nation."
77. Death of the priests is attributed to being brought *near* (c-r-e) to God (Lev. 16:1). As a corollary, Lev. 23:25 commands the bringing of sacrifices with the words, "you shall bring them near to God by fire."
78. The story of Nadav and Avihu is contained in *Parsha* (Torah portion) *Shmini*, which is read on the Shabbat following Passover. The *haphtarah* (prophetic reading) read on that same Shabbat is connected to the *parsha* by an incident concerning Utza, who was struck dead while attending the transportation of the Ark in a procession organized by King David (2 Sam. 6:3–8). In contrast to the biblical language used when the priests were killed, there is no claim that God was honored by the killing of Utza. We can surmise then that

Utza was killed as a punishment for having used laymen to stand by the side of the Ark and, when necessary, "handle" the Ark (or defecate near it—see Sotah 35a5). Although the Rabbis later explain the priests' death by alleging that they were inebriated and therefore punished, the biblical language may be seen as a wasteful sacrifice by God of those *nearest* to him.

79. Exod. 11.

80. The Hebrew root *trh*, as found in the expression *yirat shamayim* ("fear" of heaven), means also to revere and honor (Lev. 19:30; Ps. 89:7); fearing and honoring God are assumed to be one and the same.

81. Described in Lev. 16.

82. Like all *chukim* laws, the rationale for the scapegoat sacrifice is unknown (Maimonides, 1963, pp. 627–628). The analogue of this sacrifice is continued to this day, mostly by Hasidim. Called *shlogn kapores,* the ritual involves the vesting of sins upon a chicken, twirling it around by its head three times, slaughtering it, and donating it to a needy family. As a scapegoat, the chicken dies in place of the human sinner.

83. Ginzberg, 1909, p. 171.

84. Num. 19:2–13.

85. Universally, where animal husbandry is practiced, owners of attractive animals display them at fairs for sale in competition with the stock of other breeders. Finely bred "show" animals such as horses or dogs that provide no practical benefit for their owners can still be extremely valuable when offered for sale.

86. Writing specifically about the red heifer procedure, Etkin acknowledges that only the conspicuous nonutility of this ritual could render it an effective signal (1979, p. 356).

87. Quoted in N. Leibowitz, *Studies in Vayikra* (*Leviticus*) (Jerusalem: World Zionist Organization, 1980, p. 114).

88. Bulka, 1995, p. 45.

89. Biale, 1992, pp. 39, 48.

90. Ehrenreich, 1997, p. 63.

91. Ps. 45:3. Based on this verse, R. Eliezer holds that a sword may be worn on Shabbat because it displays a warrior's majesty (although "carrying" it on Shabbat is generally prohibited). R. Kahana recast "girding the sword" as a metaphor for learning and following the obligations of Torah (Shab. 63a).

92. Pinker, 1997, p. 516.

93. Wilson, 2000, p. 245.

94. See biblical references, Gen. 49:27; Exod. 15:9; Num. 31:11–12; Deut. 2:35, 3:7, 13:16, 20:14; Josh. 7:21, 8:2, 8:27, 11:14, 22:8; Judg. 5:30, 8:24–25; 1 Sam. 14:30, 32, 15:19, 21, 30:16, 19–22, 26; 2 Sam. 3:22, 8:12, 12:30; 2 Kings 3:23; 1 Chron. 20:2, 26:20; 2 Chron. 14:13, 15:11, 20:25, 24:23, 28:8, 15; Esther 3:13, 8:11; Ps. 68:12, 119:162; Prov. 1:13, 16:19, 31:11; Isa. 8:4, 9:3, 10:2, 6, 33:4, 23, 53:12; Jer. 21:9, 38:2, 39:18, 45:5, 49:32, 50:10; Ezek. 7:21, 29:19, 38:12–13; Dan. 11:24; Zech. 2:9, 14:1.

95. Hobbes, 1986, p. 185.

96. Quoted in Ehrenreich, 1997, p. 130.

97. Veblen, 1912, p. 54; see also Pinker, 1997, p. 510; Konner, 2002, pp. 93–94; Low, 2000, p. 221; Num. 31:9, 18; Judg. 21:13–14.

98. Deut. 21:10–14; Gen. Rab. 22:7; Jacobs, 1995, p. 61.

99. Meg. 7a3, n. 30.

100. Keeley, 1996, p. 86; Symons, 1979, p. 149; Buss, 1994, p. 219.

101. See the chapter "Judaism's *Yetzer* as a Biotheological Construct."

102. Dingle, 2006.
103. Num. 18:14; in the terminology of economists, a "private" good is thus turned into a "public" good.
104. See Hirsch, 1966, pp. 832–833.
105. Lev. 27:28–29.
106. Niditch, 1993, p. 28. Interpreting Deut. 20:16, the Israelites were admonished not to spare the life of any soul (Sotah 3b1).
107. Deut. 7:25.
108. Deut. 7:16–26, 13:13–18; Lev. 27:28–29; Num. 18:14; Josh. 6:15–7:1, 7:11–15; 1 Sam. 15:21; 1 Kings 20:42; 1 Chron. 2:7.
109. Smith, 1927, p. 150.
110. There is a telltale relationship between the words "חרב" (*cherev*—sword) and "חרם" (*cherem*). In biblical Hebrew, there is a convention for the interchangeability of related consonants. "ב" and "מ" are two such related consonants (along with "p"), perhaps because they are all pronounced with the lips—"b" and "m" (and "p"). As a result, the Hebrew words for "sword" (*cherev*) and "utter destruction" (*churban*) are also etymologically related.
111. Num. 14:9.
112. Ehrenreich, 1997, pp. 161–162, referring to Davidson.
113. See list in Niditch, 1993, pp. 34–35.
114. Ibid., p. 40.
115. Soloveitchik, 2002, pp. 37–38.
116. Josh. 7:19–21.
117. For a full explanation, see the chapter "The Handicap Principle in Human Social Interaction."
118. Although this can make sense from a biological perspective, Hirsch (1966), from a Judaic perspective, rejects that Temple sacrificing can be characterized as giving something of value to benefit others (Lev. I, p. 6).
119. The Talmud considers the Hebrew word for tithing, מעשר, to be homiletically similar to the word for wealth, עושר. Thus, tithing is considered a means of attaining, not dissipating, wealth (Taanit 9a1).
120. Deut. 15:21. Just as "first fruits" were surrendered to the priests, so the firstborn son belonged to Temple service unless redeemed beforehand from the priests (*Pidyon haben*—Exod. 34:19).
121. The great prestige of the High Priest carried with it the highest cost for error. Important persons are obligated to donate more than others. In addition, if the priest's intentions were found to be deficient in performing the sacrifice, he could also be liable to the individual whose sacrifice he made ineffectual (Ned. 36a1). A mistaken ruling by the Great Sanhedrin required them to offer a bull as a sin offering (Sotah 44b7, n. 29).
122. Zahavi and Zahavi, 1997, pp. 225–227.
123. Girard, 1977, p. 93.
124. Zahavi and Zahavi, 1997, pp. 134–135.
125. Durkheim, 1965, p. 384.
126. Driver, 1998, p. 105.
127. Burkert, 1996, chap. 6.
128. Ibid., p. 150.
129. Soloveitchik, 2002, p. 17.
130. Taanit 9a1.
131. Knight, 1991, pp. 30–32.

132. Bataille, 1992, pp. 49–50.

133. Intrinsic to "waste" is the element of useless, superfluous expenditure (Hoad, 1986, p. 534).

134. Bet Hillel and Bet Shammai said the *re'iyah* sacrifice must be worth more than the others (Chag. 6a2). Some animal offerings are eaten *in public* by the donor and guests (*maser behaima*—Yev. 74a1, f.n. 4).

135. Chag. 6b2. In the instructions for sacrificing, God requires that specific parts of animals be burned up entirely (wastefully) to produce a "pleasant odor" to God. Since totally charred flesh produces an *unpleasant* odor to us, why might this stench be *pleasing* to God? Possible answer: from God's perspective, incinerating flesh *smells* utterly wasteful, seemingly the objective for that sacrifice.

136. Past the point of sufficiency to wastefulness. See Durkheim, 1965, p. 380; Weber, 1963, p. 26; Burkert, 1996, p. 150.

137. Sumner, 1906, pp. 538–539. Reynolds and Tanner, 1995, p. 85, relate that fourth-century Cartaginians sacrificed many of the "best" children, especially the firstborns of high-ranking families.

138. 2 Kings 3:27, from Heschel, 1962, p. 196.

139. Zahavi and Zahavi, 1997, p. 229.

140. An example from professional sports: Drayton McLane, billionaire owner of the Houston Astros baseball team, vowed to clean the cleats on his players' shoes if the team were to qualify for postseason play after the 2005 regular season. Once the Astros reached the playoffs, McLane, true to his public promise, started cleaning baseball shoes. Of course, his picture doing this appeared in the Houston newspaper. Biological meaning: those who clean other people's shoes have low prestige in all societies. But in making good on his vow, McLane's stunt achieved the opposite effect: he increased his standing with the players and his prestige in Houston. Why? Because cleaning shoes is so beneath the station of a team owner and *wasteful* of a billionaire's time that McLane's self-imposed handicap demonstrated his worthiness and altruistic superiority as a team owner.

141. See 2 Kings 19:25; Isa. 17:13, 37:26.

142. Gruenwald, 2003, p. 216.

143. Betzig, 1986, p. 88.

144. For example, Goody, 1961, pp. 157–159, and Radcliffe-Brown (quoting Loisy), 1952, p. 174.

145. Gruenwald, 2003, pp. 199, 201.

146. "Showing off" by spending resources excessively, to the point of wastefulness, to display one's generosity.

147. Yerkes, 1952, p. 4.

148. Zahavi and Zahavi, 1997, p. 227.

149. Fehr and Gachter, 2002, Gintis, Bowles, et al., 2003.

150. The "nobility" of giving "generously" can be deduced from the fact that both Hebrew words have the same Hebrew root, n-d-v (נ-ד-ב). See Chag. 3a3.

151. For example, unemployed Hindus give what little they have as offerings to the temple gods, claiming that these sacrifices will enhance their employment opportunities (Reynolds and Tanner, 1995, p. 309). Judaically, R' Meir says those who perform altruistic services to others in the end receive benefits themselves (Ned. 83b1).

References

Bataille, G. 1992. *Theory of Religion*. Brooklyn: Zone Books.
Bergman, A., ed. 2000. *Brisk on Chumash*. Brooklyn: Mesorah Publications.
Betzig, L. 1986. *Despotism and Differential Reproduction*. New Brunswick, NJ: Aldine.
Biale, D. 1992. *Eros and the Jews*. New York: Basic Books.
Bulka, R. 1995. *Judaism on Pleasure*. Northvale: Jason Aronson.
Burkert, W. 1996. *Creation of the Sacred*. Cambridge, MA: Harvard University Press.
Buss, D. 1994. *The Evolution of Desire*. New York: Basic Books.
Dingle, G. 2006. The reproductive success of war heroes. Paper presented at the Human Behavior and Evolution Society Conference, Philadelphia.
Driver, T. F. 1998. *Liberating Rites*. Boulder, CO: Westview Press.
Durkheim, E. 1965. *The Elementary Forms of Religious Life*. New York: Free Press.
Ehrenreich, B. 1997. *Blood Rites*. New York: Henry Holt.
Etkin, W. 1979. The mystery of the red heifer: A scientific midrash. *Judaism* 28(3):351–356.
Evans-Pritchard, E. E. 1956. *Nuer Religion*. New York: Clarendon.
Fehr, S., and Gachter, S. 2002. Altruistic punishment in humans. *Nature* 415:137–140.
Funk, W. 1998. *Word Origins*. New York: Wings Books.
Gintis, H., et al. 2003. Explaining altruistic behavior in humans. *Evolution and Human Behavior* 24:153–172.
Ginzberg, L. 1909. *The Legends of the Jews*. Philadelphia: Jewish Publication Society.
Girard, R. 1977. *Violence and the Sacred*. Baltimore: Johns Hopkins University Press.
Goody, J. 1961. Religion and ritual: the definitional problem. *British Journal of Sociology* 12(2): 142–164.
Gruenwald, I. 2003. *Ritual and Ritual Theory in Ancient Israel*. Boston: Brill Publishing.
Heschel, A. J. 1962. *The Prophets*. Philadelphia: Jewish Publication Society.
Hirsch, S. R. 1966. *Commentary on the Torah,* Vol. 4, Part 2. Brooklyn: Judaica Press.
Hoad, T. F., ed. 1986. *English Etymology*. New York: Oxford University Press.
Hobbes, T. 1986. *Leviathan*. New York: Penguin Books.
Hubert, H., and Mauss, M. 1981. *Sacrifice: Its Nature and Function*. Chicago: University of Chicago Press.
Jacobs, L. 1995. *The Jewish Religion*. New York: Oxford University Press.
James, E. O. 1962. *Sacrifice and Sacrament*. New York: Barnes and Noble.
James, W. 1999. *The Varieties of Religious Experience*. New York: Modern Library.
Johnson, P. 1987. *A History of the Jews*. New York: Harper and Row.
Keeley, L. H. 1996. *War Before Civilization*. New York: Oxford University Press.
Knight, C. 1991. *Blood Relations*. New Haven, CT: Yale University Press.
Konner, M. 2002. *The Tangled Wing*. New York: Henry Holt.
———. 2003. *Unsettled: An Anthropology of the Jews*. New York: Penguin Compass.
Leibowitz, N. 1974a. *Studies in Bereshit (Genesis)*. Jerusalem: World Zionist Organization, Department for Torah Education and Culture.
———. 1974b. *Studies in Shemot (Exodus)*, Vol. II. Jerusalem: World Zionist Organization, Department for Torah Education and Culture.
Low, B. S. 2000. *Why Sex Matters*. Princeton, NJ: Princeton University Press.
Maimonides, M. 1963. *The Guide of the Perplexed*. Chicago: Chicago University Press.
Niditch, S. 1993. *War in the Hebrew Bible*. New York: Oxford University Press.

Pinker, S. 1997. *How the Mind Works.* New York: W. W. Norton.
Radcliffe-Brown, A. R. 1952. *Structure and Function in Primitive Society.* New York: Free Press.
Reynolds, V., and Tanner, R. 1995. *The Social Ecology of Religion.* New York: Oxford University Press.
Scolnic, B. E. 1984. Prayer, sacrifice and the meaning of ritual. *Conservative Judaism* 37(4):28–36.
Smith, W. R. 1927. *The Religion of the Semites.* New York: Macmillan.
Soloveitchik, J. B. 2002. *The Rav Speaks.* Brooklyn: Judaica Press.
Sumner, W. G. 1906. *Folkways.* Boston: Ginn and Company.
Swidler, W. W. 1973. Adaptive processes regulating nomad-sedentary interaction in the Middle East. In C. Nelson, ed., *The Desert and the Sown* (pp. 23–41). Berkeley: Institute of International Studies Series, University of California at Berkeley.
Symons, D. 1979. *The Evolution of Human Sexuality.* New York: Oxford University Press.
Telushkin, J. 1991. *Jewish Literacy.* New York: William Morrow.
Tiger, L. 1999. *The Decline of Males.* New York: St. Martin's Press.
———. 2000. *The Pursuit of Pleasure.* New Brunswick, NJ: Transaction Publishers.
Tylor, E. B. 1958. *Religion in Primitive Culture.* New York: HarperTorchbooks.
Veblen, T. 1912. *The Theory of the Leisure Class.* New York: B. W. Huebsch.
Watson, L. 1995. *Dark Nature.* New York: HarperCollins.
Weber, M. 1963. *The Sociology of Religion.* Boston: Beacon Press.
Wiesel, E. 2003. *Wise Men and Their Tales.* New York: Schocken Books.
Wilson, E. O. 1998. *Consilience.* New York: Alfred A. Knopf.
Wilson, E. O. 2000. *Sociobiology.* Cambridge, MA: Harvard University Press.
Yerkes, R. K. 1952. *Sacrifice.* New York: Charles Scribner's Sons.
Zahavi, A., and Zahavi, A. 1997. *The Handicap Principle.* New York: Oxford University Press.

Chapter 10

Why Are Synagogue Services So Long?

An Evolutionary Examination of Jewish Ritual Signals

Richard Sosis

Editor's Introduction

Why do traditional religious communities demand so much of their members? Why do observant Jews walk publicly to services on Shabbat instead of driving, regardless of the weather? When the Torah portion is read during the service, why must it be chanted from a handwritten parchment scroll containing no punctuation, vowels, or cantillation notes? Why does textual learning at the yeshiva, *or traditional school, consist of a roomful of paired-up boys sitting across from one another, swaying in synchrony, responding to each other's arguments in raised voices? Although these questions have time-honored religious answers, they also have answers based on costly signaling (handicap) theory.*

For those who place themselves squarely within the religious influence of their ancestors, the ongoing performance of religious arrangements requires great inconvenience: the costly expenditure of resources and, at times, the endurance of discomfort or even pain. Too often secularists dismiss the stringencies of religious observance as a residue of primitive, irrational stubbornness. In this immensely readable chapter, Richard Sosis uses costly signaling or handicap theory to explain why the cumbersome requirements of Judaic communal practices make good biological sense.

For those readers unfamiliar with the Hebrew and Yiddish terms, please consult the Glossary at the end of the chapter.

Many years ago I was visiting the northern Israeli town of Tzfat, where I currently reside, and I found myself at the Sabbath dinner table of a *Chabadnik* (*Hasidic*) couple. Over the course of the conversation, which centered on what it means to be a Jew, the husband turned to me and rhetorically asked, "Do you think keeping these *mitzvot* is easy? It's hard work doing God's commandments!" And indeed, I could not have agreed more. I was barely able to sit through all of the unfamiliar rituals that preceded the actual consumption of food, and the thought of the hours that my host would spend in *shul* the following day made me squirm in my seat. The hours at *shul* were of course just the tip of the iceberg. I knew there would be no cars, phone calling, or computers until sundown tomorrow. Never would a cheeseburger or pepperoni pizza pass their lips, lips that uttered a specified prayer liturgy at least three times every day. And all the while dressing like characters in *Fiddler on the Roof*. Little did I know that I was not even looking at my hostess's hair, but rather an impressive wig. Nor did I know that my hosts refrain from contact and marital relations for more than a third of every month.[1] So I timidly asked the obvious question: "If this is all so difficult, why do you do it?" My host's response, "Because this is what God commanded," left me unsatisfied. Aside from my simplistic theological concerns of why God would want me to do anything that seemed so demanding, I was equally mystified why anyone would obey such a deity. Indeed, the behavior of religious Jews had puzzled me since I initially encountered them on my first visit to Israel several years earlier.[2] Why do some Jews abide by countless restrictions and infringements on their behavioral freedom? If these requirements are really such a burden, how could Judaism have endured for so long? Even more curious is why some Jews who were not raised with such obligations now embrace them? And why are these religious requirements becoming increasingly more stringent in Orthodox communities?

These types of questions naturally arise with respect to other religious populations as well. Religious duties throughout the world are often challenging to perform and sometimes dangerous. Jewish preteens may complain about their bar and bat mitzvah preparations, but compared with adolescent rites of passage in many cultures, which may include hanging by one's skin, ritual scarification, and circumcisions for both males and females, learning to read Torah and lead services is a breeze. Of course, some communities barely require any sacrificial behavior of their members at all. Why do communities differ in the behavioral costs of their membership requirements, and why in the contemporary religious marketplace do Jewish costs appear to be particularly high? Moreover, how can we explain the variation in religious demands across Jewish denominations, as well as intradenominational variation in individual religious practice?

Any theory on social processes should not be applicable just to Jews, but should aim to explain the universality of religious behavior as well. Only a theory grounded in the process of natural selection can offer such a comprehensive explanation, but how? Religious behavior appears to *contradict* the principles of natural selection, which claim that to secure the resources necessary for reproduction and survival, organisms, including humans, are designed to maximize the rate at which they extract energy from the environment. Most religious behaviors seem entirely counterproductive to this goal and, indeed, some religious practices, such as ritual sacrifices, are a blatant, conspicuous display of wasted resources.[3] It is one thing that my ancestors shared their food with the Temple priests in Jerusalem, but why would they have willingly given up part of their dinner to a fire that burned it to ashes on an altar?[4] The knee-jerk response to this issue is that humans, including my ancestors and gracious *Chabadnik* hosts, engage in religious practices because they believe in the efficacy of the rituals and the tenets of the faith that give meaning to the rituals. However, this response begs the question, why has natural selection favored a human psychology that believes in the supernatural as well as the behavioral patterns that are manifestations of these beliefs?

What follows in this chapter is a description of an evolutionary signaling theory of religious behavior that aims to answer this question and its application to understanding the costliness of Jewish religious behavior and various current trends in the Jewish community. Although evolutionary theories of religion can offer insights into the origins of religion and the selective pressures that have shaped human religiosity, if they are unable to explain modern religious phenomena their value is purely academic.

Signaling Theory and Religion

Before I outline the signaling theory of religion, we need to clarify what we are trying to explain. Following previous work,[5] I will informally refer to the focus of our inquiry as the three Bs: religious behavior (ritual), badges (the physical manifestations of some ritual behaviors, such as tattoos or religious garments), and bans (behavioral restrictions known in anthropological circles as taboos). In Judaism, religious behaviors range from reciting Friday night *kiddush* to dropping coins in a *pushka*. *Kippot* and *peyos* constitute badges, and many of the laws of *kashrut, niddah*, and *shmittah* are examples of bans. The value of distinguishing between these categories will become apparent as I unpack the signaling theory of religion.

Drawing on the work of ethologists and their study of animal rituals, anthropologists have long considered religion a form of communication. This is likely to strike some as odd. Is religion not about the miraculous, mysterious, and ineffable? How can parting seas and noncombustible bushes be a system of communication? Who is communicating with whom? When Jews pray they are of course attempting to "communicate" with the God of Abraham, Isaac, and Jacob. However, for understanding the selective pressures that have shaped prayer and other religious behaviors, badges, and bans, the most relevant communicant is not God, but, rather, others in the study house and synagogue.

To understand why natural selection has universally favored religiously communicated messages requires that we approach our subject from the mindset of an evolutionary biologist. Whether studying human language, religion, the color of peppered moths, or any potentially adaptive trait, evolutionary scholars must first determine what problem the trait solved in the organisms' evolutionary history if they are to uncover the causes of its emergence. Regarding religion, if it is an adaptive strategy, it must have solved some environmental problem that all societies face. William Irons, a behavioral ecologist from Northwestern University, has suggested that this universal dilemma is how to promote cooperation.[6] Irons argues that in human history the adaptive advantage of group living was the benefit individuals attained by cooperating in activities such as hunting, food sharing, defense, and warfare. However, as Irons notes, although everyone is better off if everybody cooperates, it is often very difficult to coordinate and achieve this cooperation. The problem is that although everyone is better off if everybody cooperates than if nobody cooperates, each person is even better off if everyone else does the cooperating, while he stays at home enjoying an afternoon siesta. Throughout our evolutionary history, there were likely to have been conditions in which everyone in a group would benefit if they all worked together, possibly to kill a few bison or men in a nearby tribe. But individuals themselves could do even better by just watching everyone else expending energy and putting their lives at risk. However, if everyone pursues the latter strategy, at best there will be no bison for dinner and, at worst, your tribe will be the one decimated by other tribes who decided to cooperate. Thus, although everyone may gain if all group members invest in the cooperative goal, attaining such large-scale cooperation is often difficult to achieve without social mechanisms that prevent individuals from slacking off and free-riding on the efforts of others. Irons argues that religion is just such a mechanism.

In order to appreciate his argument, we must consider the shortcomings of messages communicated through our most common means of communication, language. A number of researchers have noted that trust lies at the heart of the problem of securing cooperation. If everyone knows that it is in everyone else's best interest to watch the hunt or war from the sidelines, how do groups of individuals develop the mutual trust that assures each individual that everybody else will participate? Of course, hunters and warriors can promise, "You have my word, I'll show up tomorrow. You can count on me." Unfortunately, unless the hunter or warrior would be severely punished if he failed to show up or there is trust already established between these individuals, such statements are not believable. But what if a man really does intend to show up to the hunt or battle; how can others be induced to rely on his promise? Well, an overused truism never seemed more appropriate: actions speak louder than words. Or, in accordance with my argument, religious behaviors, badges, and bans are a more reliable means of communicating commitment than spoken promises.

Why should this be the case? Isn't human language the evolutionary apex of communication? For an explanation I turn to the work of Israeli biologists Amotz Zahavi and Avishag Zahavi, who studied birds rather than religion, yet their writings inspired Irons and others to apply this reasoning to religious phenomena.[7] Zahavi and Zahavi recognize that when it is in an organism's best interest to send a dishonest signal (such as, "I'm really much bigger, quicker, stronger, healthier, or more beautiful than I actually am"), the signals most believable to the recipient are those that are costly to fake. Zahavi and Zahavi refer to such signals as handicaps. Handicaps are reliable because they are too costly to display or perform for individuals of low quality (in other words, those who are smaller, slower, weaker, sicker, and uglier than they would like others to believe). All behaviors incur time and energy costs, as well as the costs of missed opportunities when performing one behavioral alternative over another. Costs that extend beyond these baseline costs (also known as efficacy costs) are called strategic costs. Strategic costs can take the same form as baseline costs of production (for example, time and energy), but also can include consequences if a false signal is discovered.

Zahavi and Zahavi argued that selection has favored handicaps in a variety of species;[8] however, this has been more difficult to confirm than is generally appreciated. As the British evolutionary biologists John Maynard Smith and David Harper[9] explain, for a signal to classify as a handicap the net benefits for displaying the signal must be higher for a high-quality individual than for a low-quality individual. This could mean that the costs are higher for low-quality individuals, that the benefits are higher for high-quality individuals, or both. Critically, to classify as a handicap it must be possible to send a false signal (i.e., for a low-quality signaler to send a signal suggesting high quality). The signal must be costly to fake, but not impossible to fake. The handicap principle asserts that low-quality signalers generally do not send false signals because it simply does not pay—the net costs are too high.

So what does all this have to do with understanding the three Bs? Consider ultra-Orthodox Jews, who prefer to be known as *Haredim* (God-fearing or "trembling ones"). One of the most notable features of the Jerusalem summer landscape is how overdressed the *Haredim* are, especially for the season. Women sport long-sleeve shirts, head coverings or wigs (and occasionally both), and heavy skirts that scrape the ground. In their thick beards, long black coats, and black pants *Haredi* men spend their days fervently swaying and sweating as they sing praises to God in the desert sun. Many wear *shtriemels,* thick fur hats that were undoubtedly helpful in surviving the long and cold Eastern European winters where their ancestors lived but, from a practical perspective, should have been left at the border when they immigrated to the subtropical Holy Land. By donning several layers of clothing and standing out in the midday sun, these men are signaling to others: "Hey! Look, I'm a *Haredi* Jew. If you are also a member of this group, you can trust me because why else would I be dressed like this? Only a lunatic would spend their afternoon doing this *unless* they observed ultra-Orthodox Judaism and were fully committed to its ideals and goals." Thus, the "quality" that these men are signaling is their level of commitment to a specific religious group.

Adherence to a set of religious beliefs entails a host of ritual obligations and expected behavioral patterns. Although there may be physical or mental health benefits associated with some ritual practices,[10] the significant time, energy, and financial costs involved in imitating such behavior serve as effective deterrents for anyone who does not believe in the teachings of a particular religion. There is no incentive for nonbelievers to join this type of religious group because the costs of maintaining membership (such as praying three times a day, eating only kosher food, donating a certain part of your income to charity, growing *peyos*, and so forth) are too high. Hence, those who engage in the suite of behaviors, badges, and bans required by a religious group deserve more trust as ones who accept the doctrines of the group, which includes behaving altruistically to other group members. As a result of increased levels of trust and commitment among group members, religious groups are able to overcome free-rider problems that typically plague communal pursuits and limit overconsumption and exploitation of the mutual benefits they offer their adherents. And these mutual benefits can be quite significant. For example, during fieldwork I conducted among *Haredi* communities, I repeatedly observed invitations for meals, lodging, and rides by residents to unknown *Haredi* travelers. On several occasions I witnessed cars being loaned to complete strangers, and interviews revealed a surprising number of interest-free loans offered and accepted between people who had previously not known each other.[11] Furthermore, *Haredi* communities maintain an impressive network of *gemachs* (acronym for *gemilut chassadim*, or acts of loving kindness) that provide free or inexpensive goods and services to those within the community. The types of *gemachs* are almost countless and include medicine *gemachs*, bread *gemachs*, clothing *gemachs*, computer *gemachs*, and even dental *gemachs*. Costly ritual behaviors, badges, and bans serve to protect these benefits, and similar benefits offered by religious communities throughout the world, from free-riding nonbelievers.

These benefits may also include business dealings, as close-knit religious communities are often able to fill unique economic niches.[12] For instance, Jews, and particularly Orthodox Jews, have dominated the diamond industry throughout the world. It has been estimated that New York's diamond commerce is more than 95 percent Jewish.[13] In a rare ethnographic study of New York's diamond district, anthropologist Reneé Rose Shield describes the extraordinary level of trust among the *Haredi* Jews who work there; "handshakes, Yiddish, and trust still close multi-million dollar deals."[14] In London, Wechsberg[15] describes buyers who walk around "with a hundred thousand pounds' worth of diamonds that were handed over to them in trust."[16] The costly religious signals observed in *Haredi* communities likely facilitate these high-risk transactions.

It is also likely that, in addition to signaling group commitments, the three Bs signal mate quality. Specifically, they signal to potential mates that one has access to collective group resources and mutual insurance benefits. Of course, observing religious duties may also signal desired qualities such as dedication and self-control. For this reason, the *Haredi* courtship system is intriguing. Although *Haredi* females and their families (marriages are often arranged) clearly prefer talmudic scholars as husbands, a pattern with an apparently long history, these men generally offer little financial support, as they spend their days in *kollel*, an institute of Judaic learning for married men.[17] Indeed, since *Haredim* marry young, the wife's family often financially supports the young couple while the husband continues his learning. Although these men will indeed have access to the mutual insurance benefits that *Haredi* groups offer, their lack of earning potential means they will remain dependent on these benefits. Thus, it is not entirely clear what is driving female and familial preference for financially burdensome talmudic scholars, but it may be that fathers-in-law are signaling their wealth and group commitments by supporting these scholars. It could also be the case that the enhanced intelligence of future descendants is being selected for.

Stable Signals

Understanding the ecological problem that a trait such as religious behavior evolved to overcome provides the biologist with the reason *why* a trait evolved. In our case, I have argued that the primary ecological problem driving the emergence of religious behaviors, badges, and bans was the continuous challenge of collective action that our ancestors faced. However, equally important in any adaptationist analysis is understanding *how* the trait evolved. Why is the trait maintained within an observed population and how did it achieve stability? Anthropologists Rebecca Bliege Bird and Eric Alden Smith[18] outline four necessary conditions for the evolutionary stability of a costly signal in a population. I will address them one by one and assess how religious signals meet these conditions.

First, Bliege Bird and Smith note that there must be within-group variance in some unobservable attribute. The intensity of religious beliefs varies within communities, and this variance is unobservable. Some Jews regularly attend *shul*, but worshippers may not share the same level of belief in Judaism's tenets; dedication to their *shuls* and communities also varies. Second, group members should benefit from reliable information about this variance. Intensity of belief is related to one's commitment to the group and its goals—committed members are more likely to be cooperative and trustworthy and thus preferred social interactants, whether exchanging diamonds or offering interest-free loans. Therefore, individuals will benefit from accurate information about how beliefs and commitment vary across members. Third, signalers must be able to achieve benefits at the expense of those receiving the signal. In other words, there needs to be the potential for deceit. When diamond deals are sealed with handshakes, especially between people meeting for the first time, the potential for deceit is obviously high. Fourth, the cost or benefit to the signaler of sending the signal should be correlated with the signaler's quality with respect to the attribute. This last condition will take a little more space to explain. For the sake of simplicity, imagine a population divided between believers and skeptics. Believers will have genuinely forsaken many worldly behaviors, while skeptics have not. Israeli *Haredim*, for example, shun the secular media entirely, including secular newspapers, radio, movies, television, and the Internet (although some exceptions are made for the latter). Since they avoid these "distractions," their opportunity costs, that is, the costs associated with missed opportunities while performing a behavior, adhering to a ban, or displaying a badge, are much lower for believers than for those who have not relinquished such activities. Men in these communities are expected to dedicate their days to praying and studying religious texts. Since alternative activities are severely restricted, the cost of spending long hours in religious devotions is less for them as believers, in terms of viable missed opportunities, than for skeptics who still have all of those secular activities available to them.

Behaviors, Badges, and Bans

Thus far I have treated the obligations that religious groups demand of their members, namely the three Bs, as a suite of requirements. There is some justification for this, since most religious groups do not allow their members to pick and choose which obligations they want to fulfill and which they may ignore. You can wear the *Haredi* garb, but if you like pork chops, you would not be counted among the community. Nevertheless, it will be useful to point out some of the distinguishing characteristics of the three Bs.

We will start with bans. The astute reader is likely wondering how a taboo, such as avoiding the consumption of pig products, can be a signal. Ritual behaviors and badges can be observed by others in the community, but how can one observe something that is not done? In contrast to ritual performances and symbolic markers, bans can only be "observed" when they are at risk of being violated. The Jew who refrains from eating in a social setting because he knows the food is not kosher is signaling his identity as committed to Judaic law. Sometimes linguistic messages, such as "I don't eat nonkosher food," are required to signal adherence to a ban. Generally, however, other badges and rituals imply the adherence to a suite of taboos: wearing a *kippah* or *tzniut* (modest) clothing signals that shrimp will not be in the diet. Since bans cannot be directly displayed, they are only effective as signals when they are in jeopardy of being transgressed, such as an observant Jew who must attend a business lunch at a nonkosher restaurant.

Although bans do not constitute "complete" signals, they are especially proficient at increasing group solidarity and commitment. We can thank economists for this insight. Economists refer to what we have been calling bans or taboos as *prohibitions*.[19] They explain that prohibitions are efficient gatekeepers, eliminating those not dedicated to a group, because they effectively tax secular items. By decreeing that certain activities or goods are off limits for adherents, it becomes more costly to pursue those activities or acquire those goods because offenders will suffer the costs of punishment. This tax on secular activities and goods consequently encourages religious activity, making it "cheaper" and thus more attractive to those who accept a religious community's prohibitionary decrees. By raising the price of secular activities, the opportunity costs for religious activities (the costs of activities forgone) are lowered. For example, as mentioned above, *Haredim* are forbidden to watch television or subscribe to secular newspapers. Violation of these pastimes can be costly, because harsh communal punishments, including expelling their children from school, will be enacted if a transgression is discovered. Concomitantly, encouraged religious activities such as prayer and text study become less costly and more desirable due to fewer competing alternatives on which *Haredim* can spend their time.

Distinguishing between prohibitions (bans or taboos), ritual behaviors, and badges is useful since it underscores the separate processes that ultimately result in increased intragroup solidarity and commitment. For many religious behaviors and badges, though, both social processes seem to be at work. For instance, we can confidently categorize the black hats, pants, and frocks of the *Haredim* as badges that signal group commitments. However, these badges also deter them from participating in activities where the *Haredim* are unwelcome. The *Haredi* dress code essentially puts a tax on activities that, whether implicitly or explicitly, seek to restrict *Haredi* participation. Consequently, in addition to their role as signals, these badges impact solidarity through a process similar to how bans serve as gatekeepers, namely by making forbidden activities costly. Rituals can operate similarly, as any Jew who has donned *tefillin* and *davened shachrit* at an airport can attest.

Hard-to-Fake Handicaps or Impossible-to-Fake Indices?

It appears that religious behaviors, badges, and bans meet the conditions for the evolutionary stability of a costly signal, as outlined by Bliege Bird and Smith. So, depending on your preference, the three Bs are hard to fake, costly to fake, or using Zahavi and Zahavi's term, classified as handicaps. But are some religious behaviors, badges, and bans also *impossible* to fake?

Certain badges, such as circumcision, are permanent and quite difficult to fake, as Solomon Perel's excruciating account of his attempt to create a foreskin while masquerading as a Hitler Youth attests.[20] Roy Rappaport, the eminent cultural ecologist and anthropologist of religion, claimed that all rituals, badges, and bans are indexical signals; that is, they are signals that refer to what they denote by being truly affected by them (e.g., weathervanes denote wind direction).[21] Although the logic of his argument applies to all the Bs, here we will focus on ritual as Rappaport himself did. He argued that while ritual behaviors appear to be shrouded in mystery, they are deliberate and their message to other adherents is clear: participation in a ritual performance indexically signals acceptance of (and not necessarily belief in) the moral values encoded in the ritual. He maintained that regardless of whether or not individuals believe in the moral values encoded in a ritual performance, by participating they are signaling that they accept the moral code of the community and can be held accountable if the rules are compromised.

Rappaport stresses the distinction between belief and acceptance, a distinction that is certainly important in assessing a signal's message. Are performers of ritual signaling their religious beliefs and group commitments, or are they signaling their acceptance of a moral code that is implied by the performance of a ritual? Both are likely, but it is only acceptance that is indexical and thus nearly impossible to fake. Consider a wedding. During a wedding ceremony the bride and groom send a public signal that they accept the moral values, as defined by the community, incumbent upon the institution of their marriage. This signal is indexical—by performing the ritual the performers cannot help but indicate their acceptance of the moral code.

Nonetheless, despite their acceptance, the newlyweds may not believe in the moral code's virtues. The moral code itself varies widely by community: a *Haredi* wedding endorses very different values than does a Reconstructionist Jewish wedding involving a gay or lesbian couple.

To summarize, performing a ritual indexically signals acceptance of the moral values implicit in the ritual, but also signals belief in the doctrines that support and provide meaning for the ritual. Acceptance is nearly impossible to fake; the community observed the wedding, so one's performance cannot be denied. An individual is therefore held accountable for the moral values implicit to this marital union, such as sexual and financial fidelity. Nonetheless, the performance of these rites also signals that the actor believes in these morals (that infidelity is wrong). But it is not an indexical signal of belief, but rather a hard-to-fake signal or handicap, that faces the potential of deception. Thus, marriage vows cannot prevent a husband from committing adultery, but they do make him accountable to the community for his actions.

The Fourth B: Belief

Most scholars and laypersons alike place "belief" at the center of religion. Beliefs also play an essential role in how religious behaviors, badges, and bans operate as effective signals. To clarify this role, I will briefly discuss belief in supernatural agents, internalization of religious beliefs, and the emotional significance of these beliefs.

The renowned philosopher, physician, and rabbi Moses Maimonides (Rambam) claimed that the fundamental *mitzvah* that provides the foundation for all other *mitzvot* is belief in God.[22] How is belief in God related to the signaling function of religious practices? Evolutionary biologists distinguish between ultimate and proximate causes of behavior. Ultimate explanations refer to evolutionary explanations that either provide the historical trajectory of a trait or offer a functional explanation for its existence. In contrast, proximate explanations address the cognitive and physiological underpinnings of a behavior. An ultimate explanation for why two stags lock horns in combat is their desire for increased access to fertile females; extraordinary testosterone levels provide a proximate explanation for this same behavior. Ultimate and proximate accounts are not competing, but rather offer complementary explanations for understanding behavioral patterns. Our discussion thus far has concerned ultimate explanations, focusing on the gains individuals can achieve through costly religious practices, namely the ability to overcome problems of collective action. From the view of signaling theory, supernatural beliefs are proximate mechanisms that facilitate the efficient functioning of religious signals. But how?

There is an abundance of experimental and experiential evidence that suggests that humans have a tough time incurring immediate costs to achieve long-term gains, as anyone who has tried to stick to a low-fat diet can attest. Many people, of course, put money into retirement funds or pay the costly tuitions for a college education with the aim of increased future salaries. However, when humans pay short-term costs to achieve long-term gains their decisions are typically strategic and their information concerning the probability of ultimately achieving the long-term gains is high. The functional effects of religious practices, however, are generally hidden or ignored. I have yet to hear the *Haredi* rabbi who exclaims, "Pray three times daily and you'll reap all the mutual insurance benefits we offer!" To the contrary, when trying to motivate religious practice, rabbis often rely on exhortations that promise supernatural rewards or punishments.[23] There is a good reason for this. Supernatural rewards and punishments can change the payoffs that individuals perceive when performing religious practices.[24] If you believe an eternity in *gehennom* lies in the balance, fasting during Yom Kippur does not sound so bad. But we still have not solved our dilemma of how to encourage individuals to pay short-term costs to achieve long-term gains; indeed, introducing otherworldly payoffs seems to have exacerbated the problem. Even if supernatural rewards and punishments alter the perceived payoffs so that individuals expect gains or losses depending on their actions, the payoffs are still in the future. In fact they are even further in the future, awaiting the performer's arrival in the afterlife. Moreover, since these rewards and punishments cannot be proven or even indirectly demonstrated, why would anyone include them in their calculations when determining whether to pursue a religious practice? To understand how supernatural payoffs are effective at encouraging religious practices we turn to how these payoffs become internalized.

Consider someone who regularly attends *shul*. According to my earlier argument, by attending *shul* one indexically signals the acceptance of the moral strictures that are the foundation of the synagogue's theology. Attendance signals participation in the community and thus one is accountable for transgressing the community's moral code. Synagogue attendance also signals belief, let's say in God, but we argued that this signal is fakeable. Not all synagogue attendees necessarily believe in God, and even those who do vary in their confidence about their beliefs. However, signaling theory suggests that while such signals are fakeable, they are certainly useful indicators of belief and more reliable than uttered statements of belief. The reliability of synagogue attendance as an indicator of belief, of course, increases with intensity and costs, such as more frequent attendance, higher financial contributions, or more tedious sermons. Nonetheless, it is possible to regularly attend synagogue for ulterior motives, rather than communion with God. In fact, psychologists have distinguished between those who attend a house of worship in order to connect with their Creator (known as intrinsically motivated) and those who attend for reasons other than the religious experience (known as extrinsically motivated). For instance, some individuals ignore the majority of their religious obligations but are encouraged to attend synagogue by family members (extrinsic motivation). If not motivated by belief, they perhaps accede to familial requests because they find that the benefits of domestic stability outweigh the cost of attending synagogue.

Despite the potential for deception, repeated ritual performance, such as regularly attending synagogue, even as an atheist, may foster and enhance belief. Since ritual performance is unambiguously associated with overt group values, psychological processes, including the popularized phenomenon known as cognitive dissonance, will cause nonbelievers to either modify their belief or discontinue the ritual actions. Unless there are strong extrinsic motivations, at some introspective moment the attendee will ask, "If I don't believe in any of this, what I am doing here every week?" Two options then remain: start believing or stop attending. What is remarkable is how often the former is chosen. Ritual participation can foster and internalize belief.

The Rabbis have long appreciated that religious practices can transform attitudes and that action may precede belief. For example, the Torah relates that when the Israelites received the commandments at Sinai, they responded, "*na'aseh v'nishma,*" which translates as "We will do and we will listen."[25] This verse is one of the most widely quoted verses in the Torah and is often discussed as a core value of the Jewish faith. Rabbinic commentators emphasize the importance of the order of the declaration.[26] One would expect hearing and understanding to precede action, yet they argue that the opposite is equally true. First *do,* then you will *understand.*[27] In other words, the rabbinic recipe for attaining faith does not include studying theological or philosophical arguments for the existence of God. Indeed, they argue that one should not be concerned with the religious dogma that gives meaning to the rituals; simply perform the rituals and belief and understanding will follow. As Rabbi Avraham Heschel describes, "We do not have faith because of deeds; we may attain faith through sacred deeds.... Through the ecstasy of deeds he learns to be certain of the hereness of God. Right living is a way to right thinking."[28]

Religious practices generally possess four characteristics that enable them to promote and internalize supernatural beliefs. First, religious behaviors, badges, and bans are physically manifested displays or actions. Physical participation, which provides performers with concrete evidence of their personal involvement, contributes to psychological uneasiness if the performer does not share the values encoded in the religious action. Note, for example, that Jews follow Hannah's lead in prayer and do not sit silently while praying.[29] Worshipers are encouraged to enunciate each word so that it is audible to themselves. Similarly, blessings over food and other activities must be at least whispered—silent recitation is insufficient. Furthermore, while no law prescribes the practice, many Orthodox Jews *shokel* (sway back and forth) while praying, reciting blessings, and studying. Many religious practices are typically performed or displayed publicly. Since they are widely observed there are additional social pressures to reconcile any contradictions between belief and behavior, pressures that would be absent if the practices were performed only privately. Although prayers in Judaism can be offered alone, reciting prayers in a *minyan,* a quorum of at least ten men,[30] is highly preferred, and religious men will go to great efforts to ensure that their prayers are recited communally rather than in solitude. Religious behaviors, badges, and bans are formal; their lack of ambiguity makes them effective modes of communication. Religious practices are seldom mistaken for anything other than religious practices. When Bart Simpson incorrectly assumed three *Haredi* pedestrians with long beards were members of the rock band ZZ Top, the scene was humorous because the audience was well aware of Bart's error. Religious practices are often repetitive, cyclical, or even continuous. Although some rituals, such as a *bris milah* (circumcision) and a bar or bat mitzvah, occur only periodically, countless Jewish rituals are performed daily, weekly, monthly, or yearly. Some, such as *shmittah* (seven-year sabbaticals for the Land), occur at multiyear intervals. And many bans and badges, like pig avoidance and *tzniut* dress, are in force from cradle to grave. The repetition of formal, publicly observed religious actions demands greater reconciliation than any conflicting beliefs.

Religious emotions further serve to internalize religious beliefs. Religion is an emotional affair, and the Rabbis, especially the *Chasidim,* implore Jews to fulfill the *mitzvoth* with *kavanah* (intention, concentration, and focus). Many commentators note that it is preferable to recite a few prayers with *kavanah* than to complete the entire service without emotional energy.[31] Indeed, staid religious practices soon become the data of historians rather than the routines and principles by which living populations organize their lives. Religious practices are supported and sustained by the emotions they evoke. Moreover, supernatural religious beliefs, which cannot be verified logically, are verified by believers "emotionally." Religious practices, rituals in particular, often increase arousal in the limbic system and generate what is typically referred to as a "religious experience." Rappaport claims that the "truth of such an experience seems to the communicant to be sufficiently demonstrated by its mere occurrence, and since a sacred proposition or its symbol (e.g., the cross) is taken to be intrinsic to the experience, the sacred proposition partakes of this often powerful and compelling sense of truth."[32] Eugene d'Aquili and Andrew Newberg, pioneers in the neurobiology of religion, argue that not only are religious experiences perceived as true, they "appear to be 'more real' than baseline reality and are vividly described as such by experiencers after they return to baseline reality.... So real do these experiences appear when recalled in baseline reality that they have the ability to alter the way the experiencers live their lives."[33] In addition, since emotions are generated from limbic structures that are out of conscious control, they are difficult to "fake"[34] and can consequently serve as reliable signals of trustworthiness and commitment.[35]

So it appears that through psychological and physiological processes, as well as inherent structural characteristics such as formality and repetitiveness, religious practices are effective at internalizing the supernatural beliefs with which they are associated. Why is it important that beliefs are internalized? Internalizing religious beliefs makes the perceived payoffs for religious performance, in which supernatural punishments or rewards ensure that the religious performance is profitable, the real payoffs. The distinguished University of Chicago sociologist James Coleman observes that norm internalization is efficient when there is a range of actions that are sought to be controlled by a community.[36] This aptly characterizes Orthodox Jewish communities, which generally seek members that behave prosocially toward coreligionists under normal and adverse conditions; in other words, they wish to encourage cooperation and trust between members regardless of the situation that arises. Indeed, *ahavas Yisroel* (love of fellow Jews) is a central tenet of Judaism, one that religious children hear from their teachers and parents continuously. Furthermore, Coleman argues that external policing to encourage norm compliance becomes less efficient when members must be monitored continuously, especially if they are dispersed. Under these conditions, societies are more likely to rely on internalization strategies. The intragroup trust and cooperation promoted within religious communities are a continuous obligation not limited in time (such as just during work hours) and place (such as just in a synagogue). It is therefore not possible to monitor members' commitment to this ethic at all times. Consequently, internalizing this ethic is important.

What is particularly interesting about this whole system is that religious communities do not rely exclusively on these internalization strategies.[37] All religious communities may impose punishments, either institutionally or through informal means like cutting off social interactions. Although *cherem* (formal rabbinic excommunication) rarely occurs today, historically the threat was real. Heretics like *Tanna* Elisha ben Avuyah (second century) and philosopher Baruch Spinoza (seventeenth century) were not tolerated and were shown the door. Today, Jewish communities rely on socially ostracizing those who are not abiding by community rules. In addition, transgressions can result in lineage excommunication (*karet*). Thus, as in most religious communities, Judaism relies on both supernatural and material punishment systems to ensure conformity with community norms. Likewise, religious communities do not fully depend on the goodwill they cultivate through their moral teachings; systems that monitor behavior are completely intact. However, there is little emphasis on observing members' daily routines, which are too costly to monitor continuously anyway. Efficiently and ingeniously, the monitoring costs are shifted from observing daily life to observing adherence to religious obligations, which, due to their formality, conspicuousness, repetitiveness, and public performance, are much less costly to scrutinize. The system works because religious practices are worth watching since they are reliable signals of community commitment.

Private Practice

Our discussion on monitoring religious practices raises an important question: why do religions, including Judaism, require that their members engage in private rituals, badges, and bans even though they are rarely witnessed and compliance cannot be enforced? Two reasons are germane, the first for the individual, the second for the group.

First, engaging in private practices, that is, practices fulfilled in solitude, appears to be an extremely effective method of convincing *oneself* that one believes in the doctrine that gives meaning to the rituals. And the best way to convince others of your group commitment is to first convince yourself. When individuals engage in private religious practices, such as reciting the *Shema* in bed before falling asleep, they cannot rationalize such actions as coercion by group members. Because of the opportunity to defect on private obligations without risk of detection, engagement in such practices is the sole responsibility of the individual. However, some privately performed rituals, such as reciting Psalms and talmudic study, can be evaluated in the public sphere by assessing knowledge, thus making it difficult to fake their private performance. Moreover, many rituals, including prayer and textual study, are practiced both publicly and privately. For instance, Jews are expected to recite blessings before consuming any food, regardless of whether or not anyone else is at the table. The failure to say the required blessings when alone may result in an increased likelihood of forgetting to say them in a public setting. Nevertheless, individuals are more apt to question their own commitment if they are failing to perform ritual duties that they believe others in the community are practicing, even if the rituals are never performed in public. The performance of private religious practices reinforces group commitment when performers convince themselves of their commitment to the group.

The group-level benefits of private obligations further account for their prevalence. Somewhat paradoxically, by requiring adherents to perform private practices, the price of performing public practices is driven up for free-riding skeptics, thus enhancing the reliability of public practices as signals of group commitment. To understand the logic behind this surprising twist, we will start with a little more obvious assumption: believers perceive net gains from religious activity (which is why they engage in it), whereas skeptics perceive net costs from religious activity (which is why they refrain). The critical point is that within these internal calculations, which are of course unconscious, believers will include the costs of private practices while skeptics will not—there is no incentive for a skeptic to fake piety when nobody is watching. Since believers pay the costs of private practice while skeptics do not, and believers perceive net benefits from following the full suite of religious obligations while skeptics do not, believers must either perceive public practices to be much less costly than skeptics do, or they must perceive much greater benefits from these practices than skeptics do. Therefore, private obligations force the perceived net gains of public obligations to be significantly higher for believers than for skeptics (which is of course usually achieved through supernatural rewards), and consequently private obligations ensure that those performing public religious practices are those who are genuinely committed to the group.[38]

Applying the Theory

Any reader who has persevered to this point in the chapter is likely pondering that evolutionary signaling theory does indeed appear to explain some puzzling features of religion, but religion is so much more than growing *peyos* and refraining from pork; this theory surely cannot explain *all* of religion. And indeed, I could not agree more. I am skeptical that any lone theory can explain all of the extraordinarily diverse beliefs and behaviors that fall under the umbrella we call religion; nonetheless, signaling theory does provide many valuable insights into the selection pressures that have shaped religious practices in our evolutionary history. But as mentioned above, if evolutionary signaling theory of religion is to have any value outside the ivory towers, it must provide insights into current religious trends. Here

I offer several predictions derived from the theory and examine their relevance for understanding aspects of Jewish communities today.

Jewish Education. Signaling theory predicts that early indoctrination will be important for groups with many costly signals. Early indoctrination minimizes the opportunity costs perceived by group members, increasing their ability to tolerate costly constraints on their lives. The talmudic authors clearly recognized the importance of early indoctrination in decreasing opportunity costs. Jews who "return" to traditional Judaism are known as *ba'alei teshuva* (literally "masters of return").[39] In a well-known Talmudic statement, the Sages claim, "in the place where a penitent Jew—a ba'al teshuva—stands, even a perfectly righteous person cannot stand."[40] The Rabbis suggest that those who have sinned can achieve a higher level of spirituality than those who have been righteous all their lives. Without having ever tasted a particular sin, the temptation to transgress is not as great as for those who have. Rabbi Joseph Telushkin, who was raised in an Orthodox household, states this clearly:

> The apparent rationale of the rabbis for holding the *ba'al teshuva* in such high esteem was their belief that it is a much greater struggle for a nonreligious person to become religious and to give up formerly permitted practices, than it is for a religious person to remain religious. More than a few *ba'alei teshuva* (plural of *ba'al teshuva*) have told me that they desperately miss lobster or shrimp. As a Jew who was raised in a kosher home, I confess that these foods have never tempted me.[41]

Not surprisingly, early exposure to rituals and prayers is essential in traditional Jewish life. Indeed, arguably the central Jewish prayer, the *V'ahavta* (the first paragraph of the *Shema*), which is placed inside *mezuzot* (hung on Jewish doorposts) and *tefillin* (phylacteries), emphasizes the importance of teaching the Torah's laws to children.[42] Ironically, this is the first prayer that Jewish children learn, so children are thereby taught the importance of teaching Jewish ways to *their* children. Jewish children in religious homes are reciting prayers and performing rituals long before they are able to grasp any theological implications of their actions. And as Jewish communities across America grapple with "continuity," the importance of early exposure to Jewish life has been repeatedly emphasized. Various studies have shown that attending Jewish day school (Jewish private school) is among the most significant factors determining whether a child will remain within the tribe. Day school education is associated with much lower rates of intermarriage, higher rates of adult synagogue affiliation, and greater Jewish involvement in adulthood.[43]

Converts and Ba'alei Teshuva. The signaling theory of religion predicts that if religious practices are signals of commitment, those with the greatest need to demonstrate group commitment will display religious signals with the highest intensity.[44] If this is true, it should be particularly important for those who convert to Judaism to exhibit their newfound identity and group commitments. Although there is considerable anecdotal evidence that this is the case among Jews, there is little empirical work. As Rabbi Telushkin notes, "[i]n many contemporary American Jewish families, it's the convert to Judaism that takes religion seriously."[45] In one of the few quantitative studies on Jewish conversion, sociologists Nava Lerer and Egon Mayer found that converts on average had similar levels of religious observance and affiliation to those who were born Jewish, despite the fact that many conversions are occurring for extrinsic reasons, such as to please one's in-laws, rather than conviction in the tenets of Judaism.[46] The following joke captures the sentiment that has been understudied by social scientists.

> Before his child heads off for college a father tells his son, "Remember, don't marry someone who is not Jewish." Sure enough, the son comes home for Thanksgiving and brings his gentile girlfriend with him. Eventually, she converts and after college they marry. On the Saturday after their wedding the son has his breakfast, grabs his briefcase and begins to head out the door. His wife asks, "Where do you think you are going?" "To the office of course," he replies. "Oh, no you're not! I converted so you could go and work on the Sabbath? Put down your briefcase, you're heading to synagogue!" This went on for weeks, and in desperation the son called up the father for advice. "Dad, she won't let me go to the office on Saturday. What should I do?" His dad answers, "I told you not to marry someone who is not Jewish."

Conversion is a process that results in a change of religious community for an individual and thus occurs even when changing denominations within the same institutional religion. As most *Haredi* communities are closed to mainstream Jewry, becoming a *ba'al teshuva* can be understood as a conversion process. In order to fit in with the community, *ba'alei teshuva* often exhibit conspicuous displays of religiosity. In research on the religious practices of women in Tzfat, I found that *ba'alei teshuva* are much more likely to attend synagogue as well as pray at the gravesites of *tzadikim* (righteous ones) buried in Tzfat. The conspicuous enthusiasm of the *ba'al teshuva* is often a source of considerable humor among those who were raised in religious homes. In one joke, for example, a *ba'al teshuva* named Eliyahu, which means "my God is God," learns that God's Hebrew names should be spoken only in prayer, and thus at other times a "k" sound is inserted so that God's actual name is not uttered. In his newfound piety, the *ba'al teshuva* now refers to himself as "Kelikahu."

The signaling theory of religion also predicts that as a result of the importance of early indoctrination for minimizing opportunity costs, converts may be trusted less than those who were raised within a community. This is especially likely among groups that maintain high levels of costly signaling. Converts will perceive higher opportunity costs than members by birth, thus the willingness to pay the high cost of membership may be viewed with skepticism about the intentions of the convert. For example, it has been well documented that *ba'alei teshuva* who enter the *Haredi* community are unlikely to be welcomed as equals.[47] In his book on *Haredi* life David Landau writes:

> *Haredism's* celebration and absorption of the *teshuva* movement is not necessarily matched by a wholehearted acceptance of the individual *ba'al* or *ba'alat teshuva* into

the *Haredi* family. The litmus test is marriage, and here *ba'alei teshuva* often find their paths blocked by an informal but strongly entrenched discrimination.... The whispered assumption in *Haredi* circles is that if a *Haredi*-born boy or girl marries a *ba'al teshuva*, there must be "something wrong" with him or her: either they are poor, or they have a health disability.[48]

This bias against *ba'alei teshuva* occurs despite a recurring emphasis in Jewish liturgy and law to accept the proselyte as a full member of the community. It appears that those born into the *Haredi* community recognize that the costs of membership are too high to be paid without early indoctrination. The devotion of the *ba'alei teshuva* is not doubted by the *Haredi* born; ironically it is their rationality that seems to be in question.[49] Over the past several decades thousands of Jews have become *ba'alei teshuva*, who more often than not end up marrying each other, and whose numbers appear to be continually increasing. As Rabbi Telushkin enthuses, "it can safely be said that the explosion of the *ba'al teshuva* movement has been one of the most exciting events in post–World War II Orthodox Jewish life."[50] The causes of the success of this movement are multilayered and complex, but what is clear is that it was entirely unexpected by most non-Orthodox observers who believed that strict adherence to Jewish law would never survive the twentieth century. Certainly other religious communities have experienced religious revivals as well, so any explanation must also address the parallel phenomena in other communities. One aspect of the movement that we can understand through signaling theory is that once the Reform and Conservative denominations minimized or abandoned the time-consuming *halachic* requirements of Judaism (see below), they were also no longer able to offer the strong sense of community that had historically characterized Judaism. In the Western world's open market for leisure, less traditional Jewish life competes with other activities. Hence, when the required obligations were lessened, so that hours of religious study and prayer or dietary restrictions were not limiting the participation in alternative forms of leisure, it is not surprising that people divided their time and identities among the synagogue, tennis club, bridge group, and countless other things. By maintaining the costly rituals, taboos, and badges, Orthodox communities have been able to maintain a more exclusive hold on the time and identity of their members. What often attracts *ba'alei teshuva* is precisely this sense of community, which had otherwise been missing from their lives. It also appears that the Reform and Conservative movements have recognized the value of ritual in maintaining communities, and in recent years the rabbis of both movements have encouraged their members to take on traditional religious practices that had previously been ignored or de-emphasized.

Retention and Defection. Judaism in the United States has higher retention rates from one generation to the next than liberal Protestant denominations, but among Jews it is the Orthodox who are most successful at retaining their ranks.[51] Not only are many Jews joining the Orthodox ranks and embracing greater *halachic* observance, but Orthodox communities are much more likely to retain their members than the other Jewish denominations. Estimates vary, but probably less than 10 percent of those raised in observant homes[52] leave the Orthodox world, and this number undoubtedly decreases when taking the *Haredim* into account.[53] Signaling theory offers some insights into why those born into a ritually demanding environment are more likely to remain in it. Most importantly, those raised in strictly halachic environments are likely to have lower potential success in alternative communities and are thus less likely to seek them. As one adolescent boy who had been thrown out of one *yeshiva* and the dorm of another exclaimed, "If I don't have hasidut, I don't have life."[54] With the exception of Chabad and some Breslov *Chassidim,* the *Haredim* are isolated from other segments of society. Thus, their members generally have less knowledge about alternative groups and face higher socialization costs than if they were to join either another group or secular society. In addition, as a consequence of the necessary investment in learning religious texts and performing rituals during childhood, comparatively less time and energy is invested in acquiring the skills that are often important to compete economically in modern communities. As one English teacher in a Brooklyn *yeshiva* remarked, "English was seen as a threat and therefore dismissed as a waste of time."[55] Math, science, and history are similarly minimized or ignored in Haredi *yeshivot*. In Israel, it is not unusual for the *Haredi* school day for boys to last eleven hours, the overwhelming majority of which is spent studying Talmud (and all children in Israel attend school six days per week, with Friday being a shorter day). Long hours of Talmud study constitute a particularly effective costly signal, since they do not directly prepare students for anything other than religious life.

It should be noted that signaling theory does not predict that inborn members will never leave a community with high membership demands. Indeed, at the beginning of the twentieth century, Jews were leaving Orthodox Judaism en masse. Signaling theory assumes that as a result of the gains achieved from intragroup cooperation, religious groups offer higher benefits to their members than nonreligious groups. When this condition is not met, we expect religious groups to fail or at least experience increasing rates of defection. Economic changes, either economic difficulties within the group or improved economic conditions in other groups, are likely to have a significant impact on membership retention rates. For example, we would expect that when poverty among the Israeli *Haredim* increases relative to the growth of the Israeli economy, defection among *Haredim* should increase. Additionally, the decision to remain a member should vary predictably with individual phenotypic quality. Across religious groups, there is wide variance in the phenotypic traits that are valued and rewarded. These include such traits as diligence, manual skills, scholarship, spirituality, courage, and fierceness. Within religious communities, those who are comparatively deficient in the venerated traits are most likely to defect and seek opportunities in groups that value other characteristics.[56] For example, male *Haredi* life revolves around continual study of traditional texts. Scholars are sought after for marriage and attain the highest prestige within the community. Not surprisingly, within these communities defection rates appear to be highest among those who are less intellectually oriented,[57] although those who find their intellectual curiosity stifled are also likely to leave.[58] Signaling theory predicts that apostasy will be a function of success in one's current environment and one's potential success in alternative groups.

Proselytizing. Costly signaling theory predicts that proselytizing should be less frequent by religious groups offering greater in-group benefits, since proselytizing increases the risk of invasion by free-riders.[59] Not only have Jews not replenished their numbers through proselytizing, traditionally, those who seek to convert must be turned away several times before they can even begin the years of learning required for Orthodox conversion. Contrary to popular impressions, however, Judaism was not always a nonproselytizing religion. Jews regularly proselytized prior to the first and second centuries C.E., and possibly later.[60] Eventually, the benefits accruing to Jews through increasing membership were outweighed by the costs (death) imposed for missionary activity by Christian authorities like Emperors Hadrian, Severus, and Constantine. Interestingly, in the United States, where Jews have achieved unprecedented acceptance into mainstream society, there have been renewed discussions about proselytizing among Conservative and Reform Jews, with various Jewish organizations and congregations actively seeking converts.[61] As signaling theory would predict, the Orthodox, who maintain greater mutual benefits needing protection from exploitation, have not joined this trend.

Denominational Differences. Although much of this chapter has focused on the *Haredim*, costly Jewish practices are not the providence of the *Haredim* alone. As discussed above, signaling theory predicts that when costs become too high, those who are less committed will flee the group. Signaling theory may thus offer some insights into denominational differences in the United States.[62] As American Jews have continued to climb the economic ladder over the past century, the time investments required to maintain the successful careers of many came into conflict with the time demands of Orthodox life.[63] The Reform movement, the largest denomination of American Jewry, responded to these conditions by eliminating costly ritual practice and stigmatizing markers.[64] They also reduced the necessary investments in learning by largely replacing traditional Hebrew prayers with English translations. The distinguishing feature of the Reform movement is its abandonment of *halacha* (Jewish law); decisions of ritual practice are a personal issue decided by the individual,[65] which has resulted in very low levels of ritual observance compared to other streams of Judaism.[66] Reform Judaism is not devoid of ritual, but rituals that are communally performed tend to be convenient rather than costly, with the aim of assimilation and integration into American society rather than the isolation typical of ultra-Orthodox Judaism. For example, the two most commonly celebrated Jewish holidays among Reform Jews, Passover and Chanukah (a minor Jewish holiday), usually occur around the time of Easter and Christmas, respectively, thus minimizing the costs of holidays too "distinctive" from those being celebrated by the Christians.

Conservative Judaism emerged as a response to the Reform movement's abandonment of *halacha*, feeling that their brethren had gone too far.[67] The position of the Conservative movement was to maintain the importance of *halacha,* but to modernize it, which in almost all circumstances has resulted in reducing the costs of Jewish obligations.[68] In point of fact, very few Conservative Jews hold by the decisions of the movement in general or their particular rabbi, with members dispersing over a wide spectrum of religious observance.

Interestingly, although the Conservative and Reform movements have lessened the ritual obligations of their members, they seem to have transferred those costs into financial costs, which are more compatible with their career-oriented constituents. In other words, the Conservative and Reform movements have not eliminated the costs of membership in the Tribe, but, rather than being time intensive, they have become financially taxing. Money can serve as a costly signal; however, it is not as effective as a time commitment. Although we all face different opportunity costs on our time (thus some people's time *is* more valuable than other people's time), we are all limited to a twenty-four-hour day. The size of our respective wallets, however, is not equally constrained. Unless monetary costs are strict percentages of income, which they are not,[69] those who are wealthy can pay the costs with less burden than their poorer congregants. Nonetheless, the monetary costs of Jewish life in America may have been pushed quite high. Over twenty years ago, sociologist Jerry Winter raised alarm bells in an article in *Moment* magazine titled "Who Can Afford to be Jewish?", which reported his research on the extreme costs of Jewish life in America.[70] Aside from synagogue dues, Winter also included the costs of day school education and Jewish Community Center membership in his estimates of the affordability of Jewish life.[71] Apparently, his warnings of the excessive costs of Jewish life have not been heeded. Recent magazine articles are still addressing the issue estimate that only 10 percent of American Jews can afford the full costs of Jewish life.[72] Despite the transfer of costs from time to financial obligations in Reform and Conservative Judaism, Orthodox Jews on average likely incur the highest relative financial costs to maintain their Jewish way of life.

To maintain its own constituents, Orthodoxy has had to respond to the less costly alternative forms of Jewish religiosity offered by Reform and Conservative Judaism. Two responses seem to have occurred. Some congregations have followed the Reform and Conservative movements and eased their standards somewhat, turning a blind eye to ritual infractions, as the active parking lots on Saturday morning of many Modern Orthodox *shuls* will attest. Others have embraced the Chasam Sofer's battle cry against the Reform movement: *"Chadash asur min ha Torah"* (Anything new is forbidden by Torah), and run in the opposite direction. We now turn toward this latter group.

Fundamentalism. Fundamentalism typically refers to a religious ideology that embraces scriptural literalism and traditional religious values.[73] Current fundamentalist trends, however, have placed higher demands on their practitioners than the traditional practices that they claim to emulate. For example, the standards of *kashrut* (laws pertaining to kosher and nonkosher food) among *Haredi* Jews are more stringent now than at any time in Jewish history. Marc Shapiro of the University of Scranton notes that among the *Haredim* as well as Modern Orthodox, "a food item without a kashrut rabbinic symbol cannot be eaten, even though 40 years ago it was still acceptable to determine an item's kashrut on the basis of reading the ingredients."[74] In addition, the existence of more than one rabbinic symbol vouching for the kosher status of a food product is the result of Orthodox groups' refusal to trust each other's rabbinic supervision. The *mechitzot* (barriers separating men and women during prayer services) have gotten higher and less transparent while women's sleeves and skirts have lengthened. Separate hours at swimming pools for males and females, standard across observant communities, have now been extended to some supermarkets in Brooklyn and B'nai Brak, where men's and women's shopping hours are now separate. Although social scientists focusing on Jewish life have decried this trend, their explanations tend to be limited to only some Jewish communities;[75] Orthodox Judaism represents just one of many groups in which ritual demands are increasing. Signaling theory suggests two factors may be motivating the fundamentalist trend toward increasing ritual requirements. First, the rising costs of membership may be a direct response to increases in perceived risk of apostasy faced by religious groups. Indeed, modern fundamentalism may be partially fueled by the increased perceived risk of apostasy generated by the rapid improvement in mass media technologies, which expose wide audiences to Western secular values and culture. Second, and quite paradoxically, the multicultural openness of Western societies may also contribute to fundamentalist trends. Although embracing multiculturalism is not typical of aggressive fundamentalism, societies where group differences are tolerated and even encouraged need to increase their distinctiveness to maintain their in-group cohesion. This is because previous badges and bans, such as publicly wearing a *kippah*, are no longer as costly as they once were. Thus, multiculturalism may actually initiate movements toward fundamentalism, even while vehemently rejecting fundamentalism's message of possessing life's only true path.

Interestingly, fundamentalist trends in Judaism are not raising the intensity of all forms of religious observance. The Rabbis differentiate between *mitzvot ben adam lemakom* (religious duties between humans and God) and *mitzvot ben adam lechavero* (religious duties between humans). Although the Rabbis interpret much of Jewish suffering, such as the destruction of both Jerusalem Temples, as a consequence of Jewish failure to fulfill the latter, the former defines religious status among Jews of all denominations. As Telushkin observes, "If two Jews are speaking about a third and the question is raised as to whether or not the person is religious, the answer will be based exclusively on the person's level of ritual observance: 'He keeps Shabbat and *kashrut*, he is religious. He doesn't keep them, he is not.' Ethics are treated almost like an extra-curricular activity—nice, but not that important in defining a person's religiosity."[76]

Although Telushkin and others express dismay at this state of affairs, from the perspective of signaling theory these trends are not surprising. The rituals, bans, and badges indeed serve to define community members. Community membership is not effectively defined by altruistic actions because they can be performed for reasons other than group commitment, such as simply a desire to help others. Because *mitzvot ben adam lemakom* cannot be rationalized other than as a commitment to God's commandments, they serve as effective signals of belief in the community's goals and ideals. Psychologist Robert Cialdini has argued that fraternity hell weeks never include charitable services for similar reasons.[77] The pledge cannot rationalize (to himself or others) undergoing the pain of hell week by claiming that he was engaging in honorable or altruistic activities. These ritual requirements are thus effective signals of group commitment.

For most of the twentieth century strict observance was enough to differentiate the *Haredim* from the Modern Orthodox, but that is no longer the case. As Marc Shapiro comments, "now that the Modern Orthodox also eat *glatt* kosher, increasing stringencies must be newly deployed to up the ante."[78] As signaling theory predicts, people seem to be more interested in what others think than in what God may think, a distinction that, ironically, drives them toward doing observable *mitzvot* between humans and God, rather than less conspicuous ones between humans.

Observers of Orthodoxy's march toward greater stringency have generally accused the Rabbis of leading blind followers to certain destruction.[79] Contrary to these claims, signaling theory would suggest an inevitable tension between increasing stringencies and the willingness of the community to adhere to such demands. In Israel, it does not appear that the masses are blindly following the edicts of the Rabbis; rather, it seems that the *Haredi* religious schools are able to enforce demands that community members would otherwise be unwilling to accept. Schools serve as the great gatekeepers of the *Haredim*. Because of the high fertility rates among the *Haredim*, there is always a shortage of space in *Haredi* schools, and acceptance is highly competitive. Potential students must take entrance exams, and parents and child are thoroughly interviewed. Inappropriate socks or a woman's visible hair can prevent admittance. And once accepted, if children or parents lapse in their religious standards, the children are expelled. Nor does the pressure end once children are out of school. Given the high fertility rates among the *Haredim*, once all of their kids have graduated, they likely already have grandchildren in school. Paradoxically, building more *Haredi* schools, so that schools must compete for students rather than the converse, may actually reduce the pressures that are driving *Haredim* toward increased ritual stringencies.

Reliable Signals, Not Perfect Signals

To avoid a potential point of confusion, it is important to emphasize that religious behaviors, badges, and bans signal group commitments, but they do not guarantee them. Indeed, evolutionary biologists who have developed sophisticated models of signaling processes show that signals can be stable even with free-riders in the population.[80] Obviously, if too many of the signals are deceptive the signal will lose its value, but a minority of deceptive signals can be tolerated and still provide important information. In Tzfat, the transformation from hippie to *Chassid* can occur overnight with a haircut and a shopping spree to the local outlet selling black attire. The *peyos* resting on the ex-hippie's shoulders were the only hair left uncut, so someone who cannot read a letter of Hebrew looks as though he has been studying in *yeshiva* his entire life. Although these *ba'alei teshuva* have strong desires to be committed to the group, even if they are yet unaware of what that entails, there are others who wear the uniform but are on their way out of the community. Author Faranak Margolese describes a young Brooklyn *Chassid* who sports the full *Chassidic* garb, including *peyos* down to his chin, yet on Yom Kippur he "eats in a coffee shop" and on Shabbat "he walks outside the community, gets in a car and drives to Manhattan where he smokes and hangs out."[81] Tellingly, when the stakes are high, group members rarely rely purely on religious signals to evaluate commitment and trust. When reputational information is available it is seldom ignored; it is evaluated along with symbolic messages, often taking priority. For instance, in her study on New York's *Haredi* diamond merchants, Shield discerns that "religious piety does not substitute for ethical business practice; in fact, expressions of piety without ethical behavior garner considerable contempt. Traders are too savvy to let superficial emblems of religiosity blind them to dubious marketplace behaviors."[82]

Do We Really Need an *Evolutionary* Model?

Many of the predictions offered above did not necessarily need to be derived from an evolutionary model of signaling. Economists were the first to recognize that signaling theory was a powerful tool for understanding seemingly irrational and bizarre religious behavior. Lawrence Iannaccone observed that the satisfaction individuals get from religion depends not only on their own investment, but also on the investment of others.[83] When you are one of twenty people sitting in a sanctuary that seats five hundred, it is hard to get emotionally riveted; but when they have to put seats in the aisles and the congregants know the service and participate enthusiastically, one's own enjoyment of the experience also increases. Iannaccone argued that stigmas and sacrifices (our behaviors, badges, and bans) served to weed out those who were not fully committed to the congregation so that those who are committed can maximize their enjoyment (or in economic jargon, "utility") by being surrounded by others who are similarly committed. Iannaccone offers several elegant models to clarify his arguments, and he rigorously tests the theory with data from various sources. For example, he shows that in a sample of American Christian denominations, the communities with the strictest demands, such as the Latter-day Saints Church and Seventh-day Adventists, have the highest levels of church attendance and prayer frequency. He obtains similar results when comparing Orthodox, Conservative, and Reform Jews.

From an evolutionary perspective, the trouble with the purely economic approach is that it is hard to believe that natural selection would design humans to participate in all sorts of costly activities just so they can sit in church with others who also know the liturgy. What an evolutionary perspective offers is a reason why we might expect a correlation between rituals, taboos, badges, and church or synagogue attendance—they all serve as costly signals of group commitment that enable groups to overcome inherent problems of cooperation. Throughout our evolutionary history, humans have faced problems of cooperation, many of which were vital to our survival, including hunting and warfare. Although most of us forage in a supermarket these days, and few of us have been on a battlefront, religion continues to serve as a mechanism that solves collective action problems that arise, especially in economic domains, and allows groups to offer mutual assurance benefits that would otherwise be exploited to depletion.

The evolutionary signaling theory of religion maintains that increased commitment among the faithful will translate into successful cooperation, not just more members in the pews, and that high-prestige cooperators will leave on average more descendants than the less cooperative. Groups that require the most of their members are expected to achieve the highest levels of cooperation, whereas groups that demand less of their members will find it more difficult to achieve collective goals. In ethnohistorical work that I pursued with psychologist Eric Bressler, we found that among nineteenth-century communes, the definitive place to study human cooperation, religious communes did indeed demand more of their members than their secular counterparts, such as celibacy, relinquishing all material possessions, and vegetarianism.[84] Whereas religious communes demanding more of their members survived longer, this was not true for secular communes; there was no relationship between the requirements imposed and commune longevity. We were surprised by this latter result, since secular groups such as militaries and fraternities appear to successfully employ costly rites to sustain cohesion. Although both religious and secular practices can promote cooperation, religious practices may ironically generate greater belief and commitment because they sanctify unverifiable ideologies. Due to their reliance on supernatural elements, religious theologies are generally beyond the possibility of examination. Contemporary religions struggle when they extend beyond this border into convictions that can be evaluated, such as the claim that Earth is a less than 6,000-year-old planet orbited by the sun. In contrast, secular ideologies are subject to the vicissitudes of examination and are thus less stable than religious ideologies. Successful secular groups often incorporate unverifiable elements into their ideologies, such as "brotherhood" and "liberty," both of which are commonly trumpeted in fraternities and militaries. The ability of religious practices to evoke emotional experiences that can be associated with enduring supernatural concepts and symbols differentiates them from secular rituals, badges, and bans and may explain why they achieve greater long-term commitment and cooperation, as was evidenced in our sample of nineteenth-century communes.

Further research has extended these historical results to modern communes in Israel known as *kibbutzim*. During their hundred-year existence, until recently, *kibbutzniks* (*kibbutz* members) have lived according to the dictum "From each according to his abilities, to each according to his needs." Although sixteen *kibbutzim* are religious, the majority of *kibbutzim* are secular and often ideologically antireligious. Like their historical predecessors in the United States, religious *kibbutzim* on average have been economically more successful and stable than secular *kibbutzim*. Currently the *kibbutzim* are undergoing significant change, largely in the direction of increased privatization and reduced communality. This is a consequence of a massive economic failure that saw the *kibbutzim* collectively incur over $4 billion in debt. When news of their extraordinary indebtedness surfaced in the late 1980s, something went largely unnoticed in the academic and media reports about the inevitable collapse of the *kibbutz* movement: the religious *kibbutzim* had disproportionately survived by refusing to borrow money as did the secular *kibbutzim*. In the words of the Religious Kibbutz Movement Federation, "the economic position of the religious kibbutzim is sound, and they remain uninvolved in the economic crisis" that has affected so many of the *kibbutzim*. In fact, they have on average economically outperformed the secular *kibbutzim* in every decade of their existence.[85] The economic success of the religious *kibbutzim* is especially remarkable given that many of the religious practices performed on the religious *kibbutzim* inhibit economic productivity. For example, Jewish law does not permit Jews to milk cows on the Jewish Sabbath. Although rabbinic rulings have permitted religious *kibbutzniks* to milk their cows to prevent the cows from suffering, none of this milk can be used commercially. There are also significant constraints imposed by Jewish law on agricultural productivity. Fruits may not be eaten or sold during the first several years after a tree has been planted; agricultural fields in Israel must lie fallow every seven years; and the corners of fields cannot be harvested—the gleanings must be left for the poor. Although these constraints appear detrimental to the productivity of the religious *kibbutzim,* costly signaling theory suggests that they may actually be the key to their economic success.

I decided to study this further with economist Bradley Ruffle from Israel's Ben Gurion University. We conducted experiments on secular and religious *kibbutzim* aimed at measuring cooperative behavior in order to determine if there were differences across *kibbutzim* in members' levels of cooperation with other members of their own *kibbutz*.[86] Controlling for effects such as the age of the *kibbutz,* level of privatization, size of the *kibbutz,* and numerous other variables, we found that religious *kibbutzniks* exhibit higher levels of intragroup cooperation than secular *kibbutzniks*. Furthermore, when the data were examined more closely, an interesting pattern emerged. Religious males were significantly more cooperative than religious females. Among secular *kibbutzniks* we found no sex difference at all. This result is understandable if we appreciate the types of rituals and demands imposed on male religious Jews. Although there are a variety of requirements that are equally imposed on males and females, such as keeping kosher and not working on the Sabbath, male ritual requirements are largely public oriented, whereas female requirements are generally pursued privately or in the home. Indeed, the three major requirements imposed on women, the laws of family purity (e.g., attending a *mikvah,* or ritual bath[87]), separating a portion of dough when baking bread, and lighting Shabbat candles, are done privately. They are not rituals that signal commitment to a wider group; they appear to signal commitment within the family. Males, on the other hand, engage in highly visible ritual communal requirements, most notably public prayer three times daily. Among male religious *kibbutz* members, we found synagogue attendance to be positively correlated with our measures of cooperative behavior. There was no similar correlation among females, which is not surprising; attending services is not a requirement for women and thus does not serve as a signal of commitment to the group. Thus, the evolutionary signaling theory of religion is able to offer a unique explanation for our results, one that could not have been derived from a purely economic approach. In the economic or "club-goods" model of religion, church or synagogue attendance is analyzed as the dependent variable, and it is assumed that other religious practices are influencing attendance. In contrast, the evolutionary signaling model maintains that religious behaviors, bans, and badges all serve to facilitate cooperation.

Services Are Finally Over

To conclude, I return to the question posed in the title of this chapter: why are synagogue services so long?

Before answering this question, though, it should be pointed out that Jewish prayer services vary significantly depending on the occasion and from synagogue to temple. The weekday afternoon and evening services can each be completed in under a half-hour, while the morning service lasts about an hour. On a typical Shabbat morning, services can last more than three hours. The length of services also varies by denomination and, surprisingly to some, services at Orthodox synagogues are not always the longest. Some Conservative *shuls* hold even longer services due to the slower pace of prayer recitation and inclusion of English prayers in addition to the traditional Hebrew prayers. Nonetheless, even among Conservative *shuls* that hold all weekday and Shabbat services (which is not the majority), there is little expectation that more than a small minority of members, including the clergy, will attend most services. In contrast, in Orthodox *shuls* it is assumed that males will attend most if not all services, although attendance will vary across *shuls*. The length of services should be understood as a historical process in which prayers have been added more often than they have been omitted.[88] The goal of an evolutionary approach, however, is to understand why certain cultural practices were favored over others, thus offering insights into this historical process. Furthermore, synagogue services serve much more than the signaling function that has been emphasized here, including individuals' social, spiritual, and emotional needs.

Returning to our question, from a signaling perspective, services are so long, with much traditional knowledge required, because they serve as signals of commitment to the community. The significant time investment is a signal that a member is communally committed. In addition, the proper length of services is in the eye of the beholder. Granted, when invited to a bar or bat mitzvah, non-Jews are often surprised by the length of synagogue service, so signaling theory predicts that costs will be a matter of perception. Those who truly believe in the efficacy of their prayers and that the synagogue service offers God's traditional way to pray will not find the services too long.

Glossary (Hebrew = H; Yiddish = Y)

Ahavas Yisroel (H)   The religious obligation for Jews to love other Jews.

Ba'al Teshuva (m), Ba'alat Teshuva (f) (pl. Ba'alei Teshuva) (H) Literally, "a master or owner of return." Today *ba'al teshuva* refers to a nonreligious Jew who accepts the obligations of the Jewish laws, although historically the term referred to a religious Jew who went astray, repented, and returned to observant life.

Bar mitzvah (m), Bat mitzvah (f) (H)   Literally, "a son or daughter of a commandment"—the age of adulthood (thirteen years old for a boy and twelve for a girl) at which a Jew becomes responsible for adhering to Jewish law. The event is formalized by a ceremony in the synagogue and celebrated with a festive meal.

Bris milah (H)   A Jewish ritual circumcision conducted on boys when they are eight days old.

Chassid (pl. Chassidim) (H)   A follower of the revivalist movement founded in Eastern Europe by Rabbi Yisroel Baal Shem Tov in the eighteenth century.

Cherem (H)   A formal rabbinic excommunication, including one's property.

Chozrim B'teshuva (H)   Israeli term for *ba'al teshuva*; that is, someone who "returns" to Jewish observance.

Daven (Y)   To pray traditionally.

Gehennom (H)   Hell.

Gemach (H)   Acronym for *gemilut chassadim,* literally "acts of loving kindness." An organized network of "charity organizations" in Orthodox communities aimed at helping community members in need.

Glatt (Y)   Literally, "smooth, beyond any question." Typically used to refer to meat (*glatt* kosher) that meets a higher standard of *kashrut.*

Halacha (H)   Jewish religious law.

Haredi (pl. Haredim) (H)   Literally, "(God) fearing or trembling one." The preferred name of ultra-Orthodox Jews.

Hasidut (H)   The teachings and life of *Chassidism.*

Karet (H)   A spiritual excommunication of one's soul.

Kashrut (H)   The laws pertaining to Jewish dietary requirements (i.e., keeping kosher).

Kavanah (H)   Concentration, devotion, and inspiration during prayer and textual study.

Kibbutz (pl. Kibbutzim) (H)   An Israeli commune.

Kiddush (H)   The prayer of sanctification that ushers in the Sabbath, usually said over wine prior to dinner on Friday evening.

Kippah (pl. Kippot) (H)   A skullcap worn to show reverence for God.

Kollel (H)   An institute of talmudic study for married men.

Mechitzah (pl. Mechitzot) (H)   A divider separating men and women in synagogue and religious social events.

Mezzuzah (pl. Mezuzot) (H)   A parchment containing *Devarim* (Deuteronomy) 6:4–9, 11:13–17, that is enclosed in a narrow case and attached to Jewish doorframes.

Midrash (H)   Rabbinic literature that expounds on the Bible.

Mikvah (H)   A ritual bath required monthly by women for religious purification before commencing physical marital relations, and also used by religious men for religious purification, often prior to prayer.

Minyan (H)   A quorum of ten men (or among Conservative and Reform Jews, men and women) required to recite certain prayers.

Mitzvah (pl. Mitzvot) (H)   A religious obligation.

Niddah (H)   That period during and after menstruation when a wife is sexually unavailable to her husband.

Peyos (Y)   Sidelocks worn by men in compliance with the prohibition from *Vayikra* (Leviticus) 19:27.

Pushka (Y)   A box for small charitable donations.

Shachrit (H)   The morning prayer service.

Shema (H)   Literally, "hear" or "listen"—the name of a primary Jewish prayer, the "profession of faith."

Shmittah (H)   The laws concerning the agricultural sabbatical, particularly the law requiring the land in Israel to remain unworked and unharvested every seventh year.

Shokel (Y)   The swaying back and forth that may accompany traditional prayer and religious study.

Shtreimel (Y)   A fur hat worn by *Haredim*, especially *Chassidim*.

Shul (Y)   Literally a "school," but colloquially used to mean "synagogue."

Tanna (H)   A *Mishnaic* rabbinic scholar (first to beginning of the third centuries).

Tefillin (H)   Phylacteries consisting of two square leather boxes (containing scripture) and straps worn by adult males during morning prayers.

Tzadik (pl. Tzadikim) (H)   A righteous and holy person.

Tzniut (H)   Modest behavior, often now specifically referring to modest dress for men and women.

V'ahavta (H)   The opening word and name given to the first paragraph of the *Shema*.

Yeshiva (pl. Yeshivot) (H)   A school for the intensive study of Jewish religious texts.

Notes

1. See the chapter "Biosocial Regulation of Husband and Wife."
2. Sosis, 2004.
3. See the chapter "Making Biological Sense of Judaic Sacrificing."
4. In memory of these sacrifices, observant Jewish women today remove a piece of dough when baking bread and burn it until it is inedible.
5. Sosis, 2006.
6. Irons, 2001.
7. For example, Bulbulia, 2004a, 2004b; Goldberg, n.d.a, n.d.b; Sosis and Alcorta, 2003.
8. See Zahavi and Zahavi, 1997.
9. Smith and Harper, 2003.
10. Koenig, McCullough, et al., 2001.
11. Jewish law requires Jews to make loans to other Jews, but forbids the charging of interest on those loans.
12. See Sosis, 2005.
13. Shield, 2002, p. 15.
14. Ibid., p. 1.
15. Wechsberg, 1966.
16. Cited in Coleman, 1990, p. 109.
17. Heilman, 1992; Zborowski and Herzog, 1952.
18. Bliege Bird and Smith, 2005.
19. Berman, 2000; Iannaccone, 1992.
20. Perel, 1997.
21. Rappaport, 1999.
22. *Mishneh Torah, Hilchot Y'sodei HaTorah.*
23. Judaism is often regarded as less focused on the afterlife than other contemporary religions. Indeed, the Torah itself remains completely silent on the hereafter and the Rabbis in every generation have stressed the importance of deeds in this world. Nonetheless, the *kabbalistic, midrashic,* and *chassidic* literatures are filled with references to the eternal rewards that the righteous will receive and the suffering that awaits transgressors.
24. See Bulbulia, 2004a; Johnson, 2005; Johnson and Kruger, 2004; Sosis, 2003.
25. Exod. 24:7.
26. Shabbat 88a.
27. Lamm, 1985, pp. 20–21.
28. Heschel, 1955, pp. 282–283.
29. The Talmud (Ber. 31a) relates that we learn many of the laws of prayer from Hannah's emotional beseeching of God for a child (her prayers were answered, giving birth to the prophet Samuel).
30. In Conservative synagogues the *minyan* may also count women; most Reform synagogues do not require a *minyan.*
31. For example, Buxbaum, 1996.
32. Rappaport, 1971, p. 31.
33. D'Aquili and Newberg, 1999, p. 192.
34. Ekman, Levenson, et al., 1983; Levenson, 2003.
35. Alcorta and Sosis, 2005; Bulbulia, 2004a, 2004b.

36. Coleman, 1990.
37. Sosis, 2005.
38. Sosis, 2003.
39. In Israel, secular Jews who become religious are generally referred to as *chozrim b'teshuva*.
40. Berakhot 34b.
41. Telushkin, 1991, p. 433.
42. See the novel interpretation of this *mitzvah* in the chapter "Traditionalism and Human Evolutionary Success."
43. Dashefsky, 1992; Lazerwitz, Winter, et al., 1998.
44. Irons, 2001.
45. Telushkin, 1992, p. 140.
46. Lerer and Mayer, 1993.
47. For example, Levin, 1986; Telushkin, 1991.
48. Landau, 1993, pp. 248–249.
49. Levin, 1986.
50. Telushkin, 1991, p. 436.
51. Roof and McKinney, 1987.
52. Not all members of Orthodox synagogues are *halachically* observant, and even among self-identifying Orthodox Jews there is considerable variance in level of observance (e.g., Heilman and Cohen, 1986).
53. Margolese, 2005.
54. Guedalia and Haber, 2001, p. 328.
55. Albarelli, 2000, p. 35.
56. Sosis, 2003.
57. Landau, 1993.
58. Margolese, 2005.
59. The Church of Jesus Christ of Latter-day Saints (Mormonism) offers a notable counterexample to this prediction. Their proselytization efforts, however, which minimally require two years of commitment following high school, appear to be an effective costly signal (Sosis, 2003).
60. Baron, 1952, pp. 171–183.
61. Epstein, 1994.
62. The Jewish religious landscape in the United States and Israel differ markedly. Although the overwhelming majority of affiliated American Jews are associated with either the Reform or Conservative movements (Lazerwitz, Winter, et al., 1998), in Israel Orthodoxy dominates the religious scene and a majority of Israelis define themselves as secular (Lazar, Kravetz, et al., 2002).
63. Chiswick, 2002.
64. Agus, 1975; Fein, Chin, et al., 1972.
65. Wertheimer, 1993.
66. Lazerwitz, Winter, et al., 1998.
67. Blau, 1966.
68. One little-known exception is that according to Conservative *halakhah* it is forbidden to smoke.
69. Many synagogues do have payment scales so that wealthier members pay more, but dues are never calculated as a strict percentage of total income. And while wealthy members

tend to contribute beyond their dues requirements, the relative costs of these additional contributions are still likely to be lower than those faced by poor congregants.

70. See Winter, 1985a, 1988.
71. Winter, 1985b.
72. For example, Musleah, 2004; Bubis, 2002.
73. See Marty and Appleby, 1991; Marty, 1992.
74. Shapiro, 2005, p. 274.
75. For example, Heilman, 2005a, 2005b.
76. Margolese, 2005, pp. 222–223.
77. Cialdini, 2001, p. 81.
78. Shapiro, 2005, p. 273.
79. For example, Shapiro, 2005.
80. For example, Johnstone, 1997.
81. Margolese, 2005, p. 99.
82. Shield, 2002, p. 110.
83. Iannaccone, 1992, 1994.
84. Sosis and Bressler, 2003.
85. Fishman and Goldschmidt, 1990.
86. Ruffle and Sosis, n.d.; Sosis and Ruffle, 2003, 2004.
87. See the chapter "Biosocial Regulation of Husband and Wife."
88. Idelsohn, 1967.

References

Agus, J. 1975. The reform movement. In J. Neusner, ed., *Understanding American Judaism* (pp. 5–30). New York: KTAV.

Albarelli, G. 2000. *Teacha! Stories from a Yeshiva.* Thetford, VT: Glad Day Books.

Alcorta, C., and Sosis, R. 2005. Ritual, emotion, and sacred symbols: the evolution of religion as an adaptive complex. *Human Nature* 16:323–359.

Baron, S. 1952. *The Social and Religious History of the Jews,* vol. 1, 2nd ed. New York: Columbia University Press.

Berman, E. 2000. Sect, subsidy and sacrifice: an economist's view of ultra-Orthodox Jews. *Quarterly Journal of Economics* 115:905–953.

Blau, J. 1966. *Modern Varieties of Judaism.* New York: Columbia University Press.

Bliege Bird, R., and Smith, E. 2005. Signaling theory, strategic interaction, and symbolic capital. *Current Anthropology* 46:221–248.

Bubis, G. 2002. The costs of Jewish living: revisiting Jewish involvements and barriers: a comprehensive study of the costs, personal and communal, of living Jewishly in the U.S.-American Jewish Committee.

Bulbulia, J. 2004a. Religious costs as adaptations that signal altruistic intention. *Evolution and Cognition* 10:19–38.

———. 2004b. Area review: the cognitive and evolutionary psychology of religion. *Biology and Philosophy* 18:655–686.

Buxbaum, Y. 1996. *Real Davenning.* Flushing, NY: Jewish Spirit Publishing.

Chiswick, B. 2002. American Jewry: an economic perspective and research agenda. *Contemporary Jewry* 23:156–182.

Cialdini, R. 2001. *Influence: Science and Practice*. Boston: Allyn and Bacon.
Coleman, J. 1990. *Foundations of Social Theory*. Cambridge: Harvard University Press.
d'Aquili, E., and Newberg, A. 1999. *The Mystical Mind*. Minneapolis: Fortress Press.
Dashefsky, A. 1992. What we know about the effects of Jewish education on Jewish identification. In S. Kelman, ed., *What We Know About Jewish Education* (pp. 103–114). Los Angeles: Torah Aura Press.
Ekman, P., Levenson, R., et al. 1983. Autonomic nervous system activity distinguishes among emotions. *Science* 22:1208–1210.
Epstein, L. 1994. Why the Jewish people should welcome converts. *Judaism* 43:302–312.
Fein, L. R., Chin, J., et al. 1972. *Reform Is a Verb*. New York: Union of American Hebrew Congregations.
Fishman, A., and Goldschmidt, Y. 1990. The Orthodox kibbutzim and economic success. *Journal for the Scientific Study of Religion* 29:505–511.
Goldberg, R. n.d.a. Costly signaling in the Jewish context. Manuscript in author's possession.
———. n.d.b. Making biological sense of religious sacrifice. Manuscript in author's possession.
Guedalia, J., and Haber, L. 2001. An "Unorthodox therapy of an Ultra-Orthodox adolescent. *Jewish Medical Ethics*: 325–336.
Heilman, S. 1992. *Defenders of the Faith: Inside Ultra-Orthodox Jewry*. New York: Shocken Books.
———. 2005a. How did fundamentalism manage to infiltrate contemporary Orthodoxy? *Contemporary Jewry* 25:258–272.
———. 2005b. Jews and fundamentalism. *Jewish Political Studies Review* 17:1–2.
Heilman, S., and Cohen, S. 1986. Ritual variation among modern Orthodox Jews in the United States. In *Studies in Contemporary Jewry* (vol. 2, pp. 164–187). Bloomington, IN: Indiana University Press.
Heschel, A. 1955. *God in Search of Man: A Philosophy of Judaism*. New York: Farrar, Straus and Giroux.
Iannaccone, L. 1992. Sacrifice and stigma: reducing free-riding in cults, communes, and other collectives. *Journal of Political Economy* 100:271–291.
———. 1994. Why strict Churches are strong. *American Journal of Sociology* 99:1180–1211.
Idelsohn, A. 1967. *Jewish Liturgy and Its Development*. New York: Shocken Books.
Irons, W. 2001. Religion as a hard-to-fake sign of commitment. In R. Nesse, ed., *Evolution and the Capacity for Commitment* (pp. 292–309). New York: Russell Sage Foundation.
Johnson, D. 2005. God's punishment and public goods: a test of the supernatural punishment hypothesis in 186 world cultures. *Human Nature* 16:410–446.
Johnson, D., and Kruger, O. 2004. The good of wrath: supernatural punishment and the evolution of cooperation. *Political Theology* 5:159–176.
Johnstone, R. 1997. The evolution of animal signals. In J. Krebs and N. Davies, eds., *Behavioural Ecology: An Evolutionary Approach*, 4th ed. (pp. 155–178). Oxford: Blackwell Scientific Publications.
Koenig, H., McCullough, M., et al. 2001. *Handbook of Religion and Health*. New York: Oxford University Press.
Lamm, N. 1985. *Faith and Doubt: Studies in Traditional Jewish Thought*. New York: Ktav.

Landau, D. 1993. *Piety and Power: The World of Jewish Fundamentalism.* New York: Hill and Wang.
Lazar, A., Kravetz, S., et al. 2002. The multidimensionality of motivation for Jewish religious behavior: content, structure, and relationship to religious identity. *Journal for the Scientific Study of Religion* 41:509–519.
Lazerwitz, B., Winter, J. A., et al. 1998. *Jewish Choices: American Jewish Denominationalism.* Albany, NY: SUNY Press.
Lerer, N., and Mayer, E. 1993. In the footsteps of Ruth: a sociological analysis of converts to Judaism in America. In U. Schmelz and S. Della Pergola, eds., *Papers in Jewish Demography, 1989* (pp. 172–184). Jerusalem: Avraham Harmon Institute of Contemporary Jewry, Hebrew University.
Levenson, R. 2003. Blood, sweat and fears: the autonomic architecture of emotion. In P. Ekman, J. J. Campos, et al., eds., *Emotions Inside Out. Annals of the New York Academy of Sciences* (vol. 1000, pp. 348–366). New York: New York Academy of Sciences.
Levin, M. 1986. *Journey to Tradition.* Hoboken, NJ: Ktav.
Margolese, F. 2005. *Off the Derech: How to Respond to the Challenge.* Jerusalem: Devora Publishing.
Marty, M. 1992. Fundamentals of fundamentalism. In L. Kaplan, ed., *Fundamentalism in Comparative Perspective* (pp. 15–23). Amherst: University of Massachusetts Press.
Marty, M., and Appleby, R. 1991. Conclusion: an interim report on a hypothetical family. In M. Marty and R. S. Appleby, eds., *Fundamentalisms Observed* (pp. 814–842). Chicago: University of Chicago Press.
Musleah, R. 2004. Living Jewishly at all costs. *Hadassah Magazine* (May):20–25.
Perel, S. 1997. *Europa Europa: A Memoir of World War II.* New York: John Wiley and Sons.
Rappaport, R. 1971. The sacred in human evolution. *Annual Review of Ecology and Systematics* 2:23–44.
———. 1999. *Ritual and Religion in the Making of Humanity.* Cambridge: Cambridge University Press.
Roof, W., and McKinney, W. 1987. *American Mainline Religion: Its Changing Shape and Future.* New Brunswick, NJ: Rutgers University Press.
Ruffle, B., and Sosis, R. n.d. Does it pay to pray? Evaluating the economic return to religious ritual. Unpublished manuscript, Ben-Gurion University, Beer Sheva, Israel.
Shapiro, M. 2005. How did fundamentalism manage to infiltrate contemporary Orthodoxy? A response to Samuel C. Heilman. *Contemporary Jewry* 25:273–278.
Shield, R. 2002. *Diamond Stories.* Ithaca, NY: Cornell University Press.
Smith, J. M., and Harper, D. 2003. *Animal Signals.* Oxford: Oxford University Press.
Sosis, R. 2003. Why aren't we all Hutterites? Costly signaling theory and religion. *Human Nature* 14:91–127.
———. 2004. The adaptive value of religious ritual. *American Scientist* 92:166–172.
———. 2005. Does religion promote trust? The role of signaling, reputation, and punishment. *Interdisciplinary Journal of Research on Religion* 1:1–30.
———. 2006. *Religious Behaviors, Badges, and Bans: Signaling Theory and the Evolution of Religion.* In P. McNamara, ed., *Where God and Science Meet: How Brain and Evolutionary Studies Alter Our Understanding of Religion,* Vol. 1: *Evolution, Genes, and the Religious Brain* (pp. 61–86). Westport, CT: Praeger Publishers.
Sosis, R., and Alcorta, C. 2003. Signaling, solidarity and the sacred: the evolution of religious behavior. *Evolutionary Anthropology* 12:264–274.

Sosis, R., and Bressler, E. 2003. Cooperation and commune longevity: a test of the costly signaling theory of religion. *Cross-Cultural Research* 37:211–239.

Sosis, R., and Ruffle, B. 2003. Religious ritual and cooperation: testing for a relationship on Israeli religious and secular kibbutzim. *Current Anthropology* 44:713–722.

———. 2004. Ideology, religion, and the evolution of cooperation: field tests on Israeli kibbutzim. *Research in Economic Anthropology* 23:89–117.

Telushkin, J. 1991. *Jewish Literacy*. New York: William Morrow.

———. 1992. *Jewish Humor: What the Best Jewish Jokes Say About the Jews*. New York: William Morrow.

Wechsberg, J. 1966. *The Merchant Bankers*. Boston: Little, Brown.

Wertheimer, J. 1993. *A People Divided: Judaism in Contemporary America*. New York: Basic Books.

Winter, J. 1985a. Who can afford to be Jewish? *Moment* 10:36–42.

———. 1985b. An estimate of affordability of living Jewishly. *Journal of Jewish Communal Service* 61:247–256.

———. 1988. Income, identity and involvement in the Jewish community: a test of an estimate of the affordability of living Jewishly. *Journal of Jewish Communal Service* 65:149–156.

Zahavi, A., and Zahavi, A. 1997. *The Handicap Principle: A Missing Piece of Darwin's Puzzle*. New York: Oxford University Press.

Zborowski, M., and Herzog, E. 1952. *Life Is with People: The Culture of the Shtetl*. New York: Shocken Books.

Contributors

David Barash, Professor of Psychology, University of Washington, Seattle, since 1973. Although his work and interests are diverse, Barash's recent attention has been directed to understanding the underlying evolutionary factors influencing human behavior. He has been especially interested in male-female differences, reproductive strategies, and the troubling problem of violence in living things generally.

Laura Betzig, The Adaptationist Program, Ann Arbor, Michigan. Betzig has held research and teaching positions at Northwestern, the University of California, and the University of Michigan in anthropology, psychology, and zoology. She has lectured in departments of anthropology, biology, economics, philosophy, psychology, and medieval history.

Rick Goldberg, independent scholar in Austin, Texas, founder of Binah Yitzrit Foundation. BYF develops and funds scholarly work exploring religion, especially Judaism, from an evolutionary perspective.

Melvin Konner, Samuel Candler Dobbs Professor of Anthropology and Associate Professor of Psychiatry and Neurology at Emory University. He has held NIMH and NSF research grants and been a Fellow of the Center for Advanced Study in the Behavioral Sciences, the John Simon Guggenheim Memorial Foundation, the Social Science Research Council, and the Foundations Fund for Research in Psychiatry.

Craig Palmer, Assistant Professor of Cultural Anthropology, University of Missouri–Columbia. He focuses on incorporating cultural traditions into evolutionary explanations of human behavior. His new book, *The Supernatural and Natural Selection: The Evolution of Religion,* coauthored with Lyle Steadman, will soon be available from Paradigm Publishers.

Michael Satlow holds a joint appointment as Associate Professor in the Department of Religious Studies and the Program in Judaic Studies, Brown University. He has written extensively on issues of gender, sexuality, and marriage among Jews in antiquity; the Dead Sea scrolls; modern Jewish theology; methodology in religious studies; and the social history of Jews during the rabbinic period.

Richard Sosis is an Associate Professor and Head of the Evolution, Culture, and Cognition program in the Department of Anthropology at the University of Connecticut. His work has focused on the evolution of cooperation and the adaptive significance of religious behavior. To explore these issues he has conducted fieldwork with remote cooperative fishers in the Federated States of Micronesia and with various communities throughout Israel, including Ultra-Orthodox Jews and members of secular and religious *kibbutzim*.

Lyle Steadman, retired Professor of Biological Anthropology, Arizona State University. Steadman, a sociocultural anthropologist, spent a total of two and a half years doing fieldwork with the Hewa, stone-age agriculturalists in Papua, New Guinea. For more than three decades, he taught courses in comparative religion, kinship, the evolution of human sexuality, peoples of the Pacific, and human sociocultural evolution.

Amotz Zahavi, Evolutionary Biologist, Tel-Aviv University, a founder of the Israeli Society for the Protection of Nature.

Index

Aaron, 89, 109n25; Moses and, 70–71
Abel. *See* Cain and Abel
Abraham, 76, 80; fertility of, 46, 48, 50, 52, 54; God's covenant with, 87, 90, 93, 179–180; Isaac's sacrificing and, 180–181, 182, 193n71
abstract thinking, Jewish traditionalism and, 150, 160n76, 160n78
acquisition, of knowledge, 27–28
Adam, God's creation of, 43, 46
adaptive value, of wasting, as costly fitness displays, 187–189, 196nn133–137
adrenal enzyme defects, 105
adultery: biblical prohibition against, 86; female, 126–128, 130, 134n69, 135nn73–74, 136n92
afterlife, Judaism relating to, 22–23
aggadah, 26
ahavas Yisroel, 211, 226
altruism, as handicap, 169–170, 174, 190, 196nn150–151
ancestors, Jewish traditionalism relating to, 141–142, 145, 148, 159n37, 160nn60–61
animal world, intrafamily conflict relating to, 73
anisogamy, 5–6, 45
anthropological monism, 28
anti-Semitism, conversion relating to, 101
Ashkenaz/Ashkenazic Jewry (Northern, Central, Eastern Europe), 140; founder effect, genetic drift, and endogamy in, 102–104, 108; genetic disorders of, 102–105, 107; IQ of, 105–106, 107; as part of Jewish population, 101

Australian aboriginals, circumcision of, 92
Avihu and Nadav, God's sacrifice of, 181–182, 193n75, 194n80, 193nn77–78

ba'alei teshuva, 214–216, 222, 226, 229n39
babblers, communication between, 169–170
Babylonian exile, 99, 101
badges, behaviors, and bans, 201–207, 210
Baldwin Effect, 28
bans, behaviors, and badges, 201–207, 210
bar/bat mitzvah, 67, 226
Bathsheba, 88
b'chor, 71
behavioral propensities, of human beings, 21, 27
behavior/knowledge, of tradition, 149, 156
behaviors: badges, bans, and, 201–207, 210; Judaic, handicap principle relating to, 167; religious, signaling theory and religion relating to, 201; transformation relating to, 27–28
belief, Jewish ritual signals relating to, 208–212
benefit, definition of, 32
Bible: fertility of prominent men in, 42–61, 56n23, 57nn45–46; as history and natural history, 53–55; mating patterns in, 85–89; men unable to breed in, 52–53, 57nn45–46; prestigious men breeding in, 50–51, 107. *See also* Hebrew Bible; intrafamily conflict, in Bible and biological theory.
biblical *cherem* construct, as sacrificial, 184–186, 189, 195n110, 212, 226

237

238 ✳ *Index*

biblical commandments, for Judaic sacrificing, 177
biological implications, of monism, 18–39
biological kinsman, Jewish traditionalism relating to, 145, 159nn38–39
biological metaphors, *yetzer* relating to, 11–12
biological sense, of Judaic sacrificing, 173–198
biological theory. *See* intrafamily conflict, in Bible and biological theory
biosocial regulation, of husband and wife, 118–138
biotheological construct, *yetzer* as, 2–13
blank slates, human beings relating to, 20
The Blank Slate: The Denial of Human Nature and Modern Intellectual Life (Pinker), 21
body and soul, 20, 21, 23–25, 30
Book of Doctrines and Beliefs (Saadia Gaon), 19
breast and/or ovarian cancer, 103
breeding: slaves relating to, 53, 57n45. *See also* fertility, of prominent men, in Bible and ancient Middle East.
"bridegroom of blood," 96
brit milah (circumcision), 92, 94, 183–184, 211, 226

Cain and Abel, 70, 74; competitive sacrifices of, 178–179, 192n48, 192n57
cancer: breast and/or ovarian cancer, 103; cervical, circumcision relating to, 91–92
captive women, treatment of, 95
Catholicism, conversion relating to, 102, 108
certainty, of paternity, 128
Chabadnik, 200–201, 217
challah, 154
Chasid/Chasidim, 211, 226, 227. *See also Hasid/Hasidic*.
cherem construct, as sacrificial, 184–186, 189, 195n110, 212, 226
child, mother and, intrafamily conflict relating to, 65–67, 82nn3–6
children: intrafamily conflict relating to, 77–79, 81; stepparent relating to, 83n28, 127, 134n72
chozrim b'teshuva, 226
Christianity, 25

circumcision, 110nn57–58; of African cultures, 92; of Australian aboriginals, 92; biblical mandate of, 90; *brit milah* as, 92, 94, 183–184, 211, 226; cervical cancer relating to, 91–92; coevolutionary framework, sexual selection, and, 84–115; fertility advantages of, 90, 92, 96–98; God's covenant relating to, 90; hemorrhage or infections relating to, 91; importance of, 90, 109nn37–38; intermarriage and, 93–96; as Judaic sacrifice, 94, 183–184, 211, 226; matrilineal endogamy, sexual selection, and, 89–93, 107; of Muslims, 92; of penis, 91; persecution relating to, 91; STIs relating to, 91, 97, 98; UTIs relating to, 91, 97, 98
coevolutionary framework, sexual selection, circumcision, and centrality of texts in, 84–115
collective memory, Jewish traditionalism and, 146
commandments: biblical, for Judaic sacrificing, 177. *See also* Ten Commandments.
commentaries/writings, Jewish traditionalism and, 148–150, 160n64, 160n74
communal certainty, Judaic promotion of, 128–130
communal expiation, heifer beheaded for, 180
communal interest, in marriage, 119
communication: between signaler and receiver, 167–170; signaling theory and religion as part of, 201–205
competitive sacrifices, of Cain and Abel, 178–179, 192n48, 192n57
conjugal separation and reunion, periodic, requirement for, 118–138; family and communal certainty, Judaic promotion of, 128–130; female adultery, ritual impurity and, 127–128; female adultery, suspicion of, paternity uncertainty and, 126–127, 130, 134n69, 135nn73–74, 136n92; marital sexuality, Judaic regulation of, 119–121; men's sexual desire, hormonal variation associated with, 122–124; ovulation and menstruation, concealed, existence and

implications of, 125–126; parental reproductive choices, 121–122; women's sexual desire, hormonal variation associated with, 124–125
Conservative Judaism, 155–156, 218–219
Conservative rabbis, *halakhah* relating to, 34–35
conspicuous display, Judaic sacrificing as, 176–177, 190–191, 191nn15–16, 191nn18–24, 196n140, 196n146
conversion: anti-Semitism relating to, 101; Catholicism relating to, 102, 108; of females, 84, 101; forcing of, 102; formalization of, 101; genetic history relating to, 100–102; to Judaism, 99–100; of males, 84
converts, *ba'alei teshuva* and, 214–215
Coolidge Effect, short-term male reproductive strategy relating to, 6
costly display, of male reproductive value, 184
costly fitness displays, adaptive value of wasting as, 187–189, 195nn133–137
costly signaling theory, Jewish life and, 165–172, 174
costly signals, of handicap communicating cooperation, 186–187, 195nn118–121
covenant: "between the pieces," 179–180, 192n59, 193n63; between God and Abraham, 87, 90, 93, 179–180; of God, circumcision relating to, 90
creation: of Adam, 43, 46; of evil, 36, 38n43; of human beings, 25; Judaism and, 2–4, 22; of life, 4, 14n20; of universe, Genesis relating to, 2–3, 10
cuckoldry, 124, 126, 134nn48–49
current and future prospects: ongoing selection, 106–107

Darwin, Charles, 43, 45
Darwinian selection, 140–142
Darwinian theory, 7, 19, 22, 32, 88, 100, 139
daven, 226
David, 50–51, 68, 71, 72, 72n21, 76, 87, 95, 96
dead bodies, respect for, 27
dead, resurrection of, 26
"decline of generations," Jewish traditionalism relating to, 147, 159n50

defection and retention, 216–218, 229n52
denominational differences, 218–219, 229n62, 229nn68–69
descendant-leaving strategy, religion as, 143–144, 158
descendants, traditions relating to, 141–142
destruction, of *yetzer*, 10–11
diaspora: Rabbinical Judaism, endogamy and, 99–102. *See also* Jewish Diaspora.
dichotomy, epistemological, 19, 20–22, 27
Dinah, rape of, 93–94
DNA repair disorders, 105
drash, on maintenance of tradition, 151–155

Egypt, Israel and, 85
Elijah, 11
embodied knowledge, 28, 36
emperors and kings, reproduction relating to, 48–50
endogamy, 85–87, 108n7; diaspora, Rabbinical Judaism, and, 99–102; founder effect, genetic drift, and, in Ashkenazic Jewry, 102–104, 108; matrilineal, circumcision, sexual selection, and, 89–93, 107
epistemological dichotomy, 19, 20–22, 27
Esau, Jacob and, 72, 74–75
eunuchs, 53, 57n46
evil: God creating of, 36, 38n43. *See also* good.
evil inclination, *yetzer* as, 26
evil influence, of *yetzer*, 7–9, 15n63, 26
evil *yetzer* viewed as good, 10–12
evolution: differential success of genes relating to, 63; human, traditions in sophisticated models of, 141
evolutionary examination, of Jewish ritual signals, 199–225
evolutionary models: cooperation relating to, 223; *kibbutzim/kibbutzniks* relating to, 223–225; need for, 222–225; synagogue attendance relating to, 209, 222–223
evolutionary psychology, of short-term male reproductive strategy, 5–7, 11, 14n36, 15n82
evolutionary success, human, traditionalism and, 139–164

extramarital sex, 124
Ezra, 89, 109n25

family and communal certainty, Judaic promotion of, 128–130
family relations, *halakhah* and, 119
females: adultery of, paternity uncertainty and, 126–127, 130, 134n69, 135nn73–74, 136n92; adultery of, ritual impurity and, 127–128; conversion of, 84, 101; estrus loss of, 125, 134n57; males and, parental investment of, 6, 44–45, 55n7, 67, 129, 135n85; males v., reproductive variance of, 44; sexual allure of, short-term male reproductive strategy relating to, 6; short-term reproductive strategy of, 12; *yetzer* relating to, 12, 16nn100–103. See also women.
fertility: of Abraham, 46, 48, 50, 52, 54; menstruation and, 125, 134n60
fertility advantages, of circumcision, 90, 92, 96–98
fertility, of prominent men, in Bible and ancient Middle East, 42–61; Bible as history and natural history, 53–55; men to breed, need for, 43–47; men unable to breed, in Bible, 52–53, 57nn45–46; polygynous men breeding, in ancient Near East, 47–50, 56n23; prestigious men breeding, in Bible, 50–51, 107
first-born, intrafamily conflict relating to, 71
Flood, 4, 46
food, Judaic sacrificing relating to, 201, 228n4
food-related, biological metaphors, *yetzer* relating to, 11–12
founder effect: genetic drift, endogamy and, in Ashkenazic Jewry, 102–104, 108; selection relating to, 104–106
fundamentalism, 219–221

Gaucher's disease, 102, 105
gehennom, 209, 226
gemachs, 204, 226
generalized proposition, traditionalism relating to, 139–140
"generation to generation," 148, 157
Genesis, creation of universe relating to, 2–3, 10

genetic disorders, of Ashkenazic: adrenal enzyme defects, 105; blood clotting disorders, 105; Bloom syndrome, 102; breast and/or ovarian cancer, 103; DNA repair disorders, 105; Fanconi's anemia, 102; Gaucher's disease, 102, 105; glycogen storage defects, 105; haplotypes relating to, 103; heterozygote advantage relating to, 104–105; matrilineal/patrilineal genetic heritages, 103, 107; sphingolipid storage diseases, 105; torsion dystonia, 102, 105; TSD, 102, 105
genetic drift, founder effect, and endogamy, in Ashkenazic Jewry, 102–104, 108
genetic heritages, 103, 107
genetic history, conversion relating to, 100–102
glatt kosher, 33, 226
glycogen storage defects, 105
God, 201; Abraham's covenant with, 87, 90, 93, 179–180; Adam created by, 43, 46; blessings and, 3; contribution of, 19, 22–25; covenant of, circumcision relating to, 90; evil created by, 36, 38n43; idolatry and, 28–30; Jewish traditionalism and, 145, 159n36; as Judaism's sole creator, 4, 22; knowing/being, 28–29; *mitzvot* is belief in, 208; monistic unity of, 18, 35; Nadav and Avihu sacrificed by, 181–182, 193n75, 194n80, 193nn77–78; revelation of, 36; reward/punishment of, 23, 26
good: evil and, 3; evil and, Holocaust relating to, 35; evil *yetzer* viewed as, 10–12
good *yetzer*, 4–5, 10, 14n26

halakhah, 26, 32, 216, 218–219, 226; Conservative rabbis relating to, 34–35; family relations regulated by, 119; *niddah-tvilah* relating to, 119–122, 129–132, 133n23, 133nn17–21; Orthodox community relating to, 33, 34–35, 200; Reform Judaism relating to, 34
handicap communicating cooperation, sacrifices as costly signals of, 186–187, 195nn118–121
handicap principle, in human social interaction, 166–172; altruism,

as handicap, 169–170, 174, 190, 196nn150–151; biological meaning of, 167; Judaic behaviors relating to, 167; signaler and receiver, communication between, 167–170; social bond tested in, 169

handicaps: indices or, 207–208; signaling theory and religion relating to, 203; theory of, 166

Hannah, 210, 228n29

haplotypes: genetic disorders relating to, 103; Kohanic, 104; Y-chromosome, 103, 104

Haredi/Haredim, 203–207, 210, 215–222, 226

Hasid/Hasidic, 33, 200, 211, 217, 221–222, 226. See also *Chasid/Chasidim.*

Hebrew Bible, 22, 26, 35; reproduction and, 45

Hebrew language, 147–148, 159n55

Hebrew people, mandate to reproduce of, 45–47, 48–50

heifer: beheading of, 180; red, reverse defilement relating to sacrifice of, 182–183, 194nn85–86

heritable and replicable, traditions as, 141–142, 158nn13–14

heterozygote advantage, genetic disorders relating to, 104–105

historical overview, of Judaic sacrificing, 175

HIV, 98

Holocaust, good and evil relating to, 35

"Honor your father and your mother," 71

hormonal variation: men's sexual desire associated with, 122–124; women's sexual desire associated with, 124–125

HPV. *See* human papilloma virus

human beings: behavioral propensities of, 21, 27; blank slates relating to, 20; creation of, 25; father and mother of, 24; as indivisible, 21, 22; monistic perspective of, 21, 22

human evolutionary success, traditionalism and, 139–164

human evolution, traditions in sophisticated models of, 141

human language, signaling theory and religion relating to, 202

human nature: constructed by Jewish religious texts and liturgy, 2–4, 10; intrafamily conflict relating to, 64; monistic approach to, 36

human papilloma virus (HPV), 91, 98

human social interaction, handicap principle in, 166–172, 196nn150–151

husband: jealousy of, 127–128; wife and, biosocial regulation of, 118–138

Iberia (Sepharad), Jewish population in, 101, 108

idolatry problem, God and, 28–30

illicit desire, short-term male reproductive strategy relating to, 11, 15n82

imagination, *yetzer* relating to, 3, 7, 14n9

infants, intrafamily conflict relating to, 65, 82n2

infections: circumcision relating to, 91; infertility relating to, 97; UTIs, 91, 97, 98

infertility, infections relating to, 97

intelligence, Jewish traditionalism relating to, 152, 161n102

intergenerational continuity, 148, 154, 159n56

intermarriage, 89, 93–96. *See also* marriage.

intrafamily conflict, in Bible and biological theory, 62–83; animal world relating to, 73; children relating to, 77–79, 81; as consistent, 63; first-born relating to, 71; frequent and violent, 63; human nature relating to, 64; infants relating to, 65, 82n2; *kashrut* relating to, 66; male-male competition, 63; mother and child relating to, 65–67, 82nn3–6; parents and offspring relating to, 63–64, 67–68, 75–76, 78; pregnancy complications relating to, 75, 82n27; regression relating to, 80; royal succession relating to, 68, 82n9; sexual reproduction relating to, 65; sibling rivalry relating to, 69–75, 82n13; stepparent relating to, 76, 83n28; temper relating to, 79–80

IQ, of Ashkenaz/Ashkenazic Jewry (Northern, Central, Eastern Europe), 105–106, 107

Isaac, sacrifice of, 180–181, 182, 193n71

Jacob, 71, 81, 86, 93; Esau and, 72, 74–75; Rebecca and, 73–74, 76, 86

Jesus, rejection of, Jewish traditionalism relating to, 155
Jewish Diaspora, 101, 147, 152
Jewish education, signaling theory and religion relating to, 214, 229n39
Jewish knowing, 18–39; God and idolatry problem relating to, 28–30; implications of, 35–37; *mitzvot*, 31–35; monism relating to, 22–27
Jewish life, costly signaling theory and, 165–172, 174
Jewish monism, 36
Jewish population: current, 106–107, 108; Iberia (Sepharad), 101, 108; Middle East and North Africa, 101, 102, 107–108; Northern, Central, Eastern Europe (Ashkenaz), 101
Jewish religious texts and liturgy, human nature constructed by, 2–4, 10
Jewish ritual signals, evolutionary examination of, 199–225; applying theory relating to, 213–221; behaviors, badges, and bans, 201–207, 210; belief relating to, 208–212; evolutionary models relating to, 222–225; handicaps or indices, 207–208; in private practice, 212–213; as reliable and not perfect, 221–222; signaling theory and religion, 201–205; stable signals, 205–206
Jewish traditionalism: abstract thinking as part of, 150, 160n76, 160n78; ancestors relating to, 141–142, 145, 148, 159n37, 160nn60–61; as authoritative, 145–146, 159n40; biological kinsmen relating to, 145, 159nn38–39; collective memory relating to, 146; "decline of generations" relating to, 147, 159n50; God relating to, 145, 159n36; human evolutionary success and, 145–151; intelligence as part of, 152, 161n102; intergenerational continuity relating to, 148, 154, 159n56; land inheritance relating to, 146; legal framework for, 149; obligations, performance of, 148, 159nn57–59; Rabbinic law relating to, 147, 159n49; rationality and, 146, 159n42; recipes as part of, 154–155, 162nn116–118; rejection of Jesus as part of, 155; sharpening process relating to, 151, 152, 161n93, 161nn95–96; 161nn107–109; Temple sacrificing relating to, 146; writings/commentaries relating to, 148–150, 160n64, 160n74; *yeshiva* as part of, 150, 160nn83–86, 227
Jews: observant, traditions and, 157; sociobiology of, 84–115
Joseph, 71–72, 82n19, 87
Judaic behaviors, handicap principle relating to, 167
Judaic promotion, of family and communal certainty, 128–130
Judaic regulation, of marital sexuality, 119–121
Judaic sacrificing, 191n3; biblical *cherem* construct as, 184–186, 189, 194n110, 212, 226; biblical commandments for, 177; biological sense of, 173–198; circumcision *(brit milah)* as, 94, 183–184, 211, 226; communal expiation, heifer beheaded for, 180; competitive, of Cain and Abel, 178–179, 192n48, 193n57; as conspicuous display, 176–177, 190–191, 191nn15–16, 191nn18–24, 196n140, 196n146; costly fitness displays, adaptive value of wasting of, 187–189, 196nn133–137; as costly signals, of handicap communicating cooperation, 186–187, 195nn118–121; covenant "between the pieces," 179–180, 193n59, 193n63; definition of, 175; food relating to, 201, 228n4; historical overview of, 175; of Isaac, Abraham's obedient preparation for, 180–181, 182, 193n71; *kol nidrei*, 177; *korban*, 176; of Nadav and Avihu by God, 181–182, 193n75, 194n80, 193nn77–78; of red heifer, reverse defilement relating to, 182–183, 194nn85–86; spoils of war relating to, 184–186; vows and oaths relating to, 177, 192n30, 192n33, 192n35; warrior reputation relating to, 184, 194n91; of Yom Kippur scapegoat, 182, 193n82
Judaic traditionalism, modern implications of, 155–156
Judaism: afterlife relating to, 22–23; Conservative, 155–156, 218–219; conversion to, 99–100; creation and,

2–4; example of, 139–164; God as sole creator in, 4, 22; Messianic, 155; polythetic model of, 36; Rabbinical, diaspora, endogamy, and, 99–102; Reform, 34, 155, 156, 162n122, 218–219; scientific concepts relating to, 22

karet, 212, 226
kashrut, 32, 33, 34, 66, 201, 226; intrafamily conflict relating to, 66
kavanah, 211, 226
kibbutzim/kibbutzniks, 223–225, 226
kiddush, 201, 226
kings: polygynous, in Bible, 52; reproduction relating to, 48–50. *See also* David; Solomon.
kinship cooperation, tradition and, 142–143
kippah, 201, 206, 226
knowledge: acquisition of, 27–28; as being, 31; embodied, 28, 36; human, 20; monism relating to, 21–22; scientific, 19, 20; thought and, 22; traditional, 28; transformative, *mitzvot* relating to, 34
knowledge/behavior, of tradition, 149, 156
Kohanic haplotype, 104
Kohanim, 104
kollel, 204, 227
kol nidrei, 177
korban, 176
kosher. *See glatt* kosher

land inheritance, Jewish traditionalism and, 146
language: Hebrew, 147–148, 159n55; human, signaling theory and religion relating to, 202
law: of Moses and Israel, marriage ceremony relating to, 118; Oral, 148; Rabbinic, 147, 159n49; of Torah, 62, 87, 93, 95, 147–151, 185, 210, 214, 219
legal framework, for Jewish traditionalism, 149
leks, 101, 110n94
Levites, 104
life: creation of, 4, 14n20; Jewish, costly signaling theory and, 165–172, 174
long-term male reproductive strategy, short-term at odds with, 5–6

lust, short-term male reproductive strategy relating to, 6–7

Maimonidean hierarchy, of charitable giving, 188–189
Maimonides, 29, 70, 75, 121, 180–183, 208
male-male competition, intrafamily conflict relating to, 63
male reproductive strategy, short-term, evolutionary psychology of, 14n36; Coolidge Effect relating to, 6; female sexual allure relating to, 6; illicit desire relating to, 11, 15n82; long-term male reproductive strategy at odds with, 5–6; lust relating to, 6–7; *yetzer* relating to, 7
males: conversion of, 84; females and, parental investment of, 6, 44–45, 55n7, 67, 129, 135n85; females v., reproductive variance of, 44; reproductive value of, costly display of, 184; sex cells of, 5–6, 14n36
mandate: biblical, of circumcision, 90; of Hebrew people to reproduce, 45–47, 48–50
marital sexuality, Judaic regulation of, 119–121
marriage: ceremony of, law of Moses and Israel relating to, 118; communal interest in, 119; as monogamous, 118–119, 130, 132n6; sex/abstinence cycle in, 119. *See also* intermarriage.
masorah, 152
mate guarding, 127, 128, 129
mating patterns, in Bible, 85–89
matrilineal endogamy, circumcision, and sexual selection, 89–93, 107
matrilineal/patrilineal genetic heritages, 103, 107
matzah, 154
mechitzah, 220, 227
men: to breed, need for, 43–47; sexual desire of, hormonal variation associated with, 122–124; unable to breed, in Bible, 52–53, 57nn45–46. *See also* fertility, of prominent men, in Bible and ancient Middle East.
menstruation, 119; fertility and, 125, 134n60; ovulation and, concealed, existence and implications of, 125–126

Messianic Judaism, 155
mezuzot, 214, 227
Middle East: North Africa and, Jewish population of, 101, 102, 107–108. *See also* fertility, of prominent men, in Bible and ancient Middle East.
midrash, 31, 36, 179, 227
mikvah, 120, 133nn19–21, 227
minyan, 210, 227, 228n30
mitzvot, 22, 90, 227; belief in God is, 208; benefit relating to, 32; Jewish knowing relating to, 31–35; performance of, 31–35, 67, 200; specifications for, 34; transformative knowledge relating to, 34; transmission of, 32; understanding of, 33
mitzvot ben adam lemakom, mitzvot ben adam lechavero v., 220–221
mitzvot-performers, 33
Modern Orthodox, 219–221
monism: anthropological, 28; biological implications of, 18–39; Jewish, 36; Jewish knowing relating to, 22–27; knowledge relating to, 21–22; rabbinic, 36; Torah relating to, 19, 22, 26, 28, 29, 31, 32, 34, 35
monistic approach, to human nature, 36
monistic perspective, of human beings, 21, 22
monistic unity, of God, 18, 35
monogamous, marriage as, 118–119, 130, 132n6
Moses, 46, 51, 181; Aaron and, 70–71; law of Israel and, marriage ceremony relating to, 118; Miriam and, 71; at Sinai, 52, 149, 152; Torah of, 42, 46; uncircumcised lips of, 91, 95–96; wife of, 87, 96
mother: child and, intrafamily conflict relating to, 65–67, 82nn3–6; father and, of human beings, 24
multigenerationality, 141
Muslims, circumcision of, 92
myths/rituals, as part of religion, 143–144, 153, 189

na'aseh v'nishma, 210
Nadav and Avihu, God's sacrifice of, 181–182, 193n75, 194n80, 193nn77–78
natural order, 3, 4

natural selection, signaling theory and religion relating to, 201–203
nature, culture v., 36
"nature *versus* nurture," 20
Near East, ancient, polygynous men breeding in, 47–50, 56n23
neighboring peoples, traditions from, 147
niddah, 120–121, 126–132, 133nn17–18, 226
niddah-tvilah: *halakhah* relating to, 119–122, 129–132, 133n23, 133nn17–21; ovulatory effect relating to, 123–125, 134n52; testosterone production relating to, 123
North Africa and Middle East, Jewish population of, 101, 102, 107–108

oaths and vows, Judaic sacrificing relating to, 177, 192n30, 192n33, 192n35
observant Jews, traditions and, 157
On the Descent of Man and Selection in Relation to Sex (Darwin), 43
On the Origin of Species (Darwin), 43
Oral law, 148
Orthodox community, 131, 152, 155–156, 211; fundamentalism and, 219–221; *halakhah* relating to, 33, 34–35, 200; retention and defection relating to, 216–218, 229n52. *See also* Modern Orthodox.
ovulation: follicular phase of, 125–126, 132; menstruation and, concealed, existence and implications of, 125–126
ovulatory effect, 123–124, 125, 134n52

parental investment, of females and males, 6, 44–45, 55n7, 67, 129, 135n85
parental reproductive choices, 121–122
parents and offspring, intrafamily conflict relating to, 63–64, 67–68, 75–76, 78
paternity: certainty of, 128; uncertainty of, suspicion of female adultery and, 126–127, 130, 134n69, 135nn73–74, 136n92
patrilineal/matrilineal genetic heritages, 103, 107
pelvic inflammatory disease (PID), 97
penis, circumcision of, 91
performance, of *mitzvot*, 31–35, 67, 200
persecution, circumcision relating to, 91

personifications, of *yetzer*, 7–8
peyos, 201, 204, 227
PID. *See* pelvic inflammatory disease
pidyon ha-ben, 71
Pinker, Steven, 20–21
Plato, 21, 25
polyandry, 118, 132nn2–3
polygamy, 118
polygynous men breeding, in ancient Near East, 47–50, 56n23
polygynous patriarchs, judges, kings in Bible, 52
polygynous species, evolutionary process of, 6
polygyny, 43, 86, 88, 118
polythetic model, of Judaism, 36
power and wealth, reproduction relating to, 54, 58n47, 88, 89
pregnancy: complications of, intrafamily conflict relating to, 75, 82n27; high blood pressure in, 75; preeclampsia in, 75
prestigious men breeding, in Bible, 50–51, 107
priests (Kohanim), 104; assistants of (Levites), 104
private practice, Jewish ritual signals in, 212–213
prohibitions, 206
proselytism, 84, 99, 218, 229n59
punishment/reward, of God, 23, 26
punishments and rewards, supernatural, 209, 212, 228n23
pushka, 201, 227

Rabbinical Judaism, diaspora, and endogamy, 99–102
rabbinic construction, of *yetzer*, 7–9
rabbinic embryology, 24
Rabbinic law, Jewish traditionalism relating to, 147, 159n49
rabbinic monism, 36
rabbis, Conservative, *halakhah* relating to, 34–35
Rabbis of antiquity, 23, 24, 25, 35
Rachel, 80–81
Ramban. *See* Maimonides
rationality, Jewish traditionalism and, 146, 159n42
reason, revelation v., 19

Rebecca, Jacob and, 73–74, 76, 86
receiver and signaler, communication, between, 167–170
recipes, as part of Jewish traditionalism, 154–155, 162nn116–118
red heifer, reverse defilement relating to sacrifice of, 182–183, 194nn85–86
Reformation, 20
Reform Judaism, 155, 156, 162n122, 218–219; *halakhah* relating to, 34
regression, intrafamily conflict relating to, 80
religion: compartmentalization of, 20; as descendant-leaving strategy, 143–144, 158; myths/rituals as part of, 143–144, 153, 189; science v., 19, 20–21, 36; taboos as part of, 144. *See also* signaling theory and religion.
religious sacrifice. *See* Judaic sacrificing
reproduction: emperors and kings relating to, 48–50; Hebrew Bible and, 45; power and wealth relating to, 54, 58n47, 88, 89; wars relating to, 46–47, 52–53, 56n20. *See also* fertility, of prominent men, in Bible and ancient Middle East.
reproductive choices, parental, 121–122
reproductive strategy: of females, short-term, 12; of males, 5–7, 11, 14n36, 15n82
reproductive variance, male v. female, 44
resurrection, of dead, 26
retention and defection, 216–218, 229n52
revelation: of God, 36; reason, 19
reward/punishment, of God, 23, 26
rewards and punishments, supernatural, 209, 212, 228n23
ritual impurity, female adultery and, 127–128
ritual sacrificing. *See* Judaic sacrificing
rituals, communication between signaler and receiver relating to, 168, 169
ritual signals. *See* Jewish ritual signals, evolutionary examination of
rituals/myths, as part of religion, 143–144, 153, 189
royal succession, intrafamily conflict relating to, 68, 82n9
Ruth, 87, 95

Saadia Gaon, 19, 20, 31, 36

sacrifice: of Isaac, 180–181, 182, 193n71; wasting relating to, 175, 176–177, 180. *See also* Judaic sacrificing.
Sarah, 46, 76, 93, 181; Hagar and, 76–77
scapegoat, of Yom Kippur, 182, 194n82
science, religion v., 19, 20–21, 36
scientific concepts, Judaism relating to, 22
scientific knowledge, 19, 20
Scroll of Esther, 49–50, 90, 185
selection: Darwinian, 140–142; founder effect relating to, 104–106; natural, signaling theory and religion relating to, 201–203; ongoing, 106–107. *See also* sexual selection.
separation and reunion. *See* conjugal separation and reunion, periodic, requirement for
Sepharad, 101, 108, 140
sex/abstinence cycle, in marriage, 119
sex cells, of males, 5–6, 14n36
sex, extramarital, 124
sexual allure, of females, 6
sexual desire: of men, 122–124; of women, 124–125
sexuality: marital, Judaic regulation of, 119–121; *yetzer*-driven, 11
sexually transmitted diseases (STIs), 91, 97, 98
sexual reproduction, intrafamily conflict relating to, 65
sexual selection, 106; circumcision, matrilineal endogamy and, 89–93, 107; coevolutionary framework, circumcision, and, 84–115
shachrit, 207, 227
sharpening process, Jewish traditionalism, relating to, 151, 152, 161n93, 161nn95–96, 161nn107–109
shema/sh'ma, 5, 151, 212, 227
shmittah, 227
shokel, 210, 227
short-term reproductive strategy: of females, 12; of males, 5–7, 11, 14n36, 15n82
shtreimel, 227
shuls, 209, 219, 225, 227
"siblicide," 70, 74
sibling rivalry, intrafamily conflict relating to, 69–75, 82n13
signaler and receiver, communication between, 167–168; babblers relating to, 169–170; rituals relating to, 168, 169
signaling theory and religion: communication as part of, 201–205; converts and ba'alei teshuva relating to, 214–215; denominational differences relating to, 218–219, 229n62, 229nn68–69; financial costs relating to, 219–220; fundamentalism relating to, 219–221; handicaps relating to, 203; human language and, 202; Jewish education relating to, 214, 229n39; natural selection relating to, 201–203; Orthodox relating to, 203–204; proselytizing relating to, 218, 229n59; religious behaviors relating, 201; retention and defection relating to, 216–218, 217n52. *See also* costly signaling theory, Jewish life and.
signals: reliable and not perfect, 221–222; stable, 205–206. *See also* costly signals, of handicap communicating cooperation; Jewish ritual signals, evolutionary examination of.
slaves, breeding relating to, 53, 57n45
social bond, testing of, 169
sociobiology, of Jews, 84–115
Solomon, 10, 50–54, 68, 76, 87–88
sons-of-gods, 45–46, 55n14
sotah, 127–128
soul and body, 20, 21, 23–25, 30
stable signals, 205–206
Standard Social Science Model, 21, 37n7
stepparent: children relating to, 83n28, 127, 134n72; intrafamily conflict relating to, 76, 83n28
STIs. *See* sexually transmitted diseases
study, of Torah, 89, 101, 151–152, 186
supernatural rewards and punishments, 209, 212, 228n23
synagogue: attendance at, 209, 222–223

ta'amei mitzvot, 119, 132n12
taboos, as part of religion, 144
taharat ha-mishpakhah, 119, 129, 132n7
Talmud, 31, 151, 157, 217
Tanakh: A New Translation of the Holy Scriptures According to the Traditional Hebrew Text, 37
Tay-Sachs disease (TSD), 102, 105

tefillin, 207, 214, 227
temper, intrafamily conflict relating to, 79–80
Temple sacrificing, Jewish traditionalism and, 146
Ten Commandments, 31
testosterone production, 122–124
"theory of handicaps," 166
"thirteen attributes," 23
Torah, 149, 160n72, 160n74; law of, 62, 87, 93, 95, 147–151, 185, 210, 214, 219; monism relating to, 19, 22, 26, 28, 29, 31, 32, 34, 35; of Moses, 42, 46; reading of, 199, 200; study of, 89, 101, 151–152, 186; tradition of, 157; women relating to, 128, 132
torsion dystonia, 102, 105
traditionalism, human evolutionary success and, 139–164; *drash,* on maintenance of tradition, 151–155; generalized proposition, 139–140; Jewish traditionalism, 145–151; Judaic traditionalism, modern implications of, 155–156; religion, as descendant-leaving strategy, 143–144, 158; tradition and Darwinian selection, 140–142; tradition and kinship cooperation, 142–143
traditional knowledge, 28
traditions: Darwinian selection and, 140–142; descendents relating to, 141–142; as heritable and replicable, 141–142, 158nn13–14; kinship cooperation and, 142–143; knowledge/behavior of, 149, 156; multigenerationality relating to, 141; from neighboring peoples, 147; new, 147; observant Jews and, 157; restrictions as part of, 156; in sophisticated models of human evolution, 141; of Torah, 157
transformation, behavior relating to, 27–28
transformative knowledge, *mitzvot* relating to, 34
transmission, of *mitzvot,* 32
TSD. *See* Tay-Sachs disease
tsurah, 77, 83n29
tumah, 127
tvilah, 120, 125, 126, 133n21
tzadik, 215, 227
tzniut, 206, 211, 227

uncertainty of paternity, suspicion of female adultery and, 126–127, 130, 134n69, 134nn73–74, 136n92
understanding, of *mitzvot,* 33
universe, creation of, Genesis relating to, 2–3, 10
urinary tract infections (UTIs), 91, 97, 98
UTIs. *See* urinary tract infections

v'ahavta, 214, 227
vanishing twin syndrome, 74
vows and oaths, Judaic sacrificing relating to, 177, 192n30, 192n33, 192n35
v'shinantam l'vanekha, 151

warrior reputation, Judaic sacrificing relating to, 184, 194n91
wars, reproduction relating to, 46–47, 52–53, 56n20
wasting: adaptive value of, 187–189, 195nn133–137; sacrifices relating to, 175, 176–177, 180
wealth and power, reproduction relating to, 54, 58n47, 88, 89
wife: fertility cycle of, 119; husband and, biosocial regulation of, 118–138
women: captive, treatment of, 95; sexual desire of, hormonal variation associated with, 124–125; Torah relating to, 128, 132. *See also* females.
writings/commentaries, Jewish traditionalism and, 148–150, 160n64, 160n74

Y-chromosome haplotypes, 103, 104
yeshiva, 150, 160nn83–86, 227
yetzer: as biotheological construct, 2–13; destruction of, 10–11; evil, 3, 4–5, 7, 10–12, 14n26; as evil inclination, 26; evil influence of, 7–9, 15n63, 26; females relating to, 12, 16nn100–103; food-related, biological metaphors relating to, 11–12; good, 4–5, 10, 14n26; imagination relating to, 3, 7, 14n9; as inborn, 3, 14n12; personifications of, 7–8; rabbinic construction of, 7–9; self-control of, 10; short-tem male reproductive strategy relating to, 7
yetzer-driven sexuality, 11

Yiddish, 140
Yom Kippur scapegoat, 182, 194n82
yotzer, 2

zeitgeist, 155
Zipporah, 96
Zohar, 12